PATRONAGE, ART, AND SOCIETY
IN RENAISSANCE ITALY

THIS book is the first in a publishing series established by Oxford University Press in conjunction with the Humanities Research Centre of the Australian National University, Canberra. The OUP/HRC series includes single-author volumes by members of the HRC, past and present, and composite volumes deriving from HRC conferences. Volumes with a specifically Australian content are produced through OUP's Australian office in Melbourne; other titles are handled through their Oxford headquarters. The General Editor of the series is Professor Ian Donaldson, Director of the HRC.

Patronage, Art, and Society in Renaissance Italy

EDITED BY
F. W. KENT AND PATRICIA SIMONS
WITH J. C. EADE

HUMANITIES RESEARCH CENTRE · CANBERRA
CLARENDON PRESS · OXFORD
1987

Oxford University Press, Walton Street, Oxford OX2 6DP

Oxford New York Toronto
Delhi Bombay Calcutta Madras Karachi
Petaling Jaya Singapore Hong Kong Tokyo
Nairobi Dar es Salaam Cape Town
Melbourne Auckland

and associated companies in
Beirut Berlin Ibadan Nicosia

Oxford is a trade mark of Oxford University Press

Published in the United States
by Oxford University Press, New York

British Library Cataloguing in Publication Data

Patronage, art, and society in Renaissance
Italy.——(Humanities Research Centre/
OUP series)
1. Art patronage——Italy——History 2. Arts,
Italian 3. Arts, Medieval 4. Arts, Modern
I. Kent, Francis William II. Simons,
Patricia III. Eade, J.C. IV. Humanities
Research Centre
700'.7'9 NX705.5.18
ISBN 0-19-821978-4

Library of Congress Cataloging in Publication Data

Patronage, art, and society in Renaissance Italy.
Includes index.
1. Art patronage——Italy. 2. Art patronage——Italy——
Florence. 3. Artists and patrons——Italy. 4. Artists
and patrons——Italy——Florence. 5. Art,
Renaissance—— Italy. 6. Art, Renaissance——Italy——Florence.
I. Kent, F. W. (Francis William), 1942– . II. Simons,
Patricia. III. Eade, J. C. (John Christopher)
N5273.P38 1987 709'.9 86–28584
ISBN 0-19-821978-4

Printed in Great Britain by
Butler & Tanner Ltd, Frome and London

Preface

THE essays in this book for the most part began their lives as papers
delivered at a conference—on 'Patronage, Art and Society in the
Renaissance'—held in Melbourne in May 1983 as part of the 'Renaissance Year' organized by the Humanities Research Centre of the Australian National University. Patricia Simons convened these meetings,
which were attended by scholars from all over Australia and from
abroad, and she and F. W. Kent have undertaken, in collaboration
with J. C. Eade of the HRC, the subsequent editing for publication of
the papers. When there are differences of opinion between contributors, the editors have not intervened. The short essays by Ian Robertson
and Margaret Rose were not delivered at the conference but were
commissioned as a result of their authors' contributions to discussion.

The editors would like to thank their respective departments for
help of various kinds, and especially Bess Brudenell of the Department
of History, Monash University, who did much of the secretarial and
administrative work. At short notice J. D. Legge, Dean of the Faculty
of Arts at Monash, released funds for research assistance, which Erin
Wilson competently provided. Financial help towards compilation of
the index was forthcoming from Margaret Riddle, Chairman of the
Department of Fine Arts, University of Melbourne. F. W. Kent is
grateful to the Australian Research Grants Scheme for financial assistance, and to Carolyn James for other help. Above all, the editors and
contributors are grateful to the Director of the HRC, Ian Donaldson,
and to his staff, for their patronage of an enterprise which both reflects,
and has encouraged, the growing antipodean contribution to the study
of one of the Old World's classic periods.

F.W.K.
P.S.

Melbourne, November 1985

Contents

List of Illustrations

List of Contributors

WILLIAM EISLER is Honorary Research Affiliate of the Power Institute of Fine Arts, University of Sydney.

ROBERT GASTON is Senior Lecturer in the Department of Art History, La Trobe University, Melbourne.

RICHARD GOLDTHWAITE is Professor of History, The Johns Hopkins University, Baltimore.

HEATHER GREGORY is Lecturer in the Department of History, University of New England, Armidale.

GARY IANZITI is Senior Lecturer in European Languages at the University of Wollongong.

DALE KENT is Reader in the Department of History, La Trobe University, Melbourne.

F. W. KENT is Reader in the Department of History, Monash University, Melbourne.

GUY FITCH LYTLE is Professor of Church History and Anglican Studies at the Graduate Theological Union, Berkeley, and at the Church Divinity School of the Pacific, Berkeley.

JOHN OPPEL is Lecturer in the School of Humanities, Griffith University, Queensland.

MARGARET PLANT is Professor of Visual Arts, Monash University, Melbourne.

LORENZO POLIZZOTTO is Lecturer in the Department of Italian, University of Western Australia.

IAN ROBERTSON is Senior Lecturer in the Department of History, University of Melbourne.

MARGARET ROSE is Reader in Social Theory at the University of Melbourne.

PATRICIA SIMONS is Lecturer in the Department of Fine Arts, University of Melbourne.

TILL VERELLEN is Honorary Research Affiliate of the Power Institute of Fine Arts, University of Sydney.

RONALD WEISSMAN is Associate Professor in the Department of History, University of Maryland.

I

Renaissance Patronage: An Introductory Essay

F. W. KENT WITH PATRICIA SIMONS

THESE essays, written for a conference in Melbourne on 'Patronage, Art and Society in the Renaissance', should perhaps be read as companion pieces to those recently published, after a Folger Institute symposium, as *Patronage in the Renaissance*. There the focus was English, here it is Italian (especially Florentine); and while several of our contributors would insist on urban and Mediterranean Italy's retaining its traditional special place within European Renaissance society and culture, nevertheless all would agree with Werner Gundersheimer's assertion, made at the Washington symposium, that 'patronage, broadly defined as "the action of a patron in supporting, encouraging, or countenancing a person, institution, work, art, etc." has been clearly established as one of the dominant social processes of pre-industrial Europe'.[1] Northern Europe and princely Italy have indeed been drawn even closer together by Trevor Dean's timely reminder that the contractual bonds of clientage (*accomandigia* and *aderenza*) existing between the rulers of Ferrara and their aristocratic supporters in the later Middle Ages were comparable to those which tied members of the 'affinities' of England and the 'alliances' of France to their lords.[2] This introductory essay will further suggest that the non-contractual ties between 'friends' (patrons and clients) in an aristocratic republic such as Florence bear a family resemblance to these more formal structures of so-called bastard feudalism.

With an encouraging atmosphere of ecumenicity concerning 'the

---

[1] W. L. Gundersheimer, 'Patronage in the Renaissance: An Exploratory Approach', in G. F. Lytle and S. Orgel (eds.), *Patronage in the Renaissance* (Princeton, 1981), p. 3.

[2] T. Dean, 'Lords, Vassals and Clients in Renaissance Ferrara', *English Historical Review*, 100 (1985), 106–19; cf. G. Soranzo, 'Collegati, raccomandati, aderenti negli stati italiani dei secoli xiv e xv', *Archivio storico italiano*, 94 (1941), 3–35. See too C. Carpenter, 'The Beauchamp Affinity: A Study of Bastard Feudalism at Work', *English Historical Review*, 95 (1980), 514–32.

centrality of the patronage system[3] now established between many
Renaissance scholars of various persuasions, it seemed to the participants in the Melbourne discussions all the more important to
make careful distinctions, to explore in more detail, a concept whose
vagueness, in English though not in other European languages, could
seduce the enthusiast into claiming too much too soon; as Gary Ianziti
firmly points out, Italian distinguishes clearly between *mecenatismo*
(patronage of the arts) and *clientelismo* (political patronage).[4] This
distinction draws our attention to the fact that political and social
historians of Italy are talking more and more about 'patronage' in the
latter sense precisely at the time when some of their art historical
colleagues—two of whom contributed in Washington—are reacting
against what may fairly be called an uncritical over-use of the term
'patronage', variously defined, within their field.[5] One interesting
impulse to emerge from the Melbourne discussion was that, having
insisted on the divorce of these two sorts of patronage, contributors
often seemed to want to see them keep company again, in a more
detached spirit.

Ronald Weissman begins with a definition of political patronage and
clientage, as understood by Renaissance historians and anthropologists
of Mediterranean societies: an unequal and complex relationship, in
which the patron provides his client with far more than mere protection, over a long period and on 'a moral or social rather than a
legal basis'.[6] This complicated bond was often indistinguishable from
others, for example 'friendship'—the *amicitia* of ancient Rome, *amicizia* in Renaissance Italy—which Guy Lytle here discusses for Europe
as a whole.[7] If, as Gundersheimer says, historians can show the existence of patronal hierarchies, of networks of 'friends' or patrons and
clients, in the Italian city-states, their structure and workings are so
far clearest in Florence, thanks to the lead given by scholars such as
Gene Brucker, Dale Kent, Weissman, Richard Trexler, and Anthony
Molho, where the private evidence needed to document such informal

---

[3] S. Orgel, Preface, in Lytle and Orgel, *Patronage in the Renaissance*, pp. xi–xii.
[4] See Chapter 16.
[5] See pp. 17–21.
[6] See Chapter 2. See too the extensive bibliography in S. N. Eisenstadt and L. Roniger,
'Patron–Client Relations as a Model of Structuring Social Exchange', *Comparative
Studies in History and Society*, 22 (1980), 42–77.
[7] See Chapter 3. See too R. P. Saller, *Personal Patronage under the Early Empire*
(Cambridge, 1982).

social arrangements survives in almost embarrassing abundance.[8] (This fact, rather than a bad attack of what an historian of Milan has called 'florentinitis', explains, in part at least, why so much of the Melbourne discussion was about Florence, here assuming its role as a well-equipped laboratory in which hypotheses concerning Renaissance Italy, and European urbanism, can be formulated and tested.)[9] Dale Kent's outstanding contribution to our understanding of Florentine *amicizia*, of the bonds of 'neighbourhood, friendship and kinship', is summarized here and extended with reference to research in progress, emphasizing the intricacy and, above all, the dynamic quality of patronal ties.[10] That these permeated Florentine society and consciousness can be illustrated to readers unfamiliar with the evidence and perhaps uneasy with what may appear to be sociological abstractions by an incident drawn from the diarist Francesco Giovanni. He came near to losing a lawsuit with Albizzo Rucellai in 1444 because, as Francesco explained, not only was Albizzo a district captain but, as it happened, three of the five officials who decided the case were his 'close relations [*parenti stretti*]': his cousin Giovanni Rustichi, that man's own cousin, and one Baldassare Bonsi 'born of the Rucellai on his mother's side'.[11] It was rare that a Florentine could not assemble a group of such friends, to have recourse to 'amicitiae tam superiores quam minores'—as Pliny had put it[12]—to assist in the quest for office, tax relief, legal aid, and so forth; rarer that a man could not be influenced by this means. Antonio Nori expressed his frustration in 1427 that he could not persuade the Abbot of Vallombrosa, his debtor, to pay up: 'he's an Abbot, a person subordinate to no one save the Pope; I'm not able to squeeze him.'[13]

In Florence, the Quattrocento appears to have witnessed the heyday of political patronage (its origins and earlier functioning are difficult to make out because private evidence is lacking), but even then, as

---

[8] Gundersheimer, 'Patronage', esp. pp. 16 ff. Weissman surveys the literature in Chapter 2.

[9] V. Ilardi, 'The Visconti–Sforza Regime of Milan: Recently Published Sources', *Renaissance Quarterly*, 31 (1978), 331–42 (quotation on p. 342).

[10] See Chapter 4.

[11] Cited by B. Wilson, 'A Florentine Chronicler of the Fifteenth Century: Francesco di Tommaso Giovanni and his *Ricordanze*', unpublished MA thesis (Monash University, 1980), p. 5, to whom we are grateful for permission to quote her thesis.

[12] Cited by Saller, *Personal Patronage*, p. 12.

[13] 'E abate, e persona non sottoposto se none al papa; no' llo posso strigniere ...': Archivio di Stato, Florence, Catasto, 34, fo. 10. (All manuscript references are to collections in the Florentine State Archives, unless otherwise indicated.)

Dale Kent points out, multiple claims on a patron could strain a system which depended upon his assiduously attending to the needs of his clients. Lorenzo de' Medici's *Protocolli*, or registers of correspondence, reveal his constant care in this regard, on behalf of men and women from all social classes; little wonder that in April 1485, while trying to rest in the country, he irritably expressed his wish to be left alone, as the appointment of the new Priors drew near, 'because I've had more letters from would-be Priors than there are days in the year; and I've decided not to interfere and to live out my days as tranquilly as I can ...'.[14] However, the flood of correspondence, and of those myriad personal requests that contemporaries firmly believed were more efficacious than letters, went on, to the despair of the early sixteenth century Medici and their agents, whom Lorenzo Polizzotto shows mismanaging a log-jam of requests from clients: 'every day arrive letters from Your Lordship recommending someone or other,' wrote Lorenzo de' Medici the younger to his kinsman Giuliano on 9 October 1513, 'letters which I'm sure are written more at the request of some friend whom one can't displease by refusing, as often happens to me, rather than because you really want him to be served, etc. And therefore I desire that when Your Lordship wants someone singled out to be satisfied, that you let me know this in singular fashion, whereupon I shan't fail to do my duty.'[15] The Medici principate resolved the problem, according to Polizzotto, by ensuring that 'there was no possibility of resorting to patronage, whether private or governmental, to undermine the stability of the regime'.[16]

Contemporaries called leading patrons the 'gran maestri' (*maggiori* or *principali* in a more formal political context), a phrase close to the social anthropologist's 'Big Men' which Gundersheimer has introduced into discussions of Renaissance society,[17] while the expression 'maestro della bottega [master of the establishment]' was used of a regime's leader.[18] ('Patrone' itself became more prominent as the fifteenth cen-

---

[14] Published by M. Martelli, *Studi Laurenziani* (Florence, 1965), p. 198. See too *Protocolli del Carteggio di Lorenzo il Magnifico*, ed. M. del Piazzo (Florence, 1956).

[15] Published by O. Tommasini, *La vita e gli scritti di Niccolò Machiavelli* (Turin, 1883), ii. 974–5; cf. J. N. Stephens, *The Fall of the Florentine Republic, 1512–1530* (Oxford, 1983), p. 88.

[16] See Chapter 8.

[17] Gundersheimer, 'Patronage', pp. 13 ff. For *gran maestro* (*pezzo grosso*, or 'big shot', in modern Italian), see Alessandra Strozzi, *Lettere di una Gentildonna Fiorentina del secolo XV*, ed. C. Guasti (Florence, 1877), pp. 101, 489.

[18] This almost untranslatable phrase occurs in the correspondence of Benedetto Dei and Piero Vespucci in Conventi Soppressi, 78, 317, fo. 191, 8 Aug. 1482; 318, fo. 372,

tury went on, no doubt an example of self-conscious classicizing.)[19] In Florence, members of the Medici family became the biggest of Big Men, around whom, in the analyses of Dale Kent and others, lesser lights shone and moved, and chains of 'satellites' formed: the last noun is used by the chronicler Benedetto Dei to describe followers of Niccolò Soderini.[20] Such *gran maestri* may have been Renaissance individualists in the Burckhardtian sense, but they were 'sustained by their links with corporate structures' as Gundersheimer has observed,[21] above all by the patrilineage and, several Melbourne speakers would add, by the neighbourhood. Patricia Simons has very recently demonstrated the solidarity of the ancient magnate clan of the Tornabuoni/Tornaquinci—relatives, clients and friends of the Medici—which, as she argues here, Giovanni Tornabuoni expressed, as a patron in several senses of the word, by commissioning from the Ghirlandaio brothers the fresco cycle for the main chapel of Santa Maria Novella where so many portraits of kinsmen, and associates, appear.[22] It was to the new palaces—here discussed by Richard Goldthwaite[23]—of the great men of such leading lineages that clients and petitioners came, centres of sociability and brokerage for neighbours and allies. When in mid-1466 the Medici and their friends of thirty years split into several factions, a chronicler used the ebb and flow of people between the Medici and Pitti palaces, at opposite ends of the city, as an index of the rival leaders' fortunes. In the beginning 'Messer Luca Pitti held court at his house, where the majority of citizens went to consult about politics ... [and] few, and those not of the highest reputation, frequented [Piero de' Medici's]'. At the end Pitti, his friends disgraced and himself outmanoeuvred, 'remained out in the cold, alone at home

23 Dec. 1481, and elsewhere; when Dei uses it in his *Cronica*, ed. R. Barducci (Florence, 1985), p. 114, he certainly means Lorenzo de' Medici. One recalls that Alberti has Giannozzo criticize a man who regarded *lo stato* (the regime, or politics) as *mia bottega* (my shop, my mercantile establishment): *I libri della famiglia*, in *Opere volgari*, ed. C. Grayson (Bari, 1960), i. 181.

[19] See the examples in *Epistolario di Bernardo Dovizi da Bibbiena*, i (1490–1513), ed. G. L. Moncallero (Florence, 1955), pp. 5, 8, 11. The word 'patronus' was a 'relative rarity' in imperial Rome: Saller, *Personal Patronage*, pp. 8–9.

[20] Dei, *Cronica*, p. 69.

[21] Gundersheimer, 'Patronage', p. 19.

[22] See Chapter 12, and her 'Portraiture and Patronage in Quattrocento Florence with Special Reference to the Tornaquinci and their Chapel in Santa Maria Novella,' unpublished PhD thesis (University of Melbourne, 1985).

[23] See Chapter 9.

where no one visited him to talk politics, whereas before the house had been always full of people of all sorts'.[24]

A number of lineages, and their *palazzi*, dominated the administrative district of Lion Rosso or the Red Lion in mid-Quattrocento Florence, creating there—as described by F. W. Kent—an intimate society of neighbours, friends, and relations that also constituted a patronal hierarchy in its own right (and one which collectively patronized the arts), although it maintained vital links with other patron–client networks and with the central government of the city.[25] Robert Gaston devotes his attention to another local group of families, led by the Medici and living around the church of San Lorenzo in the district of Lion d'Oro or the Golden Lion. Neighbours and political allies, these men also co-operated as ecclesiastical patrons, in effect increasingly coming to dominate the liturgy of a local church which the Medici and they had largely rebuilt and furnished with family chapels.[26] At this point it probably comes as a relief to learn from a historian of the papal states, Ian Robertson, that it was not only the Renaissance Florentines to whom *vicini* (neighbours) and neighbourhoods, whether defined as administrative districts or more flexibly as social units, were important. In Cesena, neighbourhood administration by *contrade* continued within the seigneurial structure imposed by the Malatesta lords.[27]

Beyond lineage and neighbourhood there were other social worlds to conquer, other patronage groups to create, to influence, or to infiltrate. Marriages between houses—the creation of a *parentado*—was an obvious means, to which historians have given a good deal of attention, of forging such links; and the Melbourne conference suggested in discussion, what Christiane Klapisch has since documented in meticulous detail, that godparenthood provided another. When Giovanni Mazzuoli arranged the baptism of his children in the 1460s,

---

[24] 'Era molto abbassata in questo tempo la sua riputatione [Piero's], et M. Luca Pitti teneva residenza a casa sua, dove gran parte de' cittadini andava a consultare de' fatti dello stato . . .; pochi, et anche di non molta stima, gli frequentavano la casa [Medici] . . . [Finally Pitti] stavasi freddo, et solo a casa et niuno lo visitava per conto dello stato, usato prima d'havere sempre piena la casa d'ogni ragione [di] gente': Marco Parenti, 'Cronica', Biblioteca Nazionale, Florence, Magliabecchi xxv, 272 (cf. M. Phillips, 'A Newly Discovered Chronicle by Marco Parenti', *Renaissance Quarterly*, 31 (1978), 153–60, whose transcription of the chronicle, kindly made available to F. W. Kent, is cited here).

[25] See Chapter 5.

[26] See Chapter 7.

[27] See Chapter 6.

each decision would have been, in her view, quintessentially 'un acte politique' which reinforced old ties, or helped create new friendships;[28] 'a treacherous godfather', on the other hand, 'is a snake in one's bosom', according to Benedetto Dei.[29] One of Mazzuoli's sons was held at the font by poor people, 'for the love of God'; another had as *compari* a notary's son, Antonio, the son of the well-known painter of *cassoni* or marriage chests, Marco del Buono, and 'Mona Lucia di Francesco Schartera'. As book-keeper of the administrative district of the Unicorn, Mazzuoli would have had patronage to dispense, to clients humbler than himself as well as to his peers and superiors, from whom he would in turn have expected support. His own deferential attitude to the *gran maestri* is revealed, perhaps, by his giving the name Luca to one of his sons, apparently because the baptism took place on the day in 1463 when Luca Pitti was knighted.[30]

Although, as Klapisch shows, men were very much the preferred godparents, the appearance of women among their number should alert us to their more general role, as yet hardly studied, as users, facilitators, and dispensers of political and social patronage. The influence that able Medici women such as Lucrezia née Tornabuoni or Alfonsina née Orsini could exert, in their own right and because of their male connections, is evident in their correspondence. Such patrons, whose correspondents were often other women, provided some of their sex with a socially acceptable means of acquiring favours and influencing events. The very existence of an informal *sotto-governo*—in which women could act as intercessors, like the Virgin using and facilitating the processes and powers of a male hierarchy—gave them more access to an unrelentingly masculine polity than historians so far have thought possible.[31] Perhaps because Costanza de' Bardi was a kinswoman of his mother, she felt able to come

[28] C. Klapisch, 'Compérage et clientélisme à Florence (1360–1520)', *Ricerche storiche*, 15 (1985), 61–76; see too her 'Parrains et filleuls. Une approche comparée de la France, l'Angleterre et l'Italie médiévales', *Medieval Prosopography*, 6 (1985), 51–77.

[29] Dei, *Cronica*, p. 146.

[30] 'Ricordi di Giovanni di Niccolò Mazzuoli' (on whom see D. V. and F. W. Kent, *Neighbours and Neighbourhood in Renaissance Florence: The District of the Red Lion in the Fifteenth Century* (Locust Valley, NY, 1982), p. 47), in Compagnie religiose soppresse, 1026, 206, fos. 26, 82.

[31] See the suggestions by F. W. Kent, 'A Proposal by Savonarola for the Self-Reform of Florentine Women (March 1496)', *Memorie domenicane*, NS 14 (1983), 335–41. There is no complete edition of Lucrezia's letters; some sense of her activities as a patron emerges from those translated in Y. Maguire, *The Women of the Medici* (London, 1927), ch. 5. Alfonsina's political role is referred to by Stephens, *The Fall*, pp. 86–9, 91.

frequently to Giovanni di Cosimo de' Medici's house 'to speak to thee' about a monastery she and certain other aristocratic women wished to found, although it is true—why we do not know—that this man Costanza wanted to be their 'capo e guida e totale aiutorio' was never at home, whereupon she left a note to Contessina de' Bardi.[32] In 1496 Savonarola could be persuaded to change his mind by a determined woman follower, who worked indirectly through male acquaintances of them both.[33] If Alfonsina de' Medici was Goro Gheri's 'patrona unica',[34] further research in the correspondence of the upper classes of the Italian city-states would reveal other patronesses, and still more female clients.

In an interesting paper on 'Patronage in Florence in Anglophone Historiography', Anthony Molho has now asked, as did many contributors to the Melbourne discussions, how deep into the social structure vertical ties of clientage went, his own suggested answer being that patronage operated essentially within the urban political classes, who also had links with the élites of provincial cities and with other countrymen, such as their own factors.[35] Elsewhere, Molho has argued that 'the principal characteristic of Florentine life throughout the Quattrocento ... was the cleavage which rent political and cultural manifestations into experiences perceived and assimilated differently by the rich and the poor', a statement which provides the context for his more recent suggestion.[36] Other historians, including several participants in our conference, would point to hints of a deeper penetration by patronage chains into peasant communities and into some sections of the politically ineligible urban classes, an approach which does not necessarily sentimentalize social relations in the past, nor deny the possibility, or fact, of conflict between socio-economic groups. Rather it emphasizes patronage as a *modus operandi* which normally allowed humbler people access to their superiors, who in turn had a stake in satisfying their requests. Whether or not one says that these

---

[32] Costanza's letter to Giovanni (died 1463), without date, is in Archivio Mediceo avanti il Principato (henceforth MAP), VII, 323.

[33] F. W. Kent, 'A Proposal by Savonarola', 335–41.

[34] Gheri to Alfonsina, 14 Jan. 1517, Fondo Goro Gheri, I, fos. 307–8, a letter kindly shown to F. W. Kent by Richard Sherr.

[35] A. Molho, 'Il padronato a Firenze nella storiografia anglofona,' *Ricerche storiche*, 15 (1985), 5–16.

[36] 'Cosimo de' Medici: *Pater Patriae* or *Padrino?*', *Stanford Italian Review*, 1 (1979), 5–33 (quotation on p. 9).

clients had a 'false consciousness' imposed by their lords, the mechanism by which things were done remains more or less the same.[37]

Very likely, a harder look at the evidence by all involved will enable a consensus to be reached on the question of the connections between rural clients and urban lords. 'We want you to be lord of our persons and possessions, both in public and private,' wrote a rich Pratese to Piero di Lorenzo de' Medici on 29 July 1493, when seeking his intervention in a local dispute; we were your supporters in 1466, unlike our opponents here, Carlo d'Andrea da Prato carefully added, and 'we have your coat-of-arms mounted in our house'.[38] Urban families such as the Medici often must have gained access to rural patronage, and to peasant networks, by means of friendship with provincial leaders. Until 1456, when the commune forbade the practice by law, Florentine territorial administrators frequently forged such bonds by acting as godfathers, thereby becoming 'partigiani' of local interests.[39] Such favours were repaid when factional leaders in the city called on peasant troops during times of emergency, as when in 1466 the youthful Lorenzo de' Medici, later so much in demand as an arbiter in rural disputes, mustered 'a great crowd of peasants, especially the leaders' at feasts held in the Val d'Arno by lords 'with a great following' there; 'and everyone desiring to acknowledge himself to be Piero [de' Medici's] well-wisher, and his servant, Lorenzo received many pledges during their discussions together'.[40] More direct ties bound the prominent statesman Manno Temperani with his peasant kin, with whom he kept in touch,[41] or the wealthy Francesco Giovanni with his farmers; for six weeks in 1452 he sheltered several families of his peasant

---

[37] Cf. the remarks by Saller, *Personal Patronage*, pp. 37–8, 141, and M. I. Finley's approach in *Politics in the Ancient World* (Cambridge, 1983), esp. ch. 2.

[38] '... abiano l'arme vostre murate in chasa ...; et vogliano siate nostro signore dell'avere e delle persone in pubricho et in private': Carte Strozziane, I, 3, fo. 151. Carlo was almost certainly a member of the Gherardacci family, on whom see E. Fiumi, *Demografia, movimento urbanistico e classi sociali in Prato dall'età comunale ai tempi moderni* (Florence, 1968), pp. 381–3.

[39] Klapisch, 'Compérage et clientélisme', pp. 68–9.

[40] '[There were] molte feste dove accade essere gran concorso di contadini, et maxime de' capi, et desiderando ognuno di farsi conoscere come benivolo et servidori di Piero, nel praticare insieme fecione molte offerte a Lorenzo': Marco Parenti, 'Cronica'. Parenti adds that on this occasion the peasants did not realize that 'within a few days Lorenzo was to have them come armed to Florence in Piero's support', but throughout his account of events rural retinues loom large.

[41] D. V. and F. W. Kent, 'Two Vignettes of Florentine Society in the Fifteenth Century', *Rinascimento*, 2nd ser., 23 (1983), 237–60.

workers in his Florentine house, giving them the middle floor.[42] The Medici themselves had personal dealings with some of their farm workers. On 13 June 1439, Lorenzo di Giovanni de' Medici, in the country, gave a letter to one 'Bechone our worker [*lavoratore*]' for Cosimo in Florence, asking him to provide 50 lire of Averardo de' Medici's money for the dowry of the man's new sister-in-law, whom the writer described as 'one of those girls left alone in Campolitardi', a Medici estate. In a curious and ambiguous passage, Lorenzo goes on to exhort Ser Alesso, Cosimo's secretary, to procure a Grecian cloak for the peasant and send him 'as ambassador to the Emperor on behalf of the King of Armenia, making sure he looks the part',[43] plausibly precious and early evidence of Medicean meddling in, if not control of, one of the lower-class festive brigades of the city, the Kingdom of the Millstone (or of Armenia), which was associated with the Millstone Corner, the Canto alla Macina, just behind the Medici palace.

A group of probably plebeian youths from this precise area, the self-styled 'lads from the Millstone Corner', rushed armed to the aid of the Medici when Giuliano was killed by the Pazzi conspirators in late April 1478, an incident suggestive of the existence of ties of reciprocal dependence between *gran maestri* and at least some of the urban *popolo*, ties which neighbourhood, ritual, the dispensing of largess, and perhaps godparenthood, would have cemented.[44] Though much research on this theme remains to be done, F. W. Kent's paper suggests how rich and poor could share a certain sociability in the crowded and narrow streets of an urban quarter, to which Molho has replied, perfectly correctly, that sociability between social classes does not

---

[42] Wilson, 'A Florentine Chronicler', p. 162.

[43] 'Voi, ser Alesso, achattate una cioppa alla ghrecha a Bechone et mandatelo per imbasciadore allo' Mperadore per parte del re d'Armenia, et ghua[r]date s'elli à viso da cciò': MAP XI, 268, Lorenzo di Giovanni de' Medici to Cosimo.

[44] Kent and Kent, 'Two Vignettes', pp. 252–60. On the *potenze*, or festive brigades, see R. C. Trexler, *Public Life in Renaissance Florence* (New York, 1980), pp. 400 ff., who persuasively suggests that the territory of the King of the Millstone was identical with the Kingdom of Armenia in the Medicean Company of the Magi's realm (p. 403). While the context of this letter requires further study, the 'Emperor' mentioned presumably belonged to the Grand Monarchy or Empire of the Red City, another *potenza* based in Piazza Sant' Ambrogio, and was not the Greek Emperor then in Florence for the Council. Trexler believes that 'All signs point to the early 1470s as the time when the future *potenze* first delimited their kingdoms and placed boundary markers ...' (p. 401), but also that the Millstone Corner group 'had a deeper antiquity' (p. 403), a suggestion supported by this early letter, which F. W. Kent intends to publish in full.

necessarily mean that reciprocal bonds existed between them.[45] By their nature, such ties (which would largely have been expressed orally and in action) are hard to document, especially if a historian rules out of court, as Molho has in effect done, the scattered and anecdotal evidence which alone survives. The present writers find it instructive that, in one of his *facezie*, Poliziano can refer to an Albizzi knight's crossing verbal swords in 1378 with 'a hanger-on [*crientolo*] of his, who was one of the Ciompi'[46]—a story in which structures of both class and clientage are assumed to coexist and where, incidentally and unusually, a client is called a client—but not everyone will be persuaded that this anecdote tells us much about Laurentian society.

Perhaps we can all, at least, agree that patronage, while now very much on the Renaissance map, still resembles Australia as depicted on early charts: reasonably accurate outlines enclosing large tracts of unexplored and alien territory. Our contributors would insist that patronage had an ethos or a moral climate of its own, a claim the truth of which needs still to be demonstrated, especially to those Anglo-Saxon historians who seem uncomfortable with it. 'Clientage' has been described in *A Concise Encyclopaedia of the Italian Renaissance* as 'a loosely hierarchized practice of "I'll scratch your back if you'll scratch mine",'[47] a definition descended directly from Dr Johnson's devastating gloss on patron: 'one who countenances, supports, or protects. Commonly a wretch who supports with insolence, and is paid with flattery.'[48] The craven or extravagant language of some Renaissance letter-writers, and the professions of *amicizia* or brotherhood by men who were patently not friends in any sense of that word, might well persuade one to agree with Samuel Johnson, to deny Renaissance patronage a moral dimension. 'I am indeed yours, your creature, and with you in life as in death,' wrote Francesco Sassetti to Piero di Cosimo de' Medici, on the face of it a curiously abject claim from one who was a senior business associate of the Medici and from a family not without distinction.[49] The declaration made to Lorenzo

---

[45] See Chapter 5, and Molho, 'Il padronato a Firenze', p. 12. One needs to note, too, Klapisch's discovery that between 1450 and 1500 established families less and less recruited godparents from among the humble: 'Compérage et clientélisme', pp. 72–4.

[46] Angelo Poliziano, *Detti piacevoli*, ed. T. Zanato (Rome, 1983), p. 75; see p. 54 for another reference to a 'cliente', a word little used even in imperial Rome: Saller, *Personal Patronage*, pp. 8–9. [47] Ed. J. R. Hale (London, 1981), p. 89.

[48] *A Dictionary of the English Language* ... (London, 1785, 6th edn), ii. s.v.

[49] '... perchè sono pure vostro et vostra creatura et con voi ò a vivere et morire': MAP XVII, 127, 24 Aug. 1456. On Francesco, see E. Borsook and J. Offerhaus, *Francesco Sassetti and Ghirlandaio at Santa Trinita, Florence* ... (Doornspijk, 1981).

by Cristoforo Spini, also in the Medici firm and from a magnate lineage—my father was your servant but 'I consider myself not your servant but your house's slave and dog'[50]—calls to mind Lauro Martines's comment on a slightly earlier servile letter to this still very young Medici: 'The courtier had made his appearance in Florence.'[51] Indeed a careful (and much needed) study of the conventional language of letters of recommendation would likely reveal, broadly speaking, that as the fifteenth century went on it became more elaborate and more effusive in tone, a change suggestive of the Medici family's increasingly firm grip upon both the city's constitution and its patronal *sottogoverno*, in an Italian society which was in this and other ways becoming more courtly. 'I am, and want to be, the slave of Lorenzo and Giuliano [de' Medici]' and other *principali*, Benedetto Dei wrote in his *Memorie storiche* in 1470.[52]

This said, it is also true that an examination of the social context of letters of recommendation—of precisely who wrote what to whom, and how often and with what result—would reveal an attitude to how and why things should be done that might be less offensive to a modern sensibility. Genuine and enduring friendships, from which flowed protestations of love and fraternal regard (and scores of reciprocal favours), can be documented just as easily as insincere professions of loyalty, of which Spini's is anyway not an example, for all its extravagant language. The Florentine businessman Bartolomeo Cederni, discussed by F. W. Kent, was a master of friendship (in both the 'instrumental' and emotional senses) who kept intact his interlocking circles of patrons and clients for some forty years; like Bernardo Rucellai's friend Ser Niccolò Michelozzi, Cederni was an accomplished and beloved 'prompter and go-between [*ricordatore e intromettitore*]'.[53] Some men, moreover, did not express themselves as had Spini, and in their actions were determined to maintain a balance between the preservation of their own honour, and sense of justice, and good

---

[50] '... mi vi riputo non servidore ma schiavo e chane di vostra chasa': MAP xx, 333, 5 Sept. 1467. On Spini, see R. de Roover, *The Rise and Decline of the Medici Bank, 1397–1494* (Cambridge, Mass., 1963), pp. 92–4, 335, 345–6, 354, 357.

[51] L. Martines, *The Social World of the Florentine Humanists, 1390–1460* (London, 1963), p. 294.

[52] The passage is on p. 45 of the typed copy (in the Warburg Institute, London) of Bayerische Staatsbibliothek, Munich, Cod. Ital. 160.

[53] Biblioteca Nazionale, Florence, Fondo Ginori Conti, 29 (Carte Michelozzi), 101b, fo. 47, 23 Nov. 1486. See Chapter 5.

relations with powerful patrons, especially in cases where leniency towards a person accused of a serious crime was requested of an official. The virtuous, not to say sensible, patron would usually ask that such grace be given 'saving your honour'; an obscure provincial whom Benedetto Dei in a letter to his brother called 'Pierfilippo Pandolfini's creature'—which might seem a morally compromising description—was also 'an upright person suitable for any honest undertaking'.[54] Perhaps Florence was—we would be the first to admit that what follows needs much more working out—one of those deferential civic societies, ideally often republics, which John Pocock has described; patrons and clients had to be 'affable' together, those who deferred self-respectingly knew their rights, just as the deferred-to realized the limits of their authority and their obligations to others.[55] If a would-be client was, as the imprisoned cuirass-maker Giovanni da Milano wrote to Piero di Cosimo, 'the servant of Your Magnificence's servants', the patron also described himself as 'serving' or 'pleasing' his dependant.[56] One suspects that some of the Medici, at least, grew increasingly insensitive to or impatient of their clients' scruples, that Quattrocento-Florence's history could be usefully viewed from the perspective of the tensions created by the emergence of a family of over-mighty patrons who also (this story is better known) wrought change in its republican constitution.[57]

As the Medici and their closest friends put both the Republic and the *sottogoverno* under ever-mounting pressure, aspects of the patronage system came under criticism—tension was inseparable from Renaissance friendship as Lytle shows—the Savonarolans arguing in the 1490s that the giving of gifts to magistrates 'destroys many persons' and 'ruins the city'.[58] Yet the same pious men and women themselves

---

[54] '... Deodoro da Pistoia, una chriatura di Pierfilippo Pandolfini, persona da bbene e atta a ogni chosa giusta ...': Conventi Soppressi, 78, 318, fo. 362, 4 Sept. 1480. See too F. W. Kent, *Household and Lineage in Renaissance Florence: The Family Life of the Capponi, Ginori and Rucellai* (Princeton, 1977), pp. 80–5, 211–25.

[55] J. G. A. Pocock, 'The Classical Theory of Deference', *American Historical Review*, 81 (1976), 516–23.

[56] '... servo de' servi dela Vᵃ Mᵃ': MAP XVI, 53, 29 Nov. 1451.

[57] N. Rubinstein, *The Government of Florence under the Medici, 1434–1494* (Oxford, 1966).

[58] Domenico Cecchi made the first charge: U. Mazzone, '*El buon governo*': *Un progetto di riforma generale nella Firenze savonaroliana* (Florence, 1978), p. 191; and Domenico Bartoli the second: quoted by R. Ristori, 'Un mercante savonaroliano: Pandolfo Rucellai', *Magia astrologia e religione nel Rinascimento: Convegno polacco—italiano* (Warsaw, 1972), p. 43.

naturally formed and used networks of friends to maintain their
position in the city, so accepted and positive were many of the values
associated with patronage. It was a Prior's duty, according to an
anonymous contemporary *ricordo*, 'to honour and promote the interests of your relations and friends and neighbours ... without waiting
to be asked or entreated'.[59] The Chancellor of Florence, Lionardo
Bruni, whose ideal of impartial government and administration seemed
almost incomprehensible to his northern European contemporaries, no
doubt found it quite proper for Cosimo de' Medici, then Gonfalonier of
Justice, to attempt, in February 1439, to have the Captain of Arezzo
provide 'a kinsman of Messer Lionardo ... with a certain office which
he would like to have in this city'.[60] Friendship was a cardinal, indeed
a necessary, virtue in this 'agonistic' society, this 'paradise inhabited
by devils' as Agnolo Acciaiuoli described Florence in November 1465.[61]
Amicizia and its attendant virtues were to be cultivated, saving one's
honour, with fervour and open reverence, since one's potential enemies
were so numerous; according to Giovanni Rucellai, 'one enemy can
injure you more than four friends can help'.[62] One misunderstands
much of the moral tenor of fifteenth-century life if one dismisses
patronage and clientage as mere mutual backscratching, its rhetoric
as just that, and nothing more.

Florentine piety towards paternal forebears has been described as
'ancestor reverence',[63] the Christian cult of the saints at San Lorenzo
as, in Robert Gaston's words, 'in certain respects ... a sophisticated
and ecclesiastically orchestrated cult of patronal ancestors'.[64] The
kinship Peter Brown has detected between the emergence of the cult
of saints in late antiquity and the contemporary Roman patron–client
system, obtained still a millennium later.[65] If, however, in the beginning

---

[59] Cited by Kent and Kent, *Neighbours and Neighbourhood*, pp. 19, 23.

[60] Carlo Bonciani in Arezzo acknowledged Cosimo's recommendation of 'uno parente
di Messere Lionardo vostro cancielieri di certo offitio el quale lui disiderebe avere in
questa città': MAP XI, 159. See R. Harding, 'Corruption and the Moral Boundaries of
Patronage in the Renaissance', in Lytle and Orgel, *Patronage in the Renaissance*, pp. 47–
64, esp. p. 49.

[61] '... uno paradiso habitato da diavoli': Carte Strozziane, III, 178, fo. 14, Acciaiuoli
to Filippo Strozzi. See R. F. E. Weissman, *Ritual Brotherhood in Renaissance Florence*
(New York, 1982), esp. pp. 26–41, for the 'agonistic character of social relations'.

[62] A. Perosa (ed.), *Giovanni Rucellai ed il suo zibaldone*, I: *Il zibaldone quaresimale*
(London, 1960), p. 9.

[63] F. W. Kent, *Household and Lineage*, pp. 99 ff., 258 ff.

[64] See Chapter 7.

[65] P. Brown, *The Cult of the Saints* (Chicago, 1981), esp. chs. 2 and 3.

the language and imagery of prayers for saintly intercession by the 'invisible friends' had borrowed from the vocabulary appropriate to secular patronal hierarchies, no such analytical distinction seems applicable later. When in 1464 Giovanni Rucellai copied into his commonplace book these lines—'So, Lord, because You created me, I am; You pre-ordained that You had to create me, and to include me among Your creatures'—his prayer recalls a client's begging assurance that his patron counted him 'in the number of his friends', as the formula went, or the words of some 'creature' whose career a revered patron had literally created.[66] Fraternal love, respect, and loyalty between patron and client, a due and deferential sense of subordination of lower to higher, of son to father to change the familial image, defined the moral climate of clientage, for all that men's actions could be, inevitably, at variance with it.

In this context, to call another man a 'creature' invoked a sacred image as much as one of slavish dependence, to place oneself or one's affairs 'in the hands or arms' of the Medici—as did both Francesco Tornabuoni and the humble lads from the Millstone Corner—was to use the language of prayer and of the family.[67] Since, as John Najemy has pointed out,[68] from the later fourteenth century onwards the conception of society and the state as a family ruled by benevolent elders triumphed over a corporatist ideal, it followed logically that, on his death in 1464, Cosimo, in Niccolò Tignosi's phrase 'quasi gubernator omnium', could be proclaimed *pater patriae*,[69] his grandson later described as 'common father of all our city'.[70] The same Medici

---

[66] Perosa (ed.), *Il zibaldone quaresimale*, p. 119. See F. W. Kent, *Household and Lineage*, pp. 83–4, for the formula.

[67] 'Chome tu sai, le mie facende e la mia famigla ò lascate nelle bracca tue ...': MAP 11, 397, Francesco Tornabuoni to Averardo de' Medici, 23 Dec. 1430; Kent and Kent, 'Two Vignettes', p. 260. On 21 January 1447, Salvestro del Cicha advised his friend Bartolomeo Cederni of the willingness of two powerful men to help the latter in some enterprise: '... liberamente rimetiti nele braccia loro, perchè sono, com' è detto, discretisimi ...': Conventi Soppressi, 78, 314, fo. 247.

[68] J. Najemy, 'Guild Republicanism in Trecento Florence: The Success and Ultimate Failure of Corporate Politics', *American Historical Review*, 84 (1979), 53–71, esp. p. 69; *Corporatism and Consensus in Florentine Electoral Politics, 1280–1400* (Chapel Hill, 1982), pp. 13, 312–13.

[69] Molho, 'Cosimo de' Medici', pp. 6–9. Tignosi is cited by A. Brown, 'The Humanist Portrait of Cosimo de' Medici, Pater Patriae', *Journal of the Warburg and Courtauld Institutes*, 24 (1961), 186–221 (quotation on p. 197).

[70] Carlo del Benino to Piero Guicciardini, 13 Apr. 1492, in R. Ridolfi, 'La visita del Savonarola al Magnifico morente e la leggenda della negata assoluzione', *Archivio storico italiano*, ser. 7, 10 (1928), 205–12 (quotation on p. 210).

were not reluctant to keep blurred the distinction between sacred and secular hierarchy and patronage, as Rab Hatfield has observed in his study of the confraternity of the Magi, whose members received grace through a chain in which the Medici 'were an important link, just below the holy patrons and above the [company's] captains or governor'.[71] Earlier, one Medici placed his kinsman Averardo, Cosimo's cousin and party manager, rather higher up the chain by declaring that, 'I commend myself to you with all my heart, for my only hope is in you and in God. . . . You are my God on earth and all that I crave in this world is the honour and prosperity which I am confident I will receive by your favour.'[72] Because, in Gundersheimer's words, 'images—saints and heroes, father-figures and mother-figures, objects of deference and veneration—were part of the social ecology of everyday life',[73] the Medici patrons, in rising to dominance, drew on and fed profound social impulses, rather than created them. Lorenzo de' Medici as God the Father, or perhaps as classical deity if not *padrino* or godfather in the Hollywood sense, emerges in Gismondo Naldi's letter to Benedetto Dei, an extravagant pro-Medicean, in the grim days of early April 1492: 'I do not believe anyone else is more agonized than am I by the death of the Magnificent Lorenzo, whom I regard as a true and living god. . . . The people of Florence cannot be more loving towards Piero, whom they want in place of the father,' this last phrase, 'nel luogho del padre', perhaps intended deliberately to echo a familiar formula from letters of recommendation.[74] Hinting (prematurely, as it turned out) at the imminent announcement of Giovanni di Lorenzo's cardinalate in a letter, also to Dei, of 7 May 1488, Messer Pierantonio Buondelmonti made quite explicit his vision of the patronal chain of command: 'and everything proceeds from God by means of the virtue, worthiness and dignity of our earthly God, the Magnificent Lorenzo, to whom I beg you to recommend me as his creature.'[75]

---

[71] 'The Compagnia de' Magi', *Journal of the Warburg and Courtauld Institutes*, 33 (1970), 107–61 (quotation on p. 143). See now J. Henderson, 'Le confraternite religiose nella Firenze del tardo medioevo: patroni spirituali e anche politici?', *Ricerche storiche*, 15 (1985), 77–94.

[72] Bernardo d'Alamanno de' Medici to Averardo, cited by D. V. Kent, *The Rise of the Medici: Faction in Florence 1426–1434* (Oxford, 1978), p. 49.

[73] Gundersheimer, 'Patronage', p. 10.

[74] 'Io non chredo che altri abi più passion di me della morte del Magnifico Lorenzo, che llo tenevo per uno idi[o] vivo e vero . . . El popolo di Firenze non può essere più amorevole a Piero, e voglonlo nel luogho del padre': Conventi Soppressi, 78, 317, fo. 12, 14 Apr. 1492. Molho, 'Cosimo de' Medici', pp. 5–33, discusses Cosimo as *padrino*.

[75] '. . . tutto procede da Dio per le virtù, idonità e degnità del nostro Dio in terra,

Anthony Molho has asked what relationship students of personal patronage and clientage would suggest existed between these phenomena and the better-known development of a governing class committed 'to organizing the levers of power and to administering this power as efficiently as possible'.[76] Yet his implied distinction, or even conflict, between 'personal' ties and a 'statist' polity may be overdrawn, for the Medici and their friends might be said to have manipulated the first in the interests of the second—they would anyway have had difficulty separating the two conceptions—rather as, *mutatis mutandis*, the princes of Ferrara strengthened state control by means of personal ties with magnates.[77]

'Axiomatic as the notion that Renaissance culture flourished in an atmosphere of patronage is,' John Hale has observed, 'it remains a vague one,'[78] indeed an overworked one several recent scholars have added. All of us, we suppose, have sat through papers where the details of an art patron's life and ideas loomed larger than the commissioned artist's work, on which they anyway appeared to have had only the most general—or even far-fetched—bearing. In understandable reaction, Creighton Gilbert and Charles Hope would have us banish from our discourse the 'learned advisers' of artistic programmes;[79] Hope has insisted that 'taste played an important and on occasion a decisive part in the thinking of Renaissance patrons'[80] who were dealing with artists who possessed an increasing sense of their own 'artistic license'.[81] None of this rules out, nor (one hopes) is intended to rule out, the traditional proposition that artistic production and creativity should be examined in their precise context, part of which was a competitive social scene honeycombed with patron–client

Magnifico Lorenzo, al quale vi pregho mi racomandiate come sua creatura . . .': Conventi Soppressi, 78, 317, fo. 319.

[76] Molho, 'Il padronato a Firenze', p. 15.
[77] Dean, 'Lords, Vassals and Clients', p. 119.
[78] *Concise Encyclopaedia of the Italian Renaissance*, p. 239.
[79] C. E. Gilbert, *Italian Art 1400–1500* (Englewood Cliffs, NJ, 1980), pp. xviii ff.; C. Hope, 'Artists, Patrons, and Advisers in the Italian Renaissance', in Lytle and Orgel, *Patronage in the Renaissance*, pp. 293–343.
[80] Hope, 'Artists, Patrons, and Advisers', p. 343.
[81] H. W. Janson, 'The Birth of "Artistic License": The Dissatisfied Patron in the Early Renaissance', in Lytle and Orgel, *Patronage in the Renaissance*, pp. 344–53. Cf. M. Kemp's 'From "Mimesis" to "Fantasia": The Quattrocento Vocabulary of Creation, Inspiration and Genius in the Visual Arts', *Viator*, 8 (1977), 347–98, which shows that 'capricious creativity' was not a fifteenth-century notion, and that the patron was often expected to 'invent' the artists' subject matter (esp. pp. 358–60, 371, 373–4, 396–7).

relationships. Artists were creators who were also obliged to attract, and if possible satisfy, patrons whose continued munificence they sought and whose motives for commissioning works of art were mixed. Lorenzo Ghiberti, Benozzo Gozzoli, Piero Pollaiuolo, and Giovanni Bellini were spurred to produce their best work in the 'quality of perfect masters', Domenico Veneziano to seek Piero de' Medici's 'mediation' for a promised 'masterpiece' which 'will bring you honour'.[82] On the other hand, Gentile da Fabriano's stylistic success in Florence might illustrate a case of demand engineered by the artist with a careful eye to procuring future influential patrons, as Hatfield has proposed of Botticelli's *Adoration of the Magi*.[83] Artists continued to manipulate and to befriend patrons, and vice versa, in an environment where the possession of taste, and of egos, was the exclusive preserve of neither party. Contributors to the Melbourne conference on the whole concentrated upon more traditional themes within the study of the context of Renaissance art. Richard Goldthwaite, by way of setting the scene, continued his bravura investigation into the economics and economic imperatives of the conspicuous and massive Renaissance expenditure on an 'empire of things',[84] while, in her analysis of Carrarese patronage of painting and sculpture in fourteenth-century Padua, Margaret Plant, who does not suffer from florentinitis, demonstrated that in this 'singular culture' princely generosity constituted a political statement as well as an assertion of taste.[85] Consideration of the structures and decoration of several northern Italian palaces erected by allies of Emperor Charles V persuaded William Eisler that 'patronage in the region was to a large degree an expression of the patron's position within the new political structure created by the Emperor'.[86] This was not so, according to Heather Gregory, in the case of Palla Strozzi, the Florentine amateur humanist, whose patronage of the arts a hundred years earlier rather sprang from 'private and family motivation', even if his Medici rivals (and modern scholars) may have later read into Messer Palla's activities a political dimension he had not intended.[87]

[82] D. S. Chambers, *Patrons and Artists in the Italian Renaissance* (London, 1970), pp. 11, 14, 17, 46, 53, 91–3, 96; L. D. Ettlinger, *Antonio and Piero Pollaiuolo* (London, 1978), pp. 143–4, 155.

[83] R. Hatfield, *Botticelli's Uffizi 'Adoration'. A Study in Pictorial Content* (Princeton, 1976); see Chambers, *Patrons and Artists*, pp. 176–7, 193–4, for patronage's being attracted by the work and fame of Antonio Pollaiuolo and Fra Angelico.

[84] See Chapter 9.

[85] See Chapter 10.

[86] See Chapter 14.

[87] See Chapter 11.

In this spirit of seeking both precision and flexibility when talking of artistic patronage, Patricia Simons, who sees patronage as a process rather than a system, called for 'a more fluid, less deterministic, sense of how patron and client operated'. In her analysis, Giovanni Tornabuoni, the 'patron' in the traditional art-historical sense of Ghirlandaio's frescos in Santa Maria Novella begun in 1486, becomes almost a 'middleman'—a patronage broker or go-between in political terms—mediating between his numerous kinsmen, the friars of the Dominican convent, and the Ghirlandaio brothers.[88] In Alberti's *Ten Books on Architecture* the architect takes on a not dissimilar social and intellectual role, John Oppel would suggest, informing and co-ordinating the circles of patrons, master builders and artists for whom the book was intended.[89] The broker, variously defined, was a ubiquitous Renaissance figure—he might be a *sensale* or matchmaker, a Bartolomeo Cederni smoothing the way for his many friends, a Giovanni Rucellai acting almost as proxy patron of architecture on Palla Strozzi's behalf[90]—who moved in and around a patronage process that mediated, controlled, and expressed power and influence through a shifting realm of social forces and bonds. Perhaps in social fact, as well as in the neo-Aristotelian theory of Agricola recently expounded by Michael Baxandall, the Renaissance was 'agile and elusive' on the question of 'who was responsible for works of art and their quality', the patron, the artist or, it might be, the broker.[91] For another context—the writing of history—and another place, Sforza Milan, Gary Ianziti pointed to an example of such elasticity in Quattrocento practice, and exploited too the ambiguity in the English word 'patronage' to enter the no man's land between *mecenatismo* of the arts and *clientelismo* in ducal politics.[92]

Others, in discussion, wanted to follow Ianziti's lead, while remaining as wary as he of any tendency to conflate the several meanings of patronage. Art historians speculated about what it meant for their traditional understanding of patronage that Renaissance cities were

---

[88] See Chapter 12.

[89] See Chapter 13.

[90] F. W. Kent, 'The Making of a Renaissance Patron of the Arts', in F. W. Kent *et al.*, *Giovanni Rucellai ed il suo zibaldone*, II: *A Florentine Patrician and his Palace* (London, 1981), esp. pp. 45–51.

[91] 'Rudolph Agricola on patrons efficient and patrons final: a renaissance discrimination', *Burlington Magazine*, 124 (1982), 424–5.

[92] See Chapter 16.

composed of hierarchies of patrons and clients, some taking up, and trying to apply to other well-known commissions, Simons's conception of the patronage process in the Tornabuoni chapel as analogous to, indeed part of, the workings of a patronal society at large. Till Verellen in his paper had examined the social and artistic relationships which bound together the members of a sixteenth-century *società* of sculptors, the *setta sangallesca*, for which Antonio da Sangallo the Younger acted as a 'secondary patron' who subcontracted works of his colleagues, a mechanism which bore 'on workshop conditions, and on sculptural procedure and on the development of individual and collective styles'.[93] There is also the point that, like the Milanese secretaries-cum-historians analysed by Ianziti, some artists, Michelozzo for example, were both political clients of, and worked professionally for, their patrons;[94] 'I have always been of that house', Antonio Pollaiuolo wrote of the Medici.[95] The sculptor Bertoldo was Lorenzo de' Medici's familiar (perhaps his illegitimate kinsman) and his household artist.[96] Lorenzo, in turn, was a patron in the several senses of the word used in this book: Augustus, father of the fatherland, in command of a formidable set of clients, and also (in myth and to a lesser extent in fact) a Maecenas who was not only an arbiter of elegance and dispenser of artists' favours but a poet with an unusual belief in the creative importance of imagination, a considerable commissioner of buildings, and, it might be, an architect in his own right.[97] His methods of social control informed those by which he came to exercise so varied an artistic influence, just as he and his family (as is better known) used

[93] See Chapter 15.

[94] D. V. Kent, *Rise of the Medici*, p. 70 n. 25; M. Ferrara and F. Quinterio, *Michelozzo di Bartolomeo* (Florence, 1984), pp. 11 ff.

[95] Ettlinger, *Antonio and Piero Pollaiuolo*, p. 164.

[96] U. Middeldorf, 'On the Dilettante Sculptor', *Apollo*, 107 (1978), 310–22, esp. pp. 314–16.

[97] E. H. Gombrich, 'Renaissance and Golden Age', in *Norm and Form* (London, 1971, 2nd edn.), pp. 29–34; and the new synthesis by J. Hook, *Lorenzo de' Medici* (London, 1984), esp. ch. 6. Recent bibliography on Lorenzo as art patron is cited by C. Elam, 'Lorenzo de' Medici and the urban development of Renaissance Florence,' *Art History*, 1 (1978), 43–66; P. Foster, 'Lorenzo de' Medici and the Florence Cathedral Facade', *Art Bulletin*, 63 (1981), 495–500; F. W. Kent, 'New Light on Lorenzo de' Medici's convent at Porta San Gallo', *Burlington Magazine*, 124 (1982), 292–4. Lorenzo's idea of imagination, especially in his 'Comento ad alcuni sonetti d'amore' in *Scritti scelti*, ed. E. Bigi (Turin, 1955), p. 371, is briefly noted by Kemp, 'From "Mimesis" to "Fantasia"', pp. 363, 377 n. 152, and by D. Summers, *Michelangelo and the Language of Art* (Princeton, 1981), pp. 121–4.

their genuine passion for the arts to further their grip on Renaissance Florence. Whether such questions and propositions seem as useful to other Renaissance scholars as they did to those who participated in Melbourne, remains to be seen.

PART I

Cui Bono?: Patronage and Society

2

Taking Patronage Seriously: Mediterranean Values and Renaissance Society

RONALD WEISSMAN

THE terms patron and client have a variety of senses [noted Ernest Gellner]. In England, one often sees signs such as 'This car park is reserved for the use of patrons'. This does not mean that only men with political influence may leave their cars in the areas indicated. Or again, the non-Philistine left holds that the state should be a patron of the arts. By this they do not mean, however, that the police should wrest control of Sotheby's from the Mafia.[1]

Despite the multiple meanings of 'patron' or 'patronage', Mediterranean anthropologists are in general agreement, both as concerns the principal characteristics of patronage, and its central importance as a value system structuring politics and political values in this region.[2] Mediterranean patron–client relationships share these attributes:

1. There exists an inequality of power or resources between patron and client.
2. Patronage is a long-term relationship, having a moral or social rather than a legal basis.
3. A patronage relationship is not restricted to a single kind of transaction. It is multistranded and multipurpose.

---

[1] E. Gellner, 'Patrons and Clients', in E. Gellner and J. Waterbury (eds.), *Patrons and Clients in Mediterranean Societies* (London, 1977), p. 1.

[2] The social anthropology of patronage has produced a diverse and extensive series of studies. For comparative reviews of patronage in the Mediterranean, see Gellner and Waterbury, *Patrons and Clients*. J. Davis, *Mediterranean People* (London, 1977), pp. 132–50, presents a provisional synthesis and review of the state of patronage studies in this region. Several of the principal ethnographic studies and more general interpretations have been collected in S. W. Schmidt *et al.* (eds.), *Friends, Followers, and Factions* (Berkeley, 1977); especially useful is J. C. Scott's bibliographic review. S. N. Eisenstadt and L. Roniger, 'Patron–Client Relations as a Model of Structuring Social Exchange', *Comparative Studies in Society and History*, 22 (1980), 42–77, also contains a very complete bibliography.

4. Patronage is a relationship in which the patron provides more than simple protection. He provides brokerage, mediation, favours, and access to networks of friends of friends.

5. Mediterranean patronage has a distinctive ethos, standing outside the officially proclaimed social morality.

If Italian Renaissance patronage shared these characteristics, and all the evidence suggests that it did, what then is the significance of patronage for the interpretation of Renaissance society?

Patronage has provided political scientists, sociologists, and anthropologists with a conceptual framework for the interpretation of contemporary Mediterranean politics, social structure, social behaviour, and values. While patronage has often been the subject of Renaissance studies, it has rarely served as a key concept to guide our interpretation of fourteenth- or fifteenth-century Italian society. Students of the Renaissance have tended to use patronage to illuminate rather different areas of enquiry, most commonly, the study of the audiences for which, and the processes through which, cultural artefacts were produced, or the manner in which courts were organized.[3] When Renaissance social historians have studied patronage, it has typically been in order to examine the political history of particular communities. Few general studies of Renaissance patronage exist, and those that do have generally emphasized cultural patronage.[4] While my observations are, I hope, of some relevance for those who study cultural patronage, it is with social patronage that I am principally concerned. This discussion

---

[3] Although scholarly interest has increased in the past two decades, F. Haskell's *Patrons and Painters* (London, 1963), and E. H. Gombrich's 'The Early Medici as Patrons of Art', in E. F. Jacob (ed.), *Italian Renaissance Studies* (London, 1960), pp. 279–311, remain the classic studies of Renaissance and Baroque art patronage. On patronage at court, see A. G. Dickens (ed.), *The Courts of Europe: Politics, Patronage and Royalty, 1400–1800* (London, 1977).

[4] The most recent interpretation of Renaissance patronage is W. L. Gundersheimer's 'Patronage in the Renaissance: An Exploratory Approach', in G. F. Lytle and S. Orgel (eds.), *Patronage in the Renaissance* (Princeton, 1981), pp. 3–23. For Gundersheimer, patronage is, at its root, political. His model of patronal politics is based on Mary Douglas's 'Big Man' theory, which emphasizes the aura, powers, and dominance of chieftains and leaders, and interprets patronage as being a charismatic authority exercised over formal or informal social hierarchies. Although this interpretation illuminates the study of early modern European royalty and miscellaneous Italian Renaissance potentates, it does not describe Renaissance patronage more generally. Most studies of Renaissance patronage concern patronage of the arts. See, for example, P. Burke, *Culture and Society in Renaissance Italy* (New York, 1972), pp. 75–111. Burke provides a taxonomy of patrons, and examines the relationship between patrons, intellectuals and their markets in Italy.

will attempt to place Renaissance patronage within the broader context of Mediterranean (particularly Italian) patronage, past and present. In so doing, I wish to suggest ways in which an appreciation of patronage, if in fact it was fundamental to the Renaissance, ought to prompt us to reassess several familiar interpretations of Italian Renaissance society.

From the second decade of the twentieth century onwards, most Renaissance historians have been divided into two principal camps: those—until recently the more numerous—who emphasized the formal, corporate ordering of society into such groups as clans and guilds or sentimental solidarities such as status groups and classes, and those who argued that informal social bonds such as patronage and friendship provided the real social glue binding Renaissance society.[5] The importance of informal or noncorporate bonds was first emphasized by Antonio Anzilotti and by Nicola Ottokar. In 1912 Anzilotti provided, in the course of his explanation of the rise of the Medici principate in the sixteenth century, a brief characterization of the social basis of Medici rule during the Republic. While he did not underemphasize the importance of class and status group cohesion, he called attention to the power of informal relations, 'gli amici'. Medici power rested, he said, 'on a vast network of interests, of kinship ties, of reciprocal obligations . . .'[6]

Independently of Anzilotti, in 1926, Nicola Ottokar[7] rejected the validity of Gaetano Salvemini's[8] division of Florence into *magnati* and

---

[5] As anthropologists have long observed, patterns of social organization based on class and on informal links such as patronage are by no means mutually incompatible. J. Scott, 'Patronage or Exploitation', in Gellner and Waterbury, *Patrons and Clients*, pp. 21–39, for example, provides a sensitive analysis of the ways in which patronage may serve to legitimate or disguise certain patterns of class structures, and the ways in which the social bases of politics may shift from patronage to class as patrons lose legitimacy. See, also, S. Silverman, 'Patronage as Myth', in Gellner and Waterbury, *Patrons and Clients*, pp. 5–19.

Dependency theorists have used patronage to illuminate the ways in which Mediterranean élites have maintained traditional class hierarchies during periods of economic change and modernization. See, for example, P. and J. Schneider, *Culture and Political Economy in Western Sicily* (New York, 1976). For an analysis of Florentine social organization that compares patterns of patronage and class, see A. Molho, 'Cosimo de' Medici: *Pater Patriae* or *Padrino?*', *Stanford Italian Review*, 1 (1979), 5–33.

[6] A. Anzilotti, *La crisi costituzionale della Repubblica fiorentina* (Florence, 1912), p. 3.

[7] N. Ottokar, *Il comune di Firenze alla fine del Dugento* (Florence, 1926).

[8] G. Salvemini, *Magnati e popolani in Firenze* (Florence, 1899). For a reconsideration of Ottokar's evidence by Salvemini partisans, see G. Raveggi *et al.*, *Ghibellini, guelfi, e popolo grasso* (Florence, 1978).

popolani. Ottokar believed that this distinction was not useful for understanding political behaviour or social conflict during the late thirteenth century. For Ottokar, political cleavages could not be reduced to class or status group conflicts. Political conflict in Florence was explained by one key factor: the fluctuating personal interests of powerful individuals and families.

> Public life remained ever dominated by a network of particularistic and factional bonds, of adherents, and of clients of powerful men and families. . . . From the War between the Whites and the Blacks to the elevation of the Medici house this prevalence of fragmented power and of particularistic bonds remained, against an illusory background of anonymous democracy, the most characteristic and essential trait of the internal history of Florence.[9]

From the 1920s onwards, the Salvemini/Ottokar debate has characterized the principal positions of Florentine historians. In 1955, for example, Rudolf von Albertini broadened Anzilotti's view of the Medici. He described fifteenth-century Medici politics as a system of personal bonds between the Medici and their *amici*, a system in which the Medici dispensed favours, honours, and access to papal contacts in exchange for political support.[10]

Until 1964, relations very much like patronage and clientage had been used in analytically useful ways by Renaissance historians. But the concept of patronage—understood as a social and political system organizing certain elements of Renaissance behaviour—had not yet entered the vocabulary of Renaissance studies, until, in a brief but controversial essay, Gene Brucker formally introduced it into Florentine social history. What had been hinted at in suggestive passages by Ottokar, Anzilotti, and von Albertini was made explicit by Brucker.

For Brucker, patronage was a 'continuation and extension of the old feudal relationship between lord and dependent which never disappeared in the city and remained quite strong in the rural regions'. The spread of patronage ties was, in his analysis, occasioned by the collapse of traditional corporate loyalties such as guilds, neighbourhoods, and fraternities at the end of the fourteenth century. The demise of corporatism left the Florentine unprotected. 'To defend himself against the dangers and threats which confronted him in

---

[9] Ottokar, *Il comune*, p. 215.
[10] R. von Albertini, *Das florentinische Staatsbewusstsein im Überbang von der Republik zum Prinzipat* (Bern, 1955), ch. 1.

the very competitive Florentine milieu, he sought the support and friendship of men more powerful and influential than himself.'[11]

Since Brucker's introduction of the concept, other Renaissance historians have explored patron–client dynamics. F. W. Kent examined the uses of cultural patronage in promoting family solidarity, dynastic sentiments, and honour in the fifteenth and sixteenth centuries.[12] Anthony Molho compared the relative importance of ties of patronage and class in Cosimo's Florence.[13] For Molho, patronage, organized on the basis of neighbourhood networks, served as a form of organization and mobilization for Florence's political classes. In his view, patronage networks did not extend socially below the level of the guild community. The social depth of patron–client ties remains an open question. There is, however, increasing evidence that patronage may have been rather broadly diffused throughout the social spectrum. For example, Dale and F. W. Kent provide evidence linking the Medici, in the immediate aftermath of the Pazzi conspiracy, to neighbourhood gangs of poor Florentine youths.[14]

The historians that I have mentioned thus far described the political characteristics of patron–client relations in an overview or in summary fashion. Dale Kent's study of the elevation of the Medici offers, by contrast, a very extensive and concrete analysis of social patronage in the Renaissance. For Kent, patronage relations were an enduring feature of Florentine society.

The whole patronage system depended upon a complex of relationships; the leaders of the most powerful Florentine families functioned as brokers of patronage to which they had the greatest access, but the fulfillment of most requests required the participation of a whole chain of *amici* who clustered round them. The most successful patrons were those who managed most often to satisfy the needs of their friends; consequently successful patrons tended

---

[11] G. Brucker, 'The Structure of Patrician Society in Renaissance Florence', *Colloquium*, 1 (1964), 8–11.

[12] F. W. Kent, *Household and Lineage in Renaissance Florence: The Family Life of the Capponi, Ginori and Rucellai* (Princeton, 1977). See also his study in F. W. Kent *et al.*, *Giovanni Rucellai ed il suo zibaldone, II: A Florentine Patrician and his Palace* (London, 1981), pp. 9–95.

[13] Molho, 'Cosimo de' Medici', *passim*.

[14] D. V. and F. W. Kent, 'Two Vignettes of Florentine Society in the Fifteenth Century', *Rinascimento*, 2nd ser., 23 (1983), 237–60. Allegiances that cut across class lines were nothing new to Florentine history. Private armies arrayed on either side of patrician factional conflict, composed of peasants and possibly the urban poor, are known to have existed, for example, during the 1430s. See D. V. Kent, *The Rise of the Medici* (Oxford, 1978), p. 338.

to be those who could attract and maintain a large number of followers who constituted a pool of potential resources for each other's mutual aid.[15]

Her account of the rise of Medici power is based on her analysis of Medici use of patronage, for the Medici party was an extension of this system. The *amici* were gathered together by Medici favours, which included communal tax relief, loans, low-rent housing, intervention in law courts, manipulation of electoral scrutinies, and aid in acquiring political office. In the process of describing Medici patronage, Kent explored the mechanisms, forms of exchange, and language of patronage, and detailed the actual configuration and membership of Florentine patronage networks.

The detailed portrait of patronage in action provided by Kent leaves no doubt about the importance of patronage behaviour among the political classes of Florence. To round off the picture presented so far of Renaissance social patronage, particularly in Florence, I would add two elements: the ambiguity and the pervasiveness of patronage. The boundaries between kinship, friendship, and patronage were quite ambiguous.[16] Similar ties of obligation existed among friends, family, and patrons and clients, and the actual operation of patronage networks required the simultaneous mobilization of all relevant personal relations. In this regard, it should be stressed that examining patronage alone may be quite misleading. It would be far more appropriate to place patronage within a broader family of correlate social relations. Thus I would emphasize that in Florence most, if not all, relations were personalized. Florentines were bound by many real, imagined, or contrived reciprocal bonds, many carrying implied 'moral' obligations and overtones. To study patronage to the exclusion of friendship and kinship is to miss one of Florence's most significant social characteristics and a feature that patronage shares with other bonds: the personalized, intimate, hard-to-disentangle sense of loyalty and obligation that permeated social relations more generally.

It should also be recognized that the culture of patronage was not limited to the political classes alone. Through corporate ties, Florentines of most social classes regularly participated in ritual patron–client celebrations. The fraternities of Florence, for example, celebrated the cult of patron saints, and enacted ceremonies of spiritual clientage. And in their distributions of charity, often to Florentines

---

[15] D. V. Kent, *Rise of the Medici*, p. 92.
[16] On this point, see ibid., p. 17 n. 70.

selected through the *raccomandazione* of individual members, Florentines were able, during their terms of office, to play the patron and
distribute largess in exchange for public expressions of gratitude.
Through the cult life of Florence, patronage as a value system was
widely and regularly diffused.[17] Furthermore, the fragmentation and
dispersal of power in Florence gave many Florentines throughout the
social spectrum the chance to be political entrepreneurs, to exercise
patronage, brokerage, or influence for the purpose of creating obligations or alliances.[18]

Florence does not stand alone among Renaissance city-states as a
patronage-dominated society. Philip Jones has, for example, used
patronage-like themes to describe the personalized links between despots and local élites. Werner Gundersheimer's study of the nature of
Estensi rule in Ferrara, one of the more recent patronage studies,
reveals, additionally, the extent to which cultural patronage served the
broader aims of legitimating despots.[19]

While patronage has now entered the common vocabulary of many
Italian Renaissance historians, few have attempted to draw lessons or
conclusions about it as a general social phenomenon. And, despite the
clear evidence for the pervasiveness of patronage in Tuscan politics
and social arrangements, the concept remains troublesome for many
historians. For some, patronage, while important, is a 'feudal' patri-

[17] See further my *Ritual Brotherhood in Renaissance Florence* (New York, 1982),
chs. 2 and 3. It should be noted that Christianity is quite ambivalent about patronage.
Christian universalism tended to oppose factional partiality, while the cult of the saints
often served to legitimate patronage.

[18] In this context, it is useful to recall this observation about the political culture of
Italy and Spain:

> In the regions of the Western Mediterranean ... the fragmentation of power extends,
> by and large, throughout the social system. Everywhere power seems to be in different,
> but overlapping domains. This is an area in which individuals at all levels are
> politicians: they calculate, wheel and deal, and intrude themselves into widely diver-
> gent spheres of action. They are celebrated for their initiative and drive, notorious for
> their capacity to store information about political debits and credits, and remarkably
> skilled at interpersonal relations. The would-be entrepreneur in this context is always
> alive to opportunities for forming coalitions with others. (P. and J. Schneider, and
> E. Hansen, 'Modernization and Development: The Role of Regional Elites and
> Noncorporate Groups in the European Mediterranean', *Comparative Studies in
> Society and History*, 14 (1972); repr. in Schmidt, *Friends, Followers, and Factions*,
> pp. 472ff.)

[19] W. L. Gundersheimer, *Ferrara: The Style of a Renaissance Despotism* (Princeton,
1973). On patronage-like relations of Renaissance signories, see P. Jones, 'Communes
and Despots: The City State in Late Medieval Italy', *Transactions of the Royal Historical
Society*, 5th ser., 15 (1965), 71–96; and F. W. Kent, 'À la recherche du clan perdu',
Journal of Family History, 2 (1977), 77–86.

monial anachronism. For others, particularly neo-Burckhardtians and
some but not all Marxists, the significance of patronage is extremely
limited, being a form of behaviour that so violates theoretical assumptions about the nature of the Renaissance that its existence tends to
be either ignored or denied.

Those historians who deny the existence or the importance of
patronage generally accept a set of assumptions about the modernity
of Renaissance society and economy. These assumptions are worth re-
examining. The conventional picture of the Renaissance—and here
Florence is surely the archetype—is that what distinguishes Renaissance civilization is its precocious modernity. The modernity of the
Renaissance, conceived in Marxist, Burckhardtian, or Weberian terms,
generally involves three related developments: first, the growth of
universalistic, as opposed to personalistic, values, exemplified by civic
humanism; second, the rise of the objective, rational Renaissance state;
and third, the development of Renaissance capitalism which, like all
capitalism, is destructive of intimate, traditional social bonds. In a
Renaissance whose modernity is typified by humanism, by capitalism,
and by the development of a rational bureaucratic state, what possibly
could be the significance of a feudal anachronism like patronage?

I would suggest that these assumptions—the feudal nature of patronage and the incompatibility of patronage and modernization—are in
need of some revision. The former assumption, about feudalism, while
not incorrect, may nevertheless mislead. The latter assumption, about
modernization, is historically inaccurate, at least as far as the Mediterranean is concerned. What we now know about patronage should
lead us to re-evaluate fundamentally the conventional wisdom about
the nature of the Renaissance. If, as the title of this chapter suggests,
we should take patronage seriously, then let us begin by examining
the traditional assumptions that relegate patronage to the category of
some feudal remnant that is incompatible with Renaissance modernity.

It would be incorrect to suggest that Italian patronage is not, in some
sense, a continuation of feudal behaviour. We know that thirteenth-
century nobles emigrating to cities, did, on occasion, bring their clients
with them. And certainly, patronage is not unlike the seigneurial
culture of deference and protection associated with feudalism. As
Gellner has written,

the exchange of labour, support, rent, or tax in return for protection and
access to land, leads to many features observed both in feudalism and patron-

age relations. This is particularly so in the sphere of morals: a stress on the fidelity to persons rather than to principles, a cult of honor and loyalty, violence and virility.[20]

But several historical and theoretical problems arise when Italian Renaissance patronage is equated too closely and too simply with feudal behaviour. The patron may to some degree have entered the Renaissance in feudal garb, but his culture, his values, and his behaviour were far more ancient—and urban—in origin.[21]

Patronage was endemic to the cities of the Mediterranean well before the rise of feudalism. Ernst Badian and others have suggested that patronage was nothing less than the political and cultural system used by republican Rome to control and Romanize the Mediterranean,[22] a proposal that may, in part, help explain the universality of patronage in Mediterranean culture. And Cicero believed that *clientela*—the political and social patron–client relationship—was so embedded in the fabric of Roman politics that it must have originated with Romulus.[23]

The formal meaning of *clientela* in Rome was *in fide alicuius esse*, to be entrusted to a more powerful person. From the earliest mention of the term, it appears to have implied *fides*, or mutual moral obligation.[24] Unlike feudalism, but like Renaissance patronage, this personal moral obligation was always informal—defined in custom but not in law.[25] For the traditional Roman citizen, patronage was viewed with not a little ambivalence: it was considered, at one and the same time, to be both fundamental to the ordering of society, and dangerous for the commonwealth. For it was simultaneously recognized that, while patronage conflicted with the theoretically impersonal ideals of Roman

[20] Gellner, 'Patrons and Clients', p. 2.

[21] In this regard, N. Rouland, *Pouvoir politique* (Brussels, 1979), pp. 21–3, 260–1, believes that Roman patronage was a *peculiarly* urban phenomenon, Rome's way of managing urbanization. Patronage originated in urban social relations and, as Rome grew in importance, so too patronage increased.

[22] E. Badian, *Foreign Clientelae* (Oxford, 1958).

[23] Cicero, *De re publica*, ii. 16.

[24] See, however, R. P. Saller, *Personal Patronage under the Early Empire* (Cambridge, 1982), p. 8 n. 3, for his reasons for ignoring *fides*. Given the near universal agreement, however, among Mediterranean anthropologists about the importance of the 'moral' dimensions of patronage, Badian and others who have stressed the importance of *fides* are probably correct in this emphasis. Rouland (*Pouvoir politique*, pp. 93–8) has also noted the importance of *fides* and the difficulties of its interpretation.

[25] As Badian has suggested, '*clientela* was an extralegal institution sanctioned by *mos maiorum* and supported by the realities of power' (*Foreign Clientelae*, p. 159).

government, it was, nevertheless, the flesh and blood of actual political and social behaviour.[26] As in the case of Renaissance patronage, but unlike feudal social relations, Roman *clientela*, sometimes hierarchical in nature, could, especially in the world of kin and neighbourhood-based urban politics, become confused with the less hierarchical relationship of *amicitia*.[27]

In the city of Rome, patrons acquired clients through their patronage of neighbourhood trade guilds and burial societies. These local clients, in turn, supported their patrons for political office in Rome, through their votes, and through their participation in personal, client-based armies. At the very least, the client was obliged to accompany his patron to the Forum, increasing his retinue and, therefore, his prestige. In return, as Dionysius of Helicarnassus described *clientela*, the patron was obligated to defend his client, bring suit for him, look after his welfare and that of his family, and secure favours at home and abroad.[28]

As in the Renaissance, the most powerful Roman patrons were members of an élite (in this case senatorial) whose contacts and clients spanned the entire Mediterranean world. And it was through those contacts, largely informal, voluntary, and personal, that Rome ruled and Romanized the Mediterranean. Relations between people served as the paradigm organizing relations between states. Ernst Badian has characterized Roman dominion in the Mediterranean as based on *clientela* relations.[29] Dependant states stood to Rome as patrons to clients, owing Rome *officia* in return for Roman *beneficia*. How did the system work? Patronage provided the network of Roman and provincial interlinkages that bound the Empire together.[30] One is reminded here of Eric Wolf's description of patronage in Mexico which, in turn, has influenced much thought about patronage in the Mediterranean. For Wolf, patrons 'are those persons who stand guard over the critical synapses which connect the local system to the larger whole'.[31] Or, as Julian Pitt-Rivers has written about modern Spain: it

---

[26] K. Hopkins, *Conquerors and Slaves* (Cambridge, 1978), pp. 88–9.

[27] Saller, *Personal Patronage*, pp. 11–15, describes in detail the opportunities and ambiguities inherent in the confusion of Roman patronage and friendship.

[28] L. R. Taylor, *Party Politics in the Age of Caesar* (Berkeley, 1949), pp. 41ff.

[29] Badian, *Foreign Clientelae*, p. 262.

[30] For a case study of provincial patronage in North Africa, see Saller, *Personal Patronage*, ch. 5.

[31] E. R. Wolf, 'Aspects of Group Relations in a Complex Society: Mexico', *American Anthropologist*, 58 (1956), 1075. See also S. F. Silverman, 'Patronage and the Community–Nation Mediator in Traditional Central Italy', *Ethnology*, 4 (1965).

is, above all, the patron's 'relationship to the powers outside of the pueblo which gives him value'.[32]

Senators assumed provincial positions which made them well placed to protect the interests of foreign cities and provinces. Once such duties were acquired, the senator became the official patron of that locale. Foreign cities actively sought to acquire Roman patrons. Despite the supposed impartiality of Roman law and administration, it was often difficult for a small city to get a hearing at Rome without the intervention of a Roman patron. The patron entertained envoys, introduced them to powerful friends, acted as their sponsors, and argued their cases. When internal differences factionalized such a city, the patron was expected to intervene and provide justice. In return, client families and cities were expected to support the political career of their patron, sending official praises to Rome to bolster his reputation in the Senate, offering him hospitality if his career took a turn for the worse, and supporting his private army. And so foreign *clientelae* swelled the retinue of senators at Rome, especially during the civil wars of the late Republic. In the provinces, monuments were erected to remind the citizens of the benefits conferred by their patron. Even those states that were formally independent of Rome were customarily manipulated from Rome by means of the patronage relations existing between individual Roman patrons and local client groups. The medium of exchange of these patron–client relations, in Roman antiquity as in the Renaissance, was, of course, the ubiquitous letter of recommendation of the sort that filled the letter-books of Cicero, Pliny, and Symmachus, as well as Cosimo and Lorenzo.[33]

The frequent blurring of patronage and friendship in ancient Rome and Renaissance Florence should warn us against overemphasizing the socially hierarchical features of patronage to the exclusion of other aspects of the relationship. Inequality may take many forms in addition to those based on the hierarchies of traditional social stratification: inequality of access to news, information, friendship networks, political connections, scarce resources, of technical skills such as literacy. Thus, a man may serve as a patron to another for reasons that have little to do with great differences in property or social status. In contemporary Mediterranean communities, it is not always the wealthiest who make the best patrons, but those with the best influence

---

[32] J. Pitt-Rivers, *The People of the Sierra* (London, 1954), p. 141.
[33] Hopkins, *Conquerors and Slaves*, pp. 88–9. On letters of *raccomandazione* in Florence, see D. V. Kent, *Rise of the Medici*, pp. 83ff.

or connections. In central Italy, Sydel Silverman has described the typical patrons as professionals: administrators, schoolteachers, elected officials, priests, and notaries.[34] Similarly, in Cyprus the typical patron has traditionally been the *mukhtar*, the Muslim equivalent of a notary or petty bureaucrat.[35] To emphasize exclusively hierarchy and deference, those features most like feudalism, is surely to miss much that is essential to Roman, Renaissance, and contemporary Mediterranean patronage; for this reason, then, feudalism is a misleading analogy for the study of Renaissance patronage.

Like Roman patronage, and unlike feudalism, Renaissance patronage often contravened society's official political ethic, if not necessarily its laws.[36] While a cult of honour and loyalty openly and proudly characterized the feudal ethic, in neither Renaissance Italy nor ancient Rome did the partiality implicit in patronage serve as society's openly and officially sanctioned political morality. In terms of public political culture, patronage did not occupy the honoured place given the impartial and universal values that Renaissance civic humanism elevated as an ideal. More often than not, patronage operated as an unofficial set of assumptions and expectations. Such expectations were based on rather cynical beliefs about the importance of those pragmatic relations of power, influence, and friendship that were considered essential to making one's way in the world. Renaissance townsmen were particularly adept at sincerely professing a belief in the virtues of *buon governo*, while acting, in practice, on the assured belief that political success required loyal *amici*, and that politicians always used political office to reward friends and punish enemies. In feudal culture, such partiality and loyalty were important virtues. In ancient Rome and Renaissance Italy, the partiality of patronage relations was viewed, at best, with ambivalence.[37]

Renaissance and Roman patronage, in addition to its ambivalent moral status, was also informal and ambiguous, unlike feudalism in

---

[34] Silverman, 'Patronage', *passim*.

[35] M. Attalides, 'Forms of Peasant Incorporation in Cyprus during the Last Century', in Gellner and Waterbury, *Patrons and Clients*, p. 142.

[36] On political morality and patronage, particularly corruption, see P. Stirling, 'Impartiality and Personal Morality (Italy)', in J.-G. Peristiany (ed.), *Contributions to Mediterranean Sociology* (Paris, 1968), pp. 49–64, and R. Harding, 'Corruption and the Moral Boundaries of Patronage in the Renaissance', in Lytle and Orgel, *Patronage in the Renaissance*, pp. 47–64.

[37] As Gellner has written, 'feudalism can constitute the Great Tradition of a society; patronage does not' (Gellner and Waterbury, *Patrons and Clients*, p. 3).

which exact duties and relations were well defined and specified. And
in both Renaissance Florence and Republican Rome, the distinction
between patronage and friendship was often blurred to the mutual
advantage of both patrons and clients, who could use the moral
dimensions of friendship to manipulate the *clientela* relationship to
suit their own purpose. Finally, patronage in Roman antiquity was as
much the sophisticated influence of peddling, brokerage, trading of
favours, mediation, and local-regional interlinkage as it was the granting of physical protection. Thus, in both Republican Rome and
Renaissance towns such as Florence—again in contrast to feudalism—
it is far more accurate to speak of urban patronage networks which
included social equals, than of rural patronage hierarchies strictly
binding superiors and inferiors. In sum, in antiquity and the Renaissance, patronage should be understood broadly as a system of values
and behaviour that emphasized the necessity of having friends in
high places in a world in which all politics, indeed all important
transactions, were personalized. As such, patronage was fundamental
to the urban social processes of Mediterranean antiquity. To understand Renaissance patronage as being a feudal anachronism is to miss
its obvious links to and continuities with this far more relevant patronal
tradition that extends back in time to Roman antiquity, and forward
to contemporary Mediterranean society.

One suspects that patronal behaviour in the Renaissance has been
strongly linked to feudalism because the argument has frequently been
made that the Renaissance is a paradigm of modernization. As the
Renaissance became more modern, traditional patrimonial relations
collapsed. Much traditional modernization theory, especially as it
applies to the Renaissance, is based on cultural assumptions derived
from Burckhardt, economic assumptions derived from Marx, and
sociopolitical assumptions derived from Max Weber.

The Renaissance, in purest Marxist form, represents the triumph of
the middle class. What happens when this class dominates society?
According to Marx in the *Communist Manifesto*, 'Whenever the bourgeoisie has got the upper hand, it has put an end to all feudal,
patriarchal, idyllic relations. It has pitilessly torn asunder the motley
feudal ties that bound man to his "natural superiors", and has left
remaining no other nexus between man and man than naked self-
interest, than callous "cash payment".'[38] Historians espousing the

---

[38] This passage is cited in S. Avineri, *The Social and Political Thought of Karl Marx*
(Cambridge, 1970), p. 162. The argument is discussed by him on pp. 162–74.

concept of Renaissance individualism, or a class interpretation of Renaissance society, share to some greater or lesser extent this view. Capitalism, by its very alienating and fragmenting processes, dissolves personal bonds to kin group, neighbourhood, and patron. Abstract society invariably comes to replace community.[39]

The precise expression of such a view in Renaissance studies was first articulated by Alfred von Martin, who used Marxist assumptions to explain Burckhardtian individualism.[40] Since von Martin, assumptions about how the modernization of Renaissance society was achieved by the rise of commerce or of capitalism have become truisms for Marxists and non-Marxists alike. Explaining the outburst of artistic creativity that has come to be known as the Florentine Renaissance, one historian has recently written:

Craftsmen operated in a marketplace where social structures were loose, where relations were fluid, where the cash nexus dominated, and where contracts were protected by impersonal legal authority. Hence they were all the less inhibited in seeking to improve their skills and enlarge their imagination.[41]

Summing up the social situation of artists, Richard Goldthwaite concluded:

In Florence the opportunities were all the greater because the artisan's movement in the marketplace was not largely restricted by social structures—by guilds, by class hierarchy, by large-scale capitalist organization, or by highly personal patronage systems. Perhaps in no other city in Europe at the time was the artisan less confined by these traditional barriers.[42]

Accompanying such a fluid economy came the rationalization of the state, and its corresponding ideology, civic humanism. According to this view, best articulated by Marvin Becker, loyalty to a central state replaced loyalty to particularist groups. Left isolated in the wake of the collapse of traditional corporate bonds, the individual turned to

---

[39] Peter Burke is one of the few historians to express dissatisfaction with the conventional wisdom concerning the Renaissance and modernization. For his interpretation, see his *Culture and Society*, pp. 217ff. See also G. Brucker, 'Bureaucracy and Social Welfare in the Renaissance: A Florentine Case Study', *Journal of Modern History*, 55 (1983), 1–21, esp. pp. 17–21. Brucker notes the development, particularly in formal job classification and responsibility, of a Weberian rational–legal bureaucracy, but also recognizes, in actual practice, significant traditional patronal tendencies.

[40] A. von Martin, *The Sociology of the Renaissance* (New York, 1963).

[41] R. Goldthwaite, *The Building of Renaissance Florence* (Baltimore, 1980), p. 414.

[42] Ibid., p. 413.

the state for his sense of identity and self. In the transition from feudalism to modernity, relations based on universal law, on anonymity, impartiality, and objectivity, replaced those deriving from particularist loyalties. Relations based on contract replaced relations based on status. Individual identity was increasingly formed within a culture of civic patriotism and public sacrifice.[43]

Renaissance historians are certainly not alone in sharing this view of modernization. Anthropologists and sociologists since the turn of the century have developed models of modernization and urbanization which assume transformations similar to those described by Renaissance historians.[44] Virtually all of these models are dualistic, contrasting natural with mechanical solidarity, and the traditional rural community with the modern city, the old moral order versus the modern technical order, or community versus society. Each of these conceptions assumes a linear progression from organic, personalized, deeply interrelated, often vertically integrated societies to an atomistic, impersonal, and fragmented social order.

Much of this interpretation of modernization is based on early twentieth-century frustrations with the socially disruptive consequences of sudden, rapid urbanization in northern Europe and the United States. Whatever the experience of northern Europeans, however, the history of southern Europe does not confirm traditional models of, or assumptions about, the effects of modernization. Two decades ago, anthropologists turned their attention to southern Europe (precisely because the rapidly industrializing post-war Mediterranean basin offered the perfect environment in which to evaluate theories of social change) to study the effects of capitalism, urbanization, and political integration on traditional kinship and patronage structures.

---

[43] M. Becker, 'An Essay on the Quest for Identity in the early Italian Renaissance', in J. G. Rowe and W. H. Stockdale (eds.), *Florilegium historiale* (Toronto, 1971), pp. 299, 304–5.

[44] For a review of traditional modernization theory and a critique of assumptions underlying this theory based on recent Mediterranean research, see A. Simic, 'Urbanization and Modernization in Yugoslavia: Adaptive and Maladaptive Aspects of Traditional Culture', in M. Kenny and D. I. Kertzer (eds.), *Urban Life in Mediterranean Europe* (Urbana, 1983), pp. 203–24. For the effects of recent Mediterranean scholarship on modernization theory, see the Introduction, pp. 10–15. Proponents of modernization theory exist for every epoch. According to L. Harmand, *Un aspect social et politique du monde romain* (Paris, 1957), ancient Rome was really quite modern. During the transition from republic to empire, Rome rationalized and modernized, especially as regards its bureaucracy and administrative structures, with a consequent decline in patronage. For critiques of this argument, see Saller, *Personal Patronage*, pp. 23, 79 and Rouland, *Pouvoir politique*.

Within a decade, as community studies of Italy, Spain, Greece, southern France, and Yugoslavia began to appear, it seemed appropriate to reverse the focus of research. Students of the Mediterranean now asked: 'What were the effects of traditional kinship and patronage structures on capitalism and related "modernizing" phenomena?' Traditional *a priori* assumptions that economic relations or the growth of the centralized state determine the content and form of social relations had to be discarded or substantially refashioned.

What anthropologists have found from studying Mediterranean urbanization and modernization has been quite different from what they expected to find. Capitalism and related modernizing forces had not eliminated traditional personal bonds. Rather, it was precisely those social bonds which provided the vehicles for urbanization and modernization. And rather than being refashioned by modernization, such bonds as kinship and patronage constrained and defined the limits of modernization itself. Capitalism did not subvert patronage. What modernization did was to change its social bases, replacing older patrons with new patron groups. But the essential values and assumptions of a patronage-dominated culture did not change.

Recent studies of the Mezzogiorno offer examples of this process.[45] Until the Second World War, the traditional patron in southern Italy was the local landlord, who mediated relations between peasant towns and the outside world. These patrons were replaced by members of the local Christian Democratic Party, the official representatives of the state and the official mediators between local, regional, and national structures. While the groups exercising patronal power changed, the reality of patronage changed very little. The penetration of the state bureaucracy in southern Italy did not result in the creation of a culture of bureaucratic impartiality and anonymity. Relations between local inhabitants and party organizations, as well as between inhabitants and individual politicians, contained all of the classic features of traditional patronage behaviour: partiality, factional loyalty, personal obligation, and a lack of faith—sometimes bordering on suspicion—in political ideologies and formal institutions.

Mediterranean townsmen have failed to develop and modernize according to the historical inevitabilities sketched by Marx, or the

---

[45] For examples, see A. Blok, *The Mafia of a Sicilian Village* (New York, 1974), pp. 213ff.; L. Graziano, 'Patron–Client Relationships in Southern Italy', in Schmidt, *Friends, Followers, and Factions*, pp. 360–78; and A. Zuckerman, 'Clientelist Politics in Italy', in Gellner and Waterbury, *Patrons and Clients*, pp. 63–79.

progress of bureaucratic and economic rationalism envisioned by Weber. Why? In Palermo, the secretary of the local Communist Party characterized Italy's failure to develop abstract, ideological politics as a consequence of the continuing success of patronage. For the citizens of Palermo, he said, 'institutions as such don't exist, only individuals. Political relations are relations among people, between people who are more or less powerful. The basic fact of life is this: the people don't understand what an institution is, what its function is, its significance . . .'[46]

Recent studies, by Andrei Simic (Yugoslavia), Hans Buechler (Spain), Hans Vermeulen (Greece), and William Douglass, David Kertzer, and Alan Zuckerman (Italy), have reached quite similar conclusions about urbanization, modernization, and patronage in Mediterranean cities.[47] In all of these societies, urbanization occurred through patterns of chain migration, structured around kin groups, neighbourhoods, and patronage. And, if anything, migration has expanded opportunities for patronage and the need for *raccomandazioni*.[48] Simic's comments about Yugoslavia could easily be applied to the rest of the region:

Thus, paradoxically, the very same ethos can account for both the Yugoslav success in urbanization, as reflected in the smooth integration of millions of former peasants into city life, and the failure of the society to develop large-scale institutions based on a predominantly 'rational' or modern model. . . . The tenacity of traditional values with respect to social relationships, particularly those associated with kinship, has assured for the most part, that personal mobility has not been of an atomistic nature, but, rather, has remained rooted in an ideological system stressing familial corporacy. Thus, the relationship between kin . . . [has] not been significantly disrupted by urbanization and economic modernization.[49]

In all of these societies, bureaucratic élites have recently replaced more traditional local élites. But patronage, rather than decreasing, has increased. And the identification of formal political institutions as the

[46] V. Guarrasi, *La condizione marginale* (Palermo, 1978), pp. 152–3.
[47] Simic, 'Urbanization', pp. 203–24; Buechler, 'Spanish Urbanization from a Grassroots Perspective', also in Kenny and Kertzer, *Urban Life in Mediterranean Europe*, pp. 136–61; Vermeulen, 'Urban Research in Greece', ibid., pp. 109–32; Kertzer, 'Urban Research in Italy', ibid., pp. 53–75; Douglass, 'Migration in Italy', ibid., pp. 162–202; and A. Zuckerman, 'Clientelist Politics in Italy', in Gellner and Waterbury, *Patrons and Clients*, pp. 63–79.
[48] Douglass, 'Migration', p. 184.
[49] Simic, 'Urbanization', pp. 203, 208.

new vehicles of patronage has only reinforced traditional popular
cynicism about the worth and impartiality of institutions, thereby
increasing that particularistic and fatalistic ethos supportive of personalized patronage and kin-based politics and social relations. The
attitudes of one modern resident of Belgrade are typical of this personalized ethos, an ethos which one could easily mistake for that of
the Renaissance Tuscans, Giovanni Morelli and Paolo da Certaldo.
'How can you depend upon people you don't know?' 'At every turn,
people will fool you.' 'In the end, one can only depend upon his own!'
'In the city one needs allies, and these are usually kin.'[50]

What have we learned from this brief discussion of Mediterranean
patronage, ancient and modern? First, patronage is a recurring pattern
of Mediterranean urban organization—the unwritten rules of the
game, the ways things actually get done. This is certainly not surprising, since the Mediterranean region was urbanized and commercially
sophisticated from antiquity onwards. Mediterranean townsmen
learned to rely on personal contacts and friends of friends—for news,
for economic opportunities, for protection and support, for employment and housing—in a society lacking the impersonal means of
communication and exchange that characterizes contemporary mass
society. Second, social and economic change in the Mediterranean has
not resulted in the demise of patronage. Change has occurred, but
largely in the composition of patronage groups rather than in the ethos
or practice of patronage itself.

Finally, the personalistic culture of patronage is not at all incompatible with modernization and urbanization. Patronage in southern
Europe is not some transitional stage of development between feudalism and capitalism. It predated feudalism, and has formed the
basis of Mediterranean capitalism, a capitalism that several Italian
specialists, among them Jane and Peter Schneider, have characterized
as 'Broker Capitalism'.[51] This form of capitalism is based on kin
group, friendship, and patronage. Mediterranean capitalism, far from
destroying patronage—or most other traditional features of local social
structures—has been constrained by it. John Davis, for example, has
called attention to the 'tyranny of *Gemeinschaft*' operating in Mediterranean commerce. Formed within kinship and patronage groups,
most commercial establishments are relatively small scale. Their

[50] Ibid., p. 216.
[51] Schneider, *Culture and Political Economy*, pp. 10ff.

owners are vulnerable to the multiplicity of bonds present in such communities. As a result, a characteristic feature of Mediterranean capitalism is indebtedness. Shopkeepers are forced by their clients, with whom they share multiple ties and obligations, to play the role of patron and to extend credit in return for the client's continued business and his political support. As Davis has observed, 'the two things go together, running a shop on debts, and being an important man'.[52] From Portugal to Cyprus, from Greece to Tangiers, indebtedness and the tyranny of *Gemeinschaft* characterize Mediterranean broker capitalism, a capitalism in which commercial activity is not socially autonomous, but is constrained by patronage.[53] If capitalism, urbanization, and related forces of 'modernization' in the contemporary Mediterranean have not brought about the demise of patronage and related personalistic or kin-based systems of loyalty, one should not assume, in the absence of evidence, that Renaissance urbanization or Renaissance commerce, by their very presence, accomplished such transformations.

What, then, are the implications of patronage for the interpretation of Renaissance society? If we accept the pervasiveness of patronage as revealed by the research of Brucker, Molho, Dale Kent, F. W. Kent, and others, we must also recognize the pervasiveness of a social ethos different from the official civic ideology that has guided so many interpretations of Renaissance urban life. For I would stress with Gellner that, above all, 'patronage is a moral climate';[54] and with Boissevain, that it is a self-perpetuating 'system of belief and action grounded in the society's value system'.[55] Thus, we must consider that, in addition to the official civic ethos of the Renaissance state, there existed another ethos, sanctified by certain forms of religion and ritual, and reinforced by daily experience: the ethos of patronage.

The essential point of this ethos was that the world was divided into two camps, as Leon Battista Alberti and Paolo da Certaldo noted—friends and strangers.[56] In this world one promoted the interests of family, friends, and patrons, for one assumed that everyone else did likewise. Promoting friends, expressing gratitude to patrons,

[52] Davis, *Mediterranean People*, pp. 55–7.
[53] Ibid.
[54] Gellner, 'Patrons and Clients', p. 3.
[55] J. Boissevain, 'Patronage in Sicily', *Man*, 1 (1966), 60.
[56] On the ethos of L. B. Alberti and Paolo da Certaldo, see Weissman, *Ritual Brotherhood*, pp. 26–35.

demonstrating loyalty to kinsmen—these were key components of the private ethos of loyalty and honour, an ethos that competed with the more publicly acknowledged civic ethos. And in this world, since strangers would invariably seek their own interests before, or at the expense of, yours, one did not seek, as in the idealized vision of capitalism, to reduce all relations to the morally neutral cash nexus, or, as in the idealized vision of the Renaissance state, to treat all citizens with bureaucratic impartiality. Rather, one sought to deal whenever possible with patrons, clients, family, and friends, or, failing this, to convert all neutral relations, all necessary contacts with strangers, into ties of obligation, gratitude, and reciprocity. When, typically, Gregorio Dati made his fellow standard-bearers of the Florentine militia companies godparents to his new-born child, we observe the deliberate confusion of public office and private patronage.[57] When Giovanni Morelli advised his sons to buy powerful friends with loans, he described a means of cementing relations used not only by powerful patrons such as Cosimo de' Medici, but also by Florentines of much lesser rank, as the rich debt and credit networks of fifteenth-century Florence, now being examined, attest.[58] When Lapo Mazzei, notary to the hospital of Santa Maria Nuova, used his official position to obtain patrons for his own patron, Francesco Datini, in order to reduce Datini's taxes, one observes multiple personal networks, including networks of state notarial and treasury officials mobilized to further private ends.[59]

In towns such as Florence, competing with the sincerely held ideals of civic humanism and the rational state, one detects the realities of patronage—men seeking to honour personal loyalties and to create new obligations, by using every technique, every social bond, every resource at their disposal. And, if the experience of Roman antiquity and contemporary Italy is any guide, we must be prepared to recognize that the bureaucracy of the Renaissance state and the rise of a commercial economy, far from subverting patronage, may have served as its fundamental mechanisms. Until we re-evaluate the *a priori* conventional wisdom concerning Renaissance 'modernization' and

---

[57] G. Dati, *Diary*, tr. J. Martines, in *Two Memoirs of Renaissance Florence*, ed. G. A. Brucker (New York, 1967), p. 127.

[58] Giovanni di Pagolo Morelli, *Ricordi*, ed. V. Branca (Florence, 1956), pp. 253–4. On Florentine debt and credit networks, see my study, 'The Importance of Being Ambiguous: Social Relations in Renaissance Florence', forthcoming.

[59] The Mazzei–Datini friendship has been examined in detail by R. Trexler, *Public Life in Renaissance Florence* (New York, 1980), pp. 131–58.

review our fundamental assumptions about the relationship of social bonds and economic change; until we are willing to place Italian Renaissance cities in their broader Mediterranean context, and to view patronage not merely as the remnant of agrarian feudalism but as a genuinely urban form of social organization and behaviour that predated feudalism; and until we see in patronage not simply courts and commissions but fundamental social values—a way of viewing the world—we will not, I am afraid, have taken patronage seriously.

3

Friendship and Patronage in Renaissance Europe

GUY FITCH LYTLE

FRIENDSHIP was both a fundamental value and an essential social relationship during the Renaissance. It recurred constantly in essays, plays, poems, sermons, works of art, wills, and private letters. A friend could be many things: a soul mate, a patron, a client, a kinsman, a lover. On the one hand, friendship was an intensely private devotion, even identification, with another person, with no thought of gain or self-interest involved. On the other hand, friendship was public, utilitarian, calculating—support sought from a patron or offered to a client. Usually, in Renaissance society, it was some more or less uneasy combination of the two. Both the extravagant exaltations of friendship and their inversions—the troubled, comic, and cynical reactions to it—reflect a complex interaction between Renaissance social, economic, and political realities on the one side, and its value systems on the other.

To supplement the empirical and analytical work now being done on the way patronage actually functioned, I am here primarily concerned with the moral economy of the patronage system and the personal bonds—emotional and practical—it fostered or impaired. Others have studied these linkages in terms of 'hierarchy', 'deference', 'affability', 'fealty', and 'bastard feudalism'. But no one has focused directly on the significance of how 'friendship' could be both the synonym and the antithesis of 'patronage'. In order to understand the patronage society of the Renaissance, we must examine not only external relationships, but also the subjective understanding and ideological valuing of those encounters. Towards this end, I shall survey some of the 'speech acts' that a Renaissance person might 'perform' with regard to friendship,[1] and then consider the most important

---

[1] The terms used here derive from Q. Skinner, 'Some Problems in the Analysis of Political Thought and Action', *Political Theory*, 2 (1974), 289.

tensions involved in the personal ties of friendship and patronage in Renaissance society by examining the forces that besieged, and frequently spoiled, them: human frailty (ingratitude, betrayal), money, and the pursuit of power.

I FRIENDS, FRIENDSHIP, AND PATRONAGE: THE RHETORIC OF SOCIAL BONDS

From classical, monastic, and chivalric tradition, Renaissance Europe inherited an exalted conception of friendship, which it proceeded to heighten. It also inherited a hierarchical social structure which it refined into an elaborate system of patronage relationships that fitted many of its needs and some of its ideologies. It was, however, a Renaissance commonplace to try to keep these two bonds separate. Montaigne's essay 'Of Friendship' represents the main philosophical tradition on that topic:

This perfect friendship I speak of is indivisible: each one gives himself so wholly to his friend that he has nothing left to distribute elsewhere ... common friendships can be divided up: one may love one man in his beauty, in another his easygoing ways, in another liberality ... but this friendship that possesses the soul and rules it with absolute sovereignty cannot possibly be doubled.[2]

Marsilio Ficino also tried to explain true friendship to Giovanni Cavalcanti, his 'unique friend', by specifically isolating it from the affairs of the world:

man seeks the virtue of the soul, the pleasures of the body or abundance of riches. The first of these is sure and everlasting. The other two are transitory and mortal. Therefore ... true friendship, can only exist for those who neither seek to accumulate riches nor to satisfy sensual pleasures which change and perish ... [but] only for those who apply themselves ... to acquire and exercise the single and permanent virtue of the soul.[3]

Such purity was difficult in Renaissance society. Many of Ficino's other letters are filled with self-reproach for failing to realize this ideal, and it was widely recognized that the consummation of such a friendship was rarely, if ever, possible. Montaigne noted that even 'a single one' of such perfect friendships 'is the rarest thing in the world to find'.[4] One

---

[2] D. Frame (ed.), *The Complete Essays of Montaigne* (Stanford, 1958), pp. 141ff.; B. Weller, 'The Rhetoric of Friendship in Montaigne's *Essais*', *New Literary History*, 9 (1977–8), 503–23 provides a very useful analysis.

[3] *The Letters of Marsilio Ficino* (London, 1975), i. 96.

[4] Frame (ed.), *Complete Essays*, p. 142.

of Boccaccio's storytellers regretted the demise of 'sacred friendship' in his own time: 'Its sacred results are today most rarely seen ... for to the shame and sin of men's miserable cupidity which makes them look only to their own interest, friendship has been driven to the ends of the earth and left in perpetual exile.'[5] Sometimes the virtue of individual friendship was magnified to serve as a model for the structure and functioning of society as a whole. Thomas Starkey expressed the view that 'a multitude of people ... living together in civil life, governed by politic order and rule, should conspire together in amity ... everyone glad to help another ... to the intent that the whole might attain to that perfection which is determined to the dignity of man's nature by the goodness of God'.[6]

Leon Battista Alberti, too, expressed to Lionardo the opinion that 'God established in the human mind a strong tie to bind together human beings in society, namely justice, equity, liberality and love'. In order to live together peacefully, 'I should have need of you, and you of him, he of another, and some other of me. In this way one man's need for another serves as the cause and means to keep us all united in general friendship and alliance.'[7]

Everyday speech itself made constant reference to friends and friendship in ways that blurred the distinction between the ideal and the pragmatic. Patronage and friendship involved reciprocity. Those who sought favours also had obligations. Usually these links spread both upwards and downwards in society. Most middling men were patrons to some and clients to others. Ficino, that idealistic champion of pure friendship, could support a request for patronage by writing to his 'close friend', the 'magnanimous Lorenzo de' Medici': 'Many seek undeserved honours from you, but Gregorio Epifanio deserves far more than he asks. Even though he is a great friend of mine, I recommend him to you more for his virtue than for his friendship. For he is a friend because of his virtue.'[8] This entreaty illustrates the ambiguity of usage within the patronage process, and its justification.

One finds, too, that in the political and social relationships expressed by the terms 'good lordship', 'well-willers', 'retainer', 'servant', or

[5] Giovanni Boccaccio, *The Decameron*, tr. R. Aldington (New York, 1962), p. 609.

[6] T. Starkey, 'A Dialogue between Cardinal Pole and Thomas Lupset', in S. J. Herrtage, *England in the Reign of Henry VIII* (London, 1927), pp. 205–6.

[7] L. B. Alberti, *The Family in Renaissance Florence*, tr. R. N. Watkins (Columbia, SC, 1969), p. 15 (Watkins's Introduction).

[8] *Letters of Ficino*, i. 184.

'maintenance', 'friend' was used in ways that were demanding or cynical. During the rebellions of 1536, Henry VIII's council sought aid from loyal 'gentlemen and their servants and friends' against the 'cankered commons'. Against the Pilgrimage of Grace, the King asked the Earl of Shrewsbury and others to assemble their 'friends, tenants, and servants' in preparation for the fight.[9] This 'request' recognized that a relationship which involved 'a reciprocal exchange of patronage, support and hospitality in return for attendance, deference, respect, advice and loyalty', was still a powerful force.[10]

Lesser individuals could also trade on this form of language. John Paston wrote to his brother, Sir John: 'there be a dozen towns in England that choose no burgesses which ought to do, and you may set in for one of those towns ... [if] you be friended.'[11] And Sir Robert Sidney advised Sir John Harrington that his lawsuit required him to visit 'friends at court often and please the Queen by all you can, for all the great lawyers do much fear her displeasure'.[12] George Cavendish found that Anne Boleyn could 'work masteries with the king and obtain any suit of him for her friend'.[13] Such 'friendship' was pervasive: in 1429 the city officials of Winchester allotted a shilling to the Bishop of Winchester's treasurer's serjeant 'for making the treasurer a friend'.[14]

For the patronage seeker (or for his agent near the court whose job it was to facilitate the search) the objective was clear, even if its accomplishment was sometimes difficult. In a series of letters to the Lisles in the 1530s, John Husee sought constantly to reassure his employer that he had, or needed, friends in high places. On one occasion he wrote, 'By my faith, I cannot see the contrary but Mr. Secretary beareth my lord good mind and heart ... By utter appearance he showed that time to be your lordship's faithful friend.'[15] When a supporter died or was banished, one did whatever was necessary to secure a replacement. Husee had

---

[9] W. H. Dunham, *Lord Hastings' Indentured Retainers* (New Haven, 1955), p. 107.

[10] See L. Stone, *The Family, Sex and Marriage in England, 1500–1800* (New York, 1977), pp. 89ff.

[11] Dunham, *Lord Hastings*, p. 31.

[12] J. Harrington, *Nugae Antiquae* (London, 1769), i. 313; see also P. Williams, *The Tudor Regime* (Oxford, 1979), p. 372.

[13] G. Cavendish, *The Life and Death of Cardinal Wolsey*, ed. R. T. Sylvester (London, 1959), p. 35.

[14] J. F. Furley, *City Government of Winchester from the Records of the XIV and XV Centuries* (Oxford, 1923), p. 88.

[15] M. St C. Byrne (ed.), *The Lisle Letters* (Chicago, 1981), i. 43–4.

delivered in your lordship's name unto [Sir Thomas] Heneage eleven dozen quails, one hogshead Gascon wine, who thankfully received them. And after that I had made unto him your lordship's entire recommendations, opening unto him what losses you had by Mr. Norris's death, he said that always to his power ... your lordship shall be at any time as well assured of him as of his predecessor. So that I have good hope he will be your very friend, for he doth now totally supply Mr. Norris's whole room.[16]

The process was never-ending in the competition of advancement, or even for survival, in the Renaissance. As Husee anxiously wrote in 1537: 'Unless my Lord procure new friends, he shall do little good at their hands that he now taketh to be his friends.'[17]

The notion of 'friendship' also suffused the rhetoric of Renaissance diplomacy. The Chandos Herald said that Edward the Black Prince undertook his Spanish campaign 'out of pity and friendship' for the exiled King Pedro.[18] It was also customary to exchange respect in letters by beginning 'my trusty friend' or 'right trusty friend', and these acknowledgements could be reversed to give added impact to declarations of impending hostility. In 1455, William, Lord Bonville addressed the Earl of Devon: 'All due salutation of friendship laid apart.' 'All friendly greetings stand for naught,' came the reply.[19] 'Heavy friend', 'small friend', or 'backfriend' connoted an enemy (*OED* s.v. 6†c), and such cursings took their power from their inversion of the Renaissance chivalric code of values and behaviour.

This chivalric ideal of friendship between men in battle was still in many ways more powerful and widespread than the 'classical' conception expressed by Montaigne or Ficino. In Jean de Bueil's *Le Jouvencel*, the protagonist declares that it was a 'feeling of loyalty and pity [that] fills your heart on seeing your friend so valiantly exposing his body to execute and accomplish the command of our Creator. And then you prepare to go and live or die with him, and for love not to abandon him.'[20] Similar sentiments are manifested, for example, in a 1464 indenture by which Lord Hastings promised 'faithful, true heart,

---

[16] Ibid. iii, no. 705. Also iv, no. 943.

[17] Ibid. iii, no. 770.

[18] D. Brewer, *Chaucer in His Time* (London, 1963), p. 158; see also M. Vale, *War and Chivalry* (London, 1981), esp. ch. 2; and G. Mattingly, *Renaissance Diplomacy* (London, 1955).

[19] M. Cherry, 'The Struggle for Power in Mid-fifteenth Century Devonshire', in R. A. Griffiths (ed.), *Patronage, The Crown and the Provinces in Later Medieval England* (Gloucester, 1981), p. 123.

[20] Vale, *War and Chivalry*, p. 30 and n. 86.

love, and kind cosinage' to Lord Grey of Codnor, who promised in turn 'to bear good will to the said Lord Hastings, always taking his part . . . against all manner of persons, his ligeance, my lord of Clarence, and Sir Thomas Burgt, knight, only except'.[21] Such love and fidelity felt by a vassal for his lord and patron or between two equal knights accentuated the intermingling of friendship and patronage. Friendships could be vertical or horizontal with very much the same vocabulary and emotion.

The experience of camaraderie in arms could be strong and enduring: and there were, no doubt, some homosexual overtones. Certainly the rhetoric of mutual male love was ubiquitous, and so were its legal and moral condemnations. But more research needs to be done before we can confidently pronounce on its emotional and social implications. The same is true of similar questions about Renaissance women and their friendships, either with men or with other women.[22]

In this context, however, we may look more confidently at the relationship between 'friendship' and romantic love and marriage, since it was often repeated that 'the good or evil fortune of a man's life is in the good or evil choosing of his friend or his wife'.[23] Friends were meant to aid in the choice of a wife: 'Thomas Porayne bequeathed to Elizabeth Ordiner ten pounds to be delivered at the day of her marriage, so that the said Elizabeth do marry with such a person that shall be for the honest of her friends and at the will of her friends.'[24] But could a wife be a friend? Ian Maclean has argued that a new attitude towards marriage can be discerned in the Renaissance: 'Woman is created to be not [man's] servant or his mistress but his companion: for this reason she is created from his rib, not his foot or his head.' Reciprocal love and respect was stressed. By love, Renaissance theorists meant not passion, but 'something akin to an amalgam of Christian charity and the virtues of chastity and endurance [*tolerantia*]'. As Maclean indicates, the sixteenth-century English neo-Aristotelian, John Case, declared that a wife should be a friend; but it is also

---

[21] Dunham, *Lord Hastings*, p. 27.

[22] See J. C. Nelson, *Renaissance Theory of Love* (New York, 1963), esp. pp. 57ff.; and, for background, J. Boswell, *Christianity, Social Tolerance and Homosexuality* (Chicago, 1980). Also, L. Faderman, *Surpassing the Love of Men* (New York, 1981). Another example is in the *Letters of Ficino*, i. 110–11. But then there is Montaigne's explicit rejection of it (see Frame (ed.), *Complete Essays*, pp. 135ff.).

[23] B. J. Whiting, *Proverbs, Sentences and Proverbial Phrases from English Writings mainly before 1500* (Cambridge, Mass., 1968), F539.

[24] Public Record Office, Prerogative Court of Canterbury wills, 11 Thower (1532).

common to find passages in Renaissance moralistic literature which throw doubt on a woman's capacity for true friendship.[25] One should choose a spouse 'suited to [one's] own personality, just as one does in forming a friendship'.[26] There was also the strong misogynist exhortation to 'read well what happened to Adam, Samson, David, Goliath, Solomon, Virgil, and Aristotle', to consider that 'a noble deed of ... friendship as always in wholesome minds outweighs the madness of sexual love'.[27] But whatever the theorists said, in law and everyday affairs men were usually considered the 'patrons' of their wives.

Alberti's dialogue debated whether children should be 'less dear to their fathers and find less favour in their eyes than do other friends'.[28] But though the opinions of the time were mixed, the proposition that blood relations provided the most lasting patrons and friends was widespread. It was said in England that anyone who 'betraiyeth ... his frende carnall [kinsman] ought not to lyve nor have ever ony worshyp [honour]'.[29]

Mousnier, however, has argued that the bonds of fidelity, as distinct from those of clientage or feudal fealty, involved feelings of 'loyalty ... [and] affection and fostered the vertical relations between an inferior and his superior, with the former exchanging his devotion for the latter's protection'.[30] In accordance with this view the saints had long been known as the 'friends of God', and one's various patron saints were perhaps the most powerful friends one could hope to rely on.[31] In the best of the true personal friendships, God, according to Ficino, was a necessary element:

as God loves those who cultivate Him with devoted minds, there cannot be the two friends on their own, but there must always be three, the two men and God; God, or in other words Jupiter, the patron of hospitality, protector

---

[25] I. Maclean, *The Renaissance Notion of Woman* (Cambridge, 1980), pp. 19, 59.

[26] See Francesco Barbaro, 'On Wifely Duties', in B. G. Kohl and R. G. Witt (eds.), *The Earthly Republic: Italian Humanists on Government and Society* (Philadelphia, 1978), pp. 196–7.

[27] A. Martinez de Toledo, *Little Sermons on Sin*, tr. L. B. Simpson (Berkeley/Los Angeles, 1959), pp. 27ff.; Alberti, *The Family*, p. 103.

[28] Alberti, *The Family*, pp. 92ff.; Stone, *Family*, pp. 97ff.

[29] *OED* s.v. 'friend', sb. 3.

[30] R. Mousnier, 'Les Fidelités et les clientèles en France aux XVIe et XVIIIe siècles', *Histoire social/Social History*, 15 (1982), 35ff.

[31] On this theme, see P. Brown, *The Making of Late Antiquity* (Cambridge, Mass., 1978), ch. 3; idem., *The Cult of the Saints* (Chicago, 1981), pp. 59ff.; P. Fabre, *Saint Paulin de Nole et l'amitié chrétienne* (Paris, 1949); A. B. Orselli, *L'idea e il culto del santo patrono cittadino nella letteratura latina* (Bologna, 1945).

of friendship, and sustainer of human life ... He unites us as one; He is the unbreakable bond of friendship, and our constant guardian.[32]

In the same spirit, Pico gives us a sense of what awaits the virtuous: 'we shall fly up with winged feet, like earthly mercuries ... and enjoy that ... most holy peace ... This is that friendship which the Pythagoreans say is the end of philosophy.'[33] Yet the rewards of such friendship also entail enormous obligations and commitments: worship, restrictions of behaviour (and thought), tithes and obligations, loyalty and service. From the omnipotent patron proceeded the seemingly all encompassing demands, at least until Luther reformulated the relationship.

The tensions involved (especially those generated by money) can be further illustrated by the aphorisms of the time. Although proverbs always have a rhetorical context and cannot be said to reproduce 'reality' directly, they do provide a means of appreciating the inherent tensions within societies and value systems.[34] They often confute one another, but their very contradictions are significant.

Of course one can easily adduce the pious sentiment and cynical comment: 'Of all good thinges the worlde brought forth, A faithfulle frend ys thinge moste worthe;' Proverbs 19: 4 was often quoted, 'Richessis encressen ful many frendis'; and this was then proven by its opposite: 'the sea shall be dry when the poor man has a friend,' and 'death and poverty hath few friends'. In another very tellingly ambiguous inversion, 'the poore man hathe no frendes' became 'that man is poor that has no friend'. Folk wisdom confirmed the ubiquitous ideal that friends should have the same temperament by noticing that a 'hound and cat kiss, [but they] are not the better friends'.[35]

Popular literature made the distinction between pure friends and common friends far less often than did the philosophical treatises. A friend was a patron was a friend. One might indeed 'fynde, soth to sey, "thi purs schal be thi best(e) frende"', but 'men say it is better to have a frende otherwhils in courte than a peny in pursse'. Uncertain friends surrounded you, and 'under a shadwe off feyned freendliheed,

---

[32] *Letters of Ficino*, i. 7.

[33] G. Pico della Mirandola, *On the Dignity of Man*, tr. C. G. Wallis (Indianapolis, 1940), pp. 11–12.

[34] In addition to Whiting, see M. P. Tilley, *A Dictionary of Proverbs in England in the Sixteenth and Seventeenth Centuries* (Ann Arbor, 1950); J. W. Hassell, Jr., *Middle French Proverbs, Sentences and Proverbial Phrases* (Toronto, 1982).

[35] See Whiting, F631, R115, S109, P295, M286, H563.

ther is no frenship so pereilous for to dreed'. 'In tyme of prosperitie, a man shall not knowe his frendes', at least not which ones will stand by him; but he can be certain that 'Whan a man ys to mescheff brouht, And falle in-to adversyte, Fful few frendys than hath he'. 'With gifts a man may make friends;' but 'he is a true friend that loves me for my love and not for my good [property]', for 'friendship is more than cattle [chattels]'.[36]

One example may stand for the inevitable interpenetration between patronage and friendship. In 1538 Sir Thomas Elyot presented a copy of his *Dictionary* to Thomas Cromwell and included with it a personal letter. After congratulating Cromwell on his appointment as 'Minister ac Consiliarius', Elyot pointed out that, while he had clearly been predestined to great honour, he had won his current position through the help of fortune and God's perpetual goodwill towards the people of England. Elyot added that he valued Cromwell's friendship because of the rare fecundity of the latter's wit and the similarity of their studies, not because he (Elyot) had any personal ambition. But he did remind Cromwell that, as Cicero had said, there was no worse crime than damaging the reputation of a friend or failing to protect him when he was in danger. Elyot closed with protestations of his loyalty to his correspondent.[37] Everything is there: advancement due to patronage (from God, King, and Fortune); true friendship based on similarities of interest, temperament, and personal loyalty; the reminder both of mutual obligation and of the obloquy associated with ingratitude, as one simultaneously proclaimed the absence of ulterior motives.

Friendship and patronage were certainly not identical; nor were they wholly distinct. In Alberti's *Book of the Family*, the polished old diplomat Piero presents stylized portraits of three powerful men whom he has known and served in Milan, Naples, and Rome; and he thereby illustrates Aristotle's three types of friendship: for the sake of virtue, for pleasure, and for utility.[38] But friendships could not always maintain the neat distinctions of the parable. In reality, such relationships intertwined in the social, economic, and political milieux, in people's emotions, and in cultural and religious expression. There was a tension between them, and many writers were concerned about the failure to achieve harmony between society and its values; but they managed to reach some consensus in identifying the causes.

[36] Ibid., P445, F633, F673, P417, M312, G87, F644, F670.
[37] See S. Lehmberg, *Sir Thomas Elyot* (Austin, 1960), p. 167.
[38] Alberti, *The Family*, pp. 15, 252ff.

II   SOCIAL TENSIONS AND RENAISSANCE FRIENDSHIPS

The tension between values and needs, between ambition (to be good) and ambition (to succeed), the desire to live well (in both senses of the phrase), often took friendship beyond the breaking-point and provoked accusations of betrayal from both sides. Expressions of friendship were clothed in classical rhetoric but that virtue was also actively cultivated for use. 'True' friendships were utilized for advancement, as one was entitled to do; but reciprocity often became a problem and a cause of shame and resentment when the deficit grew too large. Remaining and maintaining friends in a patronage-based society was a continuous problem. As Elyot, borrowing explicitly from Cicero, said:

undoubtedly it is wonderfully difficult to find a man very ambitious or covetous to be assured in friendship. For where findest thou him that will not prefer honours, great offices, rule, authority, and riches before friendship? Therefore it is very hard to find friendship in them that be occupied in acquiring honour or about the affairs of the public weal.[39]

Ambition in the volatile political world of the Renaissance, avarice amid the wealth of the new money economy, and the perennial sinfulness of human beings which makes them woefully inconstant: such things, according to contemporaries, explained the lack of perfect harmony in Renaissance society. One might even suggest that the Renaissance need to emphasize 'ideal' friendships was a way to compensate for the unstable, intensely self-interested and self-promoting social relationships of that time. That is the kind of dialectic that a 'social history of values' must still determine.

One of the things that linked the concepts in Renaissance minds was that both friendship and patronage elicited the same opposite: ingratitude. This sin against friends, lords, and patrons (leading on, it was thought, to betrayal and treason) was harshly condemned. Elyot devoted an entire chapter to 'ingratitude and dispraise thereof' and named it 'the most damnable vice and most against justice'.[40]

Alas such perverse constellation now reigneth over men that where some be ... naturally disposed to amity, and findeth one, in similitude of study and manners, equal to his expectation ... it happeneth that he which is loved, being promoted in honour, either of purpose neglecteth his friend ... or else

[39] Sir Thomas Elyot, *The Book Named The Governor*, ed. S. E. Lehmberg (London, 1962), p. 151.
[40] Ibid., p. 152.

esteeming his mind with his fortune only, and not with the surety of friendship, hideth from him the secrets of his heart, and . . . trusteth no man.

For Elyot, such developments damaged both the friends and society.[41]

Ficino traced ingratitude in large part to our own mistakes and moral failings: we all too often give the wrong thing, or give to the wrong person, or do good for improper motives. We expect gratitude where we do not deserve it: 'Do not blame either the ingratitude of others or your fortune, but rather your imprudence.' 'You grieve . . . because you have been deceived by a friend . . . There are many who seem like another self who fail very often. So whenever you are deceived, do not blame . . . friends but your own rashness. Either you loved before you judged most carefully, or you loved too much or you trusted too much in the human lot.'[42]

More often the fault was attributed to others: to know one's real friends and to be assured of their faithfulness was always a problem. Alberti had Lionardo say: 'We find that there is really nothing more difficult in the world than to distinguish true friends amid the obscurity of so many lies, the darkness of people's motives, and the shadowy errors and vices that lie about us on all sides.'[43] It is not surprising, therefore, that Adovardo, while he continued to hope for 'true and perfect' friendship, understood why

the old . . . prove slower and more deliberate than young people in contracting new friendships. Perhaps they are not to be blamed either, since they have experienced in the course of many years that some go to a lot of trouble and cunningly bargain to form friendships only to exploit them and live off the labour and fortune of others. There is hardly anyone who will rush to form a new friendship with you unless he expects that it will be useful to him somehow and bring some hoped for reward.[44]

But he also recognized that he, too, had sought out 'fortunate and affluent men [who] are indeed extremely useful to friends, not so much because they will help you with their wealth and power directly but because . . . they open the way to acquaintance with all lesser . . . persons [who show] reverence toward anyone on whom their superior bestows a smile and a willing ear'.[45]

Ingratitude was not universal, but even expressions of gratitude

[41] Ibid., pp. 152–4.
[42] *Letters of Ficino*, ii. 40–1.
[43] Alberti, *The Family*, p. 228.
[44] Ibid., p. 276.
[45] Ibid., p. 282.

could carry uneasy sentiments of obligation. In one of his final letters
from the Tower, Sir Thomas More thanked the Lucchese businessman
Antonio Bonvisi for 'the sweetness of your friendship in this decay of
my fortune', and

> delighted marvelously in this your love towards me, yet when I consider ...
> that I have been now almost this forty years not a guest, but a continual
> nursling in Master Bonvisi's house, and ... have not showed myself in requit-
> ing you again, a friend, but a barren lover only, my shamefastness verily
> made that that sincere sweetness ... of your friendship, somewhat waxed
> sourish ...[46]

More's abject acknowledgement of debt no doubt represented, if in
rather dramatic circumstances and language, a situation of unequal
reciprocity that was bound to trouble a patronage society where the
obvious inequities of a hierarchical society vied with the sense of
mutual obligations between friends.

The most common instigators of strife among friends in this era
between feudalism and capitalism, between personal leadership and the
emergence of centralized despotisms, seem to have been the possibilities
offered by money and politics (or the temptations of greed and
ambition). These were also, of course, two of the fundamental reasons
why one needed patrons and friends in the first place.

Lionardo Alberti asked, 'if you will support the common view that
money is practically the first consideration in human affairs and most
to be valued. [Do you] agree with those rather shrewd characters who,
as soon as they see a friend pressed by need, suspect that they will be
asked for help and promptly block off all access to themselves ...?'[47]
In explaining why he has turned down the request for a loan from an
important friend, Petrarch earlier wrote:

> I disdain with unrestrained indignation the yoke of money which weighs down
> kings. I shall not allow, God willing, that the soul become a servant of metals
> when it is disposed to greater things. However, although I forbid money to
> dominate, it refuses to submit ... Money is ... proud ... and wishes to have
> me neither as master nor as a companion. It refuses my control, and does not
> admit my friendship.[48]

---

[46] E. F. Rogers (ed.), *The Selected Letters of St Thomas More* (New York, 1961),
pp. 253ff.

[47] Alberti, *The Family*, p. 292.

[48] Petrarch, *Rerum Familiarum Libri I–VIII*, trans. A. S. Bernardo (Albany, N.Y.,
1975), pp. 151–2.

He seems to be saying much more here than just that he does not have any money to lend. On another occasion, when he did send money to a friend in need, he feared that it would be misunderstood and viewed as shameful by the recipient. So he considered the classical reasons for giving and for either accepting or refusing gifts, and he concluded: 'I come as a friend and not as a tempter; nor, to confess the truth, am I giving you anything, but I am sharing with you what you yourself know has been held in common by us for a long time.' To refuse the gift would be 'discourteous and insolent'.[49] (A Plutarchan analogy, cited frequently in the Renaissance, argued that, like a ballgame, the patronage–friendship system only worked when thrower and catcher each fulfilled their proper function and then continuously reversed their roles.[50])

Poggio Bracciolini's dialogue *On Avarice* also debates the apparent conflicts between ideal and action. It asserts that the avaricious man 'is able neither to cultivate friendship nor be moved by kindness. For what kindness can there be in someone who holds nothing more dear than money? ... The avaricious man ... is useless to the city and ruinous to the state.'[51] But another speaker responds with a 'defence' of avarice similar to Xenophon's:

If some are more greedy ... and desirous of wealth beyond the norm, you think they ought to be expelled from the cities. On the contrary, I think they should be invited into the cities as a proper support for the people. For when money abounds the ... wretched may be helped ... and both private citizens and the state may be aided ... It seems to be preferable to have many avaricious men whom we can depend on in times of difficulty like a ... citadel. Not only do they support us with money but also with advice, wisdom, protection, and authority ... In no way have the avaricious been harmful ... I do not deny that avarice may be viewed as a vice in some people ... I also have known many avaricious noblemen—splendid, decorous, liberal, humane, and witty—whose homes are filled with guests and friends.[52]

Politics was no less a threat. Machiavelli even tied the culprits—money, politics, and ingratitude—together. In *The Prince* he declared:

[49] Ibid., pp. 327–9.
[50] It is based on Plutarch, *Moralia*, 582E–F.
[51] For important discussions of the context and other rhetorical issues, see B. Kohl's introduction to the translation of *On Avarice* in Kohl and Witt (eds.), *The Earthly Republic*, pp. 231ff. (quotation on p. 252); G. Holmes, *The Florentine Enlightenment*, 1400–50 (London, 1969), pp. 147ff., J. W. Oppel, 'Poggio, San Bernardino of Siena, and the Dialogue *On Avarice*', *Renaissance Quarterly*, 30 (1977), 564–87.
[52] Kohl and Witt (eds.), *The Earthly Republic*, pp. 262–3.

friendships gained with money, not with greatness and nobility of spirit, are purchased but not possessed, and at the right time cannot be turned to account. Men have less hesitation in injuring one who makes himself loved than one who makes himself feared, for love is held by a chain of duty which, since men are bad, they break at every chance for their own profit.[53]

Both thwarted ambition and successful ambition could hinder relationships.

But society could not exist if people functioned in solitude. Social ligatures are necessary, and all communities develop those positive and negative, functional and conflicting bonds that fit their circumstances. Of course each age does not start *ex nihilo*. Patterns of behaviour and social relationships are inherited, then modified or abandoned. Value systems which motivate or legitimate that inheritance, or sometimes confront it, also develop in a dialectic between past and present, as well as within the contemporary society itself. A fundamentally flawed human kind in a necessarily flawed human society tries to relate to what it hopes are true, or at least less flawed, ideals. No one juxtaposed the problems and the ideals better than Castiglione: 'I would ... maintain ... that without this perfect friendship men would be the unhappiest of all creatures; and because some profane persons sully the sacred name of friendship, this does not mean that we should uproot it from our souls and because of the faults of the wicked deprive the good of so much happiness.' One would succeed as a friend by being 'courteous, compassionate, generous, affable and charming as a companion, lively and diligent in serving and forwarding the advantage and honour of his friends ... tolerating their natural and excusable defects, and correcting in himself the defects that are amicably pointed out to him'.[54]

The personal and social relationships of the Renaissance were an amalgam of overlapping ties: kinship, patronage, and friendship (as well as roles as citizen or subject, communicant, etc.). Renaissance patronage was much broader than friendship and did not derive its impetus or justification from friendship *per se*. Patrons and clients did not have to be personal friends. But the convergence of linguistic usage forces the connection in all its ambiguity.

The articulated ideal of friendship remained remarkably, even suspiciously, stable throughout the Renaissance; and, even if the like-

[53] A. Gilbert (ed.), *The Chief Works and Others [of Machiavelli]* (Durham, NC, 1965), i. 62.
[54] B. Castiglione, *The Courtier*, tr. G. Bull (Harmondsworth, 1976), pp. 137–8.

lihood of finding pure friendship was always in doubt, the ideal endured in the face of persistent disappointment. Friends gave the highest and deepest meaning to social existence; yet ingratitude, betrayal, absence, constantly threatened. In many ways this is consistently parallel to the realities of the patronage society. Working properly, alliances, parties, even factions, got 'what-needed-to-be-done' done for individuals, groups, and society as a whole. It was not considered a morally inferior form of social and political organization. It could sometimes be most efficient. Yet there was always the threat of breakdown, of civil war, anarchy, and tyranny. The personal nature of social and political relationships in a patronage society was both its strength and its weakness.

4

The Dynamic of Power in Cosimo de' Medici's Florence

DALE KENT

M Y intention here is to discuss the relation between social structures—especially networks of personal relationships, obligations, and loyalties—and the way in which political power was achieved and exercised in Cosimo de' Medici's Florence. More specifically, I will raise some questions and offer some suggestions as to how one might go about establishing the precise locus of power in Florentine society between the rise of the Medici in the late 1420s and the death of Piero di Cosimo in 1469—a rather difficult thing to pin down because almost every aspect of political life in this period is dynamic. This dynamism will constitute a major theme of the study, in which I am currently engaged, of the society of early Medicean Florence, particularly from the perspective of the role of patronage in its several senses—political, social, and artistic—as a reflection of social norms and values, and as a determinant of individual and collective social and political behaviour.[1]

The most fundamental dynamic is that which operates between the three major entities involved in the political process by the 1430s. First, the traditional ruling class, defined as that group of several hundred families which by then enjoyed a tradition of participation in the leading magistracies; secondly, the *reggimento* or current regime at any given time—a more restricted group of families, or particular individuals from those families, who held major office with great

[1] This chapter, which appears here essentially as delivered as a paper to the Melbourne conference, is a report on work in progress, outlining approaches to my material, and the general pattern of the answers which are emerging. The body of the evidence as a whole—essentially some thousands of private letters, but including a range of other sources, such as laws, electoral, council, criminal, and notarial records—has yet to be systematically processed; further, since much of it is currently unavailable to me, only the most specific references will be documented. As this study was originally planned and begun with F. W. Kent as a collaborative one, extending over the period 1434–94, I should like here to acknowledge my general debt to his work.

frequency; thirdly, the Medici party—that group of men bound to the Medici family by ties of personal loyalty and obligation. These entities always overlapped to some extent, but the degree to which, and the way in which, they did so varied from time to time. If we are to understand specific political actions or events, we need to know to which of these groups the men involved in them belonged and, in order to grasp the direction of political development over the fifteenth century, we must be aware of more general alterations in the balance between these three groups, especially as the first two are based essentially on the relation of individuals to the constitutional sources of political power, whereas the third springs essentially from the personal relation of individuals to one another.[2]

The first major phase in the changing relationship between these three groups is the achievement by members of the Medici party of a preponderance of power in the *reggimento* in the late 1420s and early 1430s. When one tries to explain why certain Florentines—especially the members of the *reggimento*—either supported the attempt of the Medici family to abrogate to itself and its friends a larger share of political offices and power, or opposed this attempt, one becomes convinced that the struggle between the Medici and their opponents was not primarily an ideological conflict. The actions of most Florentines, public as well as private, political as well as personal, were largely governed by considerations of personal interest and obligation to that group of associates to whom they constantly refer—their 'relatives, neighbours and friends [*parenti, vicini e amici*]'. This was the group upon which they relied for support and assistance in any enterprise of importance to them. When the enterprise was political, as affairs of importance to Florentines so often were, a group of personal associates or patronage group turned naturally and necessarily into a political faction.[3]

Both the pro-Medicean and the anti-Medicean factions were bound together by a multiplicity of ties of blood, marriage, neighbourhood, and friendship—friendship, that is, not necessarily in the sense of emotional, but rather of instrumental association. In addition to the wealth and the influence outside Florence which the Medici family

        [2] See D. V. Kent, 'The Florentine *Reggimento* in the Fifteenth Century', *Renaissance Quarterly*, 28 (1975), 575–638, and *The Rise of the Medici: Faction in Florence 1426–1434* (Oxford, 1978); N. Rubinstein, *The Government of Florence under the Medici, 1434–94* (Oxford, 1966).
        [3] D. V. Kent, *Rise of the Medici*, esp. pp. 1–30.

derived from its bank, a crucial factor in the Medicean triumph of 1434 was the particular nature of their patronage network. The personal relationships binding them and their supporters had been systematically created or consolidated by the leaders of the family from about 1400 onwards, with a specific view to increasing their political influence and the representation of their supporters in leading offices. Their partisans had been chosen for attributes likely to be useful in a bid to gain power, and were tightly bound under the direction of a single family. Moreover, many were from 'newer' families with a comparatively limited range of obligations to consider in any concrete situation, unlike the many older families in the anti-Medicean faction, entwined in a complex morass of often conflicting interest, both with each other and with their own particular associates. When it came to the crisis, most Miceans were not subject to the sort of contrary demands which constitute one of the main problems of a complex web of patronage, and which were later to beset the Medici network itself.

In so far as the Medici victory of 1434 was achieved not by means of a putsch, but rather in accordance with the constitutional demand for government through the official magistracies, it signified that the Medici party had been successful in making itself a major force in the *reggimento*. This was demonstrated most graphically when the majority of name tickets drawn from the electoral purses to form the supreme magistracy or *Signoria* of September 1434, proved to belong to Medicean partisans who promptly recalled the exiled Medici to Florence.[4] The acquiescence in this act of the remainder of the *reggimento* ensured the subsequent increase of Medicean representation within its ranks. Thus, after 1434, we pass to the second phase in the relationship between ruling class, *reggimento*, and Medici party, in which the party becomes not a faction, but the faction within the regime, and the Medici party or patronage group and the *reggimento* are more and more closely identifiable one with the other.[5]

---

[4] Ibid., pp. 289–351.

[5] Factions developed within the Medici party (see Rubinstein, *The Government*, esp. pt II.), but not, in my view, to a point comparable with the situation before 1434; for a contrary view, see J. N. Stephens, *The Fall of the Florentine Republic, 1512–1530* (Oxford, 1983). On factions in the later fourteenth and early fifteenth centuries, see G. A. Brucker, *Florentine Politics and Society 1343–1378* (Princeton, 1962), and *The Civic World of Early Renaissance Florence* (Princeton, 1977). The growth of the contrary impulse to consensus, expressed in the progressive broadening of the governing regime's electoral base, is traced by J. M. Najemy, *Corporatism and Consensus in Florentine Electoral Politics, 1280–1400* (Chapel Hill, 1982).

The relationship between the Medici party and the *reggimento* remained dynamic, however, in at least two ways. First, many members of the ruling class who before 1434 had remained aloof from factions or even hostile to them, after the *fait accompli* of the Medici ascendancy and the disappearance of an opposition sufficient to create the civic strife which so many Florentines abhorred, became gradually favourable to Medicean government and were incorporated into the Medicean *reggimento*. Later in the century we encounter the opposite phenomenon of the readmission of those who had been actual or suspected anti-Miceans in 1434, of whom Giovanni Rucellai and the Strozzi family are particularly notable examples.[6] Indeed, as the Medicean ascendancy progressed, there was some tendency for the distinction between the three political entities to break down, under a gradual attempt to extend the Medici party to embrace the entire ruling class.[7] Secondly, the ruling class remained open to social mobility by virtue of the fact that new Medici partisans—Medici familiars among artists, humanists, and bureaucrats such as the Michelozzi family and Bartolomeo Scala spring most immediately to mind— continued to find their way into the electoral purses, and hence into the *reggimento*, through the personal favour of the Medici and their supporters.[8] This tendency, however, was counterbalanced by the gradual disaffection over the century of a number even of those who before 1434 had been among the most fervent of Medici partisans.[9] Hence the task of keeping up with the definition of the Medici party or patronage network across the period 1434 to 1469, by comparison with that of identifying it before 1434, is rather like that of turning a line drawing into an animated cartoon.

[6] See D. V. Kent, 'The Florentine *Reggimento*', esp. Table 4. On the Rucellai and the Strozzi, see D. V. and F. W. Kent, *Neighbours and Neighbourhood in Renaissance Florence: The District of the Red Lion in the Fifteenth Century* (Locust Valley, NY, 1982) and F. W. Kent *et al.*, *Giovanni Rucellai ed il suo zibaldone*, II: *A Florentine Patrician and his Palace* (London, 1981), chs. 1–6.

[7] The restitution, after the Medici return from exile, of political rights to magnates who had not opposed them, is one of the first moves in this direction; see D. V. Kent, *Rise of the Medici*, pp. 346–7.

[8] Ibid., pp. 70, 78; N. Rubinstein, 'Michelozzo and Niccolò Michelozzi in Chios 1466–67', in C. H. Clough (ed.), *Cultural Aspects of the Italian Renaissance: Essays in Honour of Paul Oskar Kristeller* (Manchester, 1976), pp. 216–28; A. Brown, *Bartolomeo Scala 1430–1497, Chancellor of Florence: The Humanist as Bureaucrat* (Princeton, 1979). See also, for example, Archivio di Stato, Florence, Mediceo avanti il Principato (henceforth MAP), XXV, 590. (All manuscript references here are to collections in the Florentine State Archives.)

[9] See Rubinstein, *The Government*, esp. pt II.

As far as the nature of Medici power in Florence is concerned, it is certainly not possible to define it by simple reference either to the family's position in relation to the constitution and its modifications of the system of appointment to offices, or, on the other hand, to the ritual, public, and particularly the foreign image of the Medici role in the Florentine state. Not only is it necessary for the historian to take all these elements equally into account; there is also an actual dynamic operating in the fifteenth century between constitutional reality and public image which indeed becomes a major factor affecting and modifying Medicean power. Moreover, the dynamic of the relations between the Medici and their fellow-citizens was different from the one which operated between them and their friends among the rulers of other states.[10]

It is clear from the Medici correspondence, and particularly from the letters of the young Francesco di Giuliano di Averardo, Cosimo's first cousin twice removed, that, when in Venice during their exile from Florence in 1433, Cosimo and his brother Lorenzo were treated on public and ceremonial occasions as the admired and respected equals of the Doge and his relatives, whose personal friendship and private hospitality they had long enjoyed as a consequence of their banking activities in Venice. This relation, and Cosimo's generous loan to the Venetian state early in 1434, induced what was then Florence's major foreign ally to interest itself in the internal affairs of the Florentine state, and to express publicly its support for the cause of the Medici. While maintaining a public stance of neutrality, the pope in fact took a similar view on similar grounds of the desirability of restoring his bankers to their native city.[11] The less partisan members of the Florentine ruling group could hardly have remained entirely indifferent to the force of such powerful foreign opinion.

After 1434, the Medici family's personal friendships with *signori* like the Manfredi, the Malatesta, and the Gonzaga gave it an advantage in diplomatic negotiations with those states based, not upon the official position of the Medici within Florence, but upon personal influence. The particular value of the Medici family as informal diplomats for

[10] See R. C. Trexler, *Public Life in Renaissance Florence* (New York, 1980); cf. his edition of *The Libro Cerimoniale of the Florentine Republic*, by Francesco Filarete and Angelo Manfidi (*Travaux d'humanisme et Renaissance*, 165, Geneva, 1978).

[11] D. V. Kent, 'I Medici in esilio: una vittoria di famiglia ed una disfatta personale', *Archivio storico italiano*, 132 (1974), 1–63, and *Rise of the Medici*, pp. 334–6; G. Holmes, 'How the Medici became the Pope's Bankers', in N. Rubinstein (ed.), *Florentine Studies* (London, 1968), pp. 357–80.

Florence was one factor that naturally increased its prestige and power within the state by comparison with its theoretically equal fellows in the ruling class, and gave it an important directive influence on Florentine foreign policy. The supreme example of this is, of course, the ultimate abandonment of the traditional Venetian connection for an alliance with Milan under the rule of the Medicean protégé, Francesco Sforza. However, even the extreme development of this influence under the later Medici cannot be seen as a totally radical departure from republican tradition, which had always acknowledged the need to select diplomats in accordance with their ability to impress foreign dignitaries, rather than in accordance with their importance as the holders of major office within the city. The most notable evidence of this was the frequent diplomatic use of *magnati* actually excluded from the major internal magistracies.[12] Nor were the Medici unique in their own society; the Acciaiuoli, for example, continued to enjoy the particular prestige which they had long derived from their foreign connections.[13]

The fact that the Medici moved in extra-Florentine circles as the equals of lords and princes necessarily helped to set them apart, however, from the majority of their fellow-citizens. In the eyes of these men, the evidence that the Medici family also shared to some extent the life-style of its princely friends must at the same time have enhanced its position, and increased unease about it. Fraser Jenkins made the point some time ago that the Medici led the way for the princes of Italy in legitimizing the expression of magnificence in architectural and artistic patronage, and further evidence confirms this in increasing detail.[14] Astorgio Manfredi consulted with Giovanni di Cosimo concerning the hangings from Bruges which he ordered via the Medici, just as he commissioned manuscripts from Piero's copies by Piero's scribe, and the Duke of Ferrara kept his eye on building projects by the Medici and their circle.[15] Richard Trexler has recently argued that

---

[12] Trexler, *Public Life*, pp. 291–301; C. Gutkind, *Cosimo de' Medici, Pater Patriae* (Oxford, 1938), ch. 5.

[13] See, for example, Brucker, *The Civic World, passim*: C. Ugurgieri della Berardenga, *Gli Acciaiuoli di Firenze* (2 vols., Florence, 1962); Rubinstein, *The Government*, esp. pp. 136–45.

[14] A. Fraser Jenkins, 'Cosimo de' Medici's Patronage of Architecture and the Theory of Magnificence', *Journal of the Warburg and Courtauld Institutes*, 33 (1970), 162–70.

[15] MAP XVI, 20, 58; IX, 36, 47, 82; F. W. Kent, '"Più superba de quella de Lorenzo"; Courtly and Family Interest in the Building of Filippo Strozzi's Palace', *Renaissance Quarterly*, 30 (1977), 311–23.

it was an important advantage to the Florentines to have citizens who could meet on equal ceremonial terms with foreign visitors, while drawing attention to the Medicean use, at the same time, of ritual to express superiority or authority in relation to various social groups and classes within Florence.[16] Similarly if, as Rab Hatfield has pointed out, the Medici palace was decorated within with a magnificence designed to impress the family's princely friends, without (if not in decoration, in the renunciation of a possible interest in unifying the site of the palace with the public piazza of San Lorenzo), the Medici acknowledged the austerity more appropriate to citizens of the republic.[17] And an incident in relation to the building of the palace recounted by the chronicler Giovanni Cavalcanti—'e se non è vero, è certamente ben trovato'—suggests that it was indeed essential that Cosimo de' Medici continue to restrain his display of wealth and power, if he wished to go on representing himself, even to some of his *amici*, as *primus inter pares* in the most powerful and successful patronage network in Florence, rather than as the city's proto-prince. According to Cavalcanti, shortly after the palace was completed, in a period when financial measures were imposing heavy burdens on much of the citizenry, Cosimo's household awoke one morning to find blood on the threshold of its new dwelling. The significance of this dramatic gesture, observes Cavalcanti, was lost on no one, least of all Cosimo, by whom it was carefully ignored, though he knew, in fact, who had done it.[18]

The more work that is done on the artistic patronage, not just of the Medici, but of their fellow-patricians over the course of the fifteenth century, the more we find confirmed Gombrich's dictum that the patronage of the Medici family was finely calculated to express superiority, but not to flaunt it.[19] We can find everywhere expressed in

[16] Trexler, *Public Life*, esp. ch. 12.

[17] R. Hatfield, 'Some Unknown Descriptions of the Medici Palace in 1459', *Art Bulletin*, 52 (1970), 232–49. San Lorenzo is presently the subject of much important work by art historians (see n. 21), which should clarify our picture of the nature and significance of Medici patronage of the church, and perhaps throw more light on its relation to the building of the adjacent palace. For some preliminary suggestions on this point, see my *Rise of the Medici*, pp. 69–71. On San Lorenzo, see J. Ruda, 'A 1434 Building Programme for San Lorenzo in Florence', and H. Saalman, 'San Lorenzo: the 1434 Chapel Project', in *Burlington Magazine*, 120 (1978), 358–61 and 361–4. I am also indebted to Margaret Haines for comments and suggestions.

[18] *Istorie fiorentine scritte da Giovanni Cavalcanti*, ed. F. Polidori (Florence, 1838–9), ii. 210.

[19] E. H. Gombrich, 'The Early Medici as Patrons of Art', in E. F. Jacob (ed.), *Italian Renaissance Studies* (London, 1960), pp. 279–311; see esp. pp. 281–2.

patronage the dynamic dialogue between the Medici family, the friends and neighbours of its party, and the other wealthy and cultured patricians of the Florentine ruling class. The examples become too numerous to mention more than a few. There is first the vivid case of the church of San Lorenzo. For some time we have been aware that the rebuilding of the church was undertaken first, in the 1420s, as a neighbourhood project by a group of the residents of the district of the Golden Lion, many of whom were already Medici partisans. After the Medici victory of 1434, the beginnings of work in 1429 were described as having been made, not by a group of neighbours, but by 'that famous citizen, Giovanni de' Medici'. While in 1440 the decision to go on with the rebuilding was made in the name of 'all the residents of the parish', when in 1442 the responsibility was finally entrusted to Cosimo himself, all reference to his friends and neighbours previously associated with the project was henceforth omitted. The Medici become not only the builders of Florence's first great Renaissance palace in the 'modern' style, but also the first family completely to remodel a public church largely at their own private expense.[20] Work now in progress by Caroline Elam on the acquisition and transfer of patronage rights over the chapels of San Lorenzo during the fifteenth century suggests that the disposition of the chapels, and especially the transfer of those in the most impressive position from one family to another, is partly a reflection of the changing relationships between the Medici and their various local partisans.[21]

It has been suggested that Andrea Pazzi's decision to build the beautiful chapel by Brunelleschi adjacent to the church of Santa Croce was ultimately a response to a desire on the part of the Medici family to assert at second-hand, through one of its leading partisans, a Medicean presence in the quarter of Santa Croce—until recently dominated by its leading political opponents—which it did not quite feel able to express directly.[22] The palace-building enterprises of Medicean partisans such as the Ginori and the Dietisalvi Neroni (the latter at present the subject of a detailed investigation by Brenda

[20] See P. Ginori Conti, *La basilica di San Lorenzo e la famiglia Ginori* (Florence, 1940).

[21] Caroline Elam reported on this research to an informal conference on San Lorenzo held at Villa I Tatti, the Harvard University Center for Italian Renaissance Studies in Florence, in mid-1982.

[22] Howard Saalman proposes this, in a draft chapter of his forthcoming book on Brunelleschi that he kindly allowed me to see several years ago.

Preyer[23]) may be seen as influenced by a desire to express appropriately in concrete form a relationship to the Medici in which a certain amount of admiration and emulation, but not too much competition, was desirable. On the other hand, both F. W. Kent and Preyer have argued that the building of Giovanni Rucellai's elegant Albertian palace not only expresses, but also affects, the long progression of his relationship to the Medici and the regime which they dominated—from finding himself, after 1434, 'suspect by the regime' as the son-in-law of Palla Strozzi, to being accepted back into the fold in the privileged position of father-in-law to Lorenzo's sister Nannina by her marriage to his son Bernardo in 1466 (a transformation of which his later sale to Lorenzo of the site for the villa at Poggio a Caiano was to some extent an acknowledgement).[24] Finally, while in the Pitti palace one can see a direct expression of that family's challenge to Medici predominance from within the Medici party,[25] the fact that Filippo Strozzi, comparatively recently accepted back into the *reggimento* after half a century of his family's exclusion, could start to build in 1489, with Lorenzo's acquiescence, a palace which Ercole d'Este was to describe as prouder ('più superba') than Lorenzo's own, is a remarkable demonstration, not just of the uses of patronage to conduct political dialogue, but of the lively continuance of that dialogue between the Medici and the ruling class right up to the death of 'il Magnifico'.

One must also be aware of changes in the relationships between the Medici and particular partisans; these remained highly dynamic in a number of ways. This is true even of what we might call the hard core of the party—that group of families, already closely identified with the Medici before 1434, who continued faithful to them at least until the end of the century. Let us look at a handful of the better examples—the Martelli, the Ginori, the della Stufa, and the Tornaquinci/Tornabuoni. While the strength of the attachment of these lineages to the Medici remained relatively constant, the nature of the bonds between them varied over time. The first three were originally neighbourhood associates, the first two from newer families, whose

---

[23] See too her 'The "chasa overo palagio" of Alberto di Zanobi: A Florentine Palace of about 1400 and its Later Remodeling', *Art Bulletin*, 65 (1983), 387–401, and the remarks of F. W. Kent in *A Florentine Patrician*, pp. 55–7.

[24] F. W. Kent, *A Florence Patrician*, passim, and also F. W. Kent's 'Lorenzo de' Medici's Acquisition of Poggio a Caiano in 1474 and an Early Reference to his Architectural Expertise', *Journal of the Warburg and Courtauld Institutes*, 42 (1979), 250–7.

[25] On the changing role of the Pitti in the Medici regime, see Rubinstein, *The Government*.

rise into the ruling class was associated with their identification with
the Medici; they formed part of that local group which provided an
important base for Medici power in the late 1420s and early 1430s.[26]
After 1434, their own promotion by Medici favour to a position of
importance within the *reggimento* narrowed the social gap between
them and their patrons. But, while the Ginori always retained something of their early attitude of subservience (which in the changing
atmosphere of later Medicean Florence was finally transmuted into
'courtiership' in its more negative sense[27]), Gismondo della Stufa and
the younger Martelli, as intimate cronies in the *brigata* of the young
Lorenzo, achieved in their relationship with him a subtle and volatile
blend of the more fundamentally instrumental friendship of their
forebears with a sharing of personal pleasures and interests (in poetry,
love, hunting, and the like) in the aristocratic courtly style.[28] The
'instrumental' roles of particular leading families in the maintenance
of Medici power also change over the century. For example, the
Martelli also became central, after 1434, to the administration of the
bank and the related cultivation of connections with foreign powers,
at councils like that of Ferrara, at the papal court in Rome, and
elsewhere. Meanwhile the Tornaquinci/Tornabuoni, closely associated with the foundation of the Medici financial fortunes in the later
fourteenth century, become less prominent (with the notable exception
of Giovanni Tornabuoni) in the bank of the fifteenth. But they maintained their intimacy with the Medici, reinforced again by marriage in
the union of Piero di Cosimo and Lucrezia Tornabuoni, and their
outstanding artistic patronage may be seen as an index and an
expression of their elevated role in later fifteenth-century Florentine
society.[29]

[26] D. V. Kent, *Rise of the Medici*, pp. 61–71.

[27] On the Ginori, see F. W. Kent, *Household and Lineage in Renaissance Florence:
The Family Life of the Capponi, Ginori and Rucellai* (Princeton, 1977).

[28] This is a complex question which requires further definition of terms through more
analysis of a range of evidence. For example, much material from letters has been
published by A. Rochon, *La Jeunesse de Laurent de Médicis (1449–1478)* (Paris, 1963),
but in the framework of a limited conception of friendship. Trexler (*Public Life*)
recognizes a much broader spectrum of the senses of that term, but continues to see
'courtly' and 'mercantile' as opposed rather than coexisting elements in this society. For
published material illustrating the activities of a not dissimilar circle which gathered
around Giovanni di Cosimo de' Medici much earlier in the century, see V. Rossi,
'L'indole e gli studi di Giovanni di Cosimo de' Medici', *Rendiconti della Reale Accademia dei Lincei, Classe di scienze morali, storiche e filologiche*, 2 (1893), 38–150.

[29] See R. de Roover, *The Rise and Decline of the Medici Bank, 1397–1494* (Cambridge,
Mass., 1963); on the Medici and their supporters before 1434, see D. V. Kent, *Rise of*

Different types of personal bond created a different dynamic between the Medici family and particular partisans, which is one reason why, in attempting to understand the relation between the Medici and the remainder of the ruling class, and the way in which the Medici party operated within it, it is not enough simply to observe the existence of personal ties (such as those created by marriage), still less merely to quantify them. The quality of each individual relationship, and the nature of its function in maintaining the party structure, has to be assessed if we are really to grasp the mechanism as a whole.[30] Moreover, the very principle by which a patronage network operates is in itself a particularly dynamic one. A request for any sort of assistance, especially in the political sphere, given that the key offices of state were usually still drawn by lot under the traditional system (however closely and ingeniously modified and manipulated by the Medici and their partisans), was likely to involve the pulling of a very complex set of strings. To obtain a particular office in these circumstances would often require the activation of quite a large proportion of the entire network, as friends called upon chains of friends of friends, in streams of requests through their letters of recommendation.

If we move on from how the Medici party operated to consider those for whom it operated, one of the more important questions which arises is on what grounds, especially as the number of their partisans grew, the Medici made a choice between their various interests and obligations. The question of choice was particularly pressing when, as so often, a large number of partisans were in direct competition for a particular office. For example, the Medici correspondence throws interesting light on the procuring for Florentine citizens of offices at the courts of their foreign friends. Here the relation between recommendations and success was much more clear-cut than for the internal offices, which involved elements of chance and manipulation,

---

the Medici, pt I. For an extensive account of Tornabuoni and Tornaquinci patronage, see P. Simons, 'Portraiture and Patronage in Quattrocento Florence, with Special Reference to the Tornaquinci and their Chapel in Santa Maria Novella', PhD thesis (University of Melbourne, 1985).

[30] While statistics concerning marriage endogamy may illuminate the strength and meaning of neighbourhood ties lower down the social scale (cf. S. K. Cohn, *The Laboring Classes in Renaissance Florence* (New York, 1980), esp. ch. 2), the evidence suggests that the governing élite pursued complex marriage strategies designed to forge a range of social links to a wide variety of ends. See F. W. Kent, *Household and Lineage*, esp. pp. 91–9, and D. V. Kent, *Rise of the Medici*, pp. 49–61.

concerning which there are obviously fewer explicit statements in the letters. What is most striking is not only the number of occasions on which different, and more or less equally influential members of the family, like Cosimo's two sons, Giovanni and Piero, would make (unbeknownst to one another) recommendations on behalf of different partisans to the same foreign friend for the same job, but also the fact that the same member of the family would himself recommend several persons in terms of the same enthusiasm. This often led to an explicit request from the recipient of these recommendations for clarification as to which candidate really enjoyed Medici support, and which should be appointed to satisfy his own obligations of friendship to the Medici family. The question of the criteria of choice operating in the resolution of these conflicts is one of some interest, but it is difficult to answer, since all those involved were usually bound to the Medici by some tie or other implying reciprocal obligations of loyalty and patronage.[31]

There is a constant dynamic between the patron and his *clientela*, in so far as his obligation to satisfy the needs of his partisans in return for their support is the nexus of the relationship. If this obligation is consistently unfulfilled, or not sufficiently fulfilled, his partisans withdraw that contingent support which makes him in the last analysis dependent upon them. There is evidence to suggest that these problems, inherent in any patronage system, were a major cause of the disaffection of individual partisans of the Medici, as their growing ascendancy over the *reggimento* as a whole increased the size of the network.[32] Not only did it become increasingly impossible to satisfy all the claims of a large number of people to a finite number of favours; there was also the problem of the growing importance—as intermediary between the major patron and his numerous clients—of the broker, whose function puts him in a position eventually to compete for the leadership of the party. A letter of warning from Filippo di Battista Arnolfi to Piero di Cosimo, shortly before the anti-Medicean conspiracy of 1466, identifies four factions within the Medici party: those who were primarily supporters of Piero himself, those who saw themselves as more

---

[31] For an explicit contemporary comment on patronage chains, see MAP v, 807; on confusion, especially concerning multiple recommendations, see ibid., VII, 54–61; XI, 53–6; XVI, 142; XX, 254.

[32] On Mediterranean patronage networks see, e.g., J. Boissevain, 'Patronage in Sicily', *Man*, 1 (1966), 18–33; J. Pitt-Rivers (ed.), *Mediterranean Countrymen: Essays in the Social Anthropology of the Mediterranean* (Paris, 1963); and E. Gellner and J. Waterbury (eds.), *Patrons and Clients in Mediterranean Societies* (London, 1977). On later Medicean patronage, see Lorenzo Polizzotto's chapter in this volume.

directly bound to Dietisalvi Neroni, or to Luca Pitti, 'and those in between'.[33] Pitti's bid for power is the most clear-cut of the evidence of an impulse, as the century wore on, to replace the Medici family's regime with another, of a similar nature but under alternative leadership.

In the case of Dietisalvi Neroni, however, though for the purposes of asserting opposition to the Medici in 1466 he had in fact joined forces with Pitti and others, we are probably dealing with a rather different phenomenon. That the greatest challenges to Medici power until the death of Lorenzo tended to come from within the ranks of the family's major supporters, was partly because, as with Pitti, the chief brokers of Medici power acquired the greatest share of it. However, I think this fact can also be explained, not only in terms of the structure of the Medici party, but also in terms of the constant dynamic in Florentine society, throughout the history of the Republic, between the pull of personal obligation and that of political idealism. I have been very concerned to stress the importance of personal relationships as determinants of political action, but the last thing that I would want to do is to take the ideas out of history. I have argued that in certain specific situations, like that of the conflict between the partisans of the Medici and Albizzi families in the 1420s and 1430s, the parties were held together by personal ties rather than by ideological considerations. However, at the point where the issue broadened to a choice between acceptance of the constitutional authority of the pro-Medicean *Signoria*, or rebellion by the Albizzi faction against it, I believe the fact that the Medicean interest happened to be identified with constitutionalism was a major factor in its gaining the support of the *reggimento* as a whole.[34]

I do not feel that the contrast drawn by some network theorists between the dynamic nature of analysis in terms of social networks, and the measurement of individual behaviour against so-called 'static institutions and social norms', has much meaning, at least in relation to this society, where I would see these elements as interconnected. Nor do I accept the view that regards network analysis as a means of understanding social behaviour in terms of self-interest and manipulation as distinct from explaining it in terms of moral imperatives. I do not see these as exclusive alternatives, and I think that to do so

---

[33] '...e quelli di mezzo': MAP XVIII, 495. I owe this reference to Rab Hatfield.
[34] D. V. Kent, *Rise of the Medici*, pp. 338–9.

may be to assume, even if unconsciously, that the tendency widespread in Mediterranean countries, both in the past and the present, to adopt a system of personal government functioning through patronage is really morally corrupt.[35] Certainly in Florence, after 1434 as before, there seems to me to be a constant dynamic or dialogue between the promotion of individual or group self-interest in politics and its expression in patronage on the one hand, and purely moral or aesthetic considerations on the other.

Letters of Medici partisans to their patrons can be couched in even the most servile language and still express the view that it is contrary to the honour of themselves, the Medici, and above all contrary to the values for which the Florentine Republic stands, to subvert justice and the constitution in the personal interests of any individual.[36] Dietisalvi Neroni and Agnolo Acciaiuoli—two of Cosimo's original, and most loyal partisans in 1434—envisaged the destruction of the Republic by the Medici party which they opposed in 1466.[37] Others, like Manno Temperani, consistently favoured by the Medici in key and sensitive offices crucial to the maintenance of their regime, remained within it but openly asserted the ideals of traditional Florentine republicanism, both in the *Consulte e Pratiche*, or informal consultations on government policy, and in such set-piece vehicles for dialogue between the Medici and their supporters as the letters written to Piero on the death of Cosimo. These, quite as much as being expressions of consolation and continuing support, were obviously intended to spell out the terms of its continuance, and their expectations of Piero's accession.[38]

Most patricians believed they had a traditional right to a share in government, even if indirectly, and they were presumably aware that the maintenance of a republican constitution was a far better guarantee of this right than any personal 'deal', however advantageous, with any patron could ever be. However, there is no reason to doubt the genuineness of their belief (whatever its relation to reality) that repub-

[35] See J. Boissevain, *Friends of Friends: Networks, Manipulators, and Coalitions* (Oxford, 1974). For a subtle analysis of Florentine social networks within a sophisticated theoretical framework, see R. F. E. Weissman, *Ritual Brotherhood in Renaissance Florence* (New York, 1982), and his chapter in this volume.

[36] See, for example, MAP V, 745; IX, 2, 30, 31, 50; XI, 563.

[37] For the correspondence of the mid-1460s between the Strozzi and Acciaiuoli (and concerning the Dietisalvi Neroni), see Carte Strozziane, ser. 3, 178, and on the latter family, see particularly MAP XVII, *passim*. Heather Gregory drew the Strozzi *filza* to my attention.

[38] MAP CLXIII. This collection includes letters from Giovannozzo Pitti and Manno Temperani, on whom see also Rubinstein, *The Government*, pp. 154–66.

licanism in the Florentine tradition was the best, the morally finest, form of government. The governing class was, after all, profoundly imbued by its education with the literature, morality, and ideals of the classical republics, and with the conviction that in both the cultural and the political spheres Florence was the modern heir of Athens and Rome.[39] The relationship between ideals and interest in Florentine politics is subtle, complex, and may well defy definition or description, but that is no excuse for historians to create an unnecessary opposition between the two which was absent from the perceptions of so many of Florence's ruling class. After all, while in 1494 the Medici were expelled from the city by general consent of that class, on primarily moral and ideological grounds, their expulsion served at the same time as an apposite reminder that the patron is ultimately accountable to his clientele upon whose collective support the maintenance of his predominance depends, and that, while a network of patronage can be an impressive instrument of political control, it is a mechanism into which is built the means of its own destruction.

[39] The literature touching on this subject is vast, but see particularly F. Gilbert, *Machiavelli and Guicciardini: Politics and History in Sixteenth-century Florence* (Princeton, 1965). For examples of the application of this education in specifically political situations, see Rubinstein, *The Government*, esp. pt II, and Brucker, *The Civic World*, chs. 3, 5, and esp. pp. 326–7.

5

Ties of Neighbourhood and Patronage in Quattrocento Florence

F. W. KENT

UNTIL quite recently, historians of fifteenth-century Florence have not been particularly interested in 'neighbourhood', in bonds of *vicinanza*, however one defines that difficult concept; nor have they much explored the relationship between artistic and political patronage and a sense of neighbourhood. The city was, of course, divided into neighbourhoods in the sense of administrative districts: after 1343 into quarters, sixteen *gonfaloni* or wards, and numerous parishes. But the nature of the political and constitutional role of these administrative subdivisions was less clear, though most scholars took for granted that these districts, and the neighbourhood loyalties that presumably developed within them, became less important as the medieval commune gave way to a more centralized and bureaucratic Renaissance city-state, one increasingly dominated by the Medici party.[1] This was in a sense a curious assumption, since the Florentines themselves, in their loquacious way, talked and wrote constantly, from Dante's time to Francesco Guicciardini's, about *vicini*, neighbours, and how important they were in their lives. Donato Velluti wrote of Cino Bonamichi, for example, that he was joined to the Velluti 'by love, kinship and neighbourhood', a complex social relationship which survived Cino's death, for Velluti further explained that the tie of neighbourhood with his friend existed 'not only here on earth on account of where we live—but even after his death, for his tomb was side by side with ours in the cloister of Santo Spirito'.[2] And one could multiply examples

---

[1] See, for example, M. B. Becker, 'An Essay on the Quest for Identity in the early Italian Renaissance', in J. G. Rowe and W. H. Stockdale (eds.), *Florilegium historiale: Essays Presented to Wallace K. Ferguson* (Toronto, 1971), pp. 294–312, esp. p. 302. On the constitutional role of the various administrative divisions, see G. Guidi, *Il governo della città-repubblica di Firenze del primo Quattrocento* (3 vols., Florence, 1981).

[2] D. Velluti, *La cronica domestica*, ed. I. del Lungo and G. Volpi (Florence, 1914), p. 22.

from a whole range of records, both personal and official, from private letters and diaries to the widely circulated works of popular writers or the sterner evidence of law or public ceremony. Belonging to a particular area of the city conferred identity on a man, as did his trade. Neri di Bicci describes himself, in the first passage of his account book, as 'a painter, from the parish of San Friano, the district of Drago and the quarter of Santo Spirito'; the far more obscure Salvestro di Ciecho di Lenzo proudly calls himself, in his tax report of 1427, 'shoemaker, *popolano* and citizen of the city of Florence, and of the parish of San Pier Maggiore and of the district of Chiavi . . .'.[3]

Now, however, taking the lead from the Quattrocento, we too are talking about neighbours and neighbourhoods. Christiane Klapisch has investigated neighbourhood in an article on the Niccolini family's 'parenti, amici e vicini', that trilogy of social relationships so ubiquitous in the Quattrocento that Dale Kent used it as the basis for her explanation of patronage relations and partisanship during the period of Cosimo de' Medici's rise to power.[4] My study on family structure in fifteenth-century Florence emphasized the importance of the *gonfalone* as a power-base for aristocratic families—a conclusion with which some others, Anthony Molho and Ronald Weissman in particular, would agree.[5] The *gonfalone*—which had originated as a defensive association of the *popolo*—increasingly became a local centre of administration. Eligibility for the city's political offices came to depend on a process of nomination and sortition which began in the *gonfalone* and for which the Gonfalonier of Company, its leading official, had much of the responsibility. Brenda Preyer supports, from yet another point of view, the suggestion that a sense of neighbourhood remained strong. Studying a number of aristocratic palace projects begun around the mid-Quattrocento, Preyer has found that in almost every case the patrician builder chose and expanded a traditional ancestral site for

---

[3] Neri di Bicci, *Le ricordanze (10 marzo 1453–24 aprile 1475)*, ed. B. Santi (Pisa, 1976), p. 1; Archivio di Stato, Florence, Catasto, 59, fo. 437ʳ. (All manuscript references here are to collections in the Florentine State Archives.)

[4] C. Klapisch, '"Parenti, amici e vicini": il territorio urbano d'una famiglia mercantile nel secolo XV', *Quaderni storici*, 33 (1976), 953–82; D. V. Kent, *The Rise of the Medici: Faction in Florence 1426–1434* (Oxford, 1978).

[5] See my *Household and Lineage in Renaissance Florence: The Family Life of the Capponi, Ginori and Rucellai* (Princeton, 1977), esp. chs. 4 and 5; A. Molho, 'Cosimo de' Medici: *Pater Patriae* or *Padrino?*', *Stanford Italian Review*, 1 (1979), 5–33, esp. pp. 21–8; R. F. E. Weissman, *Ritual Brotherhood in Renaissance Florence* (New York, 1982), esp. ch. 1.

his imposing new *palazzo*, even when such a choice was aesthetically less than satisfactory.

The concept of *vicinanza*—and what it meant to the Florentines—has, in short, become at once richer and more confused and confusing. According to Weissman, in the fifteenth century 'neighborhoods and quarters resembled cities in miniature, each with its own local services, resources and solidarities': Florence was fragmented 'into multiple communities', where the significant social relationships of 'friendship', *amicizia* and *vicinanza*, were so 'dense', 'multi-faceted' and often ambiguous ('agonistic' is Weissman's word) that men sought release from them. They did so in lay religious confraternities, whose 'confraternal ritual provided a temporary suspension of class and neighborhood loyalties' because their membership was usually city-wide.[6] For Richard Trexler, on the other hand, sectional or neighbourhood loyalties have little importance in the ritual life of the classic commune. Before Lorenzo de' Medici's time, a person was 'either a member of a family and a Florentine, or nothing at all'.[7] Towards the end of the Quattrocento, however, the commune as a ritual entity was destroyed and, as part of a 'ritual revolution', the Medici occupied the ceremonial centre of Florentine life supported by, among other groups, a wave of neighbourhood particularism, especially in the parishes. Samuel Cohn also sees the issue of neighbourhood organization and loyalties as crucial, but in another sense. His basic theme is that, after the downfall of the plebeian Ciompi, the members of the triumphant ruling class gave up their neighbourhood loyalties, to *gonfalone* and parish, to become a patriciate with city-wide connections and self-consciousness. At the same time, the *popolo minuto* lost the sense of class solidarity it had possessed in the third quarter of the Trecento, and was forced to retreat during the Quattrocento to smaller parish and neighbourhood communities, often on the periphery of the city.[8]

There is, then, suddenly an embarrassment not of riches but of

---

[6] Weissman, *Ritual Brotherhood*, pp. 9, 10, 21, 22, 163.

[7] R. C. Trexler, *Public Life in Renaissance Florence* (New York, 1980), p. 14, and *passim*. On Trexler's account of neighbourhood, see my review in *Journal of Modern History*, 54 (1982), 382–8. For his recognition of neighbourhood solidarities among the lower classes, see now his 'Neighbours and Comrades. The Revolutionaries of Florence', *Social Analysis*, 13 (1983), 53–106.

[8] S. K. Cohn, *The Laboring Classes in Renaissance Florence* (New York, 1980). Cohn considers only statistical evidence of the marital bonds made by Florentines in coming to this conclusion; but, as Weissman has written, 'marriage networks are only one dimension of social networks' (*Ritual Brotherhood*, p. 12 n. 24).

theories about neighbourhood; for all that, sustained work on the very role, and social and political structure, of the *gonfaloni* is still wanting, let alone research into 'neighbourhoods' otherwise defined. It is little wonder that there is much confusion and some contradiction; little wonder, too, that even allies can be at cross purposes. For example, Anthony Molho, who introduced with approval Cohn's idea that the labouring classes retreated in the Quattrocento to the parishes, to a more parochial consciousness, still rejected in effect the other, essential, part of Cohn's case: that the Quattrocento patriciate had simultaneously abandoned its particularistic loyalties. For, according to Molho, the *gonfaloni* were still so central to aristocratic politics in Cosimo's time that almost all patronage worked through them. In Florence there was 'created . . . a series of parallel hierarchies . . . Each of these hierarchies of clienteles tended to recruit its members primarily within a restricted geographic area in the city, most often within the *gonfalone* in which resided its most powerful members.' So the city was 'fragmented . . . into a series of patronal enclaves', and only the Medici party was strong and broad enough to transcend, and ultimately incorporate, such local patronage networks.[9] As André Chastel said in another context, Florence provides the spectacle of a city 'où les problèmes sont plus nombreuses que les certitudes'.[10] With some diffidence, therefore, I address myself to some of these questions, above all in the light of the research on neighbourhood published by Dale Kent and myself in *Neighbours and Neighbourhood in Renaissance Florence*.[11]

This work is a study of one of the smallest of the Renaissance city's sixteen *gonfaloni*, Lion Rosso (the Red Lion), situated in the quarter of Santa Maria Novella and comprising the parishes of San Pancrazio and San Paolo. The study is based upon a series of notarial acts recording the formal meetings of that *gonfalone*—some twenty in all survive for the period 1417–63—interpreted against the registers of the *catasto*, the Strozzi papers and the records of San Pancrazio, the Vallombrosan convent which played a vital part in the Red Lion's story. But the notarial acts were the core, providing the names of all

---

[9] Molho, 'Cosimo de' Medici', pp. 21, 24.

[10] *Art et humanisme à Florence au temps de Laurent le Magnifique* (Paris, 1961), p. 3.

[11] D. V. and F. W. Kent, *Neighbours and Neighbourhood in Renaissance Florence: The District of the Red Lion in the Fifteenth Century* (Locust Valley, NY, 1982). What follows summarizes this book, to which, therefore, only minimal reference will be made in the notes.

the men who attended meetings, and so enabling one to reconstruct that little local society, and how it worked. One or two meetings of other *gonfaloni* had been published earlier, but understandably their full significance had not been grasped; hundreds of such acts, for all districts, await their historians in the State Archives of Florence. I shall now try to give an account of what these records reveal about the meaning of neighbourhood. I should say at once—keeping in mind the recent historiography I have described above—that the burden of our study reinforces, without any doubt, our earlier impression (despite Trexler and Cohn) that individual *gonfaloni* preserved until well into the Quattrocento an essential political and fiscal role, and remained aristocratic strongholds where, however, local loyalties with a more popular flavour were in full play. This stated, I should add that it is clear there existed important bonds of neighbourhood which were not simply those of the *gonfalone*. Moreover, one should not over-emphasize the self-sufficiency or isolation of the *gonfaloni*, either as social or 'patronal enclaves'. At every point the *gonfalone* and its local society overlapped with other smaller and larger 'neighbourhoods', and was linked with Florence at large, with other corporations and institutions, with other social structures and networks.

The meetings of the Red Lion were almost all concerned to elect special officials called syndics (*sindachi*) to administer the district's financial affairs. These affairs were primarily to do with matters of taxation, over which each district had considerable control. Procedures varied, but basically each of the sixteen districts was allocated a sum to be raised. Then a committee of local men made the individual assessments necessary to reach the target, basing their decisions primarily on local knowledge—on 'opinione' and 'arbitrio' as contemporary language put it. The immensely sensitive business of allocating *sgravi*, or tax reliefs, was also usually put in local hands. It is essential to grasp that this traditional system of local taxation, about which we had known something for the Trecento and early Quattrocento, prevailed much longer than has been realized: to be precise, until 1458. This despite the introduction in 1426–7 of the celebrated *catasto*, which was in effect suspended from 1434 onwards.[12] Consequently neighbours remained immensely influential in a man's life, and it was essential to win the approval—by marriage, business alliance,

---

[12] Ibid., esp. ch. i, ii. See now E. Conti, *L'imposta diretta a Firenze nel Quattrocento (1427–1494)* (Rome, 1984).

or acts of friendship—of the more powerful figures in one's *gonfalone*. That this was true, scores of hitherto obscure passages in diaries and letters of the period testify;[13] and, as it happens, the Red Lion district provides some of the most explicit evidence of the various pressures that were at work, and of the different strategies for handling them. Francesco Datini, Iris Origo's 'Merchant of Prato', was taxed there, for example, and his correspondence with his wife is full of references to his attempts to restrain the 'thirst' of the red lion, as he called it.[14] For Datini, an incredibly rich outsider from Prato, was very vulnerable in a district dominated by a closely knit and long-established oligarchy of old families, such as the Strozzi and Rucellai, who could lighten their own, and their friends' and neighbours' burdens, by shifting the load on to him. Half a century later, the *gonfalone* of the Red Lion so protected one of its own, Giovanni Rucellai, decidedly 'suspect by the regime'. He had survived, he wrote in 1457, 'because I have been in the grace and benevolence of paternal kinsmen, relatives, neighbours and the rest of the men of [my] *gonfalone*, who are much to be praised because always in the tax concessions that are granted locally they have served and helped and had compassion for me'.[15]

If the Red Lion district was dominated by some ten to fifteen families otherwise prominent in the regime, much humbler men also came, though less often, to its meetings and had some part to play in local administration, which indeed was conducted in the name of 'universitas hominum dicti vexilli'.[16] Lesser guildsmen were generously represented—clearly *gonfalone* administration provided a training ground for socially mobile artisan families. But there also came local men nicknamed 'Pennuccia', 'Buonasera', 'Grassellino' or 'Pochavita', though what influence, if any, men with such risible nicknames might have exerted with a Minerbetti, a Federighi or a Strozzi we cannot be sure. More sense of community may have existed among all of them than a concentration upon gross differences in income, family antiquity and political authority might suggest was possible. At every point and in all sorts of ways (as emerged from tax reports, letters, diaries, and

[13] Kent and Kent, *Neighbours and Neighbourhood*, esp. ch. 1, iii.
[14] Ibid., pp. 56–61.
[15] Cited by me in F. W. Kent *et al.*, *Giovanni Rucellai ed il suo zibaldone*, II: *A Florentine Patrician and his Palace* (London, 1981), p. 28, where Rucellai's statement is explained in context.
[16] The social structure of the district is analysed in Kent and Kent, *Neighbours and Neighbourhood*, ch. 2, i and ii.

other papers from the district), the lives of the citizens of the Red Lion, rich and poor, powerful and humble, intersected. The wealthy frequently patronized the shops of the local poor, the poor rented these shops, and rooms and houses, from their better-off neighbours. Everybody was jumbled together in about twenty intersecting lanes and streets, and so there existed a certain neighbourhood 'sociability', however difficult a word to define that can be. There was, for instance, Luigi di Agostino, a poor man forced to hide at home so as not to be captured, whose plight was known, he wrote, in 'la vicinanza', whence came support from a local notary.[17] There was the patrician, Manno Temperani, who remembered in his first will of 1428 his humble client and tenant 'Grassellino'.[18]

Another focus of the community was the local parish church, San Pancrazio. (San Paolo played little part in district life.) It was in St Pancras that the *gonfalone* met, invoking that saint's name. Parishioners rich and poor left alms to it and most were buried there side by side, for all that the patrician tombs and chapels were far grander.[19] But the relationship between district and parish was even closer; the Red Lion district was a sacred as well as a secular institution in that special sense Richard Trexler has now made more accessible to us in his various studies. Indeed, twice in 1444, the whole corporation permanently handed over its fiscal affairs to the supervision of the abbot of San Pancrazio, the Vallombrosan Benedetto Toschi.[20] Abbot since 1428, he in effect controlled all aspects of local administration— save presumably the political side of things—until his death in mid-1464, though the district's bureaucracy and syndics of course handled the details.

Why was a permanent manager chosen, and why Toschi? For several reasons that help us to learn more about the area. One explanation is legal in nature: that in 1440 the commune passed a law which forbade too much concentration of authority in the hands of the same few elected syndics. In this sense, Toschi's appointment did not represent a narrowing of authority, but a move away from such a development, since the district was acknowledging what has been called 'the trust

---

[17] Cited ibid., pp. 28, 56, 69 n. 40.
[18] Notarile Antecosimiano, C 189 (Ser Tommaso Carondini, 1423–4), fo. 81ᵛ. On Grassellino, see Kent and Kent, *Neighbours and Neighbourhood*, pp. 113, 115, 126 n. 60. For this whole theme, see ibid., pp. 86–91, 107–21.
[19] Kent and Kent, *Neighbours and Neighbourhood*, ch. 2, iii.
[20] Ibid., pp. 135–6, and ch. 3.

function of the urban clergy',[21] above party and faction. Notably it was the district as a corporation which appointed him, and the abbot accepted in the name of the whole conventual community.[22] Toschi was an obvious choice. He was very energetic and able, as his entertaining account-books reveal and as his (presumed) portrait by Neri di Bicci, in the *S. Giovanni Gualberto Enthroned* now in Santa Trinita, suggests.[23] Toschi was also intimately in, but not of, that local society; he was, in brief, as impartial a local figure as that inbred world could find.

There was, perhaps, another reason why Toschi became permanent procurator of the men of the Red Lion. As general administrator he became the creditor of all monies owed the district by defaulting taxpayers, and in the Red Lion one mighty tax defaulter (mighty as a man and as a debtor!) stood out: Messer Palla Strozzi, in 1427 still the richest man in Florence and subsequently exiled to Padua, in late 1434, by the victorious Medici. From then onwards until his death, still in exile, in 1462, several government agencies scrambled to squeeze Palla Strozzi dry. The story is immensely complex but what seems to have happened is that Toschi decided to protect what remained of his ex-neighbour's wealth from other government agencies by taking over his affairs (including Strozzi's debt to the district). The abbot became, in effect, Strozzi's business manager, using certain income for his church but preserving what he could of the estate intact. In this he was actively aided by the patricians of the district, above all by Palla's faithful son-in-law Giovanni Rucellai and by the much respected Medicean, Manno Temperani.[24]

This ingenious scheme was, one may think, an example of aristocratic intrigue in the successful pursuit of self-interest, but it was also very much to the advantage of the whole district of the Red Lion, a product of local patriotism indeed. For, in the first instance, by keeping Strozzi afloat the district ensured the stability of its own corporate finances, and thereby also expressed its solidarity with a great local figure. Note, too, the delicious political irony by which Strozzi, an enemy of the Medici party, was protected by his ex-neighbours, most of whom were, in other respects, stout or even distinguished members

---

[21] R. C. Trexler, 'Honor among Thieves. The Trust Function of the Urban Clergy in the Florentine Republic', in S. Bertelli and G. Ramakus (eds.), *Essays Presented to Myron P. Gilmore* (2 vols., Florence, 1978), i. 317–34.

[22] See Kent and Kent, *Neighbours and Neighbourhood*, p. 141.

[23] Reproduced ibid., figs. 7 and 8. See also p. 152.

[24] Ibid., ch. 3. Rucellai's role is explained in my essay in *A Florentine Patrician*, pp. 26, 46–51.

of that Medicean regime. Further, Toschi managed Palla's and the district's finances in such a way as to ensure a profit with which, at his own and the district's insistence, he pursued his plans to rebuild and decorate the church of San Pancrazio, the sacred and civic centre of the Red Lion. Toschi, a committed builder in the Quattrocento mould, made sure that the district paid for whitewashing and stuccoing the walls, for a handsome and finely carved new choir (now at Vallombrosa), for the cloisters, for a stained-glass window, and for an organ. On all of these were placed the arms of the Red Lion, a reminder that these were local and corporate commissions.[25] Toschi, then, both symbolized and stage-managed the integration of civic and sacred in what was an intensely alive and self-conscious local community.

Judging by the case of the Red Lion, at least, one cannot concede, to Cohn for example, that a sense of neighbourhood, as identified with *gonfalone*, was not still a potent fact of upper-class Florentine life for at least a good part of the Quattrocento. To be quite sure, of course, one would need to study all fifteen other *gonfaloni*—an awesome task—but there is enough evidence available to suggest that in general terms the Red Lion was typical. While it would seem that no other district was taken over by an abbot, none the less in the *gonfalone* of the Golden Lion (which was almost identical with the parish of San Lorenzo) parochial officials did have discretion to absolve local men from certain small debts.[26] Further, the *gonfalone* of Unicorno (the Unicorn), had in Giovanni Mazzuoli, whose account books on the subject Richard Goldthwaite has recently discovered, a semi-permanent administrator.[27] Other districts, too, planned to use back-taxes for the purposes of beautifying an important local church, as did the men of Chiavi (the Keys) who met in San Pier Maggiore, in 1455.[28] There are notable other examples of district solidarity. The most obvious instance is provided by the Medicean *gonfalone* of the Golden Lion, whence came a crucial part of Cosimo de' Medici's faction in 1426–34, and his family's support for long afterwards.[29] *Gonfaloni*

---

[25] On the Red Lion district's artistic patronage, see Kent and Kent, *Neighbours and Neighbourhood*, pp. 151–62.

[26] Ibid., p. 45 n. 76.

[27] Ibid., p. 47.

[28] For this, and the well-known case of the Golden Lion district, see ibid., pp. 36, 46 n. 83, 156, 162.

[29] See D. V. Kent, *Rise of the Medici*, esp. pp. 61–71. See also Molho, 'Cosimo de' Medici', esp. pp. 26–8, and my 'New Light on Lorenzo de' Medici's Convent at Porta San Gallo', *Burlington Magazine*, 124 (1982), 292–4.

other than the Red Lion also protected men of standing, vulnerable because luke-warm towards the Medici, within the local community. Guido Baldovinetti, from an ancient family long settled in the district of Vipera (the Viper), which was centred on Borgo SS. Apostoli, anticipated Giovanni Rucellai's better known statement when he wrote in his diary in early 1455, 'I am most obliged to the district of the Viper,' where his neighbours procured for him much needed tax relief. 'And therefore I record this,' Baldovinetti continued, 'because I believe it to have been the salvation of me and of my family, in such difficulties have I been on account of taxation and wars.'[30] Even charity was dispensed locally in the 1460s by the confraternity of Santa Maria, or Sant'Agnese, delle Laudi, which met in the church of the Carmine and whose membership was principally drawn from the largely plebeian *gonfalone* of Drago Verde (the Green Dragon), in Santo Spirito. Just before Christmas 1466 Neri di Bicci, as official of the company, noted expenditure for flour 'to bake bread to give to the poor of the district of the Dragon, as we are obliged by bequest to do'.[31]

To cite such examples is not to suggest that neighbourhood communities knew little conflict or tension. On the contrary, there were strong, and frequently nasty, emotions at work in such communities, as Weissman has insisted.[32] How could it have been otherwise, given the rush to procure political eligibility and tax relief, at other people's expense, in a small and often claustrophobic community? A dispute over the purchase of a house probably caused Marco Parenti and Bernardo Rinieri, for example, who were literally 'vicini a muro commune'—neighbours sharing a common wall—in the *gonfalone* of Vaio (the Squirrel), in the quarter of San Giovanni, to feud for many years. They went to law in 1472 over the common wall because Rinieri had built on it, without Parenti's permission, a roofed terrazzo which sent torrents of rain water on to his neighbour's roof. Then in 1487 Parenti stealthily put a window in the wall, so invading Bernardo's privacy. There had been earlier prohibitions against this being done but, Rinieri wrote, Parenti 'did not bother to obey them because he is a scandalous

---

[30] Acquisti e Doni, 190, inserto 3, Ricordi of Guido di Francesco Baldovinetti (1440–63), fo. 14ʳ; see also fo. 13ᵛ.

[31] *Le ricordanze*, p. 290; see also pp. 326–7. (On this company, see Weissman, *Ritual Brotherhood*, pp. 69–72.) I am grateful to Edward Stoneham for drawing this passage to my attention. Nicholas Eckstein, also of Monash University, is currently writing a thesis on the district of Drago, Santo Spirito in the Quattrocento.

[32] *Ritual Brotherhood*, esp. pp. 21–2, 91. See too the many examples in Kent and Kent, *Neighbours and Neighbourhood*, esp. ch. 1, iii.

and perverse man', hardly the description historians would normally apply to this gifted brother-in-law of Filippo Strozzi.[33] One knows about all this because both men sat side by side in their houses furiously writing down in their diaries these and other stories. Even in this curious sense, neighbours were joined inescapably together. It is not so much that such ties were always harmonious, rather that neighbourhood mattered in people's lives, and conditioned many of the things they did and thought and wrote.

With the reintroduction in 1458 of the *catasto*, the administration of taxation left local hands, and it is almost certainly no coincidence that we have yet to find district meetings from the mid-1460s onwards. Moreover, Lorenzo de' Medici's increasingly centralized and autocratic ascendancy may also have slowly begun to rob the sixteen districts of yet another of their *raisons d'être*—as one of several clearing houses of political patronage. Indeed the Medici family's own district may have been a magnet which gradually weakened the hold of other areas on some of Florence's citizens. Piero da Gagliano wanted to buy a certain house in 1440 'because the proximity ... to yours [Piero de' Medici's] renders this a very advantageous location',[34] an argument which may also have been persuasive to the many artists and skilled artisans who clustered there, especially in the new housing areas being developed as the century went on.[35] For whatever reasons, by the early sixteenth century men no longer always invariably lived in the *gonfaloni* of their ancestors, as an acute observer noted.[36] Even so, to move 'officially' required formal permission,[37] and a sense of local identity still survived; its resurgence towards the end of the Quattrocento may have been just that, a revival, and not the new phenomenon Trexler has suggested it was. When the Medici were expelled in late 1494, the sixteen districts again acted as a popular militia against

---

[33] Conventi Soppressi, 95, 212, Ricordi of Bernardo Rinieri, fo. clxxiii; see also fo. 165. For Parenti's side of the story, see his Ricordi in Carte Strozziane, ser. II, 17 bis, fos. 41ʳ, 70ʳ, 81ʳ. See also M. Phillips, 'A Newly Discovered Chronicle by Marco Parenti', *Renaissance Quarterly*, 31 (1978), 153–60.

[34] Quoted from Mediceo avanti il Principato, XI, 552 (17 June 1440), by Molho, 'Cosimo de' Medici', p. 26.

[35] Caroline Elam noted this very interesting phenomenon in a paper on building policy in Renaissance Florence delivered on 11 March 1982 at Villa I Tatti.

[36] G. R. Sanesi, 'Un discorso sconosciuto di Donato Giannotti intorno alla Milizia', *Archivio storico italiano*, ser. 5, 8 (1891), 3–27.

[37] See the law of 24 Nov. 1512 permitting citizens to change guilds, quarters or *gonfaloni*, a reference I owe to Caroline Elam: Balìe, 44, fol. 99ʳ⁻ᵛ. Cf. my *Household and Lineage*, pp. 173–4.

them. Moreover, in 1528, the new and effective militia which later
defended the city during the siege was organized by *gonfaloni* and
quarters, the citizen soldiers of each district meeting regularly in a
local church and drilling together. They bore new flags, displaying the
emblem of their *gonfalone*, 'large or small as they saw fit, together with
the word "LIBERTY", written in big letters'.[38] Earlier, Savonarola,
debating how Florence should be ruled after the first expulsion of
the Medici, saw in the *gonfaloni* the basis of 'a kind of popular
referendum'.[39] 'You have in your city', he said in a sermon of 14
December 1495, 'sixteen gonfaloniers of company, who include under
their wing all the city and its citizens. Let the citizens meet together,
each in his own district, to consult about and consider what seems the
best form of government for you to choose.'[40] In various ways the
gonfaloni were to participate actively in the turbulent politics of the
period after 1494, and it is hardly surprising that the Medici finally
abolished them, and other components of the republican constitution,
in 1531. 'Everything was done', wrote the pro-Medicean Filippo de'
Nerli, 'to take away from the people the opportunity of being able any
longer to meet together under those ancient and popular insignia.'[41]
For certainly a spirit of aristocratic independence still lurked within
the sixteen district communities, plausibly a flavour of populism, for
all that they had their own mini-aristocracies. One wonders if it was
only a coincidence that it was the knight Messer Manno Temperani,
usually a supporter of the Medici, who led the non-partisan wing of
the republican revolt against Piero de' Medici in 1465–6: Manno
Temperani, the *éminence grise* of the Red Lion district, who believed
at heart in local prerogatives and artisan rights, in the old republican
Florence that 'more easily opens doors to able men than do other
regimes [*stati*]'.[42] Perhaps Manno was here expressing a principle (or

---

[38] F. Polidori, 'Provvisione della milizia ed ordinanza fiorentina—6 novembre 1528',
Archivio storico italiano, 1 (1842), 384–409, esp. p. 403. (On this militia in action, see
C. Roth, *The Last Florentine Republic* (London, 1925), pp. 118, 194–6.) For the
resurgence of the *gonfaloni*, see Kent and Kent, *Neighbours and Neighbourhood*,
pp. 175–8.

[39] N. Rubinstein, 'Politics and Constitution in Florence at the end of the Fifteenth
Century', in E. F. Jacob (ed.), *Italian Renaissance Studies* (London, 1960), p. 161.

[40] Quoted in Kent and Kent, *Neighbours and Neighbourhood*, pp. 176, 179 n. 17.

[41] Quoted ibid., pp. 177–8.

[42] From Temperani's unpublished 'Protestatio de Iustitia' copied, without date, in
the Ricordi of Consiglio Cerchi (1431–62), in Archivio Cerchi, 312, fo. lxx[r]. For Manno's
career and ideas, see N. Rubinstein, *The Government of Florence under the Medici
(1434–1494)* (Oxford, 1966), pp. 112, 141, 159; Kent and Kent, *Neighbours and Neigh-*

at least a belief in a style of politics) discovered and tried in the still comparatively independent sphere of district affairs.

However, a man such as Temperani also looked outwards from the *gonfalone*, not just because of the 'agonistic' nature of personal relationships there, but because his was a complex society of which the district and its community could only form a part. A *gonfalone* could not constitute a 'patronal enclave', as Molho would have it, since a man seeking a favour would almost always have to go beyond his district at some stage, even if he began to manipulate his chain of patrons from within it. The quarter was, for example, often the proper stage on which to pursue certain offices. Antonio Gherardini wrote in July 1406 to Forese Sacchetti, who was seeking election to the new *balìa*, or special council, assuring him that three neighbours from his quarter had promised support.[43] It was to two aristocrats from Santo Spirito, Luca Pitti and Luigi Ridolfi, both of them *accoppiatori* or electoral officials for that quarter, that the young Lorenzo de' Medici had recourse in September 1461, when he wanted Ser Griso Griselli, also from Oltrarno, made notary to the *Signoria*.[44] Men seem to have thought of their quarters as natural reference points. 'You may be sure', wrote Messer Piero Vespucci to Lorenzo on 7 July 1471, 'that I was never more upset in my life as when I discovered that I was not one of the men from my quarter [of Santa Maria Novella] on the magistracy of the Ten.' Vespucci, who had thought his chances were excellent since his family had long been faithful to the Medici and Lorenzo had previously promised, was also pained because 'I had closely looked at my quarter, and it seemed to me on every count I ought to have been included'.[45] Two years later Giovanni Rucellai summed up the achievements of his long life by saying that he had become 'equal or superior to any citizen in our quarter of Santa Maria Novella, and perhaps very few citizens of the whole city are my superiors'.[46] One wonders if Vespucci's disparaging remarks, on hearing of Rucellai's death in late 1481—'Giovanni Rucellai popped off.

---

bourhood, passim; and D. V. and F. W. Kent, 'Two Vignettes of Florentine Society in the Fifteenth Century', *Rinascimento*, 2nd ser., 23 (1983), 237–60.

[43] G. Brucker, *The Civic World of Renaissance Florence* (Princeton, 1977), pp. 279–80.

[44] Lorenzo de' Medici, *Lettere*, I: *(1460–1474)*, ed. R. Fubini (Florence, 1977), pp. 5–6.

[45] Published by B. Buser, *Lorenzo de' Medici als italienischer Staatsman* (Leipzig, 1879), pp. 129–30.

[46] Cited in my *A Florentine Patrician*, p. 85.

May he have God's pardon, because I know he is going to need it'[47]—
did not spring from some rivalry earlier acted out on the ample stage
provided by the quarter of Santa Maria Novella. There, as early as
1448, it had been the widow Alessandra Strozzi's intention one day to
make of her husband's ancestral home 'the most beautiful house in
this quarter',[48] a hope fulfilled almost half a century later by her son
Filippo. There was, however, solidarity as well as competitiveness
within quarters. Santo Spirito, in particular, seems to have had a
special sense of *esprit de corps*. According to Donato Velluti, whose
chronicle teems with allusions to kinsmen and friends from the
Oltrarno, the men of this area south of the river threatened in 1343
'to cut the bridges and make a city of our own' unless they were given
a fairer share of offices and taxation,[49] and this same *campanilismo*
can be found a century later, in the writings of Benedetto Dei and in
the corporate project to rebuild the quarter's main church.[50] One finds
a more homely example in the will dated May 1478 of Bernardo
Marsili, whose ancient family had long had a tower in Borgo San
Jacopo, when he left money for his daughter's son to buy a house,
stipulating, however, that it had to be in the quarter of Santo Spirito.[51]

When trying to win tax relief within one's *gonfalone*, a quintessentially local issue, it was customary to use outsiders, as well as
neighbours, to exert influence on the officials making the decision. No
unpublished source makes this clearer than the mid-fifteenth-century
correspondence of the merchant Bartolomeo Cederni, whose circle of
intimate correspondents does not, as has been argued recently, constitute part of one of those 'patronal enclaves' into which it has been
said Florence was divided.[52] Cederni lived all of his life in the district
of Bue (the Ox), in Santa Croce, opposite the Bargello in Via Vigna

---

[47] See my 'Giovanni Rucellai: An Epitaph', *Journal of the Warburg and Courtauld Institutes*, 46 (1983), 207.

[48] C. Guasti (ed.), *Lettere di una Gentildonna Fiorentina del secolo XV* (Florence, 1877), p. 39.

[49] *Cronica domestica*, p. 165.

[50] See my *Household and Lineage*, pp. 185–7. In Apr. 1436, according to Francesco Giovanni (himself from Santo Spirito), 'gli uomini del quartiere ... e i frati ... ragunatisi più volte insieme sopra l'ordinare che si principiasse a dare opera' to the project (E. Luporini, *Brunelleschi: forma e ragione* (Milan, 1964), p. 233).

[51] Notarile Antecosimiano, B 726 (Ser Antonio Bartolomei, 1455–95), fo. 245[r].

[52] Molho, 'Cosimo de' Medici', esp. pp. 24–5. In his brief analysis of the Cederni correspondence, Molho mistakenly places Bartolomeo in the district of Drago, Santo Spirito, and so fails to understand Cederni's relations with his patrons, clients and friends; see n. 53 below.

Vecchia. Precisely there, indeed, an enemy once assaulted him with a knife, shouting 'traitor, you want to rob me; you will not escape from my hands',[53] but otherwise Bartolomeo had few enemies, rather many friends. He was, a contemporary wrote, 'a young man of perfect understanding',[54] and the hundreds of letters to him—only one of his answers survives—confirm this judgement. Several of his intimates were, it is true, associated with Bartolomeo's own *gonfalone* of the Ox. A maternal relation, Giovanni Califfi, who corresponded with Bartolomeo for many years, was inscribed and taxed there but in fact lived for decades in the country (because of his poverty, 'for love of the commune', as he himself ironically wrote in 1446),[55] whence he constantly appealed to Cederni for help in getting his tax burden lowered. Bartolomeo's brother-in-law Domenico Simoni moved from his own *gonfalone* to Cederni's, where he lived near, and for years was aided by, his brother-in-law.[56] If Cederni supported such neighbours, he was helped by another man from Bue, Piero Gianni, whose name appears regularly in the correspondence.[57] On the odd occasion he was out of Florence, Cederni liked to receive news of his neighbourhood. His friend Stefano Metti reported to him in Venice on 6 July 1454, that 'thy neighbour Feo di Feo Belcari is one of the new priors', adding some lines later that 'there's married one of your neighbours, a daughter of Bernardo Gherardi, to the son of Piero di Lionardo Vanelli'.[58]

Yet Metti was not himself from Cederni's own district of the Ox, nor were the majority of Bartolomeo's intimates and correspondents; not even his 'neighbour' Bernardo Gherardi was from there, though the two men lived near one another. His main patrons and employers, the Boni family of bankers, lived quite across town; his dearest friends, the Pandolfini, were resident in the quarter of San Giovanni in the

---

[53] Conventi Soppressi, 78, 314, fo. 228ʳ (no date given). In 1480 Bartolomeo reported, correctly, that since the time of the first *catasto* he had lived in the Vigna Vecchia in Bue, Santa Croce: Catasto, 1003, i, fos. 137ʳ–8ʳ.

[54] Cited in A. Perosa (ed.), *Giovanni Rucellai ed il suo zibaldone*, I: *Il zibaldone quaresimale* (London, 1960), pp. 189–90.

[55] Catasto, 660, fo. 63ʳ. Letters from, or mentioning, Califfi are too numerous to cite here.

[56] Inscribed in Chiavi, San Giovanni, in 1427 (ibid. 80, i, fos. 156ᵛ–7ᵛ), Simoni was in Bue by 1446 (ibid. 660, fos. 294ʳ–5ʳ).

[57] In 1446, Gianni was inscribed in Bue and rented a house in Via delle Pinzochere (ibid. 661, fo. 639ʳ⁻ᵛ).

[58] Conventi Soppressi, 78, 314, fo. 588ʳ. Metti lived in the district of Chiavi, San Giovanni: Catasto, 80, i, fos. 133ᵛ–4ᵛ.

gonfalone of Chiavi.[59] The bond between Bartolomeo Cederni and these aristocratic Pandolfini was as firm and as long-lived as it could be. In his will of January 1439 Bartolomeo's father Cederno had named Agnolo Pandolfini and his sons Carlo and Giannozzo executors, giving them other discretionary powers as well,[60] and for the rest of his life the Pandolfini promoted Bartolomeo's modest public career, protected his financial position and welcomed him into their house as an intimate, indeed as godfather to several of their children. In return, Bartolomeo Cederni performed almost every imaginable service for the Pandolfini, nursing Giannozzo when he was ill, ordering books from their mutual friend, the famous Vespasiano da Bisticci, hiring a cook for Pierfilippo and giving instructions to peasants about Pandolfini lambs at Greve.

How Bartolomeo's powerful friends from outside brought influence to bear upon the men of his district is beautifully illustrated by the events of November 1447, when Cederni found himself away in Pisa, nursing Giannozzo Pandolfini, at a time when a *sgravo*, a tax reduction, was under way at home. Dozens of letters arrived in Pisa from his friends, urging him to return to Florence because that was the best, the personal, way to procure a tax deduction. Meanwhile, as the name of each new *sgravatore* for Bue was announced, his friends showered the newly elected officials with personal requests that they help Cederni.[61] However, Bartolomeo's employer, Bono Boni, knew that yet another and more complicated stratagem was available, and probably necessary. As Boni wrote on 23 November:

> thy [latest] *sgravatore* appointed is Jacopo di Niccolò di Giorgio Betti Berlinghieri and, as he was drawn for office, I spoke to him of thy need. I myself am also *sgravatore* in my *gonfalone*, and I said to thy *sgravatore* that if he wanted anybody's tax reduced in my *gonfalone* he should ask for it, but that he should graciously let me fix thy imposition in his district—and he promised me.[62]

The powerful Tommaso Soderini, also a *sgravatore* but for a district across the river in Oltrarno, also promised help for his comparatively

---

[59] See, for example, several Pandolfini reports for 1458 in ibid. 828, fos. 32ʳ–3ᵛ, 34ʳ–7ᵛ, 75ʳ; 829, fos. 326ʳ–8ᵛ. Part of Pierfilippo Pandolfini's correspondence with Cederni was published by C. Carnesecchi, 'Pierfilippo Pandolfini Vicario di Firenzuola', *Archivio storico italiano*, ser. 5, 11 (1893), 112–21.

[60] Notarile Antecosimiano, L 191 (Ser Lodovico di Antonio del Rosso, 1428–9), fos. 17ᵛ–21ᵛ. For their exercising this role, see ibid., L 191 (1436–50), fos. 128ʳ–ᵛ, 137ʳ.

[61] This series of letters is in Conventi Soppressi, 78, 314, fos. 309ʳff.

[62] Ibid., fo. 343ʳ.

obscure friend from Santa Croce.[63] Of course Bartolomeo Cederni so much needed the support of such friends from outside his *gonfalone* because he did not belong to an old and big lineage with traditional influence in its affairs. Yet such large families also had recourse, on all sorts of occasions, to friends and relatives outside their ancestral districts, increasingly, of course, as the fifteenth century went on, to the Medici.[64] The neighbourhood community of the *gonfalone* could not be sufficient unto itself, it was not a 'patronal enclave'. Beyond it was the quarter, and then the city at large.

Even so, Cederni belonged to a 'neighbourhood' in yet another, less precise but still significant, sense. Save for the Boni, most of his friends, including not only the Pandolfini but also Vespasiano da Bisticci, Salvestro del Cicha, and Stefano Metti, lived or worked close to him, coming as they did from a small area of Florence east of the church of the Badia. This area did not belong to one administrative subdistrict (indeed two quarters, San Giovanni and Santa Croce, met there), yet obviously in a social and topographical sense it was a 'neighbourhood' centred perhaps around the Badia, the Bargello, and Vespasiano's bookshop.[65] There were, as well, other such informal 'neighbourhoods' in Quattrocento Florence, rallying points situated at some key position in the city's tangled geography. The loggias and enclaves of great lineages such as the Peruzzi,[66] or the street corners known as *canti*, provided such foci. The Canto alla Macina, for example, in the parish of San Lorenzo, was in 1478 the headquarters of some thirty plebeian *bravi*, who actively helped persecute Lorenzo de' Medici's enemies in the aftermath of the Pazzi conspiracy.[67]

[63] Molho, 'Cosimo de' Medici', pp. 24–5. Molho says that 'To the best of my knowledge, Soderini occupied no public office at the time' (p. 25), but Conventi Soppressi, 78, 314, fo. 309ʳ, reveals that he was a *sgravatore* for his home district of Drago, Santo Spirito.

[64] For some examples, see Kent and Kent, *Neighbours and Neighbourhood*, pp. 50, 63–4, 93–5.

[65] The bookshop was in Via del Proconsolo, opposite the Badia; see G. M. Cagni, *Vespasiano da Bisticci e il suo epistolario* (Rome, 1969), p. 47. There are numerous references to the Pandolfini, and to Cederni and their circle, in A. D. de la Mare, 'Vespasiano da Bisticci, Historian and Bookseller', unpublished PhD thesis (2 vols., University of London, 1965). See, for example, ii. 317 n. 80; 328 n. 125; 349–50 n. 188; 364 n. 229; 371 n. 253. Del Cicha, a frequent and intimate correspondent of Bartolomeo's, came from this general area and was resident in the district of Lion Nero, Santa Croce: Catasto, 72, fos. 236ᵛ–8ʳ.

[66] D. V. and F. W. Kent, 'A Self Disciplining Pact made by the Peruzzi Family of Florence (June 1433)', *Renaissance Quarterly*, 34 (1981), 337–55.

[67] On this group, and the *canti* in general, see Kent and Kent, 'Two Vignettes', pp. 252–60.

There were still other neighbourhoods acknowledged by the Florentines themselves, even without our invoking the six 'ecological clusters' ingeniously proposed by Cohn.[68] A baker served what he called 'la vicinanza', a patrician shunned a small area within the district of the Red Lion because Jews, and woolbeaters made it 'a wretched neighbourhood'.[69] More formally, the *gonfalone* of the Green Dragon in Santo Spirito was divided into administrative 'thirds' or *terzieri*;[70] the aristocratic confraternity of the Buonuomini di San Martino distributed charity throughout the city in 1494 according to carefully defined 'sixths' or *sesti*.[71] As for the parish itself, the whole subject awaits systematic investigation, in the notarial acts of parochial meetings, a fair number of which survive in the archives, and in other, rarer, records such as parish accounts. (I should add, however, that Robert Gaston's chapter most thoughtfully points us in the right direction.[72]) There is the same need for further research into Cohn's suggestion—important as we seek to understand the complex and possibly changing meanings of 'neighbourhood'—that, during the fifteenth century, Florence 'developed a much more clearly defined class geography', the poor having been pushed out from the inner city, not least by patrician building programmes, to ghettos on the periphery.[73] The beggarish crowd (*poveraglia*) indeed lived 'near the walls [*alle pendici*] of the city',[74] but I do not think Cohn has yet satisfied us (even if one accepts his definition of working class[75]) that this had not always been the case for a fair proportion of the *popolo minuto*. As for the social effects of monumental buildings, that subject requires more detailed investigation.

To conclude, then, 'neighbourhood' seems to have been an immensely important category of Florentine experience and feeling,

---

[68] Cohn, *Laboring Classes*, pp. 28–32. Intriguingly, Cohn's six clusters bear a partial resemblance to the sixths administered by the charitable Buonuomini di San Martino (see n. 71 below).

[69] Kent and Kent, *Neighbours and Neighbourhood*, pp. 3, 11 n. 23.

[70] Weissman, *Ritual Brotherhood*, pp. 69–70.

[71] P. Bargellini, *I Buonuomini di San Martino* (Florence, 1972), doc. 28. Count Neri Capponi tells me the practice continues to this day.

[72] See Chapter 7. Accounts for San Miniato tra le Torre, kept by the parish priest from 1446 onwards, can be found in Compagnie Religiose Soppresse, 1439, i. Ronald Weissman generously provided this reference.

[73] *Laboring Classes*, p. 124. Research into this subject by Erin Wilson of Monash University does not support Cohn's suggestion.

[74] A. Fabroni, *Laurentii Medicis magnifici vita* (2 vols., Pisa, 1784), ii. 225.

[75] Cf. Richard Goldthwaite's review of Cohn in *Renaissance Quarterly*, 35 (1982), 472–3.

similar to (and often inextricable from) kinship, friendship, and patronage. Dale Kent's and mine, and Ronald Weissman's, are the only detailed studies, so far, of this phenomenon: but, interestingly, from Genoese notarial documents, Diana Owen Hughes and Jacques Heers have come recently to similar conclusions about neighbourhood's vital role in late-medieval people's ordering of their social world. Moreover, Ian Robertson, in studying the society of Cesena in the Quattrocento, has found that neighbourhoods there retained vital functions, and has suggested the survival of 'grass-roots "democracy"', at the level of the administrative subdivisions of the city and its district'.[76] In Hughes's analysis, *vicinanza* appears as one of those 'more amorphous (but nevertheless important) social phenomena whose definition has thus far eluded us'.[77] Heers is more positive: neighbourhood ties are one of the 'several essential moving forces behind social life and rivalries',[78] possibly a category of social organization and experience so important that, allied to kinship, it may even have cut across horizontal class barriers, and so divided 'many medieval and Renaissance cities, their societies and even their landscapes into vertical slices'.[79] Heers exaggerates, I suspect, for class there was in fifteenth-century Florence, though in what sense is still precisely to be defined. When that definition is satisfactorily formulated, it will take account of, perhaps incorporate rather than compete with, the ties of *vicinanza* so important to Florentines of the Renaissance.

I end by adapting a sentence by E. P. Thompson: perhaps for Quattrocento Florence—perhaps, too, if Ronald Weissman is right, for Mediterranean society in general—we should see neighbourhood like class itself, not 'as a "structure", nor even as a "category", but as something which in fact happens (and can be shown to have happened)

---

[76] The quotation is from Ian Robertson's chapter, 'Cesena: Governo e società dal Sacco dei Bretoni al dominio di Cesare Borgia', in A. Vasina (ed.), *Storia di Cesena, città e territorio*, III: *Il medioevo*, II: *Cesena dalla signoria malatestiana al ritorno papale (secoli XIV–XVI)* (Rimini, 1984–5). On this theme, see his chapter in this volume.

[77] 'Towards Historical Ethnography: Notarial Records and Family History in the Middle Ages', *Historical Methods Newsletter*, 7 (1974), 68.

[78] *Parties and Political Life in the Medieval West* (Amsterdam, New York and Oxford, 1977), p. 89.

[79] See my 'A la recherche du clan perdu: Jacques Heers and "Family Clans" in the Middle Ages', *Journal of Family History*, 2 (1977), 81 (a review article of Heers's *Le Clan familial au moyen âge* (Paris, 1974)).

in human relationships'.[80] 'I say that it is a greater rule to love one's neighbour than to love God', the Friulian miller Domenico Scandella told his inquisitor in the next century, '. . . and I believe that he who does no harm to his neighbor does not commit sin . . .'[81]

---

[80] E. P. Thompson, *The Making of the English Working Class* (1968; Harmondsworth, 1977), p. 9.

[81] Quoted by C. Ginzburg, *The Cheese and the Worms: The Cosmos of a Sixteenth-century Miller*, tr. J. and A. Tedeschi (Baltimore and London, 1980), pp. 37–9.

6

Neighbourhood Government in Malatesta Cesena

IAN ROBERTSON

THE work summarized in the preceding chapter convincingly proposes that, despite trends in the fourteenth and fifteenth centuries towards a more centralized and bureaucratic 'state', the Florentine *gonfalone*, or district, at least until the 1460s, continued to play an essential political and fiscal role in government, and to generate ties of interest and loyalty which powerfully conditioned the behaviour of Florentines. Indeed, it suggests that the *gonfalone*, with its qualified offer of political power and responsibility to a somewhat broader social spectrum in a situation in which the social base of central government was contracting, survived as a sort of living memorial to an 'ancient popular system' (to quote Manno Temperani), capable, when the ruling clique showed signs of losing its capacity to guarantee 'good government', of providing an inspiration for a challenge to the central regime. All this is significant for our understanding of the complexities of the society and polity of republican Florence.

However, a focus on neighbourhood government may help deepen our understanding of other societies and polities. There is the work of Diana Owen Hughes and Jacques Heers on Genoese neighbourhood organization; and my own on Malatesta Cesena suggests the fruitfulness of such a focus in the study of signorial regimes, sometimes assumed to have gone rather further than republican Florence towards the perfection of the centralized bureaucratic 'state'.[1]

This view of the late-medieval Italian *Signoria* has, of course, long been modified by studies demonstrating the conservatism and uninventiveness of signorial regimes, their concentration on the exercise of

---

[1] I. Robertson, 'Cesena: Governo e società dal Sacco dei Bretoni al dominio di Cesare Borgia', in A. Vasina (ed.), *Storia di Cesena*, II: *Il medioevo, 2 (Secoli XIV–XV)* (Rimini, 1985), pp. 5–92.

power rather than on institutional change.[2] In most cases, the structures and processes of communal government appear to have survived the transition to despotic rule. Communal institutions, although now located beneath a superstructure of signorially appointed officialdom and circumscribed in their powers and responsibilities, seem none the less generally to have continued to enjoy at least some substance of power in many areas of government, and not only in those that were more trivial and peripheral. Moreover, the distinctness of the coexisting *Signoria* and commune was not only institutional, but also social. Signorial patronage may have transformed the communal ruling élite, importing new 'creatures' and maintaining all, new and old, in dependence on the new fount of favour. However, the survival of communal structures, which themselves had always operated to engender a closed, self-perpetuating oligarchy, seems to have guaranteed the survival amongst the communal élite of a sense of corporate identity independent of the *Signoria*, a sense which new signorial 'creatures' came to share with the representatives of older communal families. The commune survived, then, as a socio-political entity which was always at least potentially distinct from the *Signoria*, and which stood ready to make itself actually distinct should the *Signoria*, for one reason or another, lose the capacity to satisfy its subjects.

Certainly, all this is true of the Romagnol centre of Cesena during the period of its domination by a Malatesta *Signoria* between 1378 and 1465. But the adoption of a focus on neighbourhood leads to the discovery of evidence to suggest that there also survived on the level of district government in Cesena under Malatesta rule something of the 'ancient populism' commemorated in Florence's *gonfaloni*. This adds another dimension to our picture of the complex relationship between *Signoria* and society, one which may prove to be discernible in other signorial regimes.

Cesena's surviving communal statutes detail a system of neighbourhood government which offers many parallels with the Florentine system. These details appear, in fact, in statutory collections which post-date the Malatesta *Signoria*. The earliest surviving version of the statutes is in a manuscript (now in Cesena's Biblioteca Malatestiana)

---

[2] For example (in relation to the *Signorie* of the Romagna), J. Larner, *The Lords of Romagna: Romagnol Society and the Origins of the Signorie* (London, 1965); P. J. Jones, *The Malatesta of Rimini and the Papal State: A Political History* (London, 1974); I. Robertson, 'The *Signoria* of Girolamo Riario in Imola', *Historical Studies* (Melbourne), 15 (1971), 88–117.

belonging to the period of restored direct ecclesiastical rule after 1465: it appears to date from between the end of February 1467 and the mid-1470s.[3] The appearance of the regulations regarding neighbourhood government in post-Malatesta collections raises, of course, the question (to which we shall return) of the extent to which they continued to be observed after 1465. But, although the version of the statutes in the Malatestiana manuscript incorporates the constitutional modifications introduced in 1466 and 1467, the work of correction and adaptation of the statutes to the new order has not been very thoroughly carried out. There remain in the text many indications that the greater part of the statutes date from the period of the Malatesta *Signoria*, or even earlier.[4] That the manuscript presents what is in most respects the constitution of Malatesta Cesena is confirmed by the evidence of the volumes of *bandi* and of *riformanze* of the communal councils which survive from the period of Malatesta rule.[5]

The city of Cesena in the later fourteenth and the fifteenth century was divided into ten *contrade* or districts: Chiesa Nova, Croce di Marmo, Porta Ravegnana, San Giovanni, San Severo, San Zenone, Strada dentro, Strada fuori, Talamello, and Trova.[6] Although on

---

[3] Biblioteca Malatestiana, Cesena (henceforth BMC), Cod. S.IV.6. The arguments for the dating of the manuscript are set out in Robertson, 'Cesena'. The manuscript was restored in 1980, and unfortunately rebound with its folios incorrectly ordered, although this may have been corrected by now. References are to the original pagination of the manuscript. A printed edition of the statutes appeared in June 1494 (Incip. [fo. 1ʳ]: *Incipiunt laudabilia statuta floride: & alme ciuitatis Cesene* [fo. 83ᵛ]: Impressus Venetiis per Ioannem & Gregorium de gregoriis impressores solertissimos. Anno incarnationis dominicae. M.cccc.xciiii. die. xvii. Iunii), but it lacks the fourth book in which the statutes regarding neighbourhood government appeared. The fourth book is included, however, in the later printed edition of 1589: *Statuta ciuitatis Caesenae, cvm additionibvs ac reformationibvs, pro tempore factis . . .* (Caesenae: apud Bartholomaevm Raverivm, 1589[–90]).

[4] Examples are given in Robertson, 'Cesena'.

[5] Volumes of *bandi* (decrees) survive in the Archivio di Stato, Sezione di Cesena: Archivio Storico Comunale di Cesena, Sezione Antica (henceforth ASC) for the years 1431–41, 1450–2, 1453–73; volumes of *riformanze* survive for the periods Feb. 1393 to Feb. 1394, 28 Dec. 1433 to 30 Aug. 1435, Nov. 1460 to 9 Oct. 1462. Transcripts and summaries from two volumes of *riformanze* now missing, covering the periods 10 Jan. 1452 to 29 Apr. 1453 (plus 6 Sept. 1454) and 1 Jan. 1456 to 28 July 1456, are to be found in the Cassette Carlo Grigioni in the Biblioteca Comunale, Forlì.

[6] Lists of the *contrade* may be found in ASC vol. 43, fos. 23ᵛ, 26ʳ, 52ʳ. The list in *Statuta* IV.27 (BMC S.IV.6, fo. cxxxvʳ; 1589 edn, pp. 230–1) contains only eight *contrade*, omitting Strada dentro (mentioned, however, in a document of 2 Dec. 1368 (ASC, b.11, n. II)), and San Giovanni, and describing Trova as Trova dentro. For a map of the *contrade* drawn by G. Conti, see G. Sirotti, *Città di Cesena: XVIII secoli di storia dall'arrivo del Cristianesimo a Cesena alla Cattedrale odierna* (Cesena, 1974), opp. p. 104.

occasion the city was considered for administrative or fiscal purposes in terms of other divisions, into four quarters or five *porte*,[7] the *contrada* appears to have been the fundamental division and the only one generating its own administrative structure.

The communal statutes provided that each year on 1 January the men of each city *contrada* should elect a *sindicus* (syndic), one for each *contrada*. For the purpose of making this election, all parishioners (*omnes parochiani*) were to meet in their *capelle* (a word which here seems to be used in a territorial rather than ecclesiastical sense, as a synonym for *contrada*,[8] but whose linkage with *parochiani* seems to suggest the parish church as a district focus). Election was to be achieved by a simple majority, and the elected syndic was to hold office for one year without possibility of extension. The syndic was to be paid a salary determined by the men of the *contrada*, up to the maximum of five Bolognese lire. He was required to belong to the *contrada* over which he was elected, and no one could plead immunity from serving unless exempted by statute or some special privilege, or as a result of some other just cause or excuse. The duties of the syndic were to impose and levy the *collectas* (*collette* or *colte*: direct taxes, usually nominated as destined for a particular purpose) raised in his *contrada*, to manage other business of the *contrada* and to be its legal representative or attorney in transactions and lawsuits. At the end of his term of office, he was to submit himself to an audit by representatives of the men of his *contrada*.[9]

The statutes also provided for the monthly election in each city *contrada* of two *maiores*, although allowance is made for the fact that some *contrade* may by custom have only one. Commencing with two *maiores* from opposite extremities of the *contrada*, the offices were to circulate progressively from door to door (*hostiatim*), no one being omitted: it would appear that an outgoing *maior* nominated his successor, and he could be fined 20 Bolognese soldi if he fraudulently omitted to nominate the one next in turn. Statutory exemption from the office, however, was enjoyed by judges, doctors, schoolmasters,

---

[7] For example, the provisions regarding the *estimo* in *Statuta* IV.35 (BMC S.IV.6, fos. cxxxviij^r–cxxxviiij^r; 1589 edn, pp. 236–7) speak in terms of quarters; and in October 1393, a survey of possessions was to be carried out by representatives of the five *porte* (Porta Figarola, Porta del Ponte (del Fiume), Porta dei Santi, Porta Cervese, and Porta della Trova) (ASC vol. 42, fos. 14^v–15^r).

[8] Cf. P. Sella (ed.), *Glossario latino emiliano* (Città del Vaticano, 1937) (Studi e Testi, 74), p. 70.

[9] *Statuta* IV.10 (BMC S.IV.6, fos. cxxviiij^v–cxxx^r; 1589 edn, p. 221).

and—interestingly—widows and female orphans or wards with a tax
assessment (*estimo*) below 25 lire.[10] The *maiores* themselves were
exempted from personal dues during their period of office. Within two
days of beginning their term, the *maiores* were to take an oath of office
in the hands of the notary of the communal attorneys, and to give
surety of legal exercise of their office to the extent of 25 Bolognese lire.
The duties of the *maiores* were to report to the *podestà* or his officials
crimes or deaths which occurred in their *contrade*, and to exact the
collectas levied by the *contrada* itself, those for the payment of the
plazarii and for the financing of the watch, and any other dues specific
to the *contrada*: they were not, however, given responsibility for
exacting taxes levied generally in the commune. Finally, it was provided
that the *maiores* could be subjected to an annual audit by the *Vicarius*
or his officials on the petition and in the presence of the men of the
contrada, even on the petition of two or three *hominum bone
conditionis et fame* from the *contrada*.[11]

Nor was such neighbourhood government limited to the city
contrade. The *contado* was divided into a number of extra-mural
contrade, *castra* and *ville*.[12] The men of these districts were also
required to elect various officials from amongst themselves. Districts
with five to ten *fumantes* (fiscal units)[13] were each to elect one custodian
or guardian, one *maior*, one assessor, and one bailiff (*saltuarius*);
districts with more than ten *fumantes* were each to elect two *maiores*
and guardians, two assessors and two bailiffs; districts with four or
fewer *fumantes* were to be united with a neighbouring district and to

---

[10] The last exemptions imply the possibility of widows and female orphans or wards
with higher *estimo* ratings serving as *maiores*. A priori, this seems unlikely. It may be
that the exemption clause is a fairly standard one imported from statutes regarding
personal services: as indicated, the degree of co-ordination and integration within the
text of the statutes is rather variable. Certainly, there are no surviving records of women
serving as *maiores*, apart possibly from a confused and confusing indication in the 1393
list of *maiores villarum* referred to later (cf. n. 41 below). The last of the listed names,
which are in the dative case, is difficult to read, but it appears to be *domine drude*.
However, a point preceding the name may indicate a gap, which in turn may indicate
that *domine drude* is in the genitive case and that the reference is most probably to a
son of hers whose name is unknown to the chancellor (as was the name of the father
of Zucius in the same list).

[11] BMC S.IV.6, fos. cxxxi^v–cxxxii^r; cxxxii^v–cxxxiii^r; cc^r (*Statuta* 1589 edn, pp. 224–
5, 226–7, 353).

[12] Lists of *contado* districts may be found in: BMC S.IV.6, fo. cxxxv^r (*Statuta* IV.27.
1589 edn, pp. 230–1); A. Theiner, *Codex diplomaticus dominii temporalis S. Sedis*
(Rome, 1862) ii. 498–9; ASC vol. 42, fos. 1^v–2^r, 58^r.

[13] Cf. Larner, *The Lords of Romagna*, pp. 209–19.

share its officials. The offices of custodian or guardian and assessor were to circulate 'from door to door' on a three-monthly basis, and those elected were to take their oaths of office eight days before the beginning of their term in the hands of the notary of their office. The offices could not be refused. The *maiores* of the *contado* had duties similar to those of the city *maiores*, and were similarly subject to audit. The other officials were primarily responsible for the protection of property, crops, and livestock in their districts, and for the report and assessment of *damna data*.[14]

Finally, the statutes provided that each year, at least ten days before the end of December, the syndics and *maiores* of both city and *contado* should elect for the following year thirteen town criers or beadles known as *plazarii* (*piazzari*). Seven were to be elected from the city *contrade*, and six from the districts of the *contado*. The elected, who could be compelled to serve by the *podestà* and his officials, were to swear their oath of office in the hands of the Chancellor of the Commune, and to give surety of 25 Bolognese lire to guarantee that they would exercise their office according to the statutes. The *plazarii* were to be paid a salary of 15 Bolognese lire by the place which elected them, and had the right also to charge fees for specific tasks according to a statutory scale. Nine of the *plazarii* were attached to the *podestà*, and one each to the Vicar and Judge of Appeals, the *Officialis dampnorum datorum*, the *Officialis custodie*, and the *Anziani*. As under-officers of justice (who wore red hoods emblazoned with the arms of the commune as they went about their duties) the *plazarii* had amongst their principal tasks the serving of summonses and distraint.[15]

Such were the provisions of the statutes, and it is a reasonable presumption that they antedate the Malatesta *Signoria*. How far did these provisions continue to be observed under Malatesta rule? The relevant evidence is regrettably fragmentary; no separate records of neighbourhood administration appear to have survived, nor do the communal financial and fiscal records from the Malatesta period.[16] It is interesting, however, to note listed in a chancery inventory of March 1468 a series of *estimo* registers distinguished by city *contrada* or

---

[14] BMC S.IV.6, fos. cxxxii[r], cxxxii[v]–cxxxiii[r] (*Statuta* IV.18, 21) (1589 edn, pp. 224–5, 266–7); cf. also fos. ciiij[r]–cvij[r] (*Statuta* III.4) (in the 1494 edition, cited n. 3 above, fos. 67[v]–69[v]; 1589 edn, pp. 173–7). The provisions in Book III do not altogether correspond with those in Book IV.

[15] BMC S.IV.6 fos. cxxxiiii[v]–cxxxvi[v] (*Statuta* IV.27–9) (1589 edn, pp. 230–3).

[16] With three minor exceptions: ASC b. 1396, 1697, 1728A.

contado locality.[17] Family archives from the Malatesta period also appear to be non-existent, and the valiant efforts of later antiquarian genealogists,[18] besides being inadequately documented, are so riddled with internal contradictions or inconsistencies as to be for the most part worse than useless. It is true that Cesena possesses an extensive notarial archive embracing material from at least as early as 1386. But the confusion created there by an over-enthusiastic eighteenth-century archivist makes the task of analysing the records long and arduous.[19] Some ecclesiastical records also appear to survive from the period, but indications are that they are sparse.[20] Most of what I have uncovered so far comes from references in the deliberations of the communal councils and in decrees promulgated by various governmental authorities.[21] What emerges, however, is sufficient to suggest that the provisions of the statutes concerning neighbourhood administration did not remain altogether a dead letter in the Malatesta period, and that the question of their observance deserves further investigation, particularly in the notarial archive.

Unfortunately, no records of *contrada* meetings or of actual elections of *sindici* or *maiores* have yet been uncovered. None the less there are many indications that the *sindici* and *maiores* of both city and *contado* continued to be vital links in the chain of government. They continue, firstly, to play a significant role in the apportionment and exaction of taxation. In March 1393, for instance, we find the Chancellor of the Commune ordering the *maiores* of certain *ville* of the *contado* to collect money to pay three guardians of the campanile of the *pieve* of San Vittore.[22] But more consistent evidence of this type comes from

---

[17] C. Riva, 'L'archivio del Comune di Cesena nel periodo malatestiano (1378–1465)', *Romagna arte e storia*, 1, 2 (maggio–agosto 1981), 98, 104–6.

[18] For example, Biblioteca Comunale, Cesena, MS 164.13: S. Parthi, *Memorie notabili dell'antichità, e casi seguiti nella città di Cesena con la nobiltà e fasti onorati de' suoi cittadini* ... (1572); MS 164.34: Don Carlo Antonio Andreini, *Notizie delle famiglie illustri di Cesena* (5 vols., 1809); MS 164.24: G. B. Vendemini-Rossi, *Famiglie illustri di Cesena* (1732); MS 164.36: D. De Vincentiis, *Bibliotheca Caesenatensis illustrium scriptorum, sive elogia virorum illorum ... (illustrium Caesenatensium elogia)*.

[19] He appears to have been unable to read at least the earlier documents adequately, and in most cases misidentified the notary and misdated the act. He then lovingly had the acts bound into handsome volumes in such a way as to make sections of the acts disappear into the binding!

[20] Cf. G. Mazzatinti, *Gli archivi della storia d'Italia*, ii (Rocca San Casciano, 1899), 28–30, 38–9. I have not investigated the availability of parish records from the period.

[21] Cf. n. 5 above.

[22] ASC vol. 42, fo. 58[r].

the period of war and attendant fiscal crisis in the 1430s. In January 1434, we find the General Council of seventy-two agreeing that the *colletta* of the *plazarii* should be levied in the *contrade*, and that the syndics or *maiores* of the *contrade* every three months should consign to the communal tax-collector either the moneys collected by them or receipts indicating payment of the *plazarii*. The *plazarii* themselves were to aid the syndics and *maiores* in the exaction of the tax through distraint and other means.[23] In June of the same year, the General Council agreed to the imposition of a *colletta* to provide a subsidy of 4,000 Bolognese lire for Sigismondo Pandolfo Malatesta and Malatesta Novello to help them pay their troops. When striking the rate for the *colletta*, the small executive council of the *Anziani* specifically provided, in order that the *colletta* might be more easily and more speedily levied in the *contado*, that the *maior* or syndic of each *contrada* or *villa* should levy the sum due from his district.[24] The suggestion that taxes could be levied more quickly and effectively by the *maiores* comes again in April 1435, when the General Council decided for that reason that the *maiores* of the city *contrade* should levy a *colletta* to provide funds for the repair of the city walls.[25] In the following month, the *Anziani* decreed the sums that the syndic of each city *contrada* should provide for payment of the guards of the towers of the walls;[26] and in July they decreed that the syndics should levy another *colletta* both for the payment of the guards of the towers of the walls and for the repayment of certain loans, including one from the Jews.[27]

The *maiores* also had a role in organizing corvées for the maintenance of the city's fortifications. In June 1452, for example, the *maiores* of each city *contrada* were required to provide the *podestà* with a written list of the masons of their *contrade*, so that these might be set to work on the city walls.[28] In April 1462, in the desperate situation of the Malatesta war with Pius II, the *Anziani* recognized that the burden of requisitioned labour on the city walls was becoming excessive for the inhabitants, and imposed on everyone from fourteen to seventy years of age a tax of 4 soldi, from which only new citizens and wool-workers were exempt; the *maiores* of each *contrada* were to

---

[23] Ibid., vol. 43, fo. 3^r.
[24] Ibid., fos. 20^r–21^r.
[25] Ibid., fo. 49^{r-v}.
[26] Ibid., fo. 52^r.
[27] Ibid., fo. 53^v.
[28] Ibid., vol. 44 (Grigioni transcription), fo. 59^r.

provide the Chancellor of the Commune with written lists of all the men in their *contrade*.[29]

The syndics and *maiores* continued as well to play a part in matters such as the quartering of troops and provisioning in time of war. In September 1434, for instance, we find the *Anziani* electing two citizens from each city *contrada* who, together with the *maiores*, were to conduct an inquiry into the availability of wheat and corn in the city, for the provisioning of troops of the Malatesta *signori*.[30] In May 1435, in order to maintain vital food supplies in the course of the current war with Forlì, the *Anziani* directed that the *Officialis Custodie* should order each syndic to construct a pounding-mill or bakery (*postrinum*) for his *contrada*, and two citizens were appointed to make, together with the syndics of the *contrade*, an inventory of the wheat available in the city. Three days later the proposal was modified to provide for only five mills or bakeries, each to serve two *contrade*, and it was ordered that to finance their construction each person in the city should pay his syndic one soldo per head, no one being exempt.[31]

One reference to the condemnation of a man in the court of the *podestà* on the denunciation of a *maior* of the *contrada* of San Giovanni, suggests that the *maiores* continued to perform their statutory role in that respect.[32] It also seems that the syndics and *maiores* continued to fulfil their statutory responsibilities in the matter of election of *plazarii*. In three cases in 1393 the role of syndic or *maiores* is specifically documented.[33] Moreover, we have a decree of the *podestà* of 22 December 1454 stipulating that all syndics and *maiores* of the city and *contado* should elect their *plazarii* within five days *iuxta morem et consuetudinem*.[34] And in January 1461, a decree of the *signore* himself, Malatesta Novello, laid down that no one should presume to exercise the office of *plazarius* unless 'elected and matriculated in accordance with the statutes of Cesena'.[35] Would it be wishful thinking to interpret that as reflecting also a signorial commitment to observance of the statutory provisions relating to the syndics and *maiores* themselves?

[29] Ibid., vol. 47, fo. 114^r; cf. vol. 25, fo. 58^r.
[30] Ibid., vol. 43, fo. 26^r.
[31] Ibid., fol. 51^v, 52^r.
[32] Ibid., vol. 2195 (Sentenze criminali, 1431–8), fo. 142^v (162^v) (14 Oct. 1435).
[33] Ibid., vol. 42, fos. 48^{r-v}, 60^v.
[34] Ibid., vol. 25. fo. 10^r.
[35] Ibid., fos. 50^v–51^r.

At times the *contrade* may have displayed a certain spirit of independence. A hint in the *Annales Caesenates* of a *contrada* base to partisan strife[36] finds no substantial reflection in evidence from the Malatesta period. However, at least one instance of confrontation between a *contrada* and the Commune occurs in connection with Cesena's August trade fair in 1462. The *Anziani* were perturbed to find that the men of the *contrada* of San Severo, where the fair was then held each year, were claiming the whole proceeds from the rent of the booths. This was on the basis of certain documents given them by the signorial Vicar General of the 1450s (Antonio de' Griffoli of Terranova), allegedly in accordance with the will of the *signore*. The *Anziani* protested that half of the proceeds were due to the commune. Complaint to Malatesta Novello brought a somewhat gnomic reply affirming his intention that past custom and privilege be upheld. The *Anziani* set up an inquiry to establish the commune's rights. Unfortunately, no record of the resolution of the conflict appears to survive.[37]

From the scattered evidence so far collected it is difficult to obtain a picture of the social composition and functioning of the *contrade*. The absence of fiscal records is crippling, and the surviving other governmental records rarely specify the *contrade* to which council members and officials belong. Only extensive work on the notarial records, which usually do specify *contrada* of origin, could establish the *contrada* associations of the families and clans of the ruling group and others at this period. As for those who held office in the *contrade* and *ville* as syndics or *maiores*, the few names uncovered suggest that these offices gave to men of modest status outside the conciliar and office-holding group of the central communal government the opportunity to enjoy at least some power and responsibility. In 1393, for instance, the syndic of the *contrada* of San Severo was one magister Jacobus quondam Johannis,[38] and another magister Jacobus was syndic of the *contrada* of Strada dentro.[39] In 1435, we find magister Antonius Fosschi *cimator* (cloth-shearer) serving as a *maior* of the *contrada* of San Giovanni.[40] A list of *maiores* of various *ville* in the *contado* in 1393 contains similarly modest-sounding names: Michael

---

[36] L. A. Muratori, *Rerum italicarum scriptores*, xiv (Mediolani, 1729), cols. 1154D–1155D (21 Sept. 1333).

[37] ASC vol. 47, fos. 126[r], 126[v]–126 bis [r], 127[r].

[38] Ibid., vol. 42, fo. 48[r].

[39] Ibid., fo. 60[v].

[40] Ibid., vol. 2195, fo. 142[v] (162[v]).

Mucini, Rossinus Johannini, Zucius quondam . . . (*sic*), Nardus Bartoli, Michael Venture, Ziliolus, Christofanus.[41]

As mentioned earlier, the statutory regulations regarding neighbourhood government survive in post-Malatesta collections of the communal statutes.[42] This raises the question of the extent to which these provisions continued to be implemented after the return to direct papal rule in 1465. To provide a definitive answer to this question would require further work, particularly on the considerable body of fiscal records which survive from after 1465 as well as on notarial records. None the less, it would seem that the role of the syndics and *maiores* of the *contrade* receded in importance under the papal regime. True, the communal statutes and privileges received specific papal confirmations, the Papal Governor and his officials were bound by oath to observe them, and the pre-existing system of communal government continued by and large to operate;[43] but we know that the statutory collections continued to include statutes which had been specifically abrogated,[44] let alone statutes whose observance may have been allowed to lapse. We have record of the regular election after 1465 of a *Notarius maiorum*, but it is not clear that the *maiores* in question were those of the *contrade*.[45] We know that the *plazarii* continued to figure as instruments of government, but it is not clear how they were appointed.[46] Above all, in the contexts where earlier in conciliar debates references to the syndics and *maiores* regularly occurred, such references seem no longer to appear. The same *contrade* continue to be mentioned; but when, for instance, they are to be used as a basis for revision of the *borse* (electoral purses) of the communal offices, organization of the grain supply and an attempt to restore stability in

[41] Ibid., vol. 42, fo. 58ʳ; cf. n. 10 above.

[42] Cf. n. 3 above. Concern at the loss of the fourth book of the statutes from the manuscript which was apparently then in current use in the communal chancery (evidently not BMC, Cod. S.IV.6) was expressed in the General Council in Jan. 1496: ASC vol. 60, fos. 6ʳ, 10ʳ.

[43] Cf. my 'The Return of Cesena to the Direct Dominion of the Church after the Death of Malatesta Novello', *Studi Romagnoli*, 16 (1965), 123–61.

[44] For instance, BMC S.IV.6, fo. cxlʳ (*Statuta* IV.41–2) (1589 edn, p. 240) retains the chapters *de bonis hospitalis Magistri vgolini* abrogated by the General Council in July 1452 (cf. ASC vol. 44 (Grigioni transcription), fo. 64ʳ⁻ᵛ).

[45] Archivio di Stato, Sezione di Rimini, MS formerly in the Biblioteca Gambalunga, Rimini, and formerly numbered D.I.29 (*Matricula notariorum et offitialium Civitatis Cesene* . . . [1466–77]), fos. 47ʳ–49ʳ. There were *maiores* other than those of the *contrade* or *ville*, for instance those of the *arti* (cf. ASC vol. 47, fo. 124ʳ).

[46] Cf. Archivio Segreto Vaticano, Arm. LII, t.28, fo. 13ʳ (1477); ASC vol. 855.11 (1487–91); ASC vol. 60, fo. 26ᵛ (1496).

the strife-torn 1490s, discussion centres solely on the election by the executive council of *contrada* representatives from the conciliar and office-holding group.[47] No mention is made of these representatives' collaboration with syndics or *maiores*: in fact, in March 1496, the executive council proceeds in this context to the election for each *contrada* of two *caporiones* (perhaps a Roman concept imported by the then Governor Girolamo Porcari).[48]

None the less, there does appear to be sufficient evidence to allow the conclusion that at least something of the 'ancient populism' of neighbourhood government survived as a reality in Cesena under the despotic rule of the Malatesta. This casts new light on the nature of the relationship between the *Signoria* and the commune and society which it dominated, and may in particular deepen our understanding of the ease with which that society separated itself from the *Signoria* when it became clear in the 1460s that the Malatesta no longer had the resources or prestige to guarantee their subjects the benefits of *buon governo*. And these Cesenate hints would seem also to justify the search for similar survivals in the cases of other signorial regimes;[49] their discovery could considerably enrich our general understanding of the *Signoria* as a political form in late-medieval Italy.

---

[47] ASC vol. 60, fo. 38^{r-v}; vol. 61, fos. 5^v–8^v, 13^r, 19^v–23^v.

[48] ASC vol. 60, fo. 38^{r-v}.

[49] For instance, it would be interesting to discover how far, in neighbouring Forlì, the statutory provisions concerning the election of syndics continued to be observed under the Ordelaffi *Signoria*: cf. *Statuto di Forlì dell'anno .MCCCLIX. con le modificazioni del .MCCCLXXIII.*, ed. E. Rinaldi (Rome, 1913) (*Corpus Statutorum Italicorum*, sotto la direzione di P. Sella, N.5), pp. 142–4 (Lib.I, Rub. CXXXXVI).

7

Liturgy and Patronage in San Lorenzo, Florence, 1350–1650

ROBERT GASTON

'PATRONS are patrons', the *luogotenente* of the *operai* of San Lorenzo wrote to Grand Duke Ferdinando de' Medici in 1602: 'the Patron is accountable to no one.' The Grand Duke's lieutenant was urging him to intervene with the *operai*, the men entrusted with the church's building and maintenance programme, to ensure a favourable outcome to the election of a new prior of the chapter.[1] In these years of the Grand Duchy the death of a prior was an occasion for the clergy to mount an appeal to the Medici for a better financial deal. Letters would be written detailing the great devotion with which the Grand Duke's ancestors had contributed to the building of the church; how the Medici popes Leo and Clement had granted important privileges to San Lorenzo; how the parish was the largest in the Grand Duke's state, but that the prebends and the daily distributions of cash to the clergy were unworthy of such a glorious church; how inflation was such that a priest with no outside income could scarcely keep body and soul together.[2]

[1] Archivio di Stato, Florence, Miscellanea Medicea (henceforth, Misc. Med.) 348, fo. 246[r]: 'i Patroni son' Patroni ...: il Patrone non ha a rendere conto a nessuno.' (All manuscript references are to the collections in the Florentine State Archives, unless otherwise indicated.) This chapter anticipates one in a book to be written in collaboration with Ronald Weissman, which will study the parish of San Lorenzo, 1350–1650. Research for this paper was carried out while the writer was a Fellow at the Harvard Center for Italian Renaissance Studies, Villa I Tatti, Florence, during 1981–2. I should like to thank the following scholars for their generous advice: Caroline Elam, Richard Goldthwaite, Christiane Günther, John Henderson, Bill and Dale Kent, Andrew Morrogh, June Philipp, and Ronald Weissman. Eve Borsook and Patricia Simons kindly made comments on a draft of this paper and I have gratefully incorporated some of their suggestions.
[2] 'Il Priore e Canonici del Capitolo della Chiesa di San Lorenzo devoti Servitori di Vostra Altezza con debita reverentia espongono a quella, come il detto Priore havendo esposto in Capitolo in presentia come havea conferito con Vostra Altezza qualmente la Chiesa di San Lorenzo per havere le Distributioni quotidiane del Coro, sì tenue e scarse,

The 150 scudi earned annually by canons in 1602[3] was a very substantial income, but in their view it was all relative. Since the eleventh century they had been in bitter rivalry with the canons of the cathedral,[4] and, because no self-respecting diocese could allow a parish church, however distinguished and ancient, to offer better conditions and privileges to its clergy than those available in the cathedral, the San Lorenzo canons were doomed to eternal envy and discontent. Even a cursory acquaintance with the San Lorenzo archives leaves one with the impression that the clergy were obsessed with money. It should be observed, however, that the archives of this period from many collegiate churches in Western Christendom might give the same impression. This business-like façade was largely determined by the economic structure of the newer churches run by regular canons,[5] and by the role of patronage within them. It could, indeed, be suggested that an urban collegiate church like San Lorenzo was a patronal church *par excellence*.[6] San Lorenzo derived income from rents throughout

che un Sacerdote, non havendo altro al mondo, non può di quelle vivere e sostentarsi, e gli fa di bisogno per guadagnare il vitto di servire altrove, buon tempo del'anno, e nei giorni più Festivi: D'onde la Chiesa ne veniva mal servita; et acrescere le Distributioni non si poteva senza l'aiuto di Vostra Altezza per esser la Massa Capitolare povera' (Misc. Med. 348, fo. 221ʳ: Prior and Operai to Francesco de' Medici (?), *c.*1575 (?), copy). Cf. a minute of 10 Jan. 1565: the *capitolo* and *operai* appeal to Duke Cosimo 'per ingrassare alquanto le magre et povere prebende de' Canonicati, et del Priorato'. It was concluded that 'sarebbe d'utile ed d'honore non piccolo della nostra Chiesa con augmento del culto divino fare con tale unione qualche aggiunta alle dette prebende' (Archivio del Capitolo di S. Lorenzo, 2299, Libro de' Partiti segnato G, fo. 19ᵛ; henceforth ACSL).

[3] A canon who attended all the canonical hours would earn that figure 'fra prebenda et distributioni', but the prebendal salary was absorbed by expenses during the canon's first three years in the position. The prior could hope to earn between 260 and 300 scudi per annum (Misc. Med. 348, fo. 233ʳ).

[4] P. N. Cianfogni, *Memorie istoriche della basilica di S. Lorenzo* (Florence, 1804), p. 74, on a dispute over property in 1060. From the fifteenth century onwards the conflicts focused on questions of precedence in processions for major feast-days and funerals. Cf. M. Ronzani, 'L'organizzazione della cura d'anime nella città di Pisa (secoli XII–XIII)', *Istituzioni ecclesiastiche della Toscana medioevale* (Galatina, 1980), pp. 35–85, esp. pp. 52ff.

[5] See K. Edwards, *The English Secular Cathedrals in the Middle Ages* (2nd edn, Manchester and New York, 1967); C. Bynum, 'The Spirituality of Regular Canons in the Twelfth Century: A New Approach', *Medievalia et Humanistica*, NS 4 (1973), 3–24; L. K. Little, *Religious Poverty and the Profit Economy in Medieval Europe* (Ithaca, 1978), pp. 99ff.; Y. Milo, 'From Imperial Hegemony to the Commune: Reform in Pistoia's Cathedral Chapter and its Political Impact', in *Istituzioni ecclesiastiche*, pp. 87–107.

[6] The English late-medieval chantry is a worthy rival: see K. L. Wood-Legh, *Perpetual Chantries in Britain* (Cambridge, 1965); J. T. Rosenthal, *The Purchase of Paradise: Gift Giving and the Aristocracy, 1307–1485* (London and Toronto, 1972), p. 13: 'The

Tuscany and from other provinces, but the salaries of its prior, canons, and chaplains, all of whom were beneficed clergy, were drawn predominantly from patronal endowments. The prebends were usually a rather small proportion of the total annual endowment: the residue was eked out in daily distributions as payment for the performance of liturgical duties, namely, the daily office, masses for Sundays and feasts of the church, and services specified in pious donations. For example, when Andrea di Lotaringo della Stufa endowed a canonry in San Lorenzo in 1460, he provided a prebend of 40 lire and 200 lire for the daily distributions.[7]

The distribution system guaranteed that the wishes of patrons in regard to family chapels and commemorative services were carried out. The constitutions of the church provided for the enforcement of the system: the sacristan and the treasurer of the chapter kept accurate records of who attended services and who performed the commemorative masses or offices required by donors; absentees forfeited their money, and also whatever pepper or wine or meals were distributed at major feasts.[8] Therefore the connection between the founding of chapels or the endowing of commemorative services, and the economy of the church, was a fundamental one. It was rare for a parishioner to give money to the chapter without tying it to liturgical performance in one way or another.

I have outlined these economic considerations by way of introduction to the main theme of this chapter: the development of the liturgy in San Lorenzo from the fourteenth to the seventeenth century, and the role of patronage in that development. To address oneself to such a question entails a significant shift in perception, and to some extent a rethinking of what the liturgy of the church was in the period. Liturgical history has, unfortunately, been one of the most isolated of disciplines, despite the explosion of 'relevance' in liturgical studies

---

endowments of the laity were a major source of income and a form of visibly useful employment for the clergy. As such they constituted one of the financial premises underlying and buttressing the whole system of corporate ecclesiastical institutions.'

[7] ACSL 2192, Entrata et uscita et ricordi de' partiti (1456–1462), fo. 21ʳ.

[8] For the case of a canon supported by charity during illness, see ACSL 2351, Entrata e uscita della Compagnia delle Limosine, fo. 82ᵛ. The Council of Trent (Sess. XXII, cap. III) ruled that bishops were to intervene in cathedral and collegiate churches when regulations for depriving clergy for non-performance were not provided. Cf. Archbishop Antoninus, *Summa* (Pars II, Tit. IX, Cap. XII), on simony and liturgical attendance in cathedral (and collegiate) churches. On the development of the system of distributions for canons, see P. Torquebiau 'Chapitres de chanoines', *Dictionnaire de droit canonique*, iii (Paris, 1942), 556–62.

which accompanied and followed Vatican II. Liturgiologists have concentrated their efforts on the minute and exact charting of the growth of the Roman and other major European and Eastern liturgies. But they have rarely investigated the wider historical significance of liturgy, or how liturgy was understood within Christian communities.[9]

Explicit evidence is not easy to come by. The medievalist Jean Leclercq observes: 'The monks wrote little as to their attitude towards the liturgy: its importance was quite taken for granted and for men who were living constantly under its influence it hardly needed any commentary. Rather, it was the liturgy itself which formed the usual and ordinary commentary on Holy Scripture and the Fathers.'[10] The same is true of the Renaissance period in Florence. While one can find many manuscripts of liturgical texts, there are few which actually comment on the liturgy. To find out about liturgical practice one must turn to the rich evidence of church councils, and diocesan synods, to the constitutions of individual churches, and to the records of meetings within those churches which disclose problems and conflicts arising from the liturgy. Much of this evidence is formal and abstract in its language, and disguises rather than reveals the human actions and reactions which have provoked the legislation. Using this evidence is like studying the impact of a legal code on a community through its crime statistics. The very terminology 'the liturgy' has the implication of unchangeableness, of a monolithic, almost static phenomenon. The emphasis given in the Catholic Church to the continuity of tradition has also encouraged this view. Yet, it is patently the case that at every

---

[9] The following studies are some which have addressed themselves to these questions: I. Herwegen, *Kirche und Seele: Die Seelenhaltung des Mysterienkultes und ihr Wandel im Mittelalter* (Munster, 1926); A. L. Mayer-Pfannholz, *Liturgie und Laientum: Wiederbegegnung von Kirche und Kultur* (Munich, 1927); P. Browe, *Die Verehrung der Eucharistie im Mittelalter* (Munich, 1933); L. A. Veit, *Volksfrommes Brauchtum und Kirche im deutschen Mittelalter* (Freiburg, 1936); J. A. Jungmann, *The Mass of the Roman Rite: Its Origins and Development (Missarum Sollemnia)* (New York, 1951); L. Arbusow, *Liturgie und Geschichtsschreibung im Mittelalter* (Bonn, 1951); G. Le Bras, 'Liturgie et sociologie', in *Mélanges en honneur de Msgr Michael Andrieu* (Strasbourg, 1956), pp. 291–304; J. A. Jungmann, *Pastoral Liturgy* (New York, 1962); H. B. Meyer, *Liturgie und Gesellschaft* (Innsbruck, 1970); A. L. Mayer, 'Die Liturgie in der europäischen Geistesgeschichte', in E. von Severus (ed.), *Gesammelte Aufsätze* (Darmstadt, 1971); J. L. Irwin, 'The Theological and Social Dimensions of Thomas Muentzer's Liturgical Reform', PhD Diss. (Yale University, 1971); H. B. Mayer, 'The Social Significance of the Liturgy', *Concilium*, NS 2, 10 (1974), 34–50. For an example of what can be done, see E. Borsook, 'Cults and Imagery at Sant'Ambrogio in Florence', *Mitteilungen des Kunsthistorischen Institutes in Florenz*, 25 (1981), 147–87.

[10] J. Leclercq, *The Love of Learning and the Desire for God* (New York, 1962), p. 233.

point of its history the liturgy of Rome, for example, developed under considerable pressure from interested groups and individuals. Even liturgical reform can justifiably be regarded as an example of the impact of ecclesiastical patronage.

It is time, then, to take a more flexible approach to the liturgy and to try to link its development more closely with religious, social, and political history. Here I argue that we should stop thinking of the liturgy as something like an authoritarian, institutionalized structure in which lay patrons take a passive, receptive, or merely 'participatory' role:[11] rather, lay 'control' of the liturgy was, in a significant sense, possible in Renaissance Florence.[12] The extraordinarily detailed archives from the medieval and Renaissance periods in Florence allow

---

[11] Jungmann holds the view that in the early Christian period the 'mass-liturgy was definitely cast in the form of a communal exercise', and that modern liturgical reform should aim at 're-forming and reviving the people's participation in the liturgy'. He sees 'a high level of liturgical life at the end of the Middle Ages', but also

> the onset of liturgical hypertrophy ... The people shared in this wealth of liturgical life by the endowments with which they supported the clergy and built and furnished churches. But the liturgy itself was a clerical liturgy. This was so not merely in conventional churches where the intention had always been to provide a liturgy only for the religious ... but it was true also of churches where the people were meant to worship ... where rood screens were built into churches ... the high altar of the church was no longer for the people ... Votive Masses and Masses for the Dead were employed essentially in the interests of individual families and persons ... The ties of the individual are thus loosed in the liturgy ... The most pronounced result of multiplying of Masses was the increase in low Masses, since most of them were for private requests and had no public character. This trend to the private and the subjective ... was also displayed in ... setting aside the arrangement of the ecclesiastical year and confining oneself to Votive Masses ...

Jungmann detects 'vestiges of lay participation' in singing, in the Offertory procession, and in the elevation of the Host at the Consecration. He sees the allegorical interpretation of liturgy, the vernacular sacred plays related to feast-days, and confraternities as 'fragments of faith, peripheral things' (*The Mass*, i. 130ff., *Pastoral Liturgy*, pp. 64ff.). I do not share this narrow and normative view of 'participation'; Jungmann's 'Mass-centred' approach precludes a deeper understanding of the dynamics of Renaissance piety. On the Florentine confraternities, see R. F. E. Weissman, *Ritual Brotherhood in Renaissance Florence* (New York, 1982).

[12] Jungmann's conviction that the liturgy remained 'clerical' because it was primarily performed by the clergy, must be questioned. If the liturgical requests are characterized by expert explicitness, by variety and novelty which exploit liturgical custom to its limits and beyond, and by a volume of activity which bears directly on the economic survival of the individual church, then I think we are justified in speaking of a degree of lay 'control'. In this study, liturgy is defined as any ritualized act of Christian worship performed publicly or privately by an individual cleric or layman, or by groups of clergy or laymen; such acts may take place in any context, including churches, private homes, and *palazzi*, civic buildings, confraternity halls, or public streets and squares.

us to address these problems if we are prepared to ask the relevant questions.

First, some observations on the broader developments in Florence as a background to specific comment on San Lorenzo. Synodal legislation shows that from the early fourteenth-century Florentine bishops tried to impose conformity on liturgical practice within the diocese, to bring it into line with papal stipulations.[13] This is a continuous process throughout the period, and as the Roman curia modified its requirements so in turn did the diocese. Within Florence a range of religious orders with variegated liturgical traditions all adapted in their own ways. The constitutions of churches specified many of their liturgical observances and the disciplinary action for non-observance, and the bishop, or after 1411 the archbishop, ratified all constitutions. But it would be a mistake to believe that a reading of a set of liturgical books from the Roman curia, say in 1350, or 1450, or even 1550, would tell us all we need to know about the liturgy in Florence. Certainly, the Roman Rite was by and large observed. But within the structure there existed other substructures which were particularly Florentine, and even more particularly parochial or familial or individual.

I wish here to make some preliminary remarks about one of several aspects of the liturgy in San Lorenzo which may fruitfully be explored in relation to patronage: the festal calendar.

The diocese for which a given text was produced is, of course, identifiable through the local saints mentioned in its prayers. While the Florentine bishops of the Trecento urged conformity to the Roman curia, they also promoted devotion to specific local saints, especially those associated with their own cathedral, like S. Zanobi and S. Reparata.[14] Bishops could grant indulgences and officially guarantee devotion on a larger scale. They also issued festal calendars with the dual purpose of instructing the clergy to observe specific major feasts, and of warning laymen not to work or trade on those days.[15] In

[13] Bishop Antonio d'Orso Biliotti legislated in his *Constitutiones* of 1310 to standardize minimal liturgical equipment, and also 'quod nullus sacerdos missam celebret, preterquam in nativitate domini, bis in die, nec missam etiam celebret nisi prius matutinas dixerit, tam de beata virgine quam de die. Canonem vero misse sacerdos quilibet corrigat cum missali ecclesie cathedralis' (quoted in R. C. Trexler, *Synodal Law in Florence and Fiesole, 1306–1518* (Vatican City, 1971), p. 266, and commentary, p. 30).

[14] *Constitutiones* of 1310, ibid., p. 268.

[15] Ibid., pp. 328–31; cf. B. Harvey, 'Work and Festa Ferianda in Medieval England', *Journal of Ecclesiastical History*, 23 (1972), 289–309; R. C. Trexler, 'Ritual Behaviour in Renaissance Florence: The Setting', *Medievalia et Humanistica*, NS 4 (1973), 125–44; and his *Public Life in Renaissance Florence* (New York, 1980).

addition, the diocese of Florence had its own stational liturgy which was monitored and co-ordinated by the bishop.[16] The commune also had a civic stational liturgy[17] which was intersected with this at certain points. Each religious order, and parish church too, had its more limited stational liturgy which coincided partly with both the diocesan and the communal ones, but which also included idiosyncratic elements.[18] All of this took place within the larger framework of the Roman festal calendar. It was a complex but workable system, and Rome knew better than to interfere with it. The city, the diocese, and the parish pursued their own interests for the greater glory of God.

Christian liturgical calendars are hierarchical. Some days are from time to time deemed to be more sacred than others. Just as the Roman liturgy reveals over centuries a fugal rise and fall in the importance of certain feasts, so the same process may be seen to occur within various diocesan and parochial calendars in our period. In the case of San Lorenzo this fugal process has much to do with the impact of patronage. Here the term 'patron' will be used in both of its principal meanings: one who offers his influential support to advance certain interests, and one who is a regular customer.[19]

In the fourteenth century San Lorenzo was merely one among many parish churches of venerable antiquity in the city of Florence.[20] The

---

[16] See, for example, 'Rubricae ecclesiae florentinae' (12th cent.), in Biblioteca Riccardiana, Florence, MS 3005; D. Moreni (ed.), *Mores et consuetudines ecclesiae florentinae* (Florence, 1794). Trexler, *Public Life*, p. 2 n. 3, also cites Carte Strozziane, 11, 56, which I have not seen. A later example (*c.*1500) is preserved in *L'ordine delle Processioni che si hanno a fare per la città e distretto di Firenze* (4°, n.d.; Biblioteca Nazionale, Florence (henceforth BNF), Magliabechiani Stampati, B. Cust. 9).

[17] Trexler, 'Ritual Behaviour', *passim*; *Public Life*, pp. 73ff.

[18] We are fortunate in having the *Congregationi di fuori* for San Lorenzo listed for the years 1462–3 and 1472–3; these will be published by Gaston and Weissman. An instance of 'idiosyncracy' would be the frequency with which the San Lorenzo clergy went to Sant'Ambrogio: on the special relationship between the two churches, see Borsook, 'Cults and Imagery', pp. 148ff. The *stationes* of the *clerus Florentinus* are partly recorded for the years *c.*1438–77, in two *manuali*: BNF Fondo Nazionale, 11.11.397 and 398. On the *Clerus*, see Trexler, *Synodal Law*, pp. 78ff.; R. Ristori, 'L'arcivescovo Amerigo Corsini e la sua controversia con il Clero Fiorentino (1427–29)', *Interpres*, 1 (1978), 273–84.

[19] Here I follow the definitions from *OED* as adduced by E. H. Gombrich in 'The Early Medici as Patrons of Art' (1960), in his *Norm and Form* (London, 1966), pp. 35–57.

[20] Cianfogni, *Memorie*, remains our principal source on the earlier history of San Lorenzo. (Prof. W. Bowsky is preparing a study on the period down to *c.*1350, which will clarify its administrative and economic development.) Cianfogni (pp. 88ff.) published papal and episcopal documents (11th–14th cents) which confirm *ius parochialis* and the boundaries of the parish; cf. A. Cocchi, *Le chiese di Firenze dal secolo IV al*

church had nine canonical prebends, the patron saints of which reflected its glorious early Christian origins: S. Ambrogio, who reputedly consecrated the church in AD 393, Beata Giuliana, SS. Vitale and Agricola, SS. Eugenio and Crescenzio, S. Marco Papa, S. Amato Abate, S. Concordia, S. Sisto Papa, and S. Sebastiano.[21] None of these saints was of singular importance in the current Roman festal calendar. In 1393 the day of S. Ambrogio was raised to the level of solemn feast (along with those of the other three great doctors of the church) in the diocese of Florence.[22] Under the main altar in San Lorenzo were kept the sacred bodies of the martyr Concordia, the pope S. Marco, and the holy abbot Amato.[23] But of all the above-mentioned saints, only S. Concordia gained a place among the principal feasts in the church of San Lorenzo at the time.[24] The only other saint to do so was the name-saint of the church, S. Lorenzo, whose feast had always been extraordinarily distinguished in liturgical terms in the Roman Rite, and who had a key role in the stational liturgy there.[25]

In the 1375 constitutions of San Lorenzo the major feasts were listed as: S. Concordia, S. Lorenzo, Nativity of Christ, Resurrection Sunday, Pentecost Sunday, Epiphany, the first Sunday of Lent, Corpus Domini,

secolo XX, i (Florence, 1903), pp. 18ff. P. Ginori Conti, *La basilica di San Lorenzo di Firenze* (Florence, 1940), pp. 1–43; S. K. Cohn, *The Laboring Classes in Renaissance Florence* (New York, 1980), pp. 26ff., for opinions on the demography of the parishes; Weissman, *Ritual Brotherhood*, index, p. 253; D. V. and F. W. Kent, *Neighbours and Neighbourhood in Renaissance Florence: The District of the Red Lion in the Fifteenth Century* (Locust Valley, NY, 1982), for an analysis of the parish of San Pancrazio and its administrative interaction with the district of the Red Lion. On the post-Tridentine parish, see M. Rosa, 'Le parrocchie italiane nell'età moderna e contemporanea', in *Religione e società nel mezzogiorno tra cinque e seicento* (Bari, 1976), pp. 157–81. I have not seen a very recent publication on this theme, *Pieve e parrocchie in Italia nel basso medioevo (sec. XIII–XV): Atti del VI Convegno di Storia della Chiesa in Italia, Firenze 21–25 sett. 1981* (*Italia Sacra*, 35–6) (2 vols., Rome, 1984).

[21] ACSL 2132, constitutions of 1369, fos. 4ʳ–6ᵛ; Cianfogni, *Memorie*, pp. 233–82 gives a listing of the relevant canons and their biographical details.

[22] *Constitutiones* of 1393, in Trexler, *Synodal Law*, p. 338; forty days of indulgences were granted to both the *Vigilia* and *festum*. Cf. Antoninus, *Summa*, Pars II, Tit. IX, Cap. VII, *De negligentia circa observationem festorum*. The feasts had already been given 'solemn' ranking (i.e. second class, 4 soldi distribution) in the 1375 constitutions of San Lorenzo (ACSL 2132, fo. 20ᵛ); in the 1509 constitutions, however, they had become relegated to third-class feasts (ACSL 2130, fo. 26ʳ).

[23] Cianfogni, *Memorie*, p. 195; Ginori Conti, *La basilica di San Lorenzo*, p. 72.

[24] ACSL 2132, constitutions of 1369, fo. 7ᵛ; constitutions of 1375, fo. 20ᵛ.

[25] See C. O. Nordström, *Ravennastudien* (Stockholm, 1953); G. da Bra, *Intorno alla vita e al culto di S. Lorenzo* (Rome, 1954); S. Maggio, *Il culto di S. Lorenzo martire in Italia (sec. IV–VII)* (Colle Don Bosco, 1967); P. Jounel, *Le Culte des saints dans les basiliques du Lateran et du Vatican au douzième siècle* (Rome, 1977), esp. pp. 271–2.

and All Saints. The canons were paid 5 soldi for attending these feasts. They were paid four for the next class of feasts, which included all those of the Virgin,[26] some of which were given first-rank status at other Florentine churches. The cult of S. Lorenzo had been considerably augmented during the Trecento by the granting of episcopal and papal indulgences, and by the consecration in 1338 of a new altar dedicated to *S. Lorenzo in Purgatorio*, which had a painting on it showing the saint liberating souls from purgatory. The indulgences were tied to Wednesdays, the day of the market at San Lorenzo, when the largest crowds could be expected.[27] Also, in 1394 the Republic decreed that officials of the government and guilds should proceed to the church on the feast-day of S. Lorenzo to offer candles and to hear sung mass.[28] To cap it all, new constitutions of 1418 introduced a special office for the Vigil of the feast of S. Lorenzo.[29]

But by 1415 moves were afoot to build a new church for the parish. The complex history of the building programme[30] need not concern us here, except where it has a bearing on our theme of liturgy and patronage. Howard Saalman is probably correct in assuming that 'the whole idea of enlarging the old Romanesque church had, presumably, been initiated because of strong demand by the parish patricians for suitable family chapels'.[31] And the function of the chapels, as the documents from San Lorenzo show, was 'that divine offices might be celebrated in them', that is, offices for the souls of the founders, their ancestors, and their descendants.[32]

---

[26] ACSL 2132, fos. 19ᵛ–20ᵛ.

[27] Cianfogni, *Memorie*, pp. 154–9; Borsook, 'Cults and Imagery', p. 172, on the altar; R. C. Trexler, 'Lorenzo de' Medici and Savonarola, Martyrs for Florence', *Renaissance Quarterly*, 31 (1978) 293–308, on the Wednesday markets; cf. Trexler, *Public Life*, p. 74.

[28] Cianfogni, *Memorie*, p. 178.

[29] Cianfogni, *Memorie*, pp. 186–8; ASCL 2132, fos. 30ʳ–33ᵛ.

[30] The following recent studies are relevant: V. Herzner, 'Zur Baugeschichte von San Lorenzo in Florenz', *Zeitschrift für Kunstgeschichte*, 36 (1974), 89–115; I. Hyman, 'Notes and Speculations on S. Lorenzo, Palazzo Medici, and an Urban Project by Brunelleschi', *Journal of the Society of Architectural Historians*, 34 (1975), 98–120; E. Battisti, *Filippo Brunelleschi* (Milan, 1976); J. Ruda, 'A 1434 Building Programme for San Lorenzo in Florence', *Burlington Magazine*, 120 (1978), 358–61; H. Saalman, 'San Lorenzo: The 1434 Chapel Project', ibid. 361–4; H. Burns, 'San Lorenzo in Florence Before the Building of the New Sacristy: An Early Plan', *Mitteilungen des Kunsthistorisches Institutes in Florenz*, 23 (1979), 145–54; C. Elam, 'The Site and Early Building History of Michelangelo's New Sacristy', ibid. 155–86; P. Roselli and O. Superchi, *L'edificazione della Basilica di San Lorenzo* (Florence, 1980).

[31] Saalman, 'San Lorenzo', p. 363.

[32] '... ut in ipsis celebrentur divina offita': Ruda, 'A 1434 Building Programme', p. 361, quoting the 1434 document; the same liturgical thrust is noticeable in the 1429

It is a common error of emphasis among art historians to speak of chapels as though they were built principally for architectural reasons or to house paintings on their walls or altars. This is reversing the founder's priorities. As A. H. Lloyd has noted of the medieval English patrons of colleges: 'In most cases the main motive underlying the private munificence ... was the priority enjoyed by [the founders] in the daily prayers and celebrations of such institutions.'[33] This is not to deny that the patronage of architecture or painting was a matter of intrinsic artistic value for some Renaissance patrons, or that the patronage of religious art and architecture had social and political motivations, but, however magnificent a chapel might be, its patron wanted it first and last for liturgical reasons.

Before turning to the role of the Medici in the liturgical life of the new church, it might be noted that there are significant hints in the fourteenth-century documents from San Lorenzo that lay participation in the parish and the church was being given increasing recognition by the clergy. Between 1297 and 1356 eleven choral chapels were endowed by laymen. Eight of these were suppressed for lack of funds, and the same pattern occurred between 1356 and 1422, when the bishop suppressed eleven and only three remained solvent.[34] This

document recording Cosimo de' Medici's endowment of canonries and *feste* in honour of his father, Giovanni di Bicci de' Medici: the 'two most noble and sumptuous chapels' and the *ornatissima sacristia* were seen by the clergy as contributing to the expansion and growth of the liturgy ('prout ... divinum cultum in dicta ecclesia ampliare et crescere') principally because their endowments caused them to perform liturgy on specified feast-days for the soul of Giovanni (ACSL 2132, fo. 35ʳ; D. Moreni, *Continuazione delle memorie istoriche dell' Ambrosiana R. Basilica di S. Lorenzo* 2 vols. (Florence, 1804–17), ii. 369). The phrase which occurs so frequently in documents from this period pertaining to the endowment of chapels, 'in aumentum divini cultus', should be taken more seriously. (It is here quoted from the 1442 act of the chapter conceding authority to Cosimo de' Medici to build the *cappella maggiore* and the central nave as far as the crossing: see Ginori Conti, *La basilica di San Lorenzo*, p. 241.) It is a common formula in ecclesiastical documents 1350–1650, but its frequency does not necessarily indicate that it was without significance for clergy and laity; I would argue that ecclesiastical approval of the growth of liturgy was both a confirmation of lay involvement in that field and an invitation to further co-operation. I bear in mind that the phrase could also be used in ecclesiastical contexts in which the laity had no role.

[33] *The Early History of Christ's College* (Cambridge, 1934), p. 30; quoted by E. F. Jacob, 'Founders and Foundations in the Later Middle Ages', in his *Essays in Later Medieval History* (Manchester, and New York, 1968), p. 157. See also R. O'Day, 'The Law of Patronage in Early Modern England', *Journal of Ecclesiastical History*, 26 (1975), 247–60; G. F. Lytle, 'Religion and the Lay Patron in Reformation England', in G. F. Lytle and S. Orgel (eds.), *Patronage in the Renaissance* (Princeton, 1981), pp. 65–114.

[34] Cianfogni, *Memorie*, pp. 128–9, 141–3, 150–1; Ruda, 'A 1434 Building Programme', p. 358 n.7.

indicates a strong tendency among parishioners to buy into chapels which they could not afford to maintain. There are also subtle hints in the 1369 constitutions that the clergy should be more considerate of lay wishes in connection with funerals.[35] In 1415 the first lay *operai* of the church were appointed.[36]

The new church, designed principally by Brunelleschi, was to transform the liturgy of San Lorenzo. New chapels with new dedications to new saints entailed a radical reorganization of the festal calendar. The nine old prebends carried on into the new church, but they lost their pre-eminence forever. If one cross-indexes the list of prominent parishioners who gathered in San Lorenzo in 1440 to further the building of the nave of the new church,[37] with the names of the families who had interests in those old prebends during the fifteenth century, one sees that scarcely any of the wealthiest showed interest in the old prebends. But some of the less prominent families did have relatives who later became canons in those prebends.[38] An exception was the prebend of S. Concordia, which it will be recalled was associated with a major feast-day. The youthful Cardinal Giovanni de' Medici was elected to this prebend in 1507,[39] and the Aldobrandini had taken rights of presentation to the prebend of S. Sebastiano in 1462.[40] But from 1415 onwards, the Medici and the other dominant families of the parish, many of whom were their close allies at the time when the church was in its early stages of construction,[41] primarily wanted to

---

[35] Cianfogni, *Memorie*, p. 168; ACSL 2132, fo. 10^v: the prior, canons, and chaplains, upon invitation by the family of a deceased, were to attend a prayer vigil at the home. The morning after, they were to transfer the corpse with 'maggiore o minore pompa', to the church, where the funeral service was to be performed, for rich and poor alike. Cf. ACSL 2130, constitutions of 1509, fo. 40^{r-v}; ACSL 2131, constitutions of 1531, fo. 30^r. The sacristans' books recording offices for the dead reveal that members of powerful families were likely to have their funerary services distinguished by the number of torches and candles used, and by the greater proportion of the total complement of clergy who attended. When it is recorded that 'tutto il capitolo' attended a funeral, we may assume that the deceased had special significance to the parish and chapter: e.g. ACSL Morti, segnato 3 (1507–10); ACSL Feste e Uffici e Morti, segnato 6 (1530–1).

[36] Cianfogni, *Memorie*, pp. 182, 188ff.; Ginori Conti, *La basilica di San Lorenzo*, p. 46.

[37] Document in Ginori Conti, *La basilica di San Lorenzo*, pp. 236–40.

[38] Cianfogni, *Memorie*, pp. 233–82, for the names of the holders of the prebends; the cross-indexing is offered as a simple, preliminary analysis.

[39] Cianfogni, *Memorie*, p. 263.

[40] Ibid., pp. 274ff.

[41] See D. V. Kent, *The Rise of the Medici: Faction in Florence, 1426–1434* (Oxford, 1978); one notes her warning that the allegiances evident during her chosen period were subject to change in later decades.

associate themselves with distinctively new aspects of the liturgy. Giovanni di Bicci de' Medici took for himself the sacristy burial chapel endowed with a canonry dedicated to S. Giovanni Evangelista, and the adjoining chapel and canonry of SS. Cosma and Damiano. The canons were appointed, the documents record, to say masses for Giovanni and for his parents and friends. When Giovanni died in 1428, his sons Cosimo and Lorenzo gave 900 florins to the chapter, 'to increase divine worship, for the soul of [their] father, and for offices [to be established] at the pleasure of the Capitolo'.[42]

This was the first highly significant proposal of the kind from the Medici to the chapter. It bound the chapter to a liturgically appropriate response, and it would be used repeatedly by the Medici in their dealings with the chapter in future centuries. The chapter responded with two vital innovations: a special perpetual Monday office for the dead for Giovanni and his sons and for their descendants and friends, and the promotion of the feasts of S. Giovanni and SS. Cosma and Damiano to the 5-soldi distribution level,[43] guaranteeing their perpetual significance to the clergy. In 1442 Cosimo provided money, as Saalman says, for 'the patronage of the transept and the church up to the point where the old Romanesque church still stood'.[44] In those early years other notable parishioners had bought chapels in the area of the crossing: the Neroni, Ginori, Rondinelli, da Fortuna, della Stufa, Nelli, Ciai, and Luca di Marco.[45] They clustered as closely as they could to the principal liturgical focus of the church, the main altar,[46] but of course Cosimo had acquired patronage rights to the Cappella Maggiore in 1442.[47]

[42] Ginori Conti, *La basilica di San Lorenzo*, pp. 46ff., 64; Moreni, *Continuazione*, ii. 22, 27, 366ff.; L. D. Ettlinger, 'The Liturgical Function of Michelangelo's Medici Chapel', *Mitteilungen des Kunsthistorischen Institutes in Florenz*, 22 (1978), 287–304 (esp. 298).

[43] ACSL 2132, fo. 35ʳ; instructions to the sacristan in a 1529 document read:

Nota che ogni Lunedì di ciascuna settimana s'ha a fare un Ufficio per l'Anime di Giovanni de' Medici, cioè Giovanni d'Averardo, et per tutti i passati di questa vita della Casa di detto Giovanni, et per tutti quelli che sono sepelliti nel nostro Cimitero et Chiesa con tre Orationi, il primo Inclina Domine, il 2° Deus venie largitor, et il 3° Fidelium Deus'. (ACSL 2051, inserto, Avertimento al Sacrestano, fo. 3ʳ.)

[44] Saalman, 'San Lorenzo', p. 363; Herzner, 'Zur Baugeschichte', pp. 93ff.

[45] For a useful plan showing the original allocation of chapels in the area of the crossing, see Elam, 'The Site and Early Building History', p. 164.

[46] Rightly emphasized by Herzner, 'Zur Baugeschichte', pp. 92ff.

[47] Document in Ginori Conti, *La basilica di San Lorenzo*, pp. 240–5: '... concessio dicte maioris capelle et navis in medio ecclesie consistentis usque ad altare maius antiquum eidem Cosimo et suis filiis et successoribus consignetur' (p. 243). A. Molho, 'Cosimo de' Medici: *Pater Patriae* or *Padrino?*', *Stanford Italian Review*, 1 (1979), 5–

Cosimo died on 1 August 1464. He was interred in his chosen tomb, in the pier beneath the centre of the dome of the crossing, and right in front of the high altar:[48] an unduplicatable location and of profound liturgical meaning. Cosimo may have formed the idea while travelling in Germany, and it is significant that the available models in Schaffhausen and Brunswick were royal burials.[49] The chapter provided an annual office for Cosimo which was brilliantly distinctive and must have been devised by Cosimo himself. The essential feature of it was not verbal but gestural. It was utterly simple. The office was said in the choir and the prior and all the canons and chaplains held a lighted candle in their hands during the ceremony.[50] Candles or torches were

33, is only partly correct when he writes (p. 26): 'The Medici patronage of the church of San Lorenzo, and Cosimo's sponsorship of the construction of the church's *cappella maggiore* after 1442 can be largely explained by the long-standing association between that church and the *gonfalon* Lion d'Oro.' It should not be overlooked that the documents refer continually to the parish and to the Medici's status as parishioners, as well as to the *gonfalone*; and, while the *operai* were (as Molho says) appointed from the district, they were also specified to be parishioners. Apparently the collegiate and parochial church of San Lorenzo, as it is called in these documents, provided an administrative structure for its parish which was just as real as that of the *gonfalone*, even if its susceptibility to patronage is not so clear to us. Cf. Kent and Kent, *Neighbours and Neighbourhood*, pp. 128ff., on lay patronage in the parish of San Pancrazio.

[48] D. Moreni, *Pompe funebri celebrate nell'Imp. e reale basilica di San Lorenzo* (Florence, 1827), pp. 10–14.

[49] My evidence is only circumstantial. Vespasiano da Bisticci notes that Cosimo had 'visited almost all parts of Germany and France, spending some two years in travel' (*The Vespasiano Memoirs*, tr. W. George and E. Waters (New York, 1926), p. 214). A. M. Schulz writes, in *Art Bulletin*, 62 (1980), 319:

> Eberhard, Burkhard, and Ita von Hellenburg, founders of the Münster of Schaffhausen, were interred before its altar and ... the founders, Henry the Lion, Duke of Saxony and Bavaria, and Mathilde of England were buried in the middle of the Cathedral at Brunswick. Are there other examples? Did the tradition penetrate to Italy? The answers to such questions would permit us, for instance, to place within a historical context the disposition that Cosimo de' Medici ... made for his burial ..., a disposition that has seemed till now an unqualified expression of the hubris of a Renaissance ruler.

I have simply put these two pieces of evidence together. Eve Borsook reminds me, however, that burial in the pavement in front of the high altar had a long tradition in Florence, and J. Clearfield, 'The Tomb of Cosimo de' Medici in San Lorenzo', *Rutgers Art Review*, 2 (1981), 13–30, esp. n. 74, cites medieval French and early Christian examples. Howard Saalman (in a paper presented at a seminar on San Lorenzo at Villa I Tatti in June 1982) suggested that both Cosimo's tomb and that of his father may have been inspired by Cosimo's reading of Eusebius' description of Constantine's tomb in his *Life of Constantine*.

[50] ACSL 2051, inserto, Avertimento al Sacrestano, fo. 3ʳ; ACSL 2136, constitutions of 1566, fo. 89, De officiis sive Anniversariis: 'In his officiis & Missis Congregationis, & si qua alia unquam celebranda erunt pro Illustrissima familia Medicea semper paretur Canonicus cum tribus ministris & duobus cantoribus ... salvo iure D. Prioris in

customarily set up at funeral masses and offices, and were required on the altar for the sacrifice of the mass.[51] They were also carried in procession to burials or as offerings by the commune to churches, but were very rarely handheld during church ceremonies.[52] Cosimo probably had in mind the distinctive way candles were held in the hands of the illustrious mourners of the deposed Pope John XXIII, Cardinal Baldassare Cossa, at his magnificent funeral in Florence in December 1419.[53] Cosimo's father was the cardinal's banker and, as one of his executors, had a role in planning the *esequie*.[54] The special anniversary office of Cosimo became standard for Medici dead in San Lorenzo, and it was more than a century before the chapter allowed other families to imitate it.[55]

In April 1465 the chapter gave authority to Piero di Cosimo de' Medici to allocate the north-side chapels, which were still being con-

decantandis ex his.' The offices performed in this manner were known as *offitij maggiori* (see ACSL 2325, Libro de' Partiti, segnato D., 1563–77, fo. 34ᵛ); the books recording *feste* and *ufficii*, which noted the value of candles used, include the observation *cera a mano* for all the Medici offices.

[51] See P. Bayart, 'Cierges', in *Dictionnaire de droit canonique*, iii (Paris, 1942), 718–25.

[52] Exceptions occur in the Pontifical of Durandus, in the ordination ceremonies; the candidates proceed into the choir *cum candelis accensis in manibus*, symbolizing the exorcism of demons. See M. Andrieu (ed.), *Le Pontifical romain au moyen âge*, iii (Vatican City, 1940), 342–64.

[53] See R. Lightbown, *Donatello and Michelozzo* (London, 1980), pp. 12–14; the *esequie* of Cardinal Brancaccio held in Florence in June 1427 also gave much emphasis to torches (Lightbown, pp. 81ff.).

[54] Cosimo's own funeral was held in San Lorenzo and, according to the *Ricordi* of his son Piero, he was buried 'nella sepoltura innanzi per lui ordinata senza alcuna honoranza, e pompa funebre' (Moreni, *Pompe funebri*, p. 10). However, the memorial interment ceremony held for Cosimo on 22 Oct. 1467 was of a different order, as the clergy noted: 'Facemmo ... un magnifico ossequio per la buona, e felice memoria di Cosimo ...' (Moreni, *Pompe funebri*, p. 13; the source is ACSL 1938(4), fo. 12ʳ). It is possible that S. Antoninus' modest funeral of 1459 ('At his request he was buried in S. Marco ... without any pomp'—Vespasiano, *Memoirs*, p. 163) had left its mark on the ageing Cosimo. But, as Trexler observes, 'a funeral without pomp for such a man was "more" not "less", and a typical practice of great sovereigns' (*Public Life*, p. 427). However, the account of Antoninus' funeral given by Domenico di Leonardo Buoninsegni (*Storia della città di Firenze dall'anno 1410 al 1460* (Florence, 1637), p. 124) mentions a 'gran concorso' of devotees and 'molte immagini', suggesting that the ceremony may have been less modestly observed than the pious archbishop intended. (I thank Patricia Simons for this latter reference.)

[55] The earliest example known to me of extension of the Medici office to 'outsiders' is that of Don Marco dal Giocondo, a Vallombrosan monk, who explained to the chapter in March 1572 'come desiderava far celebrare ognj anno in chiesa nostra un'offitio secondo el modo et forma si fanno quelli della Casa de' Medici ...' (ACSL 2325, fo. 65ʳ).

structed, to citizens of his choice.[56] In using the term 'citizens' and not 'parishioners' the chapter was being realistic in two senses. The chapels were proving difficult to sell.[57] Some of those purchased in the crossing area in the 1420s had already changed hands;[58] moreover, the chapter understood that in Florence patronage crossed parish boundaries. Cosimo de' Medici was not alone in cultivating chapels and commemorative masses in a range of Florentine churches.[59] The chapter also often attended funerals of families who had interests in San Lorenzo's chapels and therefore in its liturgy, but who chose to be buried in another parish's church.[60]

The phenomenon of parish consciousness needs study. Was being a parishioner a social bond? I would hesitate to extend F. W. Kent's 'great trinity of social bonds', friends, relatives, and neighbours,[61] to include parishioners. On the other hand, among the clergy, consciousness of the cohesiveness of the parish was crucial, especially to those engaged in the care of souls. When in 1575 the clergy set out to list the souls of the parish, street by street and house by house, it may be assumed that they were just formally assessing what they had previously kept in their heads. The geography of the large parish was

---

[56] Roselli and Superchi, *L'edificazione*, p. 40.

[57] Herzner, 'Zur Baugeschichte', pp. 101ff.; Saalman, 'San Lorenzo', p. 363; he notes (p. 364) that most of the northern chapels went 'to relatives and clients of the Medici family and were completed in the 1470s and 80s'.

[58] Fluctuating political relationships with the Medici, and the 'apparent ambitions of the dominant Medici' (Saalman, 'San Lorenzo', p. 363), may have precipitated the transferring of chapel ownership.

[59] Ronald Weissman and I are making a statistical survey of endowments for chapels and liturgy in the major Florentine churches, 1350–1650. For the range of Cosimo's endowments, see Gombrich, 'The Early Medici', and cf. A. Brown, 'The Humanist Portrait of Cosimo de' Medici, Pater Patriae', *Journal of the Warburg and Courtauld Institutes*, 24 (1961), 186–221; A. Fraser Jenkins, 'Cosimo de' Medici's Patronage of Architecture and the Theory of Magnificence', ibid. 33 (1970), 162–70; Molho, 'Cosimo de' Medici', esp. p. 31, on the pan-Florentine scale of Cosimo's political patronage. Trexler (*Public Life*, p. 95), exaggerates when writing that the Medici 'bought out the other families' rights to display their arms in San Lorenzo': the 1442 document which he paraphrases made that stipulation only for the choir (the *cappella maggiore*) and for the nave 'as far as the original altar' (Gombrich, 'The Early Medici', p. 42); the owners of nave chapels were free to use their family arms, and did so even on the liturgical vestments their chaplains wore.

[60] These are recorded in numerous volumes of *morti* in the Archivio capitolare; e.g. Morti, segnato 10 (1554–1558).

[61] F. W. Kent, *Household and Lineage in Renaissance Florence: The Family Life of the Capponi, Ginori and Rucellai* (Princeton, 1977), pp. 16–17; on the evidence for the perception of the Florentine parish as a 'neighbourhood', see Kent and Kent, *Neighbours and Neighbourhood*, pp. 1–5.

etched into the minds of all the clergy who kept the parish records. In 1575 some three thousand parishioners were identified,[62] presumably the active members of the parish: they were roughly one-twentieth of the city's population.

To return to the Medici and their encroachment on the liturgy in San Lorenzo, we see, in 1482, Lorenzo il Magnifico purchasing from the chapter an anniversary office for his brother Giuliano, a birthday *festa* for himself on the octave of the feast of S. Stefano (which, as Trexler rightly noticed, was the day after his actual birthdate), an anniversary office for his mother Lucrezia on the first Wednesday after the Nativity of the Virgin, and a *festa* for her on the day of the Visitation.[63] As the Medici continually interred their dead at San Lorenzo, the number of anniversary offices said for them naturally spread throughout the festal calendar, but of course in a haphazard fashion. The true anniversary office or mass fell on the actual date of death.[64] Few Medici were destined to die on very major feast-days. This is why most individuals making testaments also purchased a perpetual feast-day mass or group of masses. From a devotional viewpoint, the motivation was to obtain the greater intercessional power associated with a feast of Christ, or the Virgin, or a particular saint or martyr. But the socio-political implications of such choices are obvious. Nor should one overlook the role of personal and familial religious motivation. It is not accidental that Giovanni and Cosimo de' Medici promoted prebends and feasts for saints bearing their own names. Lorenzo did not have to bother. His name-saint was already patron of the church. He had merely to amplify the festal celebrations through banquets and gifts for *apparati*, to augment public awareness of his personal glorification in the feast.[65] But, as indicated above, by 1400 the feast of S. Lorenzo was already inscribed in the civic calendar. Lorenzo was surely aware that, by enriching the pageantry of the feast,

---

[62] ACSL Stato dell'Anime (1575–1582); the figure of 8,000 parishioners given in the documents for the 1602 election of the prior (Misc. Med. 348, fo. 232ʳ) probably refers to the number of residents rather than to those active in the sacramental life of the parish.

[63] Trexler, 'Lorenzo de' Medici and Savonarola', p. 307 (document from ACSL 2051).

[64] See A. Amanieu, 'Anniversaire', in *Dictionnaire de droit canonique*, i (Paris, 1935), 554–64.

[65] See Trexler, 'Lorenzo de' Medici and Savonarola'; A. Mannucci, *Vita di Cosimo de' Medici primo Gran Duca di Toscana* (Bologna, 1586), p. 127, describes S. Lorenzo as 'protettor della famiglia de' Medici'.

he was contributing to its civic significance, and thereby to the Medici's religious and political authority.

Feast-days were raised in significance in a number of ways. A localized devotion might attract diocesan patronage. We have seen this happen in the case of S. Lorenzo's feast. The bishop's or archbishop's patronage and indulgences encouraged regional observance of the feast. Papal patronage of the feast, however, gave it a universal significance, and papal indulgences tended to be renewed and increased by successive popes. It is hardly surprising that, when the Medici produced the two popes, Leo X and Clement VII, cults which the family had patronized in San Lorenzo were reaffirmed and strengthened, and new feasts created.[66]

In San Lorenzo there were three distinct but interrelated groups making inroads on the festal calendar. These were lay families or individuals who purchased liturgy for ancestors, descendants, or friends; secondly, the clergy of various ranks, predominantly of the chapter, but some outsiders; thirdly, devotional and caritative confraternities, and institutions like guilds. These three groups helped to shape the liturgy in San Lorenzo by purchasing patronage rights to chapels and by linking feast-days to them. They all exercised the 'reciprocal obligations of a patronage network'.[67] I have looked at the kind and quantity of liturgical services performed for parishioners, clergy, and other groups in San Lorenzo from the 1440s to the 1570s, and the following preliminary observations can be made.

By 1531 only the feasts of S. Lorenzo, SS. Cosma and Damiano, Pentecost, All Saints, the Nativity and Resurrection of Christ were given 'most solemn' status.[68] Account books listing expenditure for festal *apparati* show that the two feasts of saints were the major events of San Lorenzo's festal calendar. Despite the fluctuations in the political fortunes of the Medici in this period, their family-inspired feast-days never faltered. Only the plague in 1524–5 could temporarily reduce their popularity.[69]

From the beginning of the principate the Medici no longer had to

---

[66] Trexler, *Public Life*, pp. 422ff. and 504ff., discusses the feasts which were promoted by the Medici. He rightly emphasizes the growth of the papal 'family feasts' in San Lorenzo as having the implication of the 'sacralization' of Medici time.

[67] F. W. Kent, *Household and Lineage*, p. 27; Weissman, *Ritual Brotherhood*, p. 23.

[68] ACSL 2130, fo. 30ʳ; the constitutions of 1509 listed thirty feasts which earned 5 soldi distributions for the clergy, which included the six isolated in 1531; the constitutions of 1566 confirmed the list of 1531 (ACSL 2136, fo. 70).

[69] ACSL 2361, 2364, 2371, ranging from 1502 to 1527.

pay for their commemorative liturgy: it had become the gift of the chapter bestowed in response to ducal patronage. The documents recording these transactions are important, for they reveal much about the shaping of the church's liturgy, and of the chapter's behaviour under Medici pressure. In June 1546, ostensibly of his own initiative, the prior recommended to the chapter that, in memory of Ottaviano de' Medici, 'the devoted and affectionate benefactor of our Church and House', an anniversary mass be celebrated in the manner and form usual for persons of the illustrious house of the Medici, and that this be performed 'free of charge and without any salary'. But in the margin is written 'for one time only', to guarantee that it did not become an annual obligation.[70] One might read this case as a spontaneous gesture of gratitude on the part of the chapter. But it was more likely to have been suggested to the prior, perhaps by the Duke's secretary and auditore of the *Nove*, Lelio Torelli (himself a parishioner), that such a gesture would be deemed appropriate.

Turning to a slightly different case, one notes that in 1550 the chapter, after lengthy discussion and *maturo discorso* on the infinite benefits and favours received from Duke Cosimo, decided that on the first Wednesday after the feast of S. Lucia a perpetual anniversary office would be held for Cosimo's parents, in the usual manner reserved for the Medici. In a very significant phrase, the chapter noted that the only way in which it could demonstrate its gratitude to Cosimo was 'in cose spirituali'.[71] But one cannot imagine that a liturgical matter as vital to Cosimo as the anniversary office for his parents would have been left to the clergy of San Lorenzo. It looked much better for the chapter, however, if its records stated that the initiative had been its own. Another interesting example concerns the anniversary for the Duchess Eleonora. Shortly after she had died in 1564 the chapter received from the duke a very lucrative gift, the duchess' clothes, which would later be cut up for liturgical vestments. The chapter replied with three perpetual anniversary offices for the duchess and her deceased children, and again stated that its liturgical gifts, which of course involved annual expenses, were its only appropriate response.[72]

The Medici occasionally purchased liturgy for their friends in these

---

[70] ACSL 2299, Libro de' Partiti, segnato G (1544–62), fo. 6ᵛ.

[71] ACSL 2299, fo. 42ᵛ: 'non potendo il detto Capitolo in altro che in cose spirituali dimostrare a S.E. il pronto animo che egli ha d'esser in ciò (se non in tutto almeno in qualche particella) grato ...'

[72] ACSL 2325, fo. 16ʳ, 26 July 1564.

years,[73] and Pope Clement VII funded four chaplaincies for the New Sacristy in 1532 to say three masses per day and to recite the entire Psalter with alternating prayers, twenty-four hours a day forever— *laus perennis*[74]—but these were exceptions to the rule. By 1575, the Medici had twenty-three perpetual offices and masses, and those apart from the major 'family' feasts, the Monday office and *laus perennis*, which was already flagging in the New Sacristy.[75] Significantly, the Medici seem to have resisted the temptation to monopolize the principal feasts of Christ and Mary, at least in San Lorenzo.

Other families of the parish pursued patronage of the liturgy.[76] The della Stufa had the Conception of the Virgin and S. Giuseppe. The Aldobrandini reserved the Octave of the Conception, S. Sebastiano, and S. Concordia. The Ginori were identified with the feasts of SS. Francesco and Girolamo, S. Niccolò, and Magdalen.[77] Canons and priors, too, founded many chapels linked to important feasts and purchased perpetual offices and masses on those days.[78] As early as 1369 the chapter had instituted an anniversary office for the souls of

---

[73] ACSL 2299, fo. 100ᵛ, 3 Feb. 1558: Duchess Eleonora gave money to the chapter with the obligation of celebrating 'ogn'anno in perpetuo, uno officcio anniversario per l'anima della Signora Isabella Raynosa Matrone Spagniola, et sepolta nella chiesa nostra di San Lorenzo . . .'.

[74] See Ettlinger, 'The Liturgical Function', p. 297.

[75] Ibid., p. 295. Archival evidence fills out the details of the clergy's difficulties in observing the demanding terms of the liturgy for the New Sacristy: ACSL 2325, fo. 64ᵛ (late 1571), non-attendance at matins; ibid., fo. 73ʳ (28 Mar. 1573), problems of observance, and new Psalmbooks printed. The New Sacristy may have been opened up to liturgical purchases by outsiders: in ACSL 2120, fo. 74ʳ, a certain Luca (Ginori ?) paid for 'oratione in sacrestia nuova'. The prebend for the Sacristy paid 80 lire in 1589: see Archivio Arcivescovile, Inventaria bonorum ecclesiasticorum Diocesij Florentinae (1589), filza prima, fo. 313ʳ. A *breve* of Paul V (22 January 1610) allowed the saying of a Gregorian Mass in the New Sacristy (ACSL Pergamene, 311).

[76] What follows is drawn from the considerable number of ACSL manuscripts recording anniversary offices and masses between c.1460 and 1650. This evidence, charting the growth of family endowments in the church, will be presented in a systematic form by Gaston and Weissman. Cf. J. Chiffoleau, *La Compatibilité de l'au-delà: Les hommes, la mort et la religion dans la région d'Avignon à la fin du moyen âge (vers 1320–vers 1480)* (Paris, 1981), which uses about 6,000 wills.

[77] See F. W. Kent, *Household and Lineage*, pp. 99ff. and 258ff.

[78] For a partial list of clergy who founded chapels, see Cianfogni, *Memorie*, pp. 232, 235, 238, 252. Some examples of feast-days reserved for canons and priors may be given from ACSL, Uffici e Feste e Morti, segnato I (1492–1509); Trinity, Prior Silvestri; Corpus Domini, Canon Guelfi; SS. Pietro and Paolo and Octave of S. Lorenzo, Prior Bonichi; Purification of Virgin, Canon Mariano; Annunciation, Canon Tomaso di Bartolo; S. Benedetto, Prior Benedetto Schiattesi, etc. Cf. B. Dobson, 'The Residentiary Canons of York in the Fifteenth Century', *Journal of Ecclesiastical History*, 30 (1979), 145–73 (esp. 170), on the role of cathedral canons in endowment of chantries.

all the former priors, canons, chaplains, clerics, 'famigliari et bene-
fattori' of the church,[79] but it clearly did not satisfy their needs.

We know little about the regulating of this massive festal
programme. The sacristan took details of small liturgical requests,[80]
but the larger pious endowments must have been checked by the prior
for suitability before being submitted to the chapter's vote of approval.
I have not found any evidence of direct diocesan interference before
the 1620s, when the maximum number of masses that could be
requested from the chapter for any one day was limited to six.[81] Before
that it was possible to ask for thirty. Some Florentine churches allowed
up to one hundred. This was difficult to manage with only twenty or
thirty clergy who were forbidden to say more than one mass per day,
except on Christmas Day.[82] The problem was exacerbated in the
fourteenth and fifteenth centuries by the growth in size of the compulsory daily office. Pruning of the Roman liturgical books during the
sixteenth century helped to relieve this situation.[83]

But the bishops at Trent were fully aware of the crippling effects of
the explosion of anniversary and votive masses which had occurred
during the Quattrocento.

It often happens, in some churches [they wrote] that by reason of various
bequests from deceased persons either so great a number of masses to be
celebrated is left with them that it is not possible to take care of them on the
particular days specified by the testators, or that alms given for their celebration is so small that it is not easy to find one who is willing to accept this
obligation; the result being that the pious intentions of the testators are
defeated and occasion is given to burdening the consciences of those to whom
the aforesaid obligations pertain.

They urged bishops, abbots, and generals of orders to examine and
regulate this matter in their churches.[84]

[79] The office *della Porrea* was to be held within fifteen days of the feast of S. Lorenzo
on 10 Aug., and, if not impeded by the occurrence of a major movable feast, should fall
on the first Wednesday after the Octave of S. Lorenzo: Cf. also BNF Conventi Soppressi,
C. 10. 1409, Costituzioni dell'Ordine de' Frati de'Servi (17th cent.), fos. 8ʳ, 14ʳ.

[80] An example is in ACSL 2192, fos. 3ʳff.

[81] Details in ACSL 2051, inserto 1, where the Declarations of the Sacred Congregation
of Rites of Urban VIII (1625) are copied, together with the follow-up from Archbishop
Angelo Marzi de' Medici in July 1627.

[82] *Constitutiones* of 1310, in Trexler, *Synodal Law*, p. 266.

[83] See P. Battifol, *History of the Roman Breviary*, tr. A. Baylay (London, 1912),
pp. 149ff.

[84] Sess. XXV, Cap. IV: tr. J. Schroeder, *Canons and Decrees of the Council of Trent*
(Rockford Ill., 1978), p. 236; it was published in Florence by Archbishop Altoviti under

There is much to be gained from an investigation of this extraordinary inflation of anniversary services. The following comments
pertain only to Florence, and most particularly to San Lorenzo, but
they may well be applicable elsewhere. In the view of the Roman
Church there were sound theological and devotional reasons for the
clergy's encouragement of votive and anniversary ceremonies among
the faithful. The bishops of Trent did not question this encouragement,
any more than they questioned lay access to *ius patronatus*.[85] These
fundamental aspects of lay involvement in the architectural and liturgical life of churches had existed continuously from the early medieval period. But a very significant turning-point was the opening of
churches to lay burials, which was approved in Florence in 1221.[86]
This perhaps provides an approximate date of departure for lay
patronage of the liturgy of the kind that we have seen developing to
crisis point in the later centuries.

Intra-mural burial, even if it was relegated to the *sottochiesa*, offered
impressive psychological advantages to a believer. It permitted eternal
proximity to the sacred relics which sanctified the church. Burial within
the church proper was the most desirable condition of all,[87] and
closeness to the relics under the main altar was patently worth many
thousands of hard-earned florins to the Florentine families who could
afford it. The Christian cult of the saints, of their bodies and burial
places, may in certain respects be regarded as a sophisticated and
ecclesiastically orchestrated cult of patronal ancestors.[88] The feasts of

the rubric *De anniversariis*, in *Dioecesana synodus florentiae celebrata tertio non. Maias
MDLXIX* (Florence, 1569), p. 43.

[85] On the development of patronage rights, which were reaffirmed in Sess. XIV, Cap.
XII, but with closer episcopal supervision (Schroeder, *Canons and Decrees*, p. 113), see
P. Landau, *Jus Patronatus: Studien zur Entwicklung des Patronats im Dekretalrecht und
der Kanonistik des 12. und 13. Jahrhunderts* (Cologne and Vienna, 1975).

[86] F. W. Kent, *Household and Lineage*, p. 280; M. Becker, 'Aspects of Lay Piety in
Early Renaissance Florence', in C. Trinkaus and H. Obermann (eds.), *The Pursuit of
Holiness in Late Medieval and Renaissance Religion* (Leiden, 1974), pp. 177–99, esp.
pp. 181–2, speaks of the 'quest of a laity for spiritual authentication': 'The right to
build private chapels, bury one's dead close to the altar of the cathedral, and place
their children in one of the prestigious monasteries ... was quintessential to an urban
laity.'

[87] St Antoninus gave three reasons for the *utilitas* of burial 'in loco sacro': the
intercession of the saints in whose honour the church was built; the fact that the faithful,
when coming to the church, would see the tomb and offer prayers for the deceased; the
dead would be assured of rest undisturbed by demons (*Summa*, Pars III, Tit. X, Cap.
III).

[88] The cult of the saints is an aspect of Italian Renaissance piety that has received
little attention, despite its centrality. Until recently it has been viewed too exclusively

the saints in the liturgical calendar were always accessible to lay devotion, but they could be seen to be especially meaningful when families, who had their own ancestor cults,[89] were able to bury in churches. As families purchased patronage rights to chapels and presentation rights to prebends, both of which could be dedicated to selected saints, they could begin to increase the sacrality of their devotion to their own family ancestors by identifying one with the other. The medium of identification was the festal liturgy, and the clergy made this available, theoretically to everyone, but in significant measure only to those who could substantially endow in return.

It was only to be expected that, once the clergy opened up their churches to the lay patronage of the liturgy, they would ultimately find themselves accepting more patronage than they could repay in divine services. When a church's economy had become to a degree dependent on pious donations tied to the liturgy, the attraction of more patronage was an obvious direction to take. In the economies of the Florentine churches as a whole during this period the economic contribution of liturgical endowment may prove to be equally significant.[90]

Florence's saintly fifteenth-century archbishop, the Dominican Antoninus, warned the clergy not to introduce errors 'on account of masses for the dead or other matters proposed by laymen'. *Docendus est enim populus non sequendus*. The people are to be instructed by the clergy and not vice versa. To perform liturgy for the sole purpose of receiving the distribution constituted simony, Antoninus wrote. Priority was to be given to the canonical daily office over vigils of the

from the aspect of Protestant criticism and reform. For Florence, see Trexler, 'Ritual Behaviour', and *Public Life*; Weissman, *Ritual Brotherhood*; Borsook, 'Cults and Imagery'.

[89] On 'ancestor reverence' in Renaissance Florence, see F. W. Kent, *Household and Lineage*, pp. 99ff. Natalie Davis, working principally from French evidence, has claimed that 'The *culte des morts* was certainly not "ancestor worship"'. She rightly stresses that there was a 'corporate' aspect of liturgy for the dead, which, though endowed by private families, was said by priests, and 'gave scope to ties of family, kin, artifical kin, and sometimes of broader community': 'Ghosts, Kin, and Progeny: Some Features of Family Life in Early Modern France', *Daedalus*, 106 (1977), 87–114 (esp. 93).

[90] Becker, 'Aspects of Lay Piety', p. 177 notes: 'In the wake of the Black Death private benefactions and testamentary gifts increased astronomically.' The increase of wealth in Florence may also be relevant; see R. Goldthwaite, *Private Wealth in Renaissance Florence* (Princeton, 1968), and *The Building of Renaissance Florence* (Baltimore, 1980), for the economic context.

dead. No payment was to be exacted for burial of the dead. Usurious or simoniacal money was not to be used for the building of churches by lay patrons.[91] One has the feeling that St Antoninus knew that he was trying to hold back the flood-gates.

[91] Antoninus, *Summa*, Pars II, Tit. IX, Cap. X; on distributions and simony, Pars II, Tit. IX, Cap. XII; on priority for the daily office, Pars III, Tit. XIII, Cap. II; on patronage and simony, Pars III, Tit. XII, Cap. VII.

8

The Medici and the Savonarolans, 1512–1527: The Limitations of Personal Government and of the Medicean Patronage System

LORENZO POLIZZOTTO

THE second period of Medici ascendancy in Florence has not received from historians the close attention which has been accorded to the Medicean regimes of the fifteenth century. Both the institutional organization of the restored Medicean government and, above all, the complex network of personal ties and obligations which, taken together, constituted the equally important *sottogoverno*, have been viewed in the light of conditions which obtained under the earlier regimes.[1] There were, certainly, strong elements of continuity between past and present—elements which the restored Medici were at pains to emphasize. But during the republican interlude between 1494 and 1512 and as a result of Savonarola's apostolate in Florence, vastly different conditions had arisen which radically altered the traditional ways in which politics were viewed and by which political action was determined.

In the eighteen years of Medici exile, the Florentines had become accustomed to a more open system of government and believed themselves to have acquired not only a greater influence in the affairs of their city but also a more equitable share in the spoils of government. These benefits, real or imagined, they would not readily forego.[2]

---

[1] See, for example, A. Anzilotti, *La crisi costituzionale della repubblica fiorentina* (Florence, 1912; repr. Rome, 1969), and R. D. Jones, *Francesco Vettori: Florentine Citizen and Medici Servant* (London, 1972), esp. chs. IV and VI.

[2] As the Medicean Paolo Vettori was to remind Cardinal Giulio de' Medici, 'sempre la memoria di quel tempo vi farà guerra' ('Ricordi di Paolo Vettori al cardinale de' Medici sopra le cose di Firenze', in R. von Albertini, *Firenze dalla repubblica al principato* (Turin, 1970), p. 357).

Similarly, during the republican period, new bonds of interest had been formed and networks of patronage established which were independent of Medici wishes or interference and which, notwithstanding their restoration in 1512, continued to operate. Most importantly, however, Florentine politics, which, despite the attempts of some of the protagonists to resort to ideological arguments to justify their quest for power, had always been characterized at both the institutional and the informal levels by the absence of ideology, were now rent by ideological dissension as a result of Savonarola's message.

Insufficient account was taken of these new elements. With little reference to the changed social and political circumstances, the Medici set about ruling as their forebears had done. Once in control of the organs of government, they believed, they could win over the hostile forces in Florence by binding them to the regime with ties of interest and obligation. In this they perhaps reveal a concern more with the form of government than with its substance.[3] In the past, when applied by able heads of the family whose precedence was undisputed, these methods had served the Medici well. Now they could no longer be expected to work. Medici patronage and largess, however eagerly it was sought and however willingly dispensed, was being superimposed on pre-existing ties and obligations. These it could not easily replace, especially when they owed their origin to ideological commitment. In fact, the Medici's undiscriminating resort to patronage for political ends was to afford their enemies the means of protection and survival. In the case of the Medici's policies towards the followers of Savonarola—their most intractable enemies—the misuse of patronage was to contribute directly to the fall of 1527.

Giuliano de' Medici entered Florence on 1 September 1512, the day after Soderini had been seized and forcibly removed from office.[4] He returned ostensibly as a private citizen but, in reality, as the head of a

---

[3] For an important comment of Lorenzo de' Medici in this regard see Jones, *Francesco Vettori*, p. 82.

[4] Bartolomeo Cerretani, 'Storia in dialogo della mutatione di Firenze', MS Biblioteca Nazionale, Florence, II.1.106, fo. 149ʳ (henceforth BNF); Giovanni Cambi, *Istorie ... pubblicate ... da Fr. Ildefonso di San Luigi*, Delizie degli Eruditi Toscani, vols. 20–23 (4 vols., Florence, 1785–6), ii. 308–10; Jacopo Nardi, *Istorie della città di Firenze*, ed. A. Gelli (2 vols., Florence, 1858), i. 428–30. For the best modern studies on the revolution of 1512 see Jones, *Francesco Vettori*, ch. IV; H. C. Butters, 'Florentine Politics 1502–1515', unpub. DPhil. diss. (Oxford, 1974), pp. 168ff.; and J. N. Stephens, 'The Fall of the Florentine Republic, 1512–1530', unpub. DPhil. diss. (Oxford, 1973), chs. 2 and 3; since published under this title (Oxford, 1983).

faction dedicated to the restoration of the Medici regime as it had existed before 1494.[5] By the end of the same month with the calling of a *parlamento* and the appointment of a *balìa* or special council, which was forced through despite the bitter opposition of the republican *ottimati*, the first important steps were taken towards the realization of this aim.[6] Thus began a process which eventually resulted in the destruction of every element in the republican system of government which the Savonarolans had held dear.

Despite Savonarola's execution, the Savonarolans had not done too badly from 1494 to 1512. Always prominent in government, they had become even more influential after the creation of Soderini as *Gonfaloniere a vita* or Gonfalonier for life in 1502, playing a role out of all proportion to their numerical representation in government. With the restoration of the Medici, however—a cataclysmic event whose unexpectedness left them no time to devise a common policy—all this changed. The *parlamento* of September 1512 was called in direct contravention of a law which had been passed at Savonarola's instigation in August 1495, while the creation of a *balìa* signalled the end of the Great Council which had been the hub of the Savonarolan system.[7] In little over a year's time, under the leadership of Lorenzo de' Medici, who had taken over from Giuliano,[8] the constitutional changes were brought to their conclusion with the creation of the *Cento* or Council of the Hundred and the *Settanta* or Council of Seventy.[9]

The period that witnessed the gradual tightening of Medici control in Florence also saw their rise to power in the church. After the death of Julius II, Giovanni de' Medici was elected pope, taking the title of Leo X on 11 March 1513. Soon after, on 9 April, there followed the death of Cosimo de' Pazzi, Archbishop of Florence.[10] The Florentine See thus left vacant was immediately conferred by Leo X on his cousin

---

[5] The best account of the aims and activities of this faction is to be found in Cerretani, 'Dialogo', fos. 149ʳff.

[6] Ibid., fos. 150ᵛ–154ʳ; Filippo de' Nerli, *Commentarj dei fatti civili occorsi dentro la città di Firenze dall'anno 1215 al 1537* (2 vols., Trieste, 1859), i. 185–8.

[7] P. Villari, *La storia di Girolamo Savonarola e de' suoi tempi* (2 vols., Florence, 1930), i. 311–12; Nardi, *Istorie*, ii. 7.

[8] Cerretani, 'Dialogo', fo. 158ʳ⁻ᵛ and esp. fo. 163ᵛ; Francesco Vettori, 'Sommario della storia d'Italia', in F. Niccoli (ed.), *Scritti storici e politici* (Bari, 1972), pp. 152–3.

[9] Cerretani, 'Dialogo', fo. 166ʳ; Cambi, *Istorie*, iii. 33–7. For details of these constitutional changes, see Jones, *Francesco Vettori*, pp. 77–83; Butters, 'Florentine Politics', chs. VI, VII.

[10] Cerretani, 'Dialogo', fo. 162ᵛ.

Giulio, whom he also created cardinal later in the same year.[11] From 1513 onwards, therefore, the Savonarolans had to contend with erstwhile enemies who were not only entrenched in power in the civil government of Florence but also controlled the highest positions in the church.

The disappearance of the last vestiges of Savonarola's Florence was evident no less in matters of policy than in governmental structure. Within the first six months of the restoration, some of the Savonarolans' most cherished political and social reforms were overturned. First to go was the limit on dowries and the prohibition on contracting marriages with foreign potentates which had been instituted only the year before.[12] Then, the Jews were readmitted and empowered once again to lend money in direct competition to the Savonarolan *Monte di Pietà*.[13] Political expediency, moreover, dictated that the pro-French policy should be abandoned in favour of the Spanish alliance.[14] Finally, traditional carnivals and festivals, which Savonarola had transformed into religious celebrations, were restored to their original form, becoming once again, as Giovanni Cambi mourned, revels 'of Sodom and Gomorrah'.[15] But what most aroused the Savonarolans' fury was the desecration of the hall of the Great Council, the 'hall of Christ', the embodiment of the Savonarolan state, which was turned into a soldiers' barracks, with brothel attached.[16]

The nature of these changes and the speed with which they were effected should not, however, lead us to assume that the Medici and their supporters were in full agreement on all matters of policy. While they saw no alternative to dismantling the Savonarolan social and constitutional edifice, they were, from the very beginning, at loggerheads concerning the policy to be pursued towards the Savon-

[11] Ibid., fo. 165ʳ; Luca Landucci, *Diario fiorentino dal 1450 al 1516 continuato da un anonimo fino al 1542*, ed. I. Del Badia (Florence, 1883; repr. Florence, 1969), pp. 338–9; L. G. Cerracchini, *Cronologia sacra dei Vescovi e Arcivescovi di Firenze* (Florence, 1716), pp. 175–6.

[12] Archivio di Stato, Florence, Balìe, 44, fo. 61ᵛ (decree of 11 Oct. 1512). All manuscript references are to collections in the Florentine State Archives unless otherwise indicated.

[13] Landucci, *Diario fiorentino*, p. 348 and n. 1; C. Roth, *The Last Florentine Republic* (London, 1925), pp. 63–4.

[14] Cambi, *Istorie*, ii. 329; Landucci, *Diario fiorentino*, pp. 327, 329.

[15] Cambi, *Istorie*, iii. 24; cf. pp. 2–3, 25, 47.

[16] 'Et quivi', commented the anti-Savonarolan Giovanni Rucellai ironically, 'si faceva gran cera alla barba de' piagnoni' (Cerretani, 'Dialogo', fo. 157ʳ; see also Landucci, *Diario fiorentino*, p. 333). For details of the hall's construction, and for comments on Savonarola's part in it, see J. Wilde, 'The Hall of the Great Council of Florence', *Journal of the Warburg and Courtauld Institutes*, 7 (1944), 65–81.

arolans. The Medici friends (*amici*), well versed in the intricacies of Florentine political life, abreast of the new forces operating in it and fearing, therefore, the danger which the Savonarolans posed to the new government, advocated a policy of total repression.[17] Their arguments, however, fell on deaf ears. Throughout this initial period at least, the Medici, led by Giuliano and Cardinal Giovanni, acted in the belief that some measure of consent was essential if the regime were to prosper. They were fully aware, in other words, of the limited extent of their support, of the doubtful political expertise of their supporters and of their own lack of experience in Florentine politics.[18] They rejected, therefore, the calls by the more extreme of their friends (men like Paolo Vettori, Giovanni Rucellai, Benedetto Buondelmonti, and Luigi della Stufa), and strove, instead, to achieve some degree of continuity, if not in governmental institutions then in personnel, with the preceding regime. They did realize that, with respect to certain individuals, repression was the only answer, but on the whole they were both moderate and circumspect.[19] So, while on the one hand they dislodged both declared enemies and persons of dubious loyalty from vital governmental posts, they attempted on the other hand to ingratiate themselves with the Savonarolans, as one of the major forces in Florentine politics, by permitting them to take part in running the government.

In the experiences of Giovanbattista Ridolfi we have a key example of the Medici's complex policy. On 8 September 1512, Ridolfi had been elected Gonfalonier of Justice for the term of one year.[20] The Medici, acting at the behest of their friends, could not afford, however, to allow such an important post to remain in the hands of the acknowledged leader of the Savonarolans, especially after Ridolfi, in office, had taken decisions which they regarded as detrimental to their safety. It was essential that he be removed; and he was, accordingly, forced to resign on the specious grounds that ill-health prevented him from fulfilling the onerous duties of office.[21] Yet he was too important a

[17] Cerretani, 'Dialogo', fos. 155ʳ, 159ʳ, 160ᵛ, 162ᵛ; Vettori, 'Ricordi', pp. 357–9.

[18] Ibid., p. 358; Cerretani, 'Dialogo', fos. 157ʳ, 158ᵛ, 160ʳ; this awareness is also betrayed in Giuliano's advice to Lorenzo on how to rule in Florence: see 'Instructione al Magnifico Lorenzo', in T. Gar (ed.), 'Documenti risguardanti Giuliano de' Medici e il Pontefice Leone X', *Archivio storico italiano*, App. I (1842–3), 299–306.

[19] Supporters and opponents alike emphasized the Medici's *bontà* (good nature) (see Cerretani, 'Dialogo', fo. 154ʳ, where Giovanni Rucellai decries their excessive 'bontà et patientia'; and Niccolò Valori, 'Ricordanze', BNF Panciaticano 134, fo. 17ᵛ).

[20] Cerretani, 'Dialogo', fo. 150ᵛ.

[21] Ibid., fo. 157ʳ.

person—politically very valuable because of his large following and because of the loyalty he commanded from his friends and clients—to be summarily excluded from politics. While too risky as a Gonfalonier, especially for the period of one year, he was none the less considered suitable as a member of the *balìa*, as one of the twenty *accoppiatori*, or electoral officials, and as a member of the Council of Seventy.[22] For the same reasons, other prominent Savonarolans were encouraged to overcome their distaste for the regime, most notable amongst them Jacopo Salviati, Giovanni de' Medici's brother-in-law, and Lanfredino Lanfredini—the two men who, because of their wealth, standing, and reputation, the Medici had been most concerned to win over during the early months of consolidation.[23] Thus, while the historian Filippo de' Nerli is essentially correct when he states that the most rabid Savonarolans were excluded from the newly created councils of the state,[24] this must not be allowed to obscure the fact that the moderates and the socially prominent were well represented. Two examples will suffice. Of the fifty-five original members of the *balìa*, excluding the eleven nominated members (*arroti*), ten at least were Savonarolans.[25] Among the *accoppiatori*, upon whom the future of the regime largely depended, were five prominent Savonarolans.[26] As contemporaries clearly realized, this was a policy forced upon the Medici by an awareness of their own weakness. It is evident, however, that, as the more fiery of the Medici friends never ceased to reiterate, continued pursuit of this policy compounded the regime's weakness.[27]

A similar conciliatory course was followed by Leo X in Rome. Upon his election, he gave leading Savonarolans such as Giovanni degli Albizzi, Amerigo de' Medici, Fra Zanobi Acciaiuoli, the full benefit of his patronage, receiving them into his household, appointing them to offices within the Curia, and sponsoring their projects.[28] Later still,

---

[22] Ibid., fo. 157ᵛ; Nerli, *Commentarj*, i. 202.

[23] Gar (ed.), 'Documenti', pp. 303–4; Cerretani, 'Dialogo', fos. 151ʳ, 153ʳ.

[24] Nerli, *Commentarj*, i. 190.

[25] Giovanbattista Ridolfi, Roberto di Pagnozzo Ridolfi, Niccolò di Roberto degli Albizzi, Pandolfo Corbinelli, Piero di Jacopo Guicciardini, Lanfredino Lanfredini, Francesco di Chirico Pepi, Giuliano Salviati, Jacopo Salviati, Alessandro d'Antonio Pucci.

[26] Giovanbattista Ridolfi, Pandolfo Corbinelli, Piero Guicciardini, Francesco Pepi, Jacopo Salviati.

[27] Cerretani, 'Dialogo', fos. 157ᵛ, 160ʳ.

[28] A. Ferrajoli, 'Il ruolo della corte di Leone X (1514–1516)', *Archivio della R. Società Romana di storia patria*, 34 (1911), 11, 15; S. Salvini, *Catalogo cronologico de' Canonici della Chiesa Metropolitana fiorentina* (Florence, 1782), p. 67; W. Roscoe, *Vita e pontificato di Leone X* (10 vols., Milan, 1816–1817), x. 27–30.

Cardinal Giulio de' Medici was to adopt a like approach, when in 1519, and before his accession to the papacy, he took over the administration of the regime in Florence.[29]

It is now necessary to ask how, in view of all Savonarola's fulminations against tyrannies in general and that of the Medici in particular, some of his followers felt able to collaborate with those whom he had most detested. Some—and most notably, I would argue, Giorgio Benigno Salviati and Ugolino Verino—were obviously moved by opportunism.[30] Others—best exemplified, perhaps, by Girolamo Benivieni—collaborated because of a quietistic and passive belief that present conditions and adversities had been willed by God and should, therefore, be endured for his love.[31] Close association with the Medici, in however abject a position, meant, moreover, that Benivieni, Giorgio Benigno Salviati, and others were well placed to defend Savonarola's cause and to advocate the preferment of fellow-Savonarolans or sympathizers in important ecclesiastical and lay posts.[32] It was undoubtedly due to the efforts and activities of such men, for instance, that the Savonarolans managed to keep a large measure of control over the Tusco-Roman Congregation of the Dominican order (of which San Marco was the leading convent) for this whole period, despite the efforts of their opponents to block their appointments and to oust them from positions of prominence.[33] Unlike Benivieni, however, the

---

[29] Jacopo Pitti, 'Dell'istoria fiorentina', *Archivio storico italiano*, ser. 1, 1 (1842), 123; Nardi, *Istorie*, ii. 63; Antonio Benivieni, 'Vita di Girolamo Benivieni', MS BNF 11.1.91, p. 258.

[30] On Salviati, see C. Vasoli, 'Notizie su Giorgio Benigno Salviati (Juraj Dragišić)', in *Profezia e ragione. Studi sulla cultura del Cinquecento e del Seicento* (Naples, 1974), pp. 17–127: on Verino, see A. Lazzari, *Ugolino e Michele Verino: Studi biografici e critici* (Turin, 1897), esp. pp. 206–7. Verino had become reconciled with the Savonarolans despite the fact that he had written an invective against Savonarola in 1498.

[31] Pitti, 'Dell'istoria fiorentina', p. 123; Benivieni, 'Vita di Girolamo Benivieni', pp. 258–9.

[32] See letters of Benivieni in App. to C. Re, *Girolamo Benivieni fiorentino* (Città di Castello, 1906), pp. 315–82; see also letter of Cardinal Giulio de' Medici to Girolamo Benivieni in Biblioteca Marucelliana, Florence, B.III.66, fo. 52ʳ, dated 25 June 1523, where Giulio accedes to two requests of Girolamo. For Giorgio Benigno Salviati's role on behalf of the Savonarolan cause, see P. Burlamacchi, 'La vita di fra Girolamo Savonarola', MS BNF, G.5, 1209, fo. 221ʳ.

[33] On the Tusco-Roman Congregation in general and on the names of Vicars General and Priors of the Congregation in particular, see R. Creytens (ed.), 'Les Actes capitulaires de la Congrégation Toscano-Romaine O.P. (1496–1530)', *Archivum fratrum praedicatorum*, 40 (1970), 125–230; see also A. Gherardi, *Nuovi documenti e studi intorno a Girolamo Savonarola* (Florence, 1887; repr. Florence, 1972), p. 337, and G. Benelli, 'Di alcune lettere del Gaetano', *Archivum fratrum praedicatorum*, 5 (1935), 363–75.

majority of Savonarolans refused to accept that adversity was to
be passively endured. They embodied another strain in Savonarolan
ideology: the view that the Christian had an active role to play in
creating the conditions conducive to reform. They understood from
Savonarola's teaching that the individual was responsible for the situation in which he found himself, and responsible, also, for remedying
its defects. They refused to allow that the present regime was beyond
their reach and worked actively against it. Some accepted office in the
new government and sought to mend it from within; others refused to
have any truck with the Medici and took the course of open defiance
and even rebellion.

Those Savonarolans who accepted posts in the regime saw it as their
duty either to modify its more extreme aspects or, at the very least, to
stop it from becoming an open tyranny. In their view, accepting the
Medici's overtures did not entail a total, or even a partial, commitment
to their rule. Their outlook is epitomized in the policies of the two
most eminent Savonarolan office-holders of the time: Jacopo Salviati
and Lanfredino Lanfredini. To a certain extent, the motives of these
two men, as of other prominent Savonarolans who took office under
the Medici, were mixed. They received considerable financial benefit
from their connection with the Medici, especially after the election of
Leo X when Salviati, for instance, was given important concessions
for the farming of papal taxes; nor were they averse to passing and
then exploiting the new liberal legislation concerning marriage and
dowries.[34] Furthermore, political boycott of the regime would have
meant the end of their prominence in Florence because they would,
then, have been unable to satisfy the legitimate demands of friends
and clients for the honours and benefits of government. Although by
no means averse to serving in the new government, they nevertheless
had no wish to see the Medici's power further enhanced. Having tried,
and failed, to prevent the calling of a *parlamento* in September 1512,[35]
they continued undeterred to attempt to restrain the Medici: to lessen
the influence of the more extreme Mediceans while in the meantime
advancing the interests of their friends and of their fellow-Savon-

[34] Stephens, 'The Fall', pp. 108–9; M. M. Bullard, '*Mercatores Florentini Romanam
Curiam Sequentes* in the Early Sixteenth Century', *Journal of Medieval and Renaissance
Studies*, 6 (1976), 51–71; Butters, 'Florentine Politics, 1502–1513', pp. 199ff. Both Salviati
and Lanfredini were appointed *Riformatori del Monte* in 1513 (Cambi, *Istorie*, iii. 12).
On Salviati's subsequent career in papal service, see his letters in Archivio Segreto
Vaticano, Principi 10.

[35] Cerretani, 'Dialogo', fos. 150ᵛ, 151ʳ, 152ʳ⁻ᵛ, 153ʳ.

arolans.[36] Almost unaided, these two men resisted every attempt by the Medici, particularly Lorenzo, to increase their powers or to rule without constitutional restraint. On one occasion, when it was rumoured that Lorenzo planned to make himself sole ruler of Florence, they even threatened to rally the populace against such a move.[37] It was a threat that the Medici could not face—hence the anger of the Mediceans, who were convinced that Salviati was co-ordinating opposition to the regime and covertly working to undermine it.[38]

Naturally, the course adopted by Salviati and Lanfredini was not open to everyone. But neither was it universally attractive. For some Savonarolans there was no possibility of associating in whatever manner with a regime they held to be inimical to the advancement of true religion. So uncompromising was their attitude that they refused even to tolerate a Medici in St Peter's chair.[39] For these men there were only two alternatives. Since the loathed regime was, in their eyes, totally irreclaimable and corrupting, they had either to forsake it altogether or to work for its overthrow. Amongst those who took the former course of voluntary exile were several friars of San Marco: Tommaso Caiani, the Bettini brothers, Bartolomeo Soderini.[40] The latter course, of open defiance and rebellion, was fraught with danger. Despite this, certain Savonarolans, having little care for their own safety, adopted it.

In the first two years of the new regime seven Savonarolans, in separate incidents, dared to challenge the power of the Medici, either by refusing to accept the legitimacy of the regime or by plotting for

---

[36] Ibid., fos. 158ᵛ–159ʳ. See also Nerli, *Commentarj*, i. 191–2.

[37] Nerli, *Commentarj*, i. 208–9; Cambi, *Istorie*, iii. 150–1. Anzilotti, *La crisi costituzionale*, p. 63; Jones, *Francesco Vettori*, p. 112; Stephens, 'The Fall', pp. 65–7; letter of Galeotto de' Medici to Lorenzo, n.d., Archivio Mediceo avanti il Principato (henceforth MAP), cxvi, fo. 95ʳ⁻ᵛ. Relations between Jacopo Salviati and Lorenzo de' Medici soon became very strained; see the letter of Alfonsina Orsini de' Medici to Lorenzo, 9 Feb. 1514, ibid. cxiv, fo. 52ʳ⁻ᵛ; see also a letter by the same to Lanfredini, 10 Dec. 1513, BNF ii.v.22, fo. 48ʳ.

[38] Cerretani, 'Dialogo', fos. 158ᵛ–159ʳ where Giovanni Rucellai, voicing also the frustrations of the other *amici*, states that Jacopo Salviati 'non attese mai ad altro che r'introdurre [nello stato] e tener viva la parte del frate, di chi e' fu sì divoto et riuscivavi … di che moltissime volte fumo tra noi insieme et disperavoci' (see also fo. 181ʳ).

[39] Benedetto Luschino. *Vulnera diligentis*, Pt I, MS BNF Magl. xxxiv, 7, fo. 1ʳ and Pt III, Biblioteca Riccardiana, Florence (henceforth BRF), 2985, fos. 52ᵛ–54ᵛ, 56ᵛ–58ᵛ.

[40] Francesco Guicciardini, *Carteggi*, vol. i (Fonti per la storia d'Italia, 3), ed. R. Palmarocchi (Bologna, 1938), p. 123; Creytens, 'Les Actes capitulaires', pp. 170, 183; A. Giorgetti, 'Fra Luca Bettini e la sua difesa del Savonarola', *Archivio storico italiano*, 77, 2 (1919), 164ff.

its overthrow. The first to be arrested was Martino di Francesco Scarfi, already notorious for having arranged, in 1502, with another Savonarolan, Tommaso di Paolantonio Soderini, the pact between the Savonarolans and their opponents the *Arrabbiati* to make a common front against the Medici.[41] For plotting against the regime, Martino Scarfi was arrested, fined, and exiled for five years.[42] Shortly afterwards and for the same reasons Bartolomeo Redditi, Giusto di Piero della Badessa, and two friars of Ognissanti (Niccolò di Matteo d'Agostino and Lorenzo di Eugenio da Cigoli) were also arrested and exiled.[43] Later in 1513 and in December 1514, two other Savonarolans, Francesco del Pugliese and Bartolomeo di Pandolfo Pandolfini, were also arrested and exiled for up to ten years for agitating against the regime.[44]

To this band of activists must be added those Savonarolans who courted political and financial disaster by refusing to acknowledge the changed political situation in Florence and shunned, therefore, any accommodation with the regime: men like Ser Giuliano da Ripa, Tommaso Tosinghi, and, for a while at least, Niccolò Valori. Past misdeeds and their present attitude rendered these men so notorious that little could be done by fellow-Savonarolans on their behalf without the risk of becoming compromised. They were, accordingly, hounded out of office, ostracized, punitively taxed, placed under arrest whenever a crisis was in the offing, and, when all else failed, exiled from Florence.[45] In the words of one of them, Tommaso Tosinghi, we can

---

[41] Piero Parenti, *Istorie fiorentine*, part. ed. by J. Schnitzer, *Quellen und Forschungen zur Geschichte Savonarolas*, iv (Leipzig, 1910), 296. For biographical details on both men, see Villari, *La storia*, ii. App. pp. clvii, clix, clxxviii, cciv, cclxxxii; see also Francesco Cei, 'Cronaca', MS BNF 11.v.147, p. 155.

[42] Otto di Guardia, Ep. Rep., 155, fos. 15ᵛ–16ʳ; 230, fo. 99ʳ. See also Landucci, *Diario fiorentino*, p. 334.

[43] Otto di Guardia, Ep. Rep., 156, fos. 20ᵛ, 22ᵛ–23ʳ; 230, fo. 108ʳ⁻ᵛ. See also Parenti, *Istorie fiorentine*, p. 301. Redditi was the author of a *Breve compendio ... della verità predicata e profetata dal R.P. fra Girolamo de Ferrara*, ed. by J. Schnitzer, in *Quellen und Forschungen zur Geschichte Savonarolas*, ii (Munich, 1902).

[44] For Francesco del Pugliese's condemnation, see Otto di Guardia, Ep. Rep., 157, fo. 3ʳ. See also Cambi, *Istorie*, iii. 28. On his role in the Savonarolan movement, see Villari, *La storia*, ii. App., *passim*; and Parenti, *Istorie fiorentine*, p. 275; but see also Archivio di Stato, Milan, Potenze estere, Firenze, 947, busta 3. For Bartolomeo Pandolfini's sentence, see Otto di Guardia, Ep. Rep., 160, fo. 75ᵛ, and on him see Villari, *La storia*, ii. App., p. ccxxviii.

[45] Valori, 'Ricordanze', fo. 18ʳ⁻ᵛ; Tommaso Tosinghi, [*Vita*], BNF 11.11.325, fos. 126ʳ–130ᵛ. On Ser Giuliano da Ripa who, because of his conduct, became a symbol of Savonarolan defiance, see Cambi, *Istorie*, ii. 89; Parenti, *Istorie fiorentine*, pp. 124–6, 128; B. Varchi, *Storia fiorentina* (2 vols., Florence, 1963), i. 103; Guicciardini, *Carteggi*, i. 123. He was arraigned before the *Signoria* three times (Signori e Collegi, Deliberazioni Ord. Aut., 115, fos. 133ᵛ, 139ʳ, 140ʳ), and before the Otto di Guardia on at least one

see the consequences of this defiance and, above all, the ideological reasons behind it. As he states with ill-repressed fury, he had been spared only his life. As for the rest, apart from imprisonment and exile, he had been subjected to

most grievous imposts, forced loans beyond all reason, dishonest taxes: in effect, I was in everything dealt with as an enemy of the state. And as for the scrutinies, neither I nor my sons have ever been selected for any office ... And should someone say: 'Why have your friends not been treated like you', I reply, that had I wanted to go cap in hand and accommodate myself to today's rule, as some others have done, I believe I should have found a place, as they have; but, since I deem this rule to be totally against my taste, I have never been able to come to terms with it and ... I believe and indeed I have firm hope that in so doing I will be rewarded by God. And therefore I leave as a maxim to my sons rather to direct their attention to those things which are to the honour of God than to favour regimes which come to power by violent means.[46]

Obdurate resistance of this kind, accompanied as it was all the while by a rash of prophecies foretelling the imminent collapse of the Medici in both Florence and Rome, could have only unsettling effects on a regime that was already experiencing, as we have seen, grave internal difficulties. As the Medici friends strongly remonstrated, clearly the time had now come to do away with the problems the Savonarolans posed to the state.[47] This was also the opinion of Leo X and of Cardinal Giulio in Rome, who had been badly shaken by the reports of the inflammatory, anti-Medicean import of the prophetic sermons delivered by Fra Francesco da Montepulciano in Santa Croce, in November 1513, and by the disclosure, made at the trial of the Camaldolese Don

occasion (MAP CXVI, fo. 119^{r-v}: a letter of Galeotto de' Medici to Lorenzo, 7 Feb. 1515; CXLI, fo. 96^v: Lorenzo to Galeotto, 10 Feb. 1515).

[46] Tosinghi, [*Vita*], fo. 129^v:

albitrii disonestissimi, acchatti fuori d'ogni dovere, gravamenti disonesti, e in effetto in ogni chosa trattato come nimicho dello stato. E quanto alli squittini, nè io nè mia figliuoli mai fumo tratti a nulla ... E chi diciessi: 'Perchè non sono istati trattati gli altri tua chonpagni come te?' Rispondo che se io avessi voluto ciercare venia e achomodarmi al vivere d'oggi chome [h]anno fatto degli altri, chrederrei avere trovato lato chome loro; ma parendomi questo vivere totalmente chontro al gusto mio, non mi sono mai potuto achordare e ... chredo e [h]o ferma speranza mi sarà giovato appresso a Dio. E chosì lascio per ricordo ai figliuoli mia che più presto e' dirischino a quelle chose che sono l'onore di Dio, che favorire stati violenti.

Dr R. Pesman kindly provided me with a transcription of this document.

[47] MAP CXVI, fo. 119^r (letter of Galeotto to Lorenzo, 7 Feb. 1515).

Teodoro in January 1515, of the dangerous secret activities in which some followers of Savonarola were engaged.[48]

But, as the hapless Lorenzo realized, it was one thing to agree on the need for a repressive policy, and quite another to implement it. The problem here was not a lack of institutional or coercive powers; on the contrary, it could be argued that no Medicean regime in the past had been as powerful as the present one in terms of the control it could exercise on the institutions of government and even on the social life of the city.[49] Instead the problem was related not to the institutions but to the process of government. It concerned, in short, the Medici's inability, or unwillingness, to bring under control, to channel constructively, and to rationalize the various sources of patronage at their disposal. The ever-increasing, and conflicting, demands for office, honours, and favours were never properly sifted and co-ordinated. It was an intractable problem of both volume and evaluation.[50] And here the fault lay ultimately with individual members of the Medici family who thought they could ingratiate themselves with, and profitably manipulate, the competing forces in Florence by acceding to their requests. Lorenzo might have been, theoretically, in control in Florence; but his policy could effectively be undermined in Rome by Leo X and Giulio, who were continually harassed by a gaggle of very determined and rapacious Medici women and agents, all of them pleading for particular clients, interests and causes and all

---

[48] MAP LXVI, fo. 303 (letter of Giulio de' Medici to Lorenzo, 22 Dec. 1513, where Lorenzo is given a contemptuous lesson in politics and told, for the future, to keep 'La briglia in mano'). See also Archivio Segreto Vaticano, Arm. XXXIX, 30 (Leo X: Brevia ad Principes), fo. 161ʳ (a brief of Leo to the Florentines); Lorenzo's justifications to Giulio, of 24 Dec. 1513 (in Carte Strozziane, Ser. I, 3, fo. 29ʳ, and D. Moreni, *Continuazione delle memorie istoriche dell'Ambrosiana R. Basilica di S. Lorenzo* (2 vols., Florence, 1804–17), ii. App. 511–15. On Fra Francesco da Montepulciano and Don Teodoro, see Cambi, *Istorie*, iii. 37–9, 60–2.

[49] Already in 1513 Jacopo Salviati was complaining, through his wife Lucrezia in Rome, that Lorenzo was controlling marriage alliances in Florence (letter of Alfonsina Orsini to Lanfredino Lanfredini, 10 December 1513, BNF II.V.22, fo. 48ʳ). See also Goro Gheri, *Copialettere*, [Fuori Serie], i. fo. 3ᵛ (letter to Lorenzo de' Medici, 18 October 1516, on whether a marriage contract should be approved).

[50] Some idea of the dimensions of the problem can be obtained by consulting the letters in MAP, such as, for example, filze CV, CVIII, CXIV–CXVI, CXLI; the 5 vols. of Goro Gheri's *Copialettere* in ASF; and the private correspondence of Lanfredino Lanfredini in BNF II.V.22–4. It seems, moreover, that inability to cope with the many inopportune requests resulted in promises being made which it was not intended to fulfil. See, e.g., Gheri, *Copialettere*, iv. fos. 221ᵛ–225ᵛ, where Gheri retracts a *raccomandazione* he had made ('non mi parendo poterli denegare una tal lettera'), on behalf of Fra Filippo Strozzi.

determined to have their way regardless of the consequences for the regime.[51] Medici resources and ingenuity were great, but not endless. The strain upon the regime became more and more evident as an increasing number of Mediceans, finding erstwhile enemies preferred to office and their own legitimate expectations unfulfilled, became disenchanted with it.[52] Of even greater significance than the failure of the regime in this regard is the fact that its uncontrolled exercise of influence or patronage worked to the advantage of the Savonarolan malcontents. The leading members of the Medici family might have agreed, as a matter of policy, to bring the Savonarolans under control; but it did not follow that other members of the family—or even Leo, Giulio, and Lorenzo themselves—would abide by the decision at all times and not interfere with its proper execution.[53] Thus, of the cases already discussed, Bartolomeo Redditi was recalled from exile and relieved of all disabilities at the request, it seems, of Cardinal Giulio,[54] while Filippo del Pugliese served only two years of his ten-year term of exile because of the strong intercession of Alfonsina Orsini, Lorenzo's mother, on his behalf.[55]

Individual Savonarolans, especially if tactless and imprudent, continued to be arrested, removed from office, expelled from the convents of the city and exiled, but there was never, for the reasons already outlined, any chance that a thoroughgoing policy of repression could succeed. The regime was by now too thoroughly infiltrated by Savonarolans and the Medici too much at odds with each other for it to be otherwise. There is no clearer demonstration of this than the failure

[51] The best description of the press round Leo X, of the rivalry amongst the friends and of the clamouring for favours, is made by one of the participants, Alfonsina Orsini. See, e.g., MAP CXIV, 51 (Alfonsina to Lorenzo de' Medici, 11 Feb. 1514).

[52] Cerretani, 'Dialogo', fo. 181ʳ; Goro Gheri, *Copialettere*, i. fos. 221ᵛ–222ʳ (letter to Alfonsina Orsini, 4 Jan. 1517); v. fo. 35ʳ (letter to Benedetto Buondelmonti, 30 Apr. 1519).

[53] An example of the counterproductive meddling that went on is provided by the reactions of various members of the regime to the candidature of Girolamo Benivieni for the post of *Officiale di Studio* in Dec. 1514. Writing to Lorenzo in Rome, his deputy Galeotto de' Medici signified his and the *amici*'s disapproval because of Benivieni's 'piangnoneria'. This consideration was of little account to Lorenzo who replied that the appointment should nevertheless go ahead. With Lorenzo absent in Rome, however, Galeotto's view prevailed and Benivieni was not appointed (Galeotto de' Medici to Lorenzo, 2 Dec. 1514, MAP CXVI, 501; Lorenzo de' Medici to Galeotto, 6–8 Dec. 1514 in ibid. CXLI, fo. 82ʳ). See also Cambi, *Istorie*, iii. 53, for the names of the successful candidates.

[54] Otto di Guardia, Ep. Rep., 156, fo. 38ʳ⁻ᵛ; 159, fos. 6ᵛ, 58ᵛ.

[55] Alfonsina to Lorenzo, 16 Feb. 1514, and Lorenzo to Alfonsina, 4 Mar. 1514 (MAP CXIV, fo. 58ʳ; CXLI, fo. 4ᵛ).

of Leo X and Cardinal Giulio to have the Florentine Synod of 1516
and the tenth session of the V Lateran Council issue an unequivocal
condemnation of the Savonarolan movement.[56]

Such was the disarray amongst the Medici, moreover, and so open
were they to blandishments, that they gave their blessing to some
highly damaging Savonarolan initiatives. They lent their support, for
instance, to the proceedings for the canonization of St Antoninus:
unexceptionable and even patriotic, were it not for the fact that the
friars of San Marco were behind it and that it revived the flagging
fortunes of that convent as a spiritual and civic centre.[57] Similarly ill-
advised was Cardinal Giulio's and Leo X's blessing, and financial
support, for a newly founded confraternity which was to finance,
build, and manage the hospital of the *Incurabili*. The confraternity
was of Savonarolan inspiration and was controlled by them from the
beginning.[58]

In the circumstances, it is not surprising to find that after Leo X's
accession no important member of the Medici family wished to remain
in charge in Florence. They tended, instead, to flee to Rome on the
slightest pretext. Lorenzo for instance, who had not wanted the job in
the first place, went to Rome on at least four separate occasions, once
for as long as nine months, and the last time was received so 'rudely
and with words and in ways [so] offensive' by the Pope that he went

---

[56] Despite the secrecy with which the proceedings against the Savonarolan movement
was shrouded, his followers found out what was afoot from two informants at the papal
court—Fra Bonifacio Landino and Fra Mariano Fetti; they then were able to mount a
successful defence; see Zaccaria di Lunigiana, *Defensio Fratris Zachariae Lunensis qua
tuetur Hieronymum Savonarolae sociosque ab haeresi* (MS BNF, Conventi Soppressi,
J.1.46, fos. 1^r–18^v); Luca Bettini, *Opus Fratris Luce Bectinis ... in defensionem fratris
Hieronymi Savonarolae ferrariensis ... tempore Synodi compositum florentinae
MDXVI* (MS BRF, 2053, fos. 1^r–21^v); and letters of Lorenzo de' Medici to Galeotto
and to Luigi della Stufa, both dated 10 Feb. 1515 (MAP CXLI, fos. 96^v, 97^r). On the
whole issue, see G. Schnitzer, *Savonarola* (2 vols., Milan, 1931), ii. 476–7.

[57] S. Orlandi, 'La canonizzazione di S. Antonio nella relazione di Fra Roberto Ubaldini
da Gagliano', *Memorie domenicane*, NS 40 (1964), 85–115, 131–62. For indications that
the money collected for the expenses of canonization was diverted to other uses, see
Archivio Generale dell'Ordine Domenicano, Santa Sabina, Rome, Tabularium Ordinis
Praedicatorum, IV.19., fo. 32^v.

[58] Cambi, *Istorie*, iii. 159–61; L. Passerini, *Storia degli stabilimenti di beneficenza e
d'istruzione elementare gratuita della città di Firenze* (Florence, 1853), pp. 203–9; G.
Conti, *Fatti e anedotti di storia fiorentina* (Florence, 1902), pp. 450–1. Of the thirteen
officers appointed to lead the confraternity, four (including the Prior) were Savonarolan
(i.e. Alessandro d'Antonio Pucci, Simone del Nero, Marco Strozzi, and Bartolomeo
Redditi).

1. Tomb of Ubertino da Carrara. Padua, Eremitani.

2. Tomb of Jacopo da Carrara. Padua, Eremitani.

3. Guariento, Old Testament cycle. Padua, Reggia Carrarese, Capella dei Principi (now the Accademia).

4. *The Thebaid*, Canto 4. Dublin, Chester Beatty Library.

6. Altichiero, Medallion inset, *Crucifixion*. Padua, Oratory of St George.

5. Altichiero, Medallion inset, *Crucifixion*. Padua, Oratory of St George.

7. Guariento, *Luna*. Padua, Eremitani, Chapel of St Augustine.

8. Guariento, *Mars*. Padua, Eremitani, Chapel of St Augustine.

9. Altichiero, *Council of Ramiro*. Padua, Sant'Antonio, Chapel of Sant Felice.

10. (*above*) Altichiero, *Baptism of King Sevio*. Padua, Oratory of St George.

11. (*right*) Altichiero, *Martyrdom of St George*, detail. Padua, Oratory of St George.

12. Giusto de Menabuoi, frescos. Padua, Baptistery, interior.

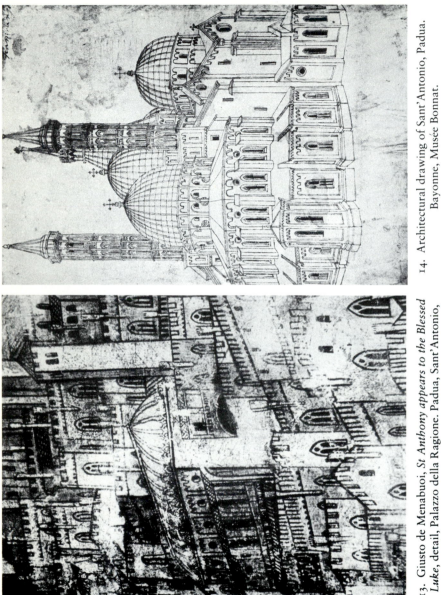

13. Giusto de Menabuoi, *St Anthony appears to the Blessed Luke*, detail, Palazzo della Ragione. Padua, Sant'Antonio,

14. Architectural drawing of Sant'Antonio, Padua. Bayonne, Musée Bonnat.

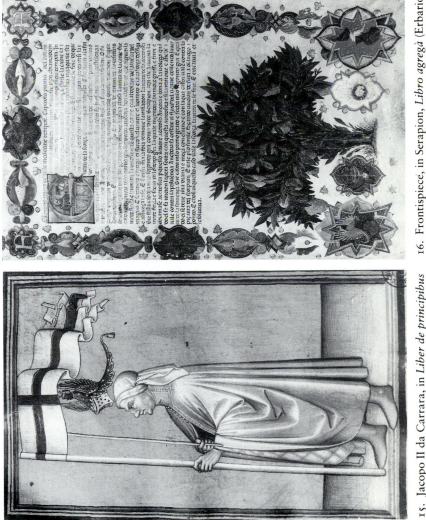

15. Jacopo II da Carrara, in *Liber de principibus Carrariensibus*. Padua, Museo Civico, MS BP 158.

16. Frontispiece, in Serapion, *Libro agregà* (Erbario Carrarese). London, British Museum, Eg. 2020.

17. Domenico Ghirlandaio, *Annunciation to Zacharias*. Florence, Santa Maria Novella, Tornaquinci Chapel.

18. Domenico Ghirlandaio, *Expulsion of Joachim*. Florence, Santa Maria Novella, Tornaquinci Chapel.

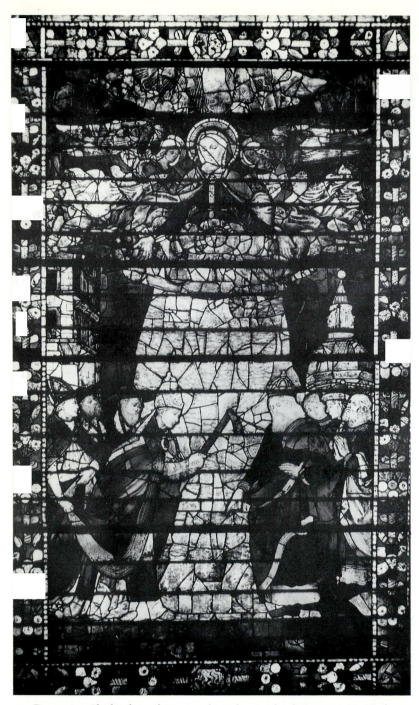

19. Domenico Ghirlandaio (design) and Sandro Agolandi (execution), *Madonna of the Snow*, stained glass. Florence, Santa Maria Novella, Tornaquinci Chapel.

20. Guidotti, *View of the Palazzo Doria*, Genoa (1769).

21. Reconstruction of the garden façade of the Palazzo del Tè in Mantua, from E. Verheyen, *The Palazzo del Tè in Mantua: Images of Love and Politics* (Baltimore and London: Johns Hopkins University Press, 1977).

22. Magno Palazzo, Castello del Buonconsiglio, Trent.

23. Marcello Fogolino, Ceiling decoration, c. 1532. Trent, Magno Palazzo, Stanza del Torrione.

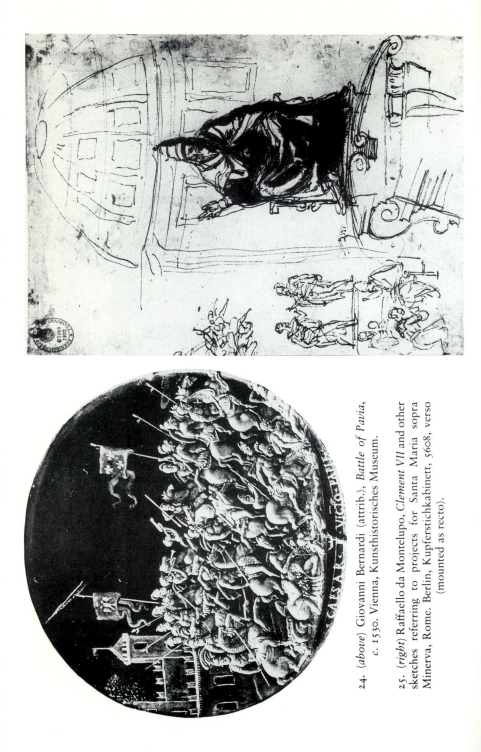

24. (*above*) Giovanni Bernardi (attrib.), *Battle of Pavia*,
c. 1530. Vienna, Kunsthistorisches Museum.

25. (*right*) Raffaello da Montelupo, *Clement VII* and other
sketches referring to projects for Santa Maria sopra
Minerva, Rome. Berlin, Kupferstichkabinett, 5608, verso
(mounted as recto).

back to Florence in a huff.[59] It was not, I emphasize, because pickings were better in Rome—though they undoubtedly were—but because being in power in Florence was a thankless task. As a result, recourse was had more and more to deputies, who were charged with the administration of government in Florence: Galeotto de' Medici, Goro Gheri, and Silvio Passerini, Cardinal of Cortona. The appointment of these men, though highly resented by all Florentines of whatever political persuasion and therefore a major contributing factor to the Medici's fall in 1527, was, nevertheless, a blow to the Savonarolans. Because they had owed their appointment and therefore their allegiance to only one member of the Medici household, they had been able to use delaying tactics against unwelcome pressure by citing their orders or by referring matters back to their 'padrone'.[60] By these means they were, in effect, bureaucratizing the whole process of patronage. It was under the stewardship of the Medicean deputies, especially of the Cardinal of Cortona after 1523, that repression of the Savonarolans was most successful. Even though important Savonarolans, by now well entrenched in the regime, could not be touched, their influence was greatly reduced, especially in matters relating to the prosecution of the campaign against fellow-Savonarolans. Devoid of protection, some of the socially less eminent Savonarolans were forced to come to terms with the regime.[61] Others joined their brethren in exile, especially in such centres as Mirandola, Bologna, Venice, and Lyons, which became the new centres for printing Savonarolan texts. By far the greater majority, however, remained in Florence, their devotion to Savonarola undiminished, though they were by now forced to display it only in private shrines or in secret conventicles of infiltrated legitimate confraternities.

The experiences of the final few years of Medici rule before their overthrow in 1527 inform the whole history of the last Florentine Republic from 1527 to 1530. The Republic, which came increasingly under Savonarolan control and which relied from the beginning on Savonarolan ideology to justify its policies and its very existence, presented throughout a rigid and uncompromising face to the world.

---

[59] Cerretani, 'Dialogo', fos. 179^v–180^r: 'salvaticamente et con parole e modi [sì] ingiuriosi.'

[60] See, e.g., Goro Gheri, *Copialettere*, i. fos. 11^v, 161^v, 164^r; iii. fo. 27^r; iv. fos. 58^v–59^r.

[61] Such as Niccolò Valori, Lorenzo Violi, and Carlo del Benino, all of whom were to obtain official posts in the regime for the first time. Valori was appointed Florentine ambassador to Rome, Violi as Second Chancellor, and del Benino as Gonfalonier of Justice.

Intolerant and revengeful, it persecuted not only declared Mediceans, but also those Savonarolans who had collaborated with the preceding regime and who had thus become guilty of betraying God and of exposing their less well-placed brethren by failing to protect them: Jacopo Salviati, Pier Ridolfi, Carlo del Benino, and many others, including the harmless Girolamo Benivieni.[62] Neither past merits nor status now stilled suspicion or stopped the bloodshed. When the Mediceans made their return to the city in 1530, they had learned their lesson. As Clement VII made abundantly clear, there would be no repetition of past errors. The Medici would by no means countenance a restoration of the political system which had served them so badly between 1512 and 1527.[63]

The settlement imposed on Florence in 1532 was notable as much for the constitutional changes that did away with traditional institutions as for the way in which power was now concentrated in the hands of the new *principe*, Alessandro de' Medici, to the almost complete exclusion of other Florentines, however highly placed.[64] In the way in which first Alessandro and then Cosimo interpreted the new constitution, in their concern for control and centralization, there was no possibility of resorting to patronage, whether private or governmental, to undermine the stability of the regime.[65] Political survival now depended entirely on the will of the Dukes; and prominent Savonarolans, like the other Florentines of the same class, were forced to come to terms with the Medici. Savonarolan activity was forced underground. A radicalized Savonarolan ideology became almost exclusively the preserve of the socially humble and of the politically disenfranchised.[66]

---

[62] Balìe, 46, fos. 104^r, 107^{r-v}, 108^r; also a letter of Girolamo Benivieni to Jacopo Salviati, Sept. 1530 (in Re, *Girolamo Benivieni fiorentino*, App., p. 348).

[63] Nerli, *Commentarj*, ii. 181ff., esp. p. 200; and 'Discorsi intorno alla riforma dello stato di Firenze', ed. G. Capponi, *Archivio storico italiano*, ser. 1, 1 (1842), 413–77.

[64] A. Anzilotti, *La costituzione interna dello Stato Fiorentino sotto il duca Cosimo I de' Medici* (Florence, 1910), pp. 12–16, 25–30.

[65] As Anzilotti saw, it was crucial to this achievement of centralization that Alessandro and Cosimo relied on 'persone di fiducia' (predominantly they were secretaries), to run the affairs of state rather than relying on the Council of State (see ibid., pp. 30–1, 46–50, 142 and *passim*).

[66] See, e.g., the social composition of the conventicle of the *Capi rossi*, formed exclusively of *sottoposti* (BNF Magl. VIII, 1398, fos. 32^r–34^r).

PART II

Cui Bono?: Patronage and the Artist

9

The Empire of Things: Consumer Demand in Renaissance Italy

RICHARD GOLDTHWAITE

THE patronage of art in Renaissance Italy is a subject that would seem not to lend itself to economic analysis. Tradition, going back to the Renaissance itself, has so loaded the term with notions about the individuality of patron and artist and about the uniqueness of the work of art that almost by definition patronage defies generalization. Some obvious economic questions—where the money came from, how much art cost, what constraints the patron's financial interests imposed on the artist—have been raised in studies of specific instances of patronage, but the subject has yet to be placed in the larger context of the economic and social life of the times.[1]

Yet, as Pierre Bourdieu has written, art cannot remain isolated on 'a sacred island systematically and ostentatiously opposed to the profane, everyday world of production, a sanctuary for gratuitous disinterested activity in a universe given over to money and self-interest'.[2] It too has a price and is acquired, in part at least, as a result of economic decisions. One way to get a broader perspective on the patronage of art, therefore, is to regard it as a form of consumption. In this light, art looks somewhat different from what we are usually told about it—less 'beautiful', perhaps, as something that exists in and of itself on its own terms, but none the less interesting as an aspect of the material culture of its time. In fact, it was only in the course of the

---

[1] Cf. Francis Haskell in the preface to his classic study of patronage in Italy, *Patrons and Painters: A Study in the Relations Between Italian Art and Society in the Age of the Baroque* (London, 1963):

> I have also fought shy of generalisations ... Inevitably I have been forced to think again and again about the relations between art and society, but nothing in my researches has convinced me of the existence of underlying laws which will be valid in all circumstances ... I hope that the bringing together of so much material may inspire others to find a synthesis where I have been unable to do so.

[2] P. Bourdieu, *Outline of a Theory of Practice* (Cambridge, 1977), p. 197.

Renaissance that art created consciously as such emerged as a specific kind of object; and much of the 'art' that fills our museums today never achieved that distinctive status at the time. Indeed, our museums are, in a very real sense, monuments to the luxury consumption of the past—temples, even, where a consumer society pays homage to the passion for spending that gives life to the capitalist system of the West.

As a consumption phenomenon the patronage of art in Renaissance Italy represents something new in the history of art in a quantitative as well as a qualitative sense, for men not only redirected their spending habits according to new canons of taste but they demanded substantially more art and a greater variety of it. Secular architecture came into its own, especially with the house, or palace, and its wider spatial setting, the city as a whole; and with the country house, or villa, and its wider spatial setting, the garden. Sculpture broadened its range to take in everything from miniatures and medals to equestrian monuments for the adornment of all these places, both inside in palaces and villas and outside in gardens and city squares. Furnishings of every kind, from pottery and beds to paintings and frescos, proliferated to fill up interior spaces. In the area of religious art it is difficult to say that the kind of goods changed in any appreciable way during the Renaissance. Churches and their decoration, from paintings and liturgical utensils on altars to frescos on walls, were of course nothing new; but, if the demand for these things in the Renaissance simply continued old habits, now with a taste for a new style, the level of consumption was nevertheless extraordinarily impressive, both in building and furnishing new churches and in rebuilding and renovating older ones.

Apart from stylistic innovation, all this consumption was a notable economic activity. Had palaces and churches, villas and gardens, sculpture and painting, domestic and liturgical furnishings all been produced in the traditional medieval style, we would still be confronted with an abundance and variety of goods that add up to a veritable 'empire of things'. The phrase is from Henry James; and although the world had become infinitely more cluttered by the time he was writing, the consumer society of which he was such a keen observer had its first stirrings, if not its birth, in the new habits of spending that possessed the Italians in the Renaissance. As much as anything else, these habits marked what is new about the Renaissance and what sets Italy off, economically as well as culturally, from the rest of Europe at the time.

The 'empire of things' the Italians built up for themselves in the Renaissance looms large in the economic historian's view of the period —but as a vast wasteland of spending that has repulsed rather than invited exploration. It has been taken for granted that such a massive appropriation of resources is in one way or another to be associated with economic decline, although there has not been much more than casual speculation about whence the money came to finance so much consumption. The nature of this material culture, however, and what gave rise to these consumption habits in the first place, have been remote from the interests of economic historians. We have never been very comfortable with demand: it is generally thought to arise from the psychic depths of personality, the cultural depths of society, or some such abyssal place in the realm of motivations well beyond the economist's pale.[3]

It ought to be possible, however, to make some economic sense out of demand by regarding consumption very much as Henry James did, as a basic economic and social process. Rather than buying goods just for private enjoyment, inspired by his own individual tastes, man fills up his environment to give order to his world, a meaning that justifies his very existence. Man buys intentionally as the result of a deliberate decision informed by the values of his culture; the totality of his consumption, therefore, has a certain coherence. To the extent that the goods man surrounds himself with help establish, and maintain, his relations with other men, consumption involves him in a sort of ritual activity; and even if certain kinds of consumption seem only to satisfy personal pleasure rather than make a social statement, it is nevertheless likely that those pleasures themselves are socially conditioned.[4]

If consumption is regarded in this way, we obviously cannot be satisfied to explain the rise of the Italian 'empire of things' as merely the result of greater wealth, for greater wealth alone does not explain why men wanted new kinds of objects. Nor is it enough to say that 'conspicuous consumption' was a form of social competition motivated by the desire for prestige, for prestige alone does not explain why the particular things men wanted had prestige value. What is proposed

---

[3] Carlo Cipolla discusses demand in a general way in *Before the Industrial Revolution: European Society and Economy, 1000–1700* (New York and London, 1976); but as editor of *The Fontana Economic History of Europe* he was not able to persuade his contributors to make any breakthrough in dealing with it in specific historical contexts.

[4] See M. Douglas and B. Isherwood, *The World of Goods* (New York, 1979).

here, in short, is an approach that regards any particular historical configuration of consumption habits as a function of the culture of that moment—and an approach, incidentally, that looks at consumption as a whole, blurring the distinction between luxury goods and necessities, between taste and needs, between, even, art and other kinds of objects.

For art, too, belongs in this context. Considered simply as a consumer object, art is as much an index of culture as the style in which those goods were made and as any of the scholarly, literary, and religious ideas that make up its intellectual content. Whereas we know something about how art eventually achieved its intellectual status in the Renaissance, we do not know very much about why many kinds of art objects came into existence in the first place. In any case, the eventual emergence of an attitude about art as a particular kind of object, consciously endowed with style and with content, is one of the most notable features of the Renaissance; and by the same token the emergence of self-conscious patronage of the arts, in practice and as an ideal, marks one distinctive way consumption habits changed in the Renaissance.

Goods, in short, communicate something about culture; and, since they have value and require economic decisions, the study of preferences in men's spending habits ought to be one way the economic historian can explore the material world in order to reach into the higher realms of cultural history and yet keep his feet solidly on his own ground. In the following discussion some of the evidence about men's spending habits in the private domestic world of Renaissance Italy is organized along these lines in an attempt to propose a hypothesis for further research into the consumer culture which is the context in which the specific demand for art—that is, patronage—can eventually be studied.

The problem, then, is to explain the Renaissance 'empire of things' as a validation of a way of life that was sustained by more and more possessions. The habits of spending that gave rise to this material culture signals something new in the history of the West. The traditional values of medieval Europe found only a limited outlet in the purchase of goods. The religious rationale for private expenditures was obviously limited; and, indeed, for urban residents in the expanding commercial centres of Italy who were constantly reminded that avarice, usury, and cheating were ubiquitous threats to the prevailing moral order, it was simply better not to spend money at all in any way that would draw attention to the fact of one's wealth.

Feudalism provided the only real secular model for luxury expenditures, but it was an expression of values and attitudes that were remote from the realities of Renaissance Italy. However transformed feudalism had become by the time it reached its 'bastardized' form in England and its 'non-feudal' form in France at the end of the Middle Ages, it still survived in many spheres—in the hierarchical structure of the upper class, in the organization of the social life of nobles around the households of great magnates, in their military ethos, and in their landed interests. At a time when central monarchical government was generally unstable, common interests drew landowners together in 'affinities' or 'alliances' under the auspices of a local magnate who could use his power to offer protection and dispense patronage. The bonds that held these groups together were mutual self-interest rather than contractual obligations of a classical feudal kind; but the system was personalized by the cult of lordship, with its emphasis on service, fidelity, and obedience, and by a sense of class, with a heightened feeling for the solidarity of the lineage—all traditional feudal values.[5]

The chivalric code expressed these very values; and it therefore could still be evoked by the upper class as a rationale for its social behaviour. The model of the knight loomed larger than ever, both for great magnates and kings who needed to inspire loyalty and military ardour, and for the nobility as a whole which needed to sharpen its definition of itself at a time when its ranks were becoming increasingly diversified and its privileges threatened. That the late medieval affinity was no longer primarily military did not weaken the appeal of the chivalric code; as Maurice Keen has written, the greater emphasis that came to be put on nobility of blood rather than on the actual taking of knighthood 'clearly did not, in any significant degree, undermine the conception of the essential role of the secular aristocracy as being a martial one'.[6] Hence, for Keen and for others, the resurgence of

---

[5] P. S. Lewis, 'Decayed and Non-feudalism in Later Medieval France', *Bulletin of the Institute of Historical Research*, 37 (1964), 157–84; idem., *Later Medieval France: the Polity* (New York, 1968), pp. 175–208; C. Carpenter, 'The Beauchamp Affinity: A Study of Bastard Feudalism at Work', *English Historical Review*, 95 (1980), 514–32; G. L. Harriss, Introduction to *England in the Fifteenth Century: The Collected Papers of K. B. McFarlane* (London, 1981).

[6] M. Keen, *Chivalry* (Oxford, 1984), pp. 152–3. Keen's notes serve as guides to the literature on chivalry, especially for the later middle ages; and his view of the importance

chivalry at the end of the Middle Ages was not, as Huizinga regarded it, an attempt to escape the harsh realities of life into a dream world of play and fantasy. There was no divorce between dream and reality; if anything, chivalry was at its height in the fourteenth and fifteenth centuries, never stronger as a force shaping attitudes and behaviour because it represented a powerful traditional ideal that aroused men's nostalgia for a model of corporate class behaviour they could still cling to as relevant to their lives in a period of rapid social and political change.

The ideal determined the way men spent their money. Training in arms was expensive; it required outlays for horses and equipment, and continual exercise in tournaments and the hunt. Even more important than military expertise, however, was the assertion of status as, on the one hand, a landlord in the eyes of tenants and, on the other, a member of the hierarchy of nobility. It was above all hospitality, therefore, that marked the noble way of life. Largess was the supreme medieval aristocratic virtue, with strong Christian overtones; by opening his house to all comers—friends, followers, and even men unknown to him—and offering them food, drink, and accommodation, the noble lived up to the highest expectation of his class. Lesser nobles attended the households of greater lords and appeared in their retinue on specific occasions wearing their livery and badges; and the poor noble found honour even in menial service of the most personal and intimate kind in the lord's household. This gregarious life centred on the great hall of the lord's house and was highly ritualized by elaborate ceremony. Consumption was directed to the rounding out of this scenario for the assertion of status. Clothes, plate for the table, and retinues of liveried servants, dependents, and clients dominated expenditures; and most of those precious objects which we consider to be the typical art forms of the period had the function of ceremonial display, either liturgical or secular, 'condensing pomp and circumstances' (in the words of Georges Duby) to something 'which one could clasp in the hand'. For this way of life, conspicuous consumption was a kind of investment in the noble's social position that secured service and paid dividends in the universal recognition of his dignity and status.[7]

of chivalry at that time is reiterated in Georges Duby's review in *The Times Literary Supplement*, 29 June 1984, p. 720.

  [7] On the English household, see D. Starkey, 'The Age of the Household: Politics, Society and the Arts *c.* 1350–*c.* 1550', in S. Medcalf (ed.), *The Late Middle Ages* (London, 1981), pp. 225–305. The quotation from Duby comes from his *The Age of the Cathedral: Art and Society 980–1420* (Chicago, 1981), p. 204.

In short, underlying the consumption habits of the landowning class of northern Europe was a coherent social ideology, a concept of nobility that, far from being submerged still inchoate in the subconscious, had long found explicit expression in literary and even (by standards of the time) scholarly writings on chivalry. It incorporated an aristocratic ethos with Christian and military components, and it organized social life around the virtues of service, largess, and pride in ancestry and status. These were all the old values, and this is why traditional material culture remained intact: nothing had changed in the noble's basic way of life that made new functional demands on the kinds of things he surrounded himself with. For all the flamboyance, exaggeration, and even vulgarity that characterized the aristocratic world of goods at the end of the Middle Ages, nobles were spending their wealth in essentially traditional ways.

As the expression of the ideology of a European-wide élite, which had in addition the full sanction of the church, chivalric culture also took root in Italy, even though feudalism as a legal and political system was stunted in its growth in much of Italy by the emergence of towns as the centres of political and economic power. Feudalism had its presence in the person of the German emperor, the nominal overlord of much of the peninsula, and in the various royal houses in southern Italy, so that nobles who were attracted into the northern towns did not lose sight of the chivalric model. Indeed, in the potentially threatening environment of urban life they may have looked to it all the more intensely to maintain their class identity as landowners who clung to their independence, as knights who fought for the commune, and as an élite who found strength in family unity and a sense of lineage. Amidst the turbulence of communal political life these nobles established corporate groups of relatives, followers, and hangers-on of other kinds—like the *consorterie* in Florence and the *alberghi* in Genoa— that were probably not very different from the affinities in northern Europe. And it is very likely, too, that they used their wealth in the traditional ways of the feudal nobility: they asserted their presence in large palaces, notable more for their dominating towers than for any other architectural feature, and they directed their consumption to satisfying their gregarious instincts as public figures, both as heads of family clans and of client groups and as magnates active in civic life. Ultimately, however, the chivalric model was bound to become unrealistic for the urbanized nobles of Italy. On the one hand, they saw their independent basis of power in the countryside slowly eroded by the extension of communal authority over the countryside, and meanwhile they had no feudal authority around which to rally outside the city, once it was clear the imperial cause was lost. Within the city, on the other hand, nobles had to confront the fact that urban residence required adjustments. As a sense of public authority gradually asserted itself against the amorphous corporatism of the earlier commune, the nobility found its room for independent behaviour more constricted and its idiosyncratic ways curbed; and it eventually lost what had been its unique contribution to the commune with the increasing recourse to professional soldiers in the fourteenth century. Inevitably nobles joined in the life of the city, investing and participating in capitalist enterprise and marrying into the new entrepreneurial class, so that it became increasingly difficult to identify them in economic and social terms. By the fifteenth century in Florence, where this process of assimilation went as far as anywhere else, magnate status was little more than a category for those who had lost their right to participate in political affairs; it hardly referred any more to a social élite with traditional rights and a distinctive life-style.

Even with the assimilation of the nobility into urban life, the feudal model—precisely because it was the only fully legitimated model for secular behaviour—continued to have its appeal to common city folk, as the popularity of chivalric literature in Italy testifies. It became increasingly clear, however, that this kind of public display of status was not appropriate to city life. The proliferation of anti-magnate legislation to curb behaviour and of sumptuary legislation to limit display, especially during ceremonial festivities, was symptomatic of the growing disenchantment. So too was the declining expenditure of the urban classes on ostentatious military gear. It is prominent, for example, in Florentine inventories as late as the second half of the fourteenth century; but thereafter account books do not record many new acquisitions and we can infer from later inventories that older, inherited equipment of this kind was not even kept around. Nor did public office in republican Florence require much of a show. If a Florentine was called into highest government service on the *Signoria*, he joined the others in the same simple garb and lived confined to a dormitory in the Palazzo Vecchio for the duration of his tenure, one of the number even having to scribble away at daily accounts to keep track of purchases for the table. If he took a more conspicuous office in the countryside, as a vicar, captain, or *podestà*, where he had to

make a ceremonial entry as the representative of central government
and to keep up a conspicuous presence, he took along, to be sure, a
helmet, shield, sword, standard, and other such feudal trappings of
office; but many men did not personally possess such objects and so
had to borrow them, apparently unbothered by taking charge of a
new post decked out in gear bearing the arms of some other family.
Florentines still enjoyed playing at jousts throughout the fifteenth
century; and some of them paid a great deal for the sake of putting on
a good appearance. They were not prepared, however, to bear the cost
of real armour and the attendant expenses of keeping fit through
continual exercise and of maintaining the staff and stable required to
play the real game. Venetian nobles enjoyed it as much—but as a
spectacle organized by their professional military captains which they
watched from a healthy distance, without incurring the personal
expense of participation.[8]

By the end of the Middle Ages, when in the north the chivalric
tradition enjoyed a highly romanticized—and very expensive—
resurgence, in urban Italy it had long receded into the realm of literature. And whatever the so-called 'refeudalization' of Italy's upper
classes meant in the sixteenth century, it certainly did not mean that
they spent any more money on these knightly pursuits. The only
secular order in Italy, the Order of the Knights of S. Stefano, set up
by the Grand Duke of Tuscany, defined an 'honourable' life-style as
the prerequisite for membership; but the Order did not attract many
of the older families, and the numerous men it took in from the
business and industrial world—including even sons of brickmakers—
hardly knew anything about military games.[9] Not even the nobles of
Verona, who more than any other in Italy 'kept faith with their ancient
feudal and knightly pretensions',[10] were really prepared to bear the
cost of belonging to the military academy they set up in the sixteenth
century to get themselves in shape to play military games; and eventually it could not compete for their attention with another academy
(the first ever) founded to promote music, an art that in its taming
sociability could hardly have been more remote from war—and one

[8] M. Mallett, *Mercenaries and their Masters: Warfare in Renaissance Italy* (Totowa,
NJ, 1974), pp. 114–15.

[9] F. Angiolini and P. Malanima, 'Problemi della mobilità sociale a Firenze tra la metà
del Cinquecento e i primi decenni del Seicento', *Società e storia*, 4 (1979), 17–47.

[10] M. Berengo, 'Patriziato e nobiltà: Il caso veronese', in E. Fasano Guarini (ed.),
Potere e società negli stati regionali italiani fra '500 e '600 (Bologna, 1978), p. 196.

that perhaps cost as much in time if not in money. Elsewhere in the Veneto in the late sixteenth and early seventeenth centuries military academies popped up here and there; but the best indication that the noble's heart was not really in this kind of activity was his unwillingness to pay the ridiculously low share of the cost of operating them. These academies were able to open only after the Venetian Senate was prevailed upon to grant them subsidies (which it did out of its concern for the state's defences); and they all degenerated into social clubs within a generation of their founding.[11] Writers like Castiglione and Montaigne commented on the Italians' incapacity for fighting. Duels, for example, had become extinct in Italy by the end of the sixteenth century, at a time when Henry IV of France was punishing duellists by the thousands.[12] Travellers to Italy were impressed that Italians did not even carry swords. 'So,' as David Hume later observed (talking 'Of Refinement of the Arts'), 'the modern Italians are the only civilized people, among Europeans, that ever wanted courage and a martial spirit.'

Nor did Italians imitate the rural nobility of the north in what Lawrence Stone has called their 'old country ways'—maintaining hoards of servants and a large kitchen so that they could, in the words of one late-sixteenth-century English writer, 'keep open houses for all comers and goers'.[13] In the city there was much less occasion for hospitality. A man's status was not to be judged by the number of his attendants and the scale of his hospitality, and servants and a kitchen were not a major part of household expenditure. It is an amazing fact, especially in view of the size of their palaces, that rich men in Florence did not have many servants at all. A man as wealthy as Giovanni Rucellai had only eight between his country house and his town palace, including stable-hands and two female slaves. Other rich households at the time had no more than two or three servants and these were mostly women, many of whom, incidentally, did not stay very long, with the result that a normal household staff underwent continual change in its ranks. Many Florentines preferred a female slave, probably to assure themselves of a little stability in their household affairs;

[11] J.R. Hale, 'Military Academies on the Venetian Terra ferma in the Early Seventeenth Century', *Studi veneziani*, 15 (1973), 273–95.

[12] F.R. Bryson, *The Sixteenth-century Italian Duel: A Study of Renaissance Social History* (Chicago, 1938), pp. 132–3.

[13] Fynes Moryson, *An Itinerary* (Glasgow, 1907–8), iv. 94–5.

but few households had more than one.[14] What kind of retinue could a great man like Rucellai, or any of his friends, put together with a few women, a slave, a stable-hand? Montaigne found Venice 'the city in the world where one lives most cheaply, as a train of valets is here of no use whatsoever ... Everybody going about by himself'; and in Padua he observed that 'it is not the custom here to ride about the town on horseback, and not many are followed by a lackey'.[15] Other travellers made the same observation about Italians in general—they did not have servants, horses, swords. Fynes Moryson added a great deal about how little Italians spent at table, both for the purchase of food and for the entertainment of guests—which led him repeatedly to tirades, by way of contrast, against the good old ways in which the English were spending their money at the time.[16] 'The natural hospitality of England' led Sir Henry Wootton, in 1624, to regard certain aspects of Italian palace design as unsuitable for imitation in England—namely, the small size of the service rooms and the fact that they were confined to the basement and therefore not 'more visible'.[17]

Things were somewhat different at the courts of the northern Italian princes, but not very much. Ceremony was obviously more elaborate than in merchants' homes, and much of it had a feudal gloss to it. Many of these men were, after all, military men, and what other model was there to follow? These Italian princes wanted the legitimacy that a feudal title could nominally confer, and their courts had all the trappings of feudal rites and ritual; but how successful could feudal ceremony be in holding together a state, like that of the Visconti, the Gonzaga, or the d'Este, which stayed afloat on mutual-defence pacts drawn up in terms of sheer power, not claims of tradition or legitimacy; where local lords held their distance and resisted being absorbed into the court life of the ruler; where claims of family—the strongest of feudal bonds—were continually answered by violence or rejected in favour of illegitimacy? Under these circumstances feudal consumption habits did not arise from the real exigencies of life; and this is why the

[14] On servants in Florence, see my study, *The Building of Renaissance Florence: An Economic and Social History* (Baltimore, 1980), pp. 106–8; C. Klapisch, 'Célibat et service féminins dans la Florence du XVe siècle', *Annales de démographie historique: Démographie historique et condition féminine* (Paris, 1981), pp. 289–302.

[15] *The Diary of Montaigne's Journey to Italy in 1580 and 1581*, ed. E. J. Trechmann (London, 1929), pp. 92, 94.

[16] Moryson, *An Itinerary*, i. 192–3; iv. 93–9, 172–4.

[17] Quoted in F. Heal, 'The Idea of Hospitality in Early Modern England', *Past and Present*, 102 (1984), 71.

chronicles of these places do not have anything like the chivalric orgies
and spectacles that fill northern court records, just as the treasury
accounts of these Italian princes, more tellingly, do not record such
heavy expenditures for these kinds of activities and the household
accounts of nobles are not full of expenditures for 'pomp and cir-
cumstance' in attendance and service at court. 'Yet no doubt they of
all Nations can worst judge what it is to keepe a plentifull house, or
a Princes Court and Trayne,' observed Moryson at the end of the
sixteenth century. In Florence Moryson 'saw nothing in the trayne, or
Tables of the Court, wherein many of our Earles and Barons doe not
equall it'; and he found the court of Mantua 'after the Italian manner,
faire for building but solitary for trayne of Courtiers'.[18] The 'style of
a Renaissance despotism', to use Werner Gundersheimer's formulation
for his study of Ferrara, was something very different from the traditional feudal mode.

The appearance of the city in the midst of feudal Europe set the stage
for the eventual emergence of an alternative set of values, and the cities
in northern Italy were the most precocious in realizing this potential.
As the residence of the dominant groups within society, the city became
the unchallenged centre of culture in Italian life, where an appropriate
ideology with ethical–religious, juridical, historical, and aesthetic components slowly worked itself out.[19] Nothing indicates more clearly
how life in the city thus conditioned men's values and behaviour than
the way they spent their money.

Life in the city meant above all subordination to a more complex
and demanding collectivity, to a fluid society based more on contract
than on status. One direct cost this kind of life carried was self-
taxation, an item the Italian urban élites were more prepared to enter
in their budgets than most northern Europeans. The greater autonomy
of the city as a territorial state and the relative political instability in
Italy imposed a correspondingly greater responsibility for security.
The history of taxation of nobles in feudal kingdoms points up, by
contrast, the importance of the more highly socialized conscience

---

[18] *Shakespeare's Europe*, ed. C. Hughes (Manchester, 1902), pp. 106–7, 117–18.
[19] S. Bertelli, *Il potere oligarchico nello stato-città medievale* (Florence, 1978), pp. 149–
64; M. C. De Matteis, 'Societas christiana e funzionalità ideologica della città in Italia:
Linee di uno sviluppo', in R. Elze and G. Fasoli (eds.), *La città in Italia e in Germania
nel medioevo: Cultura, istituzioni, vita religiosa* (Bologna, 1981). See also G. C. Argan
and M. Fagiolo, 'Premessa all'arte italiana', in the Einaudi *Storia d'Italia*, i (Turin,
1972), 734–6.

among the urban upper classes. This sense of collectivity among urban residents also expressed itself, in a more private and voluntary way, in the forms of their charity. The feudal noble dispensed charity in a characteristically personal gesture, literally handing it out in an act of hospitality on his own premises; or he simply made blanket gifts to the church as intermediary, in a sense abdicating any direct responsibility for society at large.[20] Life in the city, however, generated more pressing problems of social control; and urban élites assumed the responsibility for dealing with general welfare through institutions like orphanages, hospitals, and confraternities dedicated to the distribution of alms. Taxes and charitable contributions are two expenditures men were prepared to make that indicate how the city—and not only the Italian city—came to represent a different kind of social organization with its own system of values that slowly took possession of urban élites, setting them off from the rural nobility of feudal Europe.

The most obvious physical expression of this cultural outlook was the city itself; and the proof of the real loyalties it could inspire is that disposition (so notable among Italians) to spend money co-operatively on urban monuments. Public spending of this kind—both official and private—is much more impressive in Italian cities than in northern ones. The great cathedrals of Italy, just to take the example of the most conspicuous monument in most medieval cities, were public projects, whereas many a Gothic cathedral in northern Europe was erected by an ecclesiastical authority, usually a noble-dominated cathedral chapter, which was often capable of explicitly excluding the local burghers from participation in the enterprise.[21] In the classical Mediterranean tradition, architecture thus reasserted itself as the concrete, material—and therefore costly—expression of a cultural ideal.

This urban ideology informed private behaviour in putting architecture at the centre of that 'empire of things' the Italians began to build up for themselves in the Renaissance. As the communes evolved into more oligarchical and despotic states, the ruling élites began to build more assertively for themselves; but, if building shifted from the public to the private sphere, it still belonged in a civic context. For all the egotism one may wish to see in the building activities of both oligarch and despot, ranging from chapels in public places to ambitious

[20] J. T. Rosenthal, *The Purchase of Paradise: Gift-giving and the Aristocracy, 1307–1485* (London, 1972), pp. 130–1.

[21] W. H. Vroom, *De financiering van de kathedraalbouw in de middeleeuwen in het bijzonder van de dom van Utrecht* (Maarssen, 1981), pp. 106–8.

urban renewal schemes (the likes of which were not seen in any northern town until much later), we cannot discount altogether the appeal of the arguments made by Alberti, Palmieri, and others, both humanists and architectural theorists, about the contribution of the beauty of such things to the common good. Architecture, as Alberti observed, is pre-eminently an urban art form; and, as virtually every Renaissance treatise on architecture asserts—and as most architectural historians ever since repeat—architecture is also pre-eminently an expression of power. For the Italian oligarchs and despots it was the focus of their preoccupation with publicity, which was perhaps all the more keen once it became clear how inappropriate the older feudal forms of ritualistic spectacle were. Moreover, Italians as no other peoples in Europe, had tangible evidence of the grandeur and immortality of architecture in the Roman ruins that were everywhere around them. The Romans gave the Italians a model to follow. In this sense style, too, came to have profound cultural meaning; and it was style that elevated their buildings to the level of architecture. And style, consisting of conspicuous embellishment, thrived all the more in the competitive atmosphere of urban life.

Architecture thus became the principal means by which Italians staked out their claim to grandeur and magnificence; it was certainly the chief luxury they spent their money on; and it was the one art form the upper classes were interested in reading about and showed a passionate intellectual and even creative interest in. It was the chief term by which they redefined the traditional aristocratic concept of magnificence.[22] Architecture, indeed, became the most important sign of nobility in Italian society. Already by the time Vespasiano da Bisticci was writing his lives, its status—more than that of painting or sculpture—had given rise to the concept of patronage of the arts as ennobling. At the more mundane level of conspicuous consumption, the importance of the town palace and the family chapel had, by the sixteenth century, clearly won over even the most recalcitrant rural feudal nobility—in southern Italy, for instance, where nobles let their traditional country seats fall into ruin by abandoning them for residence in Naples; and in the even more provincial backwashes of the Marches, where the nobles came into town and built palaces and chapels in accordance with the new mode of asserting one's social

[22] A. D. Fraser Jenkins, 'Cosimo de' Medici's Patronage of Architecture and the Theory of Magnificence', *Journal of the Warburg and Courtauld Institutes*, 33 (1970), 162–70.

status.[23] The geography of Italian art in the sixteenth century—that is, the appearance of new centres in Rome, Naples, Genoa, and elsewhere—was partly determined by the urbanization of rural élites and the consequent changes in the spending habits of men in search of a new definition of their nobility.

Economic values show just how important buildings were both as expenditures in themselves and in the way they in fact determined further spending and thereby defined new consumer habits. Buildings were by far the most important expenditure many of these men made. How many men can be found in the annals of great builders (before the industrial era of high salaries) who, like Filippo Strozzi, spent more than one-third of the value of their entire estate just to put up a house, without counting its furnishings? This palace of a Florentine merchant cost one-third to one-half of what Henry VII, king of England, paid out, in these very same years, for his great palace at Richmond, a building that 'was destined to be the architectural symbol of the Tudor dynasty . . . a symbol [by which] all Europe would measure this upstart king'.[24]

It is well known how men in the Renaissance justified their spending on building by developing the concept of magnificence as a public virtue, but magnificent building also had implications for one's private living expenditures that raised moral questions. At the end of the fifteenth century Giovanni Pontano developed this theme in his treatise on the social virtues, which he linked with that part of ethics that presupposes the spending of money, and so in a sense he subjected possessiveness itself to moral analysis. At the centre of this scheme is a new virtue, splendour, which is the complement of magnificence, being the logical extension of magnificence into the private world. Whereas magnificence is manifest in public architecture, splendour expresses itself in the elegance and refinement with which a person lives his life within buildings; it therefore consists in the furnishings, ornaments, and adornment of town houses as well as in the gardens of country villas. It is the beauty of all these things that excites admiration for the possessor of objects, and moreover that beauty

---

[23] G. Labrot, *Baroni in città: Residenze e comportamenti dell'aristocrazia napoletana, 1530–1734* (Naples, 1979), esp. pp. 31–6; B. G. Zenobi, *Ceti e potere nella Marca pontificia* (Bologna, 1976), pp. 270–1.

[24] G. Kipling, *The Triumph of Honour: Burgundian Origins of the Elizabethan Renaissance* (Leiden, 1977), pp. 3–4.

consists not in utility and inherent value but in variety and crafts-manship. Hence Pontano clearly 'translates the ethical principle as an end in itself into a principle of beauty', in a sense endowing pos-sessiveness with an aesthetic as well as an ethical quality.[25]

material

The possessiveness that slowly overcame Florentines manifests itself consciously in their most basic economic records—the account books covering their busy economic lives and carefully kept in double entry. As if taking up a novelty, they began to open separate accounts for individual pieces of furniture, for the furnishings of rooms, and for the particular artisans who supplied these goods. As the pace of acquisition increased, however, the world of goods grew beyond accounting control, and by the sixteenth century the accounts of household furnishings become more generalized and the individual object loses its particular identity. Thus possessiveness came to be taken for granted.[26]

This process of accumulation can also be traced in the internal history of many a palace. When the Strozzi palace, for example, was finally ready for occupancy, about a decade after the builder's death, his widow did not have much furniture to take with her on moving day; but the household accounts of subsequent generations (up to the end of the line in this century), along with complete inventories at each juncture when the palace passed from one generation to the other, reveal the slow process by which the house was adapted for use, and readapted with changes in fashion. A century after it was begun, the family still occupied principally only one floor, the *piano nobile*, which was, however, now crammed with furnishings, including many kinds of things that had not even existed at the time the building was put up; but there were still many empty rooms on this floor, and on the top floor all the rooms were empty or used for storage, one of these extravagant spaces being used for the keeping of chickens. Clearly, there was no need for so much space when such a great palace was put up; but once the space became available, men learned how to use it and adjusted their way of life accordingly. In short, form preceded and, in a sense, determined function.

The history of how life evolved inside the Strozzi and many other early palaces can also be written around the adaptation of the great generalized spaces of the original plan to the more particular needs

---

[25] F. Tateo, *Umanesimo etico di Giovanni Pontano* (Lecce, 1972), pp. 171–7. Tateo has edited Pontano's *I trattati delle virtù sociali* (Rome, 1965).

[26] See my discussion in *The Building of Renaissance Florence*, pp. 77–83.

the family developed as it adjusted to life inside. The considerable modification of interior space over the sixteenth and seventeenth centuries is dramatized in the radical transformations that had to be made when an older Renaissance palace was remodelled in the seventeenth century for more modern living. When the Riccardi bought the Medici palace they found that what had been in its time the grandest palace in Florence, if not all of Italy, could not even begin to satisfy the needs of a rich family almost two centuries later. No sooner did the new owners take possession than they virtually gutted it, putting in two staircases in the new fashion—one a spiral, the other grandly sweeping through the height of the building; needing a larger reception room than any the house then had, they threw several of the larger older rooms together and even raised the already high ceiling on the *piano nobile* well into the floor above; the loggias were enclosed to make galleries around the courtyard; an extension was added virtually doubling the size of the house and including an even grander hall, the famous library, and accommodations for stable and carriages; and, finally, no fewer than four chapels were opened, besides the space which had been the Medici chapel, itself apparently an anomaly in fifteenth-century town houses.[27] In short, the history of domestic architecture over the period of the Renaissance is the history of the redefinition of the use of interior space, and this has enormous implications for the history of luxury consumption—including, of course, art.

While these urban élites were enlarging their world of goods within their town houses, they were also extending it beyond the city with the villas they built all over the surrounding countryside. Even the feudal nobility of central and south Italy, once it was thoroughly urbanized, preferred villas on the outskirts of Rome or Naples (in addition to their town house) to the seats of their more remote ancestral estates, which they now let fall into ruin. The great ecclesiastical princes in Rome and the secular princes in Ferrara, Mantua, Florence, and elsewhere built villas across town from their town palaces, and others just outside the city walls, and yet others somewhat beyond in the more remote countryside. We know that the first Grand Duke of Tuscany did not spend much time during his long reign in any one place: he was continually on the move, going from one villa to another, each place just down the road no more than an hour or so away at

[27] F. Böttner, 'Der Umbau des Palazzo Medici–Riccardi zu Florenz', *Mitteilungen des Kunsthistorischen Institutes in Florenz*, 14 (1970), 393–414.

the most. And these villas—like those of other princes—were not located at the centre of great rural estates; they were not in provincial towns, where they might have served conspicuously to remind subjects just who the prince was; they were not fortified places strategically located in the defence network of the state. In short, this ceaseless villa-hopping had a different purpose from the mobility of the itinerate courts of the feudal north. Nor did the villa in Italian life represent the refeudalization of the Italian upper classes; their move to the country was, rather, an extension of urban life into the countryside, and the fuss they made about the *otium* they found there presupposes an urban point of view. With the villa, in any case, they added another corner with its own distinctive character to their newly created, ever-expanding physical world: it was just that much more space to be filled up with goods, goods that expressed the new life-style that gave their world its meaning.

Many account books of the rich tell the story of how, across the fifteenth and sixteenth centuries, merchants and nobles, princes, and prelates, spent more and more of their wealth on building and furnishing, and then remodelling, as successive generations settled down to life inside such enormous spaces. With the construction of these spaces in the Renaissance, Italians created a world in which they could develop a different style of life, and in which a new culture came to be defined. This is why so much was spent on objects, why so many new kinds of objects came into existence, why in the final analysis the arts flourished now in the domestic world as they had earlier in the religious world.

All too little is known about this culture, about the coherence of this 'empire of things', about its enlargement and transformation. We are only now beginning to learn just how central the bedroom was in the home of the early Renaissance Florentine. The first accounts kept by a young man who had at last reached financial independence often open with the detailed expenditures for the fitting-out and furnishing of this room, which in fact added up to a kind of counter-gift to the dowry of the wife he would eventually lead there. In Alberti's treatise on the family, when the husband takes his wife on a tour of her new home, it is the last room he leads her to, and he closes the door behind her to show her all those things he keeps there for his private enjoyment. Inventories confirm this absolute priority of the bedroom as the place in the house where objects of all kinds—many of those things we today call art—begin to appear in notable quantities. And yet, given the current state of research into this social background for art, who could think of opening a study of the history of secular art in the Renaissance with a first chapter entitled 'Bedroom Art'?

We know a little more about the private study—the *studiolo* or *scrittoio*.[28] Whether in the homes of merchants in Florence and Venice, or of princes in Mantua and Urbino, these rooms came to be filled up with all those curiosities men enjoyed in privacy, giving rise to new art forms and to the collecting of older ones, to the refinement of taste and to the improvement of learning. Almost a quarter of the famous inventory of the Medici palace made on the death of Lorenzo the Magnificent in 1492 is taken up with the list of items in his minuscule and remotely located study; and these included his most valuable possessions. Here was a kind of mini-'empire of things' that reveals another aspect of these new spending habits. Lorenzo's study was not the treasury of a feudal prince: the value of his precious objects was not inherent in their materials, and they did not have the function of ceremonial display, either liturgical or secular, of the typically feudal kind. Nor was hoarding the characteristic behaviour of men who lived in the economic world of the Italian towns; instead, behind their collecting impulse was a new cultural ideal—one that emphasized craftsmanship rather than intrinsic value of materials, learned content rather than ceremonial function, private pleasure rather than public display. Here, in short, was a programme for altogether new consumer habits.

Much more needs to be learned about bedrooms and studies—and other rooms, too—and about their further evolution and transformation as the demands on domestic space changed. The movement of a picture like Botticelli's *Primavera* from the bedroom of a town house (where we now know it was originally) to the hall of a villa (where Vasari saw it some years later), involved much more than a rehanging, just as it is more than a mere quantitative leap from the intimate Renaissance *studiolo* or *scrittoio* to the sumptuous library and collection gallery of a baroque palace. That history is recorded in the changing and enlarging constellation of goods that men bought to furnish and decorate these rooms to make them livable and usable; and historians have yet to chart the underlying patterns of these

[28] W. Liebenwein, *Studiolo: Die Entstehung eines Raumtyps und seine Entwicklung bis um 1600* (Berlin, 1977); J. von Schlosser, *Die Kunst- und Wunderkammern der Spätrenaissance: Ein Beitrag zur Geschichte des Sammelwesens* (Leipzig, 1908).

kaleidoscopic changes in consumption habits, let alone explain the deeper impulses that gave rise to them.[29]

The dynamic behind the expansion of this 'empire of things' was the working out of what might be called a new life-style. The famous description of Niccolò Niccoli by Vespasiano da Bisticci already in the early fifteenth century points to the new model:

Of all men ever born he was by far the cleanest, in his eating habits as in all else. When he was at table he ate from the most beautiful antique dishes, and he drank from cups of crystal or some other fine stone. To see him at table, as old as he was, gave one a sense of refinement. He always insisted that the table cloth before him be of the whitest, like all his other linens. Some may be astonished to hear that he possessed such a vast quantity of tableware, and to these may be answered that in his day things of this sort were not so much in vogue or so highly prized as they have been since ... There was no house in Florence that was more adorned than his or where there were more refined things than in his, so that whoever went there, whatever his interests, found an infinite number of worthy things.[30]

Gentilezza or refinement is the repeated word in Vespasiano's text; and this was the new model of behaviour Italians expressed in the goods they bought—from the increasing quantity and variety of tableware that conditioned their dining habits, to the books, musical instruments, and art works with which they cultivated taste and learning.

The backwardness of northern Europe served to put the relative refinement of the Italians into relief. It was not simply that Italians thought themselves the cleanest people in Europe. Machiavelli observed that Italian princes ate and even slept with greater 'splendour', and Pontano criticized the French at table for exactly this reason—they ate to satisfy their gluttony rather than with any sense of splendour.[31] Northerners regarded the forks they saw in Italy as strange, if not positively suspicious; like Montaigne, they were impressed that each diner had his own napkin and complete service of silverware, so that he did not even touch his plate with his hands while

[29] This subject is now being studied by J. Kent Lydecker, of the National Gallery of Art in Washington.

[30] *Vita di uomini illustri del secolo XV*, ed. P. d'Ancona and E. Aeschlimann (Milan, 1951), pp. 442–3.

[31] Cited by C. De Frede, '"Più simile a mostro che a uomo": la bruttezza e l'incultura di Carlo VIII nella rappresentazione degli Italiani del Rinascimento', *Bibliothèque d'Humanisme et Renaissance*, 44 (1982), where the Italian attitude is discussed, esp. 577–81.

eating. When the poet Tasso went north he found it curious, if to their credit, that the French used glass to make church windows for the glory of God rather than table utensils 'for display and for the pleasure of drinkers'.[32] Even Marie de' Medici, who went as Queen of France, found the Louvre more fit for use as a prison than as a royal residence.

By the end of the sixteenth century Italians had created a style of living with its own world of goods that clearly set them off from other Europeans. Fynes Moryson was much impressed by the Italian passion for buildings, furnishings, and ornamental gardens: 'for', he says, 'they bestow their money in stable things, to serve their posteritie, where as [he adds, referring to the value the English put on feasting] our greatest expenses end in the casting out of excrements.' Moryson criticizes the Italians for never travelling abroad, which, he explains, is because they 'are so ravished with the beauty of their own Country ... holding Italy for a Paradise'. 'In truth,' says Giovanni Botero, 'we Italians are too much friends to our own selves and too much involved admirers of our own things, when we prefer Italy and its cities to all the rest of the world.'[33]

By the second half of the sixteenth century no one would think of describing the nobility in Italy in the way that applies to France: 'a group living on the land for the most part, rough, usually unlettered, often brutal, and perhaps just as often courageous, with a tradition of fighting as its profession even if all did not fight.'[34] *Civile* is the word Italians used to describe what these northern rural nobles were not; and by that they meant everything that is implied by residence outside a city, something that struck all Italian observers as peculiar about the northern nobility. According to an old Tuscan proverb, already cited by Paolo da Certaldo in the late fourteenth century, only animals lived in the country; and in the words of a Florentine exile a century later, to be sent away from the city was to be expelled from *civiltà*.[35] The full evolution of a thoroughly urbanized way of life eventually conferred on the Italian upper classes, even on courtiers like Tasso in

---

[32] *Le lettere di Torquato Tasso*, ed. C. Guasti, I (Florence, 1854), p. 42.

[33] Moryson, *An Itinerary*, iv. 82, 94; G. Botero, 'Delle cause della grandezza e magnificenza delle città', in *Della ragion di stato*, ed. L. Firpo (Turin, 1948), bk. II, ch. 12.

[34] E. Schalk, 'The Appearance and Reality of Nobility in France during the Wars of Religion: An Example of How Collective Attitudes Can Change', *Journal of Modern History*, 48 (1976), 23.

[35] D. V. and F. W. Kent, *Neighbours and Neighbourhood in Renaissance Florence: The District of the Red Lion in the Fifteenth Century* (Locust Valley, NY, 1982), p. 29.

one of the most feudal-like courts in Italy, a completely new concept of culture.

It is urban life that made much of the difference in Italian civilization, and that difference still sets Italians off today, when they confound foreigners with their judgements about whether other people's comportment is, or is not, *civile*. As Botero observed, trying to explain this difference at the end of the sixteenth century: the closer proximity of noblemen in the city, where they are continually on view, breeds a keener sense of competition and changes the terms of that competition, so that the urban nobility spend more lavishly than the rural nobility, and this leads 'necessarily' to more building and the multiplication of crafts. Perhaps, too, we could further extend this argument along the lines of David Hume's observation about the course of civilization in England at a time when consumerism was becoming a notable phenomenon there—that is, says Hume, luxury heightened the gratification of the senses and hence led to refinement in taste and in the arts generally. In any case, these new spending habits were induced by the urban residence of the dominant classes in Italian society and by the redefinition they gave to the noble life-style.

It is nothing new to say that the city has always been at the centre of Italian life, but the implications of urban residency for the development of a distinctive way of life have not been explored. Rather, the social history of Italian urban élites takes its cue from how the earlier relations between the traditional rural nobility and the new mercantile classes affected the formation of the commune, and the emphasis is on the ensuing dialectic, with its themes of the 'betrayal of the bourgeoisie', its 'aristocratization', and, finally, in the sixteenth century, 'the return to the land' and 'refeudalization'—to use the slogans of the argument as it is currently formulated. In the final analysis, all this leaves the city as a mere transitional stage in the long history of the traditional nobility, rather than a formative one in the evolution of a new kind of nobility. It sets up a class dialectic without regard to the synthesis that was ongoing from the very beginning, as the rural aristocracy and the new urban élites merged on their common ground, the city—something that did not happen in northern Europe; and it underplays the distinctive difference between the Italian and northern traditions of culture by exaggerating the influence of the north on Italy and overlooking the later influence of Italy on the north. To understand the social fusion and the emergence of a new concept of nobility that found such self-conscious expression by the sixteenth century, we need to know more about the peculiar ways in which city life impinges on man's habits, shapes his attitudes, determines his relations with other men—in short, programmes his behaviour according to the rituals of social life. How men spent their money is not the whole story, but it is one way in which the economic historian can explore the distinctive sociology of urban élites.

In any case, the material culture of the Italian Renaissance does not reveal anything like the so-called 'class mentalities' that have given rise to so many flights of scholarly fancy in the traditional historiography of the social and cultural life of Italy.[36] The consumption habits noted here do not appear peculiar to merchants, bankers, and manufacturers—the so-called bourgeoisie—or to princes and aristocrats, any more than they resemble the ways the feudal élites of northern Europe were then spending their money. This consumption was an index to a new concept of nobility that was engendered in the city and that asserted itself in co-operative political action and social control, in the magnification of public space, in the cultivation of new forms of private and domestic social life, in the refinement of taste and education, and—finally—in the definition of art and in the patronage of it. In these ways it was city life, not class behaviour, that gave rise to that 'empire of things' we call the Renaissance.

---

[36] A criticism of this historiographical tradition, with special reference to the recent literature on the earlier period, can be found in R. Bordone, 'Tema cittadino e "ritorno alla terra" nella storiografia comunale recente', *Quaderni storici*, 52 (1983), 255–77. This tradition has been reinforced by the popularity in Italy (as marked by recent translations) of the work of Otto Brunner and Norbert Elias, neither of whom, however, addresses the Italian situation—nor, indeed, do they take it into consideration as an influence on the evolution of the concept of nobility in northern Europe.

Patronage in the Circle of the Carrara Family: Padua, 1337–1405

MARGARET PLANT

In its period of domination in Padua from 1337 to 1405, the house of Carrara sustained a singular chapter in the history of patronage.[1] Beginning with Marsilio da Carrara, elected in 1337 Gonfalonier and Captain General of the commune of Padua, the Carrara princes reconsolidated the city and rebuilt its walls, initiated the building of their palace, the Reggia, and its decoration, and entombed themselves splendidly in a manner that became standard among the élite of the Veneto.

Carrarese supporters in Padua imitated these tombs and commissioned frescoed chapels which introduced portraits of themselves and their city. While the support of the military was necessary to the survival of the Carrara rule, their patronage disinterestedly embraced the Studium, Padua's famous university. The most eloquent scholar of the Trecento, Petrarch, sought after by many princes, endorsed the enlightened Carrara patronage, living out his last years in Arquà, near Padua, by courtesy of Francesco da Carrara.

Among his first gestures upon assuming power in 1338, Ubertino da Carrara interred his predecessor, Marsilio II, in the abbey church of Carrara San Stefano, after a provisional funeral of notable magnificence held in Sant'Antonio.[2] Paduan chroniclers make plain that the Carrara funerals were stately and moving occasions; the tombs that remain confirm the prestige of their ceremonies of death and the desirable status of their memorials. Marsilio's sarcophagus takes a monumental wall form, carved and richly panelled in marble; sur-

---

[1] The basic source used here is G. and B. Gatari, *Rerum italicarum scriptores*, XVII, I. i: *Cronaca carrarese*, ed. L. A. Muratori *et al.* (Città di Castello, 1914) (referred to hereafter as Gatari). Although providing some detail on the 'Vita cultura ed arte durante la Signoria Carrarese', A. Simioni's *Storia di Padova* (Padua, 1968), is inaccurate, particularly in dating. See also B. G. Kohl, 'Government and Society in Renaissance Padua', *Journal of Medieval and Renaissance Studies*, 2 (1972), 205–21.

[2] Gatari, p. 22.

mounted by a classical acanthus plinth, the carved central panel shows the deceased and saints presented to the Madonna and Child.[3] Ubertino da Carrara, who died in 1345, and Jacopo da Carrara, assassinated five years later, were more splendidly personalized as recumbent effigies with surmounting arches filled with frescos (Plates 1 and 2).[4] In Venice, by comparison, representation of the defunct was surprisingly rare: only the Frari tomb of the soldier Duccio degli Alberti[5] (dated between 1345 and 1351), and the tomb of the distinguished doge, Andrea Dandolo, are comparable.[6] Sculpted sarcophagi were, in general, less numerous than in Padua.

The death of Ubertino da Carrara occasioned a grand funeral leading to entombment in the church of Sant'Agostino, in 'un'archa realisma'.[7] The homage of the Studium on this occasion was appropriate, since Ubertino had been responsible for various university initiatives;[8] his effigy is laudatory, showing him with a model of the walled city of Padua at his feet, epitomizing his role as a city father reconsolidating Padua after her wars with Verona. The 'royal' quality in the tomb of Ubertino, remarked upon in the Gatari chronicle, was extended by later rulers of his house and expressed in Padua by a remarkably sustained tradition of portraiture. Deliberately cultivated by the Carrara themselves, the emulation of features giving permanence and status were sought also by the *nobili*, who perpetuated themselves and their families, and recorded their proximity to the ruling house, in chapel frescos as well as tombs.

Although it was by no means unusual for civic seals to carry schematic views of the city's buildings enclosed in walls,[9] the portrait of

[3] W. Wolters, *La scultura veneziana gotica 1300–1460* (Venice, 1976), i. 162–3; ii, figs. 95–8.

[4] Ibid., pp. 168–9. The tombs are now in the Eremitani. The wall type with fresco was not confined to Padua, but was widespread in the Veneto, and particularly popular in Verona. Cf. P. Pettenella, *Altichiero e la pittura veronese del Trecento* (Verona, 1961).

[5] Wolters, *La scultura*, i. 166–7; ii, figs. 114, 121–6.

[6] Ibid. i. 190; ii, fig. 311.

[7] Gatari, p. 24.

[8] For Ubertino's contact with the Studium, see N. G. Siraisi, *Arts and Sciences at Padua. The Studium of Padua before 1350* (Toronto, 1973), who notes on p. 29:

Once the Carrara were established . . . they proved to be notable patrons of the schools, not only confirming and extending scholarly privileges granted by the communal government, but also actively seeking to recruit students from other *studia* and to improve academic standards. The *studium generale* of Padua was, after all, one of the principal ornaments of the city.

[9] On the representation of the Trecento city and its civic overtones, see L. Puppi, 'Temi di urbanistica simbolica Trevisana nell'opera di Tomaso da Modena', in *Tomaso*

Padua found more monumental and consistent presentation, not only in model form at the feet of Ubertino, but in frescos where the distinctive buildings—the Palazzo della Ragione, the Duomo, and the Basilica Sant'Antonio—display their characteristic silhouettes.[10]

Already, in the first decade of the fourteenth century, the Cappella Scrovegni, named after the most famous of Padua's lay patrons in the fourteenth century, Enrico Scrovegni, had no fewer than three representations of its donor: in Giotto's *Last Judgement*, where Scrovegni presents the model of his chapel; as a sculpted figure presenting himself in life as the pious man in prayer; and in death, recumbent in his wall-tomb in the apse of his domestic chapel.[11] In the standing sculpture he appears as a young man; the figure on the tomb, on the other hand, has features some sixteen years older. The brow has become wrinkled and the lower eyelids sag, although the full mouth is still distinctive. There is a hint of the commemorative portrait revived from the antique: of a concern with exact physiognomy which consistently enters portraiture only in the fifteenth century. Might we not, in these sequences of Paduan family features, glimpse a revival of the Roman *imagines*, the wax death masks occasionally displayed by living family members to keep the familial spirit alive and exalted? It is a speculative point, but not alien to the antique themes which, in Padua, confirm the cultivation of ancient Rome. Such a gesture of familial continuity is evident in Ubertino da Carrara's insignia of a Saracen's head, used by his descendants.[12]

Following the example of the Carrara family, like-minded citizens, from *condottieri* to *dottori*, participated in the programme of entombment. No doubt Scrovegni (an eminent citizen with brothers well-placed in the ecclesiastical hierarchy) gave early popularity and prestige

da Modena e il suo Tempo, Convegno Internazionale di Studi per il sesto centenario della morte (Treviso, 1980), pp. 309–23. One of Padua's saints, S. Prosdocimo, appears on the *carrarino* issued by Jacopo II (before 1350), holding a model of the city: see G. Gorini, 'Iconografia monetale e cultura figurativa a Padova nei secoli XIV e XV', in L. Grossato (ed.), *Da Giotto al Mantegna* (Milan, 1974), pp. 81–5; S. Daniele is represented on a coin and by Nicoletto Semitecolo in a panel for the Duomo sacristy, holding a model of the city (ibid., catalogue nos. 41, 120).

[10] L. Gaudenzio, 'Profilo urbanistico di Padova', in *Padova: guida ai monumenti e alle opere d'arte* (Venice, 1961), pp. ccxxxi–ccliii.

[11] Wolters, *La scultura*, pp. 153–4. He concludes, after discussion of dating ranging from 1300 to 1360: 'Sembra che la scultura di Enrico Scrovegni abbia avuto un ruolo innovatore nella storia del ritratto veneziano.' For the tomb, see pp. 161–2.

[12] C. Gasparotto, 'Gli ultimi affreschi venuti in luce nella Reggia dei da Carrara e una documentazione inedita sulla camera di Camillo', *Atti e memorie dell'Accademia Patavina di Scienze, Lettere ed Arti*, 81 (1968–9), 238.

to the wall-tomb in Padua. His sister, Bartolomea, became the wife of Marsilio II da Carrara, and her tomb, though it lacks an effigy, participates in the fashion for monumental enshrinement in a sculpted sarcophagus;[13] the judge Corrado Sala (who died around 1340 and was entombed in Sant'Antonio) preferred the acanthus-plinth model close to that of Marsilio II, but presented himself—with some daring— on the central relief, standing and offering his hand to the Christ Child;[14] Rainiero degli Arsendi, a prominent lawyer in the Studium, presented his features in effigy, resting his legal tomes forever at his feet;[15] Federico da Lavellongo, *podestà* in the service of Francesco il Vecchio, remains a knight-at-arms in death, surmounted by a frescoed Madonna presented to the kneeling knight and his saints.[16]

The programme of funerary chapels in Trecento Padua may be seen as an extension of the earlier self-consciousness of the sculpted tomb. The military class provided conspicuous patrons. In Padua, during the years of constant hostility with her Veneto neighbours, the prestige of the soldier was obviously high: chronicles record the military in conference with the ruling house. Two soldier clans of the Lupi family, come to the service of the Carrara from Parma, endowed chapels that vied with the earlier splendour of Scrovegni's.[17] Bonifacio Lupi endowed the Cappella di San Giacomo (now San Felice) in Sant' Antonio with architectural and sculptural designs by Andriolo de' Santi, sculptor of the Carrara tombs, and a sustained cycle of frescos by Altichiero, the most notable painter active in Padua from around 1370 until the 1380s. One of the most complete of Trecento chapels, it features an unusual number of portraits of contemporaries within a frescoed bay commemorating the intervention in the 1370s of the King of Hungary, Louis the Great, in the successful battles against Venice.[18] In having himself represented among the Carrara court and in the presence of Petrarch, the patron, Bonifacio, gains a precise temporal context (Plate 9), in contrast with the Cappella Scrovegni's heavenly presentation of its donor. Bonifacio had acted as Francesco il Vecchio's

[13] Wolters, *La scultura*, i. 159–60; ii, fig. 76.

[14] Ibid. i. 187–8; ii, fig. 301.

[15] Ibid. i. 191; ii, fig. 312.

[16] Ibid. i. 203–4; ii, figs. 377, 379.

[17] The documents have been published in detail: see A. Sartori, 'Nota su Altichiero', *Il Santo*, 3 (1963), 291–326, and 'La Cappella di S. Giacomo al Santo', ibid., 6 (1966), 267–359.

[18] See my 'Portraits and Politics in late Trecento Padua: Altichiero's Frescoes in the S. Felice Chapel, S. Antonio', *Art Bulletin*, 63 (1981), 406–25.

ambassador to King Louis of Hungary in 1373, and the context of his presentation in the fresco must have been fully understood at the time of its unveiling.[19] Raimondino Lupi responded to the example of his kinsman with an endowment of an oratory in honour of St George, a separate edifice in the precincts of Sant'Antonio.[20] Only fragments of the ambitious tomb remain: an upper torso of an armoured soldier with the Lupi breastplate, and the sarcophagus mounted on columns, perpetuating the form of a public tomb of Padua's fabled founder, Antenore, familiar to the city.[21]

The Paduan tombs remain more or less intact, but palaces and their decorations have been less fortunate. The obliteration of much of the Reggia Carrarese has destroyed the evidence of the grandeur and continuity of the patronage of the Carrara house, dissipating evidence of their proto-humanist sympathies. In 1779, when the Reggia became the home of the Accademia Patavina, the frescoed rooms were (ironically, in an Academy), almost obliterated, although destruction and alteration had begun with the Venetian domination that ended Francesco Novello's rule in 1405. Reconstruction of what was once a singular sequence of decorated chambers follows the invaluable research initiated by three historians: Julius von Schlosser in the 1890s, Theodor Mommsen in the 1950s, and Cesira Gasparotto a decade later.[22]

The palace building and decoration commenced under Ubertino da Carrara. The principal painter was Guariento, an artist who gained prestige in the Veneto, and was later called to Venice to decorate the Palace of the Doges.[23] In part the frescos of his Old Testament cycle have been recovered, surviving today mainly on one wall.[24] They are

---

[19] Gatari, pp. 54, 61, 144.

[20] The initial document is 4 May 1378; see Sartori, 'Nota', p. 307. See also M. Savonarola, *Libellus de magnificis ornamentis regie civitatis Padue*, ed. Arnaldo Segarizzi (Rerum Italicarum Scriptores, ed. L. A. Muratori, XXIV, XV. 33, Milan, 1902).

[21] For the Antenore Tomb, see the comments by R. Weiss, *The Renaissance Discovery of Classical Antiquity* (Oxford, 1969), pp. 18–19. For a reconstruction of the Lupi tomb, see G. L. Mellini, *Altichiero e Jacopo Avanzi* (Milan, 1965), fig. 157.

[22] J. von Schlosser, 'Ein Veronesisches Bilderbuch und die höfische Kunst des XIV Jahrhunderts', *Jahrbuch der kunsthistorischen Sammlungen des allerhöchsten Kaiserhauses*, 16 (1895), 144–230; T. Mommsen, 'Petrarch and the Decoration of the Sala Virorum Illustrium in Padua', *Art Bulletin*, 34 (1952), 95–116; C. Gasparotto, 'La Reggia dei Da Carrara', *Atti e memorie dell'Accademia Patavina di Scienze, Lettere ed Arti*, 79 (1966–7), 71–116; idem, 'Affreschi venuti,' 237–61.

[23] F. d'Arcais, *Guariento* (Venice, 1965), pp. 25ff.

[24] F. d'Arcais, 'Gli affreschi del Guariento dell'Accademia di Padova', *Arte veneta*, 16 (1962), 7–18.

novel in their continuous narrative form, using rock-strewn mountains and architecture as bridges between episodes (Plate 3).

Guariento's decoration for the Cappella dei Principi no longer remains *in situ*. But surviving panels, now in the Museo Civico in Padua, suggest a splendour Byzantine in aspiration, certainly *aulica* in style, with armoured ranks of archangels, the Madonna and Child, and a tondo of St Matthew, on gilded grounds. Their rectangular and trapezoidal shapes suggest they originally had soffit positions, with corner tondi providing, no doubt, a scintillating fascia above frescoed walls. The dating and placement of the decoration remain hypothetical: D'Arcais suggests the 1360s, the time of Francesco il Vecchio.[25] But the fashionable archaic style and the fact that the building of this part of the Reggia was complete by 1345 under the initiative of Ubertino, favours a date earlier (perhaps in the rule of Jacopo II between 1347 and 1350). Indeed the Cappella may well have been accorded priority in the scheme of interior decoration, since there was a lavish reception granted to the Cardinal Legate, Guido da Boulogne-sur-Mer, on two occasions: in 1349 when he officiated in the re-entombment of St Anthony in his basilica, and in 1350. Gauriento is known to have been living in the immediate area of the Reggia in 1348, and was therefore at hand for the project.[26]

Only fragments remain of the secular decorations of the Reggia: heraldic decorations and architectural fragments have been recovered, but there are few traces of the frescoed rooms, which must have formed a unique sequence and proudly proclaimed a continuous family enterprise. The taste of Francesco il Vecchio was notable for its classical orientation, evident not only in his friendship with Petrarch, but also confirmed by accounts of the lost decorations.[27] Two schemes were clearly outstanding: the Theban room and the Sala Virorum Illustrium, later to be known as the Sala dei Giganti. In his mid-fifteenth-century description of Padua, Michele Savonarola wrote of

[25] D'Arcais, *Guariento*, p. 70.

[26] Gasparotto, 'Affreschi venuti', p. 255.

[27] Petrarch's influence on the decorations in the Reggia is remarked by A. Schmitt, 'Zur Wiederbelebung der Antike im Trecento Petrarcas Rom-Idee in ihrer Wirkung auf die Paduaner Malerei', *Mitteilungen des Kunsthistorisches Institutes in Florenz*, 18 (1974), 191ff. Gasparotto, 'La Reggia', p. 100, remarks on Petrarch's significance even for the programme of the chapel, as a consequence of his closeness to Bishop Ildebrandino de' Conti and his position from 1349 as a canon. On Petrarch and the figurative arts, see G. Contini, 'Petrarca e le arti figurative', in A. S. Bernardo (ed.), *Francesco Petrarca: Citizen of the World* (Padua and Albany, 1980), pp. 45–131 (emphasizing the early period of contact with Giotto and Simone Martini).

Two spacious and most ornately painted rooms, the first of which is called
the Thebarum and the other is named the Imperatorum: the first is both larger
and more glorious, in which the Roman emperors are depicted marvellously
with figures and with triumphs in the best gold and with colour.[28]

The 'Anonimo', a chronicler identified as 'Michiel', writing between
1521 and 1543, presents the Theban room as one of the chief salons:
'The Theban room, which contains the history of Thebes, was painted
by ... [*sic*] who seems to have also painted the history of Spoleto in
the Council Room in Venice, which Titian covered with other
pictures.'[29] The battle room ('representing the exploits of the Carraresi
with squadrons of soldiers') was possibly undertaken in the 1350s in
the initial period of Francesco's consolidation of power, with its
predictable glorification of familial achievement. Additional battle
rooms reconstructed by Gasparotto staked a claim for the antique
glory of Padua in calculated concordance with her recent return to
power.[30] The inspiration of Livy, famed son of Patavium, is notable;
the Stanza delle Navi represented the siege of Patavium by the Spartans
(*c.*302 BC) as recorded by him. The Brenta room paralleled the antique
room, showing battle between Verona and Padua in 1314. A Sala di
Nerone, with an antique narrative providing a prototype of familial
murder, would seem to have been occasioned by the assassination of
Jacopo II in 1350.[31] There are further antique parallels: a Room of
Camillus, recognized by Livy as the second founder of Rome, and a
Room of Lucretia, again suggest the inspiration of Livy whose description of the triumph of Camillus is the culmination of the fifth book of
Ab urbe condita, giving the account of the virtue of Lucretia, violated
by Tarquinus and revenged by Brutus.[32] Padua must have witnessed
an early monumental treatment of this latter theme, to become popular
with later painters. The rooms of Camillus and Lucretia probably
formed a sequence with a Camera of Hercules, similarly extolled for
his antique *virtù*.[33] There were further rooms decorated with Carrara

[28] Savonarola, *Libellus*, p. 49.
[29] *The Anonimo: Notes on Pictures and Works of Art in Italy Made by an Anonymous
Writer in the Sixteenth Century*, tr. P. Mussi and ed. G. C. Williamson (London, 1903),
p. 37.
[30] Gasparotto, 'La Reggia', p. 108.
[31] Ibid., p. 103.
[32] Gasparotto, 'Affreschi venuti', pp. 250ff.
[33] Ibid., p. 252.

maps and emblems, and a Sala Bestiarum, no doubt painted with hunting scenes.[34]

The sustained interest in antique themes vindicates the reputation of Padua in her early Trecento years as a centre of proto-humanist activity. It is appropriate (if hypothetical) to attribute the impetus for such programmes largely to Francesco il Vecchio, since the Sala di Thebe would seem linked in conception, as it is by proximity, with the better-known Sala dei Giganti, persuasively associated with Francesco il Vecchio, in consultation with Petrarch. It is now customary to link Petrarch's name with Francesco's scheme for the Sala Virorum Illustrium in the later 1360s, but Petrarch could well have earlier acted as adviser to the Carrara before he took up permanent residence in Padua in 1367. In 1349 he had been appointed a Paduan canon and he was close to the Paduan bishop, Ildebrandino de' Conti, and familiar with Jacopo da Carrara before Jacopo's assassination in 1350, to which Petrarch responded with marked grief.[35] Although it may be retrospective mythologizing, Michele Savonarola in his later history of Padua's glories linked Petrarch, the Laureate, with the famed early circle of humanists, Lovato and Mussato, and their guiding spirit, Livy.[36] The Theban room might well be seen in relation to an antiquarian circle in Padua, stimulated by Petrarch's presence. Again the artist associated with the programme is Guariento, who demonstrates a remarkable flexibility of style in the Cappella decorations. For art historians endeavouring to recreate the original scheme of the Sala Virorum Illustrium, manuscripts of Petrarch's *De viris illustribus* have played a determining role. The illustrated manuscript of Statius' *Thebaid* (now in the Chester Beatty collection in Dublin) is revealing: it has a known Paduan provenance and may well reflect the lost decorations of the Theban Room.[37] Not only the coincidence of subject matter, but also the *grisaille* mode of illustration in the manuscript, and the extended horizontal format of the twelve folios, have counterparts in the continuous narrative lay-out of Guariento's Old Testament

---

[34] Gasparotto, 'La Reggia', pp. 114–15; Schmitt, 'Zur Wiederbelebung', p. 172 n.19.

[35] See n. 27 above. See also E. H. Wilkins, *Petrarch's Later Years* (Cambridge, Mass., 1959), pp. 3, 41.

[36] Savonarola, *Libellus*, pp. 29–30. See also G. Billanovich, 'Petrarch and the Textual Tradition of Livy', *Journal of the Warburg and Courtauld Institutes*, 14 (1951), 137–208, and Weiss, *The Renaissance Discovery*, ch. 2.

[37] Cf. Mellini, *Altichiero e Avanzi*, pp. 98ff. One should note a continuity in a monumental tradition of narrative that both artists, as mentioned above, absorbed upon coming to Padua.

frescos in the Reggia (Plate 3). The stylistic affinities are telling, especially since the *grisaille* mode of illustration (in imitation marble relief sculpture) is *all'antica* in implication, as in Giotto's Virtues and Vices in the Scrovegni Chapel. Paduan taste for *grisaille* illustration is borne out by the late-fourteenth-century *Bibbia istoriata padovana*[38] and the manuscripts of Petrarch's *De viris illustribus*, first decorated around 1380. The presentation is in contrast to the highly coloured and still medieval style of manuscripts issuing from nearby Venice, such as Benoît's *Roman de Thèbes*, from the 1350s.[39]

The exchange of motifs and styles between fresco and miniature has long fascinated art historians and confirmed (though not without ambiguity) the dependence of one upon the other. In the fourth canto of the Statius manuscript of the *Thebaid* (Plate 4), a figure drinking at a river has been observed to be close to one similar in the contemporary frescos of the Oratory of Mezzaratta in Bologna.[40] Recent historians have noted a connection between the Paduan and Bolognese schools of painting, given the documented presence in Padua of Jacopo Avanzo from Bologna.[41] But the motif's appearance in the Statius manuscript might well derive from a source closer to home—in the Theban Room of the Reggia. A connection with the Theban programme and Altichiero's later Lupi frescos can also be observed through the medium of the manuscript, as the dramatic fall of a horse in the sixth lunette of Altichiero's cycle in Sant'Antonio is close to a similar motive in the ninth canto of the Statius.[42]

The description of the lost Reggia decorations highlights the battle and cavalry scenes, which constitute a distinct tradition in Paduan art. The chivalric subject was favoured by the military élite in Trecento Padua, since it legitimized the soldier as the agent of Christ and *virtù*.[43] Central to the choice of St James as the saint of the cycle of Altichiero's frescos in the Santo was his connection with the pilgrimage centre of Santiago de Compostela in Spain, and his auspicious intervention in

---

[38] G. Folena and G. L. Mellini, *Bibbia istoriata padovana della fine del Trecento* (Venice, 1962).

[39] For the Venetian manuscripts, see H. Buchthal, *Historia Troiana: Studies in the History of Medieval Secular Illustration* (London, 1971).

[40] C. L. Ragghianti, *Stefano da Ferrara: Problemi critici tra Giotto a Padova, l'espansione di Altichiero e il primo Quattrocento a Ferrara* (Florence, 1972), pp. 36–7.

[41] See in general Mellini, *Altichiero e Avanzi*, for discussion of the authorship problem; and R. Simon, 'Altichiero versus Avanzo', *Papers of the British School at Rome*, 45, NS 22 (1977), 252–71.

[42] Mellini, *Altichiero e Avanzi*, p. 102, figs. 98, 326.

[43] Plant, 'Portraits', pp. 418–20.

battle. To a degree, the battle piece in northern Italy reflected a French-based fashion of the *cavalleresco*, but in Padua it was modified by an *all'antica* spirit[44] which, if lost from the walls of the Reggia, can be sighted in manuscripts and in Altichiero's frescos. In the following century, the reaction of Pisanello to Altichiero's work (seen in Pisanello's study based on another fallen horse in the sixth lunette of the Santa Felice chapel) and the continued relevance of chivalric inspiration, is in evidence in Pisanello's frescoed battle cycle for the Gonzaga palace in Mantua.[45] The recognition afforded him by contemporary humanists suggests that the chivalric subject was not seen as irrelevant or obsolete in the mid-fifteenth century.[46]

There is, in Padua, also a tradition of rendering antique motives in medallion format, painted in *grisaille* (Plates 5 and 6). To an extent, it is an imported tradition brought by Altichiero from Verona, where Vasari noted Altichiero's work, as painter to the Scaligeri, in frescos of battles based on Flavius Josephus and a medallion series featuring antique emperors, produced for the Loggia of Can Grande.[47] The Verona medallions no doubt reflect the antiquarian interests of the contemporary Veronese, Giovanni Mansionario, a pioneer numismatist. Petrarch's similar interests and, indeed, his inclusion in the Verona medallion frescos, are documented.[48] The Carrara (traditional enemies of the Scaligeri as well as patrons of Petrarch, who appeared in the Verona medallions) doubtless were well aware of Verona's propagandist art in fresco and funerary monuments.[49] However, the medallion style in Padua is earlier in evidence in Guariento's work in the apse of the Eremitani, where there appears a remarkable socle in *grisaille* with representations of the planetary gods and goddesses: Luna, Venus, Mercury, Mars, and Saturn (Plates 7 and 8).[50] Rather

[44] Ibid., p. 418.

[45] G. Paccagnini, *Pisanello* (London, 1973), esp. ch. 3; Mellini, *Altichiero e Avanzi*, figs. 100, 289.

[46] M. Baxandall, *Giotto and the Orators: Humanist Observers of Painting in Italy and the Discovery of Pictorial Composition, 1350–1450* (Oxford, 1971), pp. 91ff.

[47] G. L. Mellini, 'La "Sala Grande" di Altichiero e Jacopo d'Avanzo', *Critica d'arte*, 35 (1959), 313–14; Schmitt, 'Zur Wiederbelebung', pp. 190ff.

[48] See E. Rossini, 'Francesco Petrarca e Verona: Documenti vecchi e nuovi', in G. Padoan (ed.), *Petrarca, Venezia e il Veneto* (Venice and Florence, 1976), pp. 23–51, and G. Mardersteig, 'I ritratti del Petrarca e dei suoi amici di Padova', *Italia medioevale e umanistica*, 17 (1974), 253–5.

[49] For the Scaligeri funerary monuments, see G. L. Mellini, *Scultori veronesi del Trecento* (Milan, 1971).

[50] D'Arcais, *Guariento*, p. 109–15.

than being ostensibly religious, these figures appear astrological in inspiration, anticipating the often-observed Renaissance marriage between antique form and content. In this detail of Guariento's decoration we perhaps witness a reflection of the dominant position of astrology in the Studium of Padua and the fame, earlier in the century, of Pietro d'Abano and Jacopo Dondi.[51] Astrology had a public face in Padua since, during the rule of Ubertino da Carrara, Jacopo Dondi installed his novel astronomical clock in 1344 in the tower of the Carrara palace.[52] Subsequently, Jacopo's son, Giovanni Dondi dall'Orologio, called by Petrarch 'easily prince of astronomers', was famed for his planetarium begun about 1348: 'the most splendid clock of the Renaissance'.[53]

The astrological fresco cycle of the Palazzo della Ragione also reflects the early importance of the Studium. In scale it is the most ambitious cycle in Padua: the pre-eminent embodiment of the days of the commune. Giotto is frequently invoked as the first decorator, working in conjunction with Peter d'Abano.[54] The existing scheme, a repainting after a fire of 1423, preserves the general dispensation of the original, but through a veneer of International Gothic. The Ragione scheme was presumably complete in its presentation of the months and their associated activities and religious images according to a unique scheme devised in the early Trecento, but it continued to be decorated thereafter by painters in Carrara service, such as Guariento and Altichiero.[55] It is a monumental and conspicuous example, too often bypassed, of the decorative ambitions of Padua.

If only in its vast scale the surviving Sala dei Giganti mirrors the original room of the Reggia, which, too, was prodigious in ambition. Michiel comments on the prominent position given to the portraits of Petrarch and his secretary, Lombardo della Seta, at the head of the

---

[51]   Siraisi, *Arts and Sciences*, pp. 77ff.

[52]   Savonarola, *Libellus*, pp. 49; Gasparotto, 'La Reggia', p. 83.

[53]   The planetarium was later installed in the Castello Sforzesco at Pavia; see P. L. Rose, 'Petrarch, Giovanni de' Dondi and the Humanist Myth of Archimedes', in Padoan (ed.), *Petrarca, Venezia e il Veneto*, pp. 101–8. Dondi was an eloquent witness to Petrarch's death; see B. G. Kohl, 'Mourners of Petrarch', in A. Scaglione (ed.), *Francis Petrarch Six Centuries Later: A Symposium* (Chapel Hill, 1975), p. 341.

[54]   See G. C. Mor *et al.*, *Il Palazzo della Ragione di Padova* (Venice, 1964); G. H. Hartlaub, 'Giottos zweites Hauptwerk in Padua', *Zeitschrift für Kunstwissenschaft*, 4 (1950), 19ff., and C. L. Ragghianti, 'Giotto a Padova, 1303–1309', in his *Stefano da Ferrara*, pp. 11ff.

[55]   Ragghianti, 'Il nuovo ciclo pittorico del Palazzo della Ragione', in his *Stefano da Ferrara*, pp. 93–7.

great hall (where they can still be seen).[56] It is not necessary here to retrace the footsteps of Schlosser and Mommsen who established Petrarch's link with the decoration; nor to re-rehearse the connection with Altichiero and his school. As a collaborative venture between painter and poet, the Sala dei Giganti may well have extended an association first established in Verona when Petrarch and Altichiero were both at the Scaligeri court.[57] And Francesco il Vecchio was no doubt aware of the embellishments of the rival Veronese and was inspired to vie with neighbouring princes, however scholarly and informed the records tell us was his interest in Petrarch's *De viris illustribus*.

Certainly Petrarch's capacity to inspire the patronage of princes was the most perfected of his period. As well as Jacopo II and Francesco il Vecchio, Robert of Naples, Azzone Visconti, Pandolfo Malatesta of Rimini, the Can Grande of Verona, and Doge Andrea Dandolo sought his favours.[58] Petrarch himself left an admiring record of the decorations of Robert of Naples, and it has been recently assumed that Giotto's lost fresco, the *Gloria* painted in Milan for Azzone Visconti, reflected the inspiration of the poet's *Trionfi* and his authority and charisma in the eyes of another princely patron.[59]

In the culminating bay of Altichiero's Lupi chapel, Petrarch appears in the *Council of Ramiro* as a near-centre figure, seated at the king's right hand and visibly associated with learning by the attribute of a book (Plate 9). Identification of the members of the Carrara family has been uncertain, but they are inevitably present and deliberately emphasized close to the patron, Bonifacio Lupi and his wife.[60] In a sustained tribute to his posthumous fame and prestige in Padua, Petrarch appears again around 1380 in the frescos commissioned by Raimondino Lupi for his Oratory.[61] His proximity to the bearded Francesco il Vecchio is most evident; the hooded Petrarch on our left accompanies the ruler to the baptism of the king who was witness to St George's slaughter of the dragon and was converted (Plate 10). As witness to the martyrdom of St George, Francesco appears on horse-

[56] *The Anonimo*, p. 38: 'In the same room are the portraits of Petrarch and Lombardo, who, I believe, suggested the subjects of these paintings.'

[57] See G. L. Mellini, 'Considerazioni su probabili rapporti tra Altichiero e Petrarca', in Grossato (ed.), *Da Giotto al Mantegna*, pp. 51–4; and Plant, 'Portraits', *passim*.

[58] E. H. Wilkins, *Life of Petrarch* (Chicago, 1961).

[59] C. Gilbert, 'The Fresco by Giotto in Milan', *Arte Lombarda*, 47–8 (1977), 31–72.

[60] See Mardersteig, 'I ritratti', pp. 251–80; and Plant, 'Portraits', pp. 413ff.

[61] See Plant, 'Portraits', p. 410.

back wearing the Saracen-head escutcheon of his forefather, Ubertino (Plate 11). The Carrara family are again present on the opposite wall, attendant at the funeral of St Lucy with members of the Lupi clan. In a representation of patronage within patronage, *signori* and donors, rulers and favoured poets, are painted together. Since previous representation of contemporaries was limited to their portrayal in heaven or hell, or on funerary or donor memorials, the Paduan parade is without precedent. Indeed, on these walls are anticipated the celebrated frescoed appearance of fifteenth-century Florentines: the Medici journeying in the retinue of the Magi, the Tornaquinci attendant at the *Annunciation to Zacharias* in Santa Maria Novella (Plate 17).

In Trecento Padua, the proximity of scholars, *nobili*, and the ruling house is celebrated in Altichiero's frescos; the cohesion is endorsed by the records of ambassadors and councillors listed in the chronicle of the Gatari.[62] Yet the frescos do not cater merely to political expediency. The central figure of Altichiero's *Council of Ramiro*, King Louis of Hungary (Plate 9), was certainly honoured as the formidable ally of the Paduans against the Venetians; but the king's presence is perhaps ideal rather than actual, since there is no record of his presence in Padua. His appearance is replete with allusions to the Christian ruler's *virtù* and he is enthroned, elevated above the house of Carrara. His centrality is as telling as the written records of Paduan alliance with Hungarian power.[63] Too great an emphasis on the politics of Paduan circles should not be allowed to distort the Christian legacy and the importance of patronage which confirmed the patrons' piety.

The visual schemes commissioned by the Carrara did not only annex antique and chivalric battles to dignify their own exploits; traditional Christian themes were also sought, particularly by Francesco il Vecchio's devout wife, Fina da Buzzacarina. The church of Santa Maria dei Servi had her special interest, as did the Baptistery which she planned as her funerary monument.[64] The artist concerned was Giusto de' Menabuoi, another of the major figures in northern Italian art, come to Padua from Milan in 1369, and first documented in the Eremitani, in a commission from another close associate of the

---

[62] For example, the 'Consiglio del Signore di Padova' in 1372, Gatari, pp. 62–3; the ambassadors to Citadella in 1381, ibid., p. 199.

[63] On a ruler's centrality, see Lauro Martines in his articulate but overstated ch. XII: 'The princely courts: a paradise for structuralists', in *Power and Imagination: City-States in Renaissance Italy* (London, 1980), pp. 317ff.

[64] See S. Bettini, *Le pitture di Giusto de' Menabuoi nel Battistero del Duomo di Padova* (Venice, 1960), *passim*.

Carrara, Tebaldo de' Cortellieri. Michiel describes that chapel with Virtues on the one side, Vices on the other, together with portraits of men famous in the Augustinian order and the donor represented on the right side of the altar, with accompanying eulogistic inscription.[65] There is documentary evidence that Giusto was summoned to Padua by the Carrara, who are revealed as initiators and facilitators of unique schemes.[66] Schlosser found in this encyclopaedic Eremitani programme, remaining now only in fragments, an intimation of Raphael's Stanza della Segnatura itself.[67]

The interior of Fina's Baptistery is fully frescoed with an ambitious programme from both Old and New Testaments, and an apsidal area with Apocalyptic scenes and altar-piece (Plate 12). Fina and Francesco appear in the crowd in *Christ before Pilate* and Fina also is shown presented to the Enthroned Virgin. Her tomb, designed by Andriolo de' Santi, was destroyed after the Venetian invasion and survives only in unhelpful fragments—supports of griffins and lions.[68] Francesco's bier was carried in full ceremony to the Baptistery after his death in exile at Monza in 1393, but no traces of the funerary monument remain.[69] Michiel records the obliterated inscription 'in four lines, now perished, probably in memory of the Signori de' Carrara, who had caused that work to be done'.[70]

---

[65] *The Anonimo*, pp. 28–9:

> The chapel on the right, which contains on the one side a representation of the Virtues, and on the other side a representation of the Vices, together with the portraits of the men who were famous in the Order of St Augustine, and the titles of the works of the Saint, was painted by Giusto of Padua (Giusto Padovano), or, as some people will have it, of Florence. It was founded by Messer Tebaldo de' Cortellieri of Padua, in 1370, and his portrait is to be seen on the right side of the altar, as it appears from the eulogistic inscription underneath.

Cortellieri was one of the seven ambassadors invited by Francesco da Carrara to address the *Signoria* of Venice in 1360.

[66] Bettini, p. 32: 'magistro Justo Pictore q. Joh. de Menaboibus de Florentia habitatore Padue in contrada Scalumnae cive civitatis Paude cum privilegio M. et potentis D. D. Francisci de Carrara.'

[67] J. von Schlosser, 'Giusto's Fresken in Padua und die Vorläufer der Stanza della Segnatura', *Jahrbuch der kunsthistorischen Sammlungen des allerhöchsten Kaiserhauses*, 17 (1896), 13–100.

[68] For the fragments of Fina's tomb, see *Da Giotto al Mantegna*, catalogue no. 91. For the funeral of Fina da Buzzacarina in 1378, see Gatari, pp. 158–9: 'Sotto la ditta archa era scritti a sua laude alchuni verssi, i quali qui di sotto dinoteremo.'

[69] See Gatari's extended account: 'Quando morì il Signor Misser Francesco Vecchio da Carrara in lo Castello do Monza a dì vi de Otore 1393', and 'Come il Signore fe' aportare el corpo de suo padre a Padova e l'onore che li fu fato, che fu a dì XVIII de Novembre 1393', pp. 440–4.

[70] *The Anonimo*, p. 36.

Less fluent than Altichiero in organization, the tight, box-like com-
partments of the Baptistery's painted bays is evidence, none the less,
of Giusto de' Menabuoi's considerable compositional skill, though
somewhat rigid in its application. Where greater fluency is evident
(in the architectural renderings) the intervention of the workshop of
Altichiero has been suggested, but this is by no means a necessary
thesis, given the development of Giusto's architectural renderings in
his later commission for the Cappella Belludi, in Sant'Antonio (Plate
13).[71] A significant city vista (we have already remarked on its Paduan
importance) occurs in the Baptistery's *Meeting of Abraham and the
Three Angels*. In the apsidal area the seven churches of the Apocalypse
are indubitably Paduan—among them the Santo, San Giustino,
Sant'Agostino, San Niccolò and Santa Sofia. The portrayal of Paduans
was extended by portraits of Padua.

Giusto was occupied with the Baptistery scheme during the 1370s,
when Altichiero was active in the service of the Lupi. In 1382, Giusto
received a further commission for the frescoing of the Cappella Belludi.
This came from the Conti family, yet again in close contact with the
Carrara.[72] Indeed, the arms of the patrons Naimerio and Manfredino
de' Conti are intertwined with those of the Carrara. The chapel is
named for the Blessed Luke, who had particular local relevance as the
companion of St Anthony and was notable for intercessions in Paduan
affairs. Donor portraits are again conspicuous, with the presentation
of Naimerio and Manfredino, their wives and sons. Again local monuments are specific, too, with the representation of the Basilica of
Sant'Antonio and a panorama of the city appearing in bird's-eye view
in the scene of St Anthony's revelation.

As often observed, the representation of architecture in proto-
Renaissance painting is closely linked with the emergence of theoretical
perspective and an intellectual, mathematical shift in the premises of
painting. In the representation of architecture in Paduan painting,

[71] On the attributions of architectural renderings to Altichiero rather than Giusto,
see ibid., p. 8. See also C. L. Ragghianti, 'Problemi padovani: Battistero, Cappella
Belludi', *Critica d'Arte*, 8 (1961), 1ff., and C. Bellinati, 'La Basilica del Santo in un
affresco di Giusto de' Menabuoi nel Battistero della Cattedrale di Padova (1376)', *Il
santo*, 18 (1978), 111–26.

[72] See *The Anonimo*, p. 10: 'In the year 1382, as it is written there on a stone, it was
dedicated to San Giacomo and San Filippo, whose lives are painted there for Messer
Renier, Messer Conte, and Messer Manfredino de' Conti, Paduan noblemen, originally
from Genoa'. Also Savonarola, *Libellus*, p. 16: 'Paucisque deinde passibus a sinistris
cappellam comperies, manu Iusti pictoris ornatissimam, nobilium de Comitibus: Luce
beato, eius Antonii fideliter commensali, ab eis magna cum devotione confectam.'

Altichiero's precise buildings have seemed sufficiently accurate to allow identification, for instance, of the house of Lombardo della Seta,[73] and allusions to the architecture of the Santo seem intentional in the Oratory frescos of the *Funeral of St Lucy* and the *Presentation in the Temple*. Earlier, in the 1350s and 1360s, the accomplishment of Guariento's perspective in the apsidal area of the Eremitani and the surviving fragments of the *Coronation of the Virgin* in the Palazzo Ducale in Venice, must have seemed a triumphant demonstration of Paduan perspective—the *tour-de-force* elaboration of the Virgin's throne in the Palazzo Ducale remains impressive in its intricacy.[74] It is tempting to seek a dynamic connection between such sophistication in architectural rendering and the Studium's pursuit of optics and related *prospettiva* which had constituted a notable tradition since the Paduan residence of Witelo in the previous century.[75] No thorough account of the Studium in the later Trecento has yet been undertaken; but the fame of Biagio Pelacani, author of *Questiones perspectivae* and master at Padua for periods between 1377 and 1411, has been noted.[76] Biagio's authority in Padua has been thought sufficient to have redirected the Quadrivium of the Studium in favour of mathematics over astrology.[77] Paolo da Pozzo Toscanelli, trained at the Studium in the second decade of the fifteenth century and a key figure in the circle of Brunelleschi and Alberti, was familiar with Biagio's teachings,[78] as was the famous Vittorino da Feltre, appointed to the chair of rhetoric

---

[73] See A. Calore, 'La casa di Lombardo della Seta in Padova', *Italia medioevale e umanistica*, 17 (1974), 491ff. The house has been located as Nos. 8, 10, 12, Via Marsilio da Padova.

[74] See D'Arcais, *Guariento*, pp. 45–6, with reference also to the later expertise of Altichiero.

[75] D. C. Lindberg, 'Lines of Influence in Thirteenth-century Optics: Bacon, Witelo and Pecham', *Speculum*, 46 (1971), 66–83, and Siraisi, *Arts and Sciences*, pp. 72–5.

[76] See G. F. Vescovini, *Studi sulla prospettiva medievale* (Turin, 1965), ch. XII: 'Biagio Pelacani da Parma e l'impostazione Gnoseologica delle sue questioni di Prospettiva', pp. 239ff., and her 'Le questioni di "Perspectiva" di Biagio Pelacani da Parma', *Rinascimento*, 12 (1961), 163–243; R. Klein, 'Pomponius Guaricus on Perspective', *Art Bulletin*, 43 (1961), 211–30, repr. in his *Form and Meaning* (Princeton, 1981), pp. 102ff. J. White, in *The Birth and Rebirth of Pictorial Space* (London, 1957), which pursues the history of empirical but not theoretical perspective in the Trecento, does not mention Biagio.

[77] Siraisi, *Arts and Sciences*, p. 67 n. 3, citing an article by A. Favaro.

[78] S. Y. Edgerton, Jr., *The Renaissance Rediscovery of Linear Perspective* (New York, 1975), pp. 61–2: 'Toscanelli was undoubtedly influenced by Blasius' book.' The coincidence of Biagio's *Questiones* being available in transcription to Alberti (with his Paduan background) from 1428 has been insufficiently examined: see F. Borsi, *Leon Battista Alberti* (Oxford, 1977), pp. 297–8.

in Padua in 1421.[79] The interconnected disciplines of mathematics, optics, and the pursuit of the classics customary in the Studium, inspired crucial figures active in the later Renaissance.[80]

A drawing persuasively linked with the Padua of the late Trecento is perhaps sufficient to demonstrate the sophistication of applied architectural theory. The subject is the Basilica of St Anthony, presented, it would seem, as an architectural study for its own sake, demonstrating a two-point or bi-focal system of perspective rendering, with particular virtuosity in the complex apsidal chapel system (Plate 14). The drawing stands early in the lineage of architectural detailing which will come to constitute a distinctive northern Italian tradition of architectural portraiture.[81] We know of Jacopo Bellini's later documented contact with the Paduan study of perspective.[82] His sketch-book studies synthesize aspects of the favoured one-point Florentine system with the Paduan bi-focal tradition. A treatise on sculpture, written in Padua in 1504 by Pomponius Gauricus, holds to the bifocal tradition apparently still relevant in Padua; Robert Klein has spiritedly argued that the treatise is a culmination of Paduan practice.[83]

In the history of art, one piece of writing may sometimes be made to assume an undue burden as typical of its time. One of the few treatises remaining from the late fourteenth century is the *Libro d'arte* of Cennino Cennini, a Florentine from the studio of Agnolo Gaddi, who was engaged in the service of the Carrara in the 1390s, though no details of his employment are known.[84] Though the work, as is often remarked, is scarcely more than a recipe book with moral instruction added, its contents may reflect rather on the current Florentine practice than a supposed conservatism in Paduan art.[85]

[79] Baxandall, *Giotto and the Orators*, pp. 127–8, connecting Vittorino da Feltre with Padua and Biagio Pelacani.

[80] Siraisi, *Arts and Sciences*, pp. 173–4.

[81] Mellini, *Altichiero e Avanzi*, fig. 290, pp. 73–7, with reference also to Ragghianti.

[82] Cf. C. L. Joost-Gaugier, 'Jacopo Bellini's Interest in Perspective and its Iconographical Significance', *Zeitschrift für Kunstgeschichte*, 38 (1975), 5 n. 5, and figs. 8a, 8b.

[83] See Klein, 'Pomponius Guaricus on Perspective'.

[84] L. Venturi, 'La critica d'arte alla fine del Trecento: Filippo Villani e Cennino Cennini', *L'arte*, 20 (1925), 237.

[85] It should be clear from the above that the present writer is in disagreement with the view that Padua was trapped at the end of the century in a position of overstated loyalty to Giotto: cf. E. Panofsky, *Renaissance and Renascences in Western Art* (New York, 1970), p. 13 n. 2: 'a new wave of admiration for Giotto ... can be observed, characteristically, in Padua, the scene of Altichiero's activity in the last quarter of the fourteenth century.' This is based on Vergerio's view that one should study Giotto

The sophisticated basis of Paduan art is surely apparent in the late Trecento—in the potency of its perspective theory and in its sustained interest in human and architectural naturalism.

An ease within a variety of disciplines and an accompanying sense of civic responsibility has long been the hallmark of the humanist. Giovanni Dondi dall'Orologio is a Paduan paradigm: he was creator of the planetarium; lecturer in medicine, astrology, philosophy, and logic at the Studium; possessor of a library rich in classical texts (as well as in recent Paduan 'classics' by Alberto Mussato); friend of Petrarch; on occasion ambassador for Francesco il Vecchio; and proto-archaeologist in Rome, where in 1375 he made his famous annotations and measurements.[86] The versatility of the Paduan Studium and of the *signori* in a variety of scholarly and artistic fields, as in politics and diplomacy, is impressive. It is sufficient to indicate a consistent pattern of intellectual appreciation in the ambience of the Carrara. Such a climate led naturally to speculation on the rule of the just lord and his relation to the tyrant: a debate taken to be central to emergent 'civic humanism' in Florence. In 1373 Petrarch's invited address to Francesco il Vecchio articulated the issues of justice and generosity in the public arena.[87] Writing around 1406, Giovanni Conversino da Ravenna, who had come to Padua in 1392 to a chair of grammar and rhetoric, lamented the aggrandizing policies of the son, Francesco Novello, but praised the father:

who after taking over the rule of Padua repaired the walls of the city, adorned empty spaces with the construction of homes, encouraged the arts, introduced wool-working, increased the prosperity of citizens, and fostered humanistic studies to an extraordinary degree ... And in a short time, when not yet an

alone, but there is no evidence that Vergerio showed a progressive insight into the visual arts. M. Baxandall takes a similar conservative position in *Giotto and the Orators*, pp. 43–4, 49. Indeed, the view that it was Florentine painting that was retrograde, could be sustained by reference to the work of Agnolo Gaddi in Florence (cf. B. Cole, *Agnolo Gaddi* (Oxford, 1977)). The continuity in Padua of the Giottesque tradition has been seen to be augmented and deepened consistently throughout the fourteenth century from Guariento to Altichiero, Avanzo, Giusto de' Menabuoi, and Jacopo da Verona.

[86] See n. 53 above, and Weiss, *The Renaissance Discovery*, pp. 49–53. See also N. W. Gilbert, 'A Letter of Giovanni Dondi dall'Orologio to Fra Guglielmo Centueri: A Fourteenth-Century Episode in the Quarrel of the Ancients and the Moderns', *Viator*, 8 (1977), 299–346; V. Lazzarini, 'I libri, gli argenti, le vesti di Giovanni Dondi dall'-Orologio', *Bollettino del Museo Civico di Padova*, 18 (1925), 11–36.

[87] *Epistolae Seniles*, lib. xiv, I (28 Nov. 1373). See also B. G. Kohl, 'Political Attitudes of North Italian Humanists in the Late Trecento', *Studies in Medieval Culture*, 4 (1974), 419–20.

old man ... brought Padua's circumstances to such a degree of beauty and richness as a popular ruler could not have reached in a whole century.[88]

This was the common assessment of the older Francesco, whose fall from power on 29 June 1388 the Gatari chronicle records, with moving allusion to the Trojan wars and 'le lagrime degli ochy'.[89]

Francesco Novello's restoration of Carrara power in 1390 also brought with it positive, if not spectacular, acts of patronage. In the manner of his forefather, Ubertino, he first proceeded to celebrate his house's return to power by striking a set of coins, *alla romana*, which bore his own profile and those of the previous princes.[90] Modelled on the Roman sesterce, they were larger and more impressive than earlier Carrara currency, which even so, since Ubertino's innovatory rule, had not neglected the propaganda value of the coin, and had used the familiar chariot wheel device on the obverse of coins bearing Padua's saints, Prosdocimo and Daniele. The medallions of 1390 have remained central to numismatics since they presented a clear model, soon to be widely imitated, for the Renaissance. The patrons of Pisanello, author of the most famous Renaissance sequence of medals, are again inheritors of Paduan practice.[91]

In the context of Padua's precocious portraiture, the profile presentation is again relevant in frescos painted during Francesco Novello's period of power. The frescos of the Capella Bovi in the Oratory of San Michele, attributed to Jacopo da Verona, are not of the same importance as Altichiero's earlier schemes, but they do continue a tradition, by presenting the Carrara princes in close proximity to the commissioning Bovi, both in the *Adoration* and in the *Death of the Virgin*.[92]

---

[88] *Dragmalogia de Eligibili Vite Genere*, ed. and tr. H. L. Eaker and intro. B. G. Kohl (New Jersey and London, 1980), p. 129.

[89] Gatari, p. 313.

[90] See the fundamental article by J. von Schlosser, 'Die ältesten medaillen und die Antike', *Jahrbuch des kunsthistorischen Sammlungen des allerhöchsten Kaiserhauses*, 18 (1897), esp. 64–8; G. Gorini, 'Iconografia monetale e cultura figurativa a Padova nei secoli XIV e XV', in Grossato (ed.), *Da Giotto al Mantegna*, pp. 81–5; and F. Cessi, 'Monetazione e Medaglistica dei Carraresi', ibid., pp. 86–9, and catalogue nos. 116ff.

[91] R. Weiss, *Pisanello's Medallion of the Emperor John VIII Palaeologus* (London, 1966), p. 11 and plate II.

[92] L. Rizzoli, 'Ritratti di Francesco il Vecchio e di Francesco Novello da Carrara in medaglie ed affreschi padovani nel secolo XIV', *Bolletino del Museo Civico di Padova*, 25 (1932), 104–14; F. d'Arcais, 'Jacopo da Verona e la decorazione della Cappella Bovi in S. Michele a Padova', *Arte veneta*, 27 (1973), 9–33.

The fame of the coin portraits has led to a connection between them and the illustrations to a key chronicle of the 1390s: the *Liber de Principibus Carrariensibus et gestis eorum* by Pier Paolo Vergerio (Plate 15). Another notable scholar active in Padua in the 1390s, Vergerio was initially attached to the Studium and then (as did Conversino) became Chancellor to Francesco Novello.[93] Participating in the novel construction of contemporary history (a key feature of the culture of Padua) Vergerio presented biographies of the six Carrara lords.[94] Of interest to those art historians who seek a continuity of portrait intention in Padua are the nine full-page *grisaille* illustrations of the princes.[95] Here again the influence of fresco painting might be detected, specifically the influence of the lost balcony of Carrara notables in the Reggia, as described by Michiel.[96] The particularity of Guariento's portraiture (still to be seen in his tomb fresco for Ubertino) may well have had its influence on these late Trecento medallions and illustrations:[97] it would be characteristic, not to say expedient, for Francesco Novello to recall his ancestors' initiatives.

Vergerio's history of the Carrara princes has been described (by Hans Baron) as 'imbued with admiration for the ruthless power politics by which the Carrara ... had imposed their tyranny'.[98] It might well appear that Vergerio's admiration for Francesco Novello was a vested interest, but he was patently willing and able to vindicate it publicly: his oration of 1392 commemorated the Carrara recovery of Padua, insisting that the regime had the support of Paduans and that Carrara interests were those of Padua at large.[99] Vergerio's loyalty seems to have continued unabated; he believed in the efficacy of the lineage. It was to Ubertino II da Carrara, son of Francesco Novello, that he dedicated his *De ingenuis moribus*, written between 1400 and 1405,

---

[93] See Kohl, 'Political Attitudes', pp. 422–5; and D. Robey, 'P. P. Vergerio the Elder: Republicanism and Civic Values in the Work of an Early Humanist', *Past and Present*, 58 (1973), 3–37.

[94] Kohl, 'Political Attitudes', p. 425; Robey, 'P.P. Vergerio the Elder', pp. 20ff.

[95] A. Medin, 'I ritratti autentici di Francesco il Vecchio e di Francesco Novello da Carrara ultimi principi di Padova', *Bollettino del Museo Civico di Padova*, 11 (1908), 104–14.

[96] 'The balcony at the back, where the Signori of Padua are portrayed life-size in green colour ...' (*The Anonimo*, p. 38).

[97] Grossato (ed.), *Da Giotto al Mantegna*, illus. opp. catalogue no. 55, the donor portrait of Ubertino, and D'Arcais, *Guariento*, figs. 34–5.

[98] H. Baron, *The Crisis of the Early Renaissance* (Princeton, 1966), p. 132.

[99] For a critique of Baron's emphasis on the tyranny of the Carrara princes, see Robey, 'P. P. Vergerio the Elder'; for the oration, see ibid., pp. 8–9.

before proceeding to his history of the princes: *De principibus car-rariensibus*. The connection of Vergerio with the emergent humanists of Florence has long been recognized as a dialogue of Paduan con-servatism with greater Florentine progressiveness but, for our purposes, the debate does not concern the republicanism, lapsed or otherwise, of Padua, or the testimonies, solicited or spontaneous, of court subjects. Rather it is the capacity of the ruling house to elicit chronicles and a *memento vitae*.[100] The house of Carrara sustained this panegyric for more than half a century, and its success is dem-onstrated in the chronicles: the last years of Francesco Novello's rule, to 1405, are recorded in the anonymous *Gesta magnifice domus carrariensis*; and Galazzo and Bartolomeo Gatari's *Cronaca carrarese* sustains the praise. Indeed, the very derivativeness of such chronicles as Vergerio's confirms the acceptance of Carrara rhetoric and declares its effectiveness. If the manuscript illustrations are indeed a reflection of the monumental frescos in the Reggia, this too signals the visual efficacy of the programme.

The medallions, with the chronicles and their illustrations, suggest that Francesco Novello was a consolidating leader, as befitted the circumstances by which he had come to power and the uneasy nature of peace in the 1390s. He devoted attention to the restoration of the Cathedral[101] and to the expansion of the Carrara library[102]—in the former case, probably in response to the piety of his mother, Fina da Buzzacarina, who was patron of the Baptistery; and, in the latter, to the inheritance of his father, whose library included codices presented by Petrarch. The younger Francesco also continued patronage of the Studium—indirectly in his choice of scholarly chancellors, and directly as inheritor of issues concerning the autonomy of the faculties. His agreement of 1399, granting the right of faculties to elect their rectors and professors, refers back to a controversy in 1360, the time of his father's rule.[103] Outstanding among Francesco Novello's additions to the Library was the (so-called) Carrarese Herbal—the *Libro agregà* of Serapion, now in the British Museum (Plate 16). It is a product of the wide-ranging patronage of the Studium and here, in particular, of the

---

[100] Ibid., pp. 22–3, remarking that Vergerio's testimonies are 'extremely suspect, since it has now been established for some time that they are of an almost entirely derivative character'.

[101] C. Bellinati and L. Puppi, *Padova: Basiliche e chiese* (Vicenza, 1975), pt 1, p. 85.

[102] V. Lazzarini, 'Libri di Francesco Novello da Carrara', *Atti e memorie dell' Accademia Patavina di Scienze, Lettere ed Arti*, 18 (1901–2), 25–36.

[103] Siraisi, *Arts and Sciences*, p. 23.

Paduan interchange between medicine and the then embryonic science of botany.[104] Described as 'the first modern collection of naturalistic plant portraits ever made . . .',[105] the illustrations are unique in the period. The heraldic Carrara frontispiece binds it to the ruling house.

It is clear that many forms of art and scholarship (including the production of local history) served the Paduan alliance of power and spread it to a circle that included soldiers, *nobili*, and *dottori*. To grasp how it emanated from the ruling house, it is necessary to reconstruct the Reggia Carrarese, sustained and splendid (if we can judge from the records) even beside the edifices of such Paduan enemies as the Visconti and the Scaligeri. The ambition of the *nobili*, planning their tombs and embellishing their chapels, would seem to have gone hand in hand with fealty to the Carrara, whose portraits and arms are intertwined with their own in the chapels of the Cortellieri, the Contini, the Bovi, and of Bonifacio and Raimondino Lupi. The *scriptoria* of Padua were connected with the *botteghe* of the leading painters: the illustrated Statius, a manuscript of Petrarch's *De viris illustribus*, the so-called *Bibbia istoriata padovana* and the Serapion were decorated during Francesco Novello's rule, sustaining the Paduan interest in a novel, *all'antica*, mode of illustration, at the service of the distinguished tracts of their resident scholars and writers.

When the conquering Venetians entered Padua in 1405, imprisoning Francesco Novello and his sons and removing their heads in the Palazzo Ducale in January 1406, a singular culture was terminated. The house of Carrara had presented itself as the physical and the metaphorical centre of the city, from Ubertino in 1338 to Francesco Novello in 1405, in a unique and prophetic example of familial leadership borne up by a patronage both politically expedient and yet open in its encouragement of scholars. The branches of art and learning that were nourished consistently by the house of Carrara established a positive link between learning and 'tyranny', perhaps sufficient to modify the negative implications of the latter. As contemporary witnesses, the Gatari recognized the closing of an era as they concluded their history

[104] S. Bettini, 'Le miniature del "Libro Agregà de Serapiom" nella cultura artistica del tardo Trecento', in Grossato (ed.), *Da Giotto al Mantegna*, p. 55; Siraisi, *Arts and Sciences*, ch. iv: 'Scientia Naturalis et Metaphysica.'

[105] O. Pächt, 'Early Italian Nature Studies and the Early Calendar Landscape', *Journal of the Warburg and Courtauld Institutes*, 13 (1950), 31.

of Padua with 'the death of Signor Messer Francesco da Carrara and the sons Francesco Terzo and Jacopo Carrara ... and the death of Messer Ubertino da Carrara, which finishes the tragedy of our chronicle'.[106]

---

[106] Gatari, p. 579.

Palla Strozzi's Patronage and Pre-Medicean Florence

HEATHER GREGORY

ONE of the most common and tempting historical fallacies is the belief that those events or developments of which we lack a detailed knowledge are probably much the same as superficially similar events which have been investigated in some detail. Hence the example of Medicean artistic patronage in fifteenth-century Florence can exercise a kind of tyranny over our consideration of other patronage there, and more generally in Italy, during the Quattrocento. Perhaps beginning with the publication of Ernst Gombrich's 'The Early Medici as Patrons of Art' in 1960, there has been an increasing tendency to view patronage of the arts in a political context and, in particular, as part of the assertion or maintenance of a status appropriate to a substantial or dominant role in the government of a particular city.[1] Thus Werner Gundersheimer has borrowed from anthropology the notion of the 'Big Man' and applied it to the princely rulers of Quattrocento states such as Ferrara: the problem such 'Big Men' faced was 'how to satisfy the philosophical and personal requirements of a clientele committed to magnificence, splendour and fame'.[2] Useful as the framework undoubtedly is for the examination of much Renaissance patronage, it may not, however, be universally applicable. In particular, a recent suggestion that a 'Medicean pattern' can usefully be applied to the

---

[1] E. H. Gombrich, 'The Early Medici as Patrons of Art', in E. F. Jacob (ed.), *Italian Renaissance Studies* (London, 1960), pp. 279–311. Central to much recent writing on this subject is A. D. Fraser Jenkins, 'Cosimo de' Medici's Patronage of Architecture and the Theory of Magnificence', *Journal of the Warburg and Courtauld Institutes*, 33 (1970), 162–70; see also C. Clough, 'Federigo da Montefeltro's Patronage of the Arts, 1468–1482', ibid. 36 (1973), 129–44; and W. Gundersheimer, 'The Patronage of Ercole I d'Este', *Journal of Medieval and Renaissance Studies*, 7 (1977), 1–18.

[2] Gundersheimer, 'Patronage of Ercole I d'Este', pp. 3–4, and his 'Patronage in the Renaissance: An Exploratory Approach', in G. F. Lytle and S. Orgel (eds.) *Patronage in the Renaissance* (Princeton, 1981), pp. 3–23.

patronage of Palla Strozzi in Florence in the early Quattrocento—
indeed, that Palla's patronage provided a model which Cosimo de'
Medici later followed[3]—needs to be reconsidered. The dominance of
the Medici wrought many changes in the political behaviour of the
Florentine patriciate,[4] and it would not be surprising if such changes
included the redirection, whether wholly or in part, of the purposes of
individual patronage.

The notion of a connection between the cultural patronage of Palla
Strozzi and that of Cosimo de' Medici is at once suggested to the
reader of the most voluminous and frequently quoted source for Palla's
biography, the *Life* by Vespasiano da Bisticci.[5] Yet when subjected to
close examination, Vespasiano's claim to credence is far from absolute
where the details of Palla's patronage are concerned, and it becomes
clear that the power of the Medicean example exercised at least as
much fascination over him as it might over any modern historian.
Vespasiano's portrait of Palla in fact represents what he might have
been, had he been very like Cosimo de' Medici. It is necessary to take
a fresh look at this early Quattrocento patron, without the aid or
hindrance of such governing preconceptions. From such a re-exam-
ination, there emerges an example of early Quattrocento patronage of
the arts and of learning which, while influenced by considerations of
fashionable humanist taste and of family tradition, was nevertheless
not primarily motivated by political considerations. Because Palla's
activities after his exile in 1434, in collaboration with his son-in-law
Giovanni Rucellai, have recently been examined in detail, the present
chapter will be devoted to the period before Palla's expulsion.[6] I will
concentrate on those areas of his patronage which are, at least to some

[3] D. D. Davisson, 'The Iconology of the S. Trinita Sacristy, 1418–1435: A Study of
the Private and Public Functions of Religious Art in the Early Quattrocento', *Art
Bulletin*, 57 (1975), 323.

[4] N. Rubinstein, *The Government of Florence under the Medici, 1434–1494* (Oxford,
1966); D. V. Kent, *The Rise of the Medici: Faction in Florence 1426–1434* (Oxford,
1978); D. V. Kent, Chapter 4 in this volume. A recent attempt to relate political, cultural,
and patronage changes in fifteenth-century Italy may be found in L. Martines, *Power
and Imagination: City-States in Renaissance Italy* (London, 1980).

[5] Vespasiano da Bisticci, *Le vite*, ed. A. Greco (Florence, 1976), ii. 139–65.

[6] See F. W. Kent, 'The Making of a Renaissance Patron of the Arts', in F. W. Kent *et
al.*, *Giovanni Rucellai ed il suo zibaldone*, II: *A Florentine Patrician and his Palace*
(London, 1981), pp. 9–95; see also D. V. and F. W. Kent, *Neighbours and Neighbourhood
in Renaissance Florence: The District of the Red Lion in the Fifteenth Century* (Locust
Valley, NY, 1982), pp. 145–50.

extent, illuminated by his own writings: the building of the Santa Trinita chapel and his manuscript collection.[7]

Palla Strozzi has received rather curious treatment at the hands of modern historians. There are many cursory references to him, in which he features as a 'representative' citizen–humanist, or as one of the circle of students around Manuel Chrysoloras;[8] single aspects of his intellectual activity—most commonly his collection of Greek and Latin manuscripts, or the chapel in Santa Trinita—have also been studied.[9] But in general little has been done to illuminate the man, his personality, or the motivation for his patronage. In addition, there has been little or no consideration of his role in Florentine and Italian politics, or of his eminence as a Florentine ambassador. The only modern biography of Palla unfortunately makes little use of his writings, and tends to be uncritical in its use of the accounts of his early biographers.[10]

One reason why Palla has been poorly served is the lack of a single accessible and coherent source by means of which his career may be approached. The evidence on Palla's life and activities is scrappy and incomplete, particularly for the period after his exile. While there is a variety of evidence for the Florentine period, in the form of some private letters, account books, and tax returns,[11] almost no letters

---

[7] His participation in guild patronage is not considered here: nor is his activity as a collector, except of MSS. Giovanni Rucellai refers to Palla's possession of *arienti* and *gioie* in the *zibaldone*: see A. Perosa (ed.), *Giovanni Rucellai ed il suo zibaldone*, I: *Il zibaldone quaresimale* (London, 1960), p. 63.

[8] So L. Martines, *The Social World of the Florentine Humanists, 1390–1460* (London, 1963), pp. 12, 166–7, 249, 316–18; R. Weiss, *The Renaissance Discovery of Classical Antiquity* (Oxford, 1969), p. 54. His finances were treated in A. Molho, *Florentine Public Finances in the Early Renaissance, 1400–1433* (Cambridge, Mass., 1971), pp. 157–60.

[9] Davisson, 'Iconology'; G. Poggi, *La cappella e la tomba di Onofrio Strozzi nella chiesa di Santa Trinita (1419–1423)* (Florence, 1903); G. Fiocco, 'La biblioteca di Palla Strozzi', *Studi di bibliografia e di storia in onore di T. De Marinis*, ii (Verona, 1964), 289–310; idem., 'La casa di Palla Strozzi', *Memorie dell'Accademia dei Lincei: Classe di Scienze Morali*, Ser. vii, 5, 7 (1954), 361–82; A. Diller, 'The Greek Codices of Palla Strozzi and Guarino Veronese', *Journal of the Warburg and Courtauld Institutes*, 24 (1961), 313–21; and M. L. Sosower, 'Seven Manuscripts Palla Strozzi Gave to the S. Giustina Library', ibid. 47 (1984), pp. 190–1.

[10] L. Belle, 'A Renaissance Patrician: Palla di Nofri Strozzi, 1327–1462', unpublished PhD thesis (University of Rochester, 1975).

[11] The most important archival materials for the Florentine period are contained in Archivio di Stato, Florence, Carte Strozziane (hereafter CS), ser. 3 (esp. *filze* 280–1, 284–6 and 345). (All manuscript references are to collections in the Florentine State Archives, unless otherwise indicated.) There are also some private letters in Biblioteca Laurenziana, Florence (Ashburnham 1830, Carteggio Acciaiuoli, Casetta II), and in the Biblioteca Nazionale, Florence (henceforth BNF), Fondo principale, V, 10.

survive from the period of exile (from 1434 till 1462); nor is there any coherent financial record.[12] While the two very long wills which Palla wrote during his exile are invaluable,[13] they only illuminate certain areas: the chapel in Santa Trinita, to some extent his collection of manuscripts, his relationship with his immediate family, and his attitude to various ancestral Florentine properties. But on other matters—the degree of his involvement in the planned Albizzi coup of September 1434,[14] the precise reasons for his exile, the nature of his friendship with Cosimo de' Medici—Palla's surviving writings tell us nothing at all. Despite their length, and their unusually discursive and descriptive nature, the wills of 1447 and 1462 are fundamentally arrangements for the disposition of property, and it is necessary here to be cautious about any argument from silence. Because of an unfortunate combination of circumstances, both the letters and the accounts illuminating Palla's property and financial dealings after 1434, and perhaps also his attitude to his exile, were either destroyed or lost.[15] So far as his patronage in particular is concerned, the deliberate burning of the master account book (in which were recorded all the financial dealings conducted by his eldest son, Lorenzo, on his father's account in Florence during the 1430s) almost certainly destroyed crucial evidence relating to the history of the Santa Trinita chapel after 1434.[16]

To one assessing the accuracy of Vespasiano's *Life* of Palla Strozzi, not the least of the problems is that it is not contemporary biography.

---

[12] Biblioteca Riccardiana, Florence, 4009 (unfol.) contains a single letter of Palla to Francesco Caccini, Padua, of 27 May 1450. On the difficult nature of the evidence for Palla's period in exile, see F. W. Kent, 'Making of a Renaissance Patron', pp. 22ff.; for the events of these years in so far as they can be reconstructed, see ibid., pp. 22–39, and my thesis, 'A Florentine Family in Crisis: the Strozzi in the Fifteenth Century', unpublished PhD thesis (University of London, 1980), pp. 221–46.

[13] Archivio di Stato, Ferrara, Archivio Bentivoglio (hereafter Arch. Bent.), lib. IV.I.2, and lib. III.34.

[14] On this ambiguous and puzzling episode, see D. V. Kent, *Rise of the Medici*, pp. 333–4; we are in fact reliant entirely on Cavalcanti for the suggestion that Palla had agreed in advance to join Rinaldo degli Albizzi's coup. Vespasiano, perhaps predictably, states only that his support (and that of the 'parecchi centinaia de' fanti che gli guardassino la casa sua') was unsuccessfully sought by Rinaldo (*Le vite*, ii. 153); but cf. the slightly different account in the *Life* of Agnolo Pandolfini, ibid., p. 277.

[15] F. W. Kent, 'Making of a Renaissance Patron', p. 10.

[16] Arch. Bent., lib. IV.I.2. fo. 18: ·

Ancor perchè dopo e mie confini ... decto Lorenzo rimase a Firenze e stettevi alcuni anni e fece tutte le faccende di là e di possessioni e d'altro. Et molte cose gli convenne fare, di che mal potrebbe render ragione. Spetialmente essendosi arso certo libro e quaderno dove aveva scritto tutto. Che dice si fece a bonissimo fine e che cosa fu consigliato e per lo meglio. E così mi pare essere certo, che a buon fine facesse.

While Vespasiano's precise date of birth is uncertain, he was no older than fourteen at the time of Palla's exile, and may well have been only twelve.[17] It is equally impossible to date the composition of the *Lives* precisely, but Albinia de la Mare has argued that the *Life* of Alessandra de' Bardi, Palla's daughter-in-law—in which a substantial part of the material in Palla's *Life* also appears—was written between 1478 and 1482; the four Strozzi *Lives* were certainly completed by 1491.[18] The *Life* of Palla is neither wholly accurate nor wholly inaccurate. Vespasiano's account, for example, of Manuel Chrysoloras' coming to Florence to teach Greek, and Palla's involvement here, seems true in its broad outline.[19] However, his attribution to Palla of a major role in obtaining manuscripts of works hitherto unknown in Italy, while bearing a certain relation to the truth, is almost certainly exaggerated. Vespasiano refers to the 'Cosmographia, colla pittura' which he claimed Palla had had sent to Florence from Constantinople.[20] Palla in his will of 1462 made it clear that Chrysoloras had brought the manuscript to Florence and had later given it to him.[21] Some of Vespasiano's statements about Palla's family are obviously inaccurate, most notably the assertion that all his sons (and Nofri is specifically mentioned) predeceased him.[22] However on other matters, such as the patronage of Palla's youngest son Carlo by Pope Nicholas V, and the

---

[17] On the evidence of *catasto* returns, Vespasiano's age was given as eight in 1427, as nine in 1430/1, as twelve in 1433 (A. de la Mare, 'Vespasiano da Bisticci, Historian and Bookseller', unpublished PhD thesis (2 vols., University of London, 1966) ii. 292; G. Cagni, *Vespasiano da Bisticci e il suo epistolario* (Rome, 1969), p. 13). He claimed to have known Niccoli as early as 1433/4 (*Le vite*, ii. 230–1), which is even more remarkable if he was only eleven in that year, as his notarized deposition of 1477 suggests (cited by Cagni, *Vespasiano*, p. 13).

[18] De la Mare, 'Vespasiano da Bisticci', i. 26; the four Strozzi *Lives* (of Palla, Matteo di Simone, Messer Marcello, and Benedetto di Pieraccione) were presented to Filippo Strozzi at some time before his death in that year. The *proemio* addressed to Filippo exists in two substantially different versions (*Le vite*, ii. 429–33, 434–8).

[19] Here the difficulty encountered is that the available accounts are all largely dependent on that of Vespasiano. The later biographies of Palla, such as Lorenzo Strozzi's (*Le vite degli uomini illustri della casa Strozzi*, ed. P. Stromboli (Florence, 1892) and that of A. Fabronio (*Pallantis Stroctii vita* (Parma, 1802)) are clearly derivative, and most modern historians have been prepared to accept Vespasiano's authority.

[20] Greco (ed.), *Le vite*, ii. 140.

[21] Arch. Bent., lib. III, 34, fo. 27. The same probably applies to the copy of Plutarch's *Lives*, which Vespasiano mentions; see my article, 'A Further Note on the Greek Manuscripts of Palla Strozzi', *Journal of the Warburg and Courtauld Institutes*, 44 (1981), 184; and Greco (ed.), *Le vite*, i. 140.

[22] Greco (ed.), *Le vite*, i. 162. Nofri, with his brother Giovanfrancesco, was the recipient of a letter of consolation on their father's death from Francesco Filelfo; published in Fabronio, *Pallantis Stroctii vita*, pp. 39–50.

assassination of his eldest son in Gubbio, he is quite correct.[23] Elsewhere, as in the case of the story of Palla's having borrowed 20,000 florins from Cosimo de' Medici (or perhaps it was an investment on Cosimo's part) and how, when unable to repay it, he made over to Cosimo property to that value in Empoli and Prato, we must remain sceptical without other evidence.[24]

What, then, was the likely source of Vespasiano's information? He was a close friend of one of Palla's grandsons, Bernardo Rucellai, whose father, Giovanni, had made a modest beginning to the biographical tradition about his father-in-law in the late 1450s.[25] The most famous part of Giovanni's portrait, Lionardo Bruni's attribution to Palla of the 'seven parts of happiness', also appears in Vespasiano's *Life*, and it seems probable that Vespasiano knew of this story through his friendship with Bernardo.[26] However, we can discount the possibility that Vespasiano had actually read Giovanni Rucellai's *Zibaldone*, or at least that he had read all of it, otherwise it is difficult to understand why he neglected to use the other valuable information which it contained about his subject; for example, Giovanni's statement that Palla 'went 50 years at a time without having had a fever, and for 86 years had all his teeth, without ever losing one'.[27]

Vespasiano had a number of other contacts with Palla's kinsmen and friends, but in all cases these were at one generation removed. He

---

[23] Greco (ed.), *Le vite*, ii. 162. The Strozzi correspondence makes clear what Vespasiano tactfully forbore to mention, that Lorenzo's assailant was a Bardi and therefore a kinsman of Lorenzo's wife, variously identified as Lorenzo or as Jacopo di Lionardo de' Bardi: CS 3, 131, fo. 65—Niccolò Strozzi to Filippo Strozzi, Florence, of 6 Mar. 1451; fo. 66—Smeraldo Strozzi to Filippo Strozzi, Rome, of 20 Mar. 1451; fo. 67—a certain Francesco (surname uncertain) to Filippo Strozzi, Florence, of 3 Apr. 1451.

[24] Greco (ed.), *Le vite*, ii. 149–50. Palla's *catasto* 'portata' of 1427 (not autograph) is at CS 3, 129, fos. 23ff. The *campione* entry is Catasto, 76, fos. 169–202. Vespasiano emphasized Palla's friendship with Cosimo de' Medici, a matter on which corroborating evidence is lacking; see, e.g., Greco (ed.), *Le vite*, ii. 152. Lorenzo Strozzi in his *Life* of Palla, although following Vespasiano closely in other respects, omitted this material entirely.

[25] Perosa (ed.), *Il zibaldone quaresimale*, p. 63.

[26] Greco (ed.), *Le vite*, ii. 142–3. The *proemio* to the *Lives* of Ser Filippo di Ser Ugolino, Niccolò Niccoli and Franco Sacchetti was addressed to Bernardo Rucellai (ibid., ii. 459–60).

[27] Perosa (ed.), *Il zibaldone quaresimale*, p. 54. The interpolation of which this passage forms a part, on the 'Quattro Grandi di Firenze', was clearly written after the death of both Palla and Cosimo de' Medici (ibid., p. 157 n. 34). Baron does not consider this passage in his investigation of Palla's age (see H. Baron, 'The Year of Leonardo Bruni's Birth and Methods for Determining the Ages of Humanists Born in the Trecento', *Speculum*, 52 (1977), 583–6).

was a close friend of the brothers Donato and Piero Acciaiuoli, who
were also Palla's grandsons, and who maintained contact with their
grandfather and maternal uncles after their exile, although they had
only been children in 1434.[28] Vespasiano also knew Messer Piero
Strozzi, whose father, Benedetto, had been Palla's friend, political ally,
and copyist.[29] Last but not perhaps least, Vespasiano was a friend and
probably a client of Filippo Strozzi, whose father Matteo had been a
next-door neighbour and intimate of Palla's whole household; Matteo
had, for example, taken a leading part in arranging Lorenzo di Palla's
betrothal to Alessandra de' Bardi in 1428.[30] Because of his father's
early death and his own departure from Florence at the age of twelve,
it is uncertain how much Filippo knew about his much older kinsman.[31]

When we come to what must be the most controversial aspect of
Vespasiano's *Life*, the story that Palla planned to build and furnish
with manuscripts a public library in the church of Santa Trinita,[32] it
is clear that none of Vespasiano's probable informants was old enough
to have contemporary memories of such a plan. But the fact that
Vespasiano's *Life* of Palla, together with the other three Strozzi *Lives*,
was presented to Filippo, is likely to have influenced its composition
in another way. Vespasiano may have wished to flatter this ambitious
builder through his portrait of Palla. The question of whether Palla
ever in fact planned such a project will be discussed in detail below.
What must be stressed here is that Vespasiano was not in a position

---

[28] They were the sons of Lena di Messer Palla by her first marriage, to Neri di Donato
Acciaiuoli. On their friendship with Vespasiano, see de la Mare, 'Vespasiano da Bisticci',
ii. 17–18, 301, 304–5; on their relationship with Palla, see E. Garin, 'La giovinezza di
Donato Acciaiuoli, 1429–1456', *Rinascimento*, 1 (1950), 47–9. Piero Acciaiuoli wrote in
1451 that Lorenzo di Messer Palla had been 'a noi in spezialità singulare padre'
(Biblioteca Riccardiana, 4009, unfol.—Piero Acciaiuoli to Francesco Caccini, Florence,
of 5[?] Mar. 1451).

[29] A. de la Mare, 'Messer Piero Strozzi, a Florentine Priest and Scribe', in A. S. Osley
(ed.), *Essays Presented to Alfred Fairbanks on his Seventieth Birthday* (London, 1975),
pp. 55–68.

[30] On Vespasiano's friendship with Filippo, see de la Mare, 'Vespasiano da Bisticci',
ii. 387; Cagni, *Vespasiano*, pp. 172–4, publishes a letter of Vespasiano to Alfonso,
Filippo's eldest son, in which he refers to two new *Lives* he was sending Alfonso, 'in
memoria dell'amicitia ho tenuto con phillipo tuo padre e del simile in tu'. In 1487 Filippo
had recorded a gift of cloth worth 12 florins to Vespasiano (CS 5, 41, fo. 29ʳ). For
Matteo's role in the Strozzi–Bardi marriage, see CS 3, 132, fos. 278–9—Palla Strozzi to
Matteo Strozzi, Ferrara, of 7 Mar. 1428, and Nofri di Palla Strozzi to Matteo Strozzi,
Ferrara, of the same date.

[31] R. Goldthwaite, *Private Wealth in Renaissance Florence: A Study of Four Families*
(Princeton, 1968), pp. 53–4.

[32] Greco (ed.), *Le vite*, ii. 146–7.

accurately to describe Palla's patronage of up to fifty years before he wrote, as he was able to do for that of Cosimo de' Medici, of which he was a contemporary witness and in which he was an active participant.[33]

There is one other factor which must be taken into consideration when assessing the reliability of Vespasiano's biography. It is extremely probable that, at least by the time he wrote the *Lives*, he was seriously disenchanted with the Medicean regime.[34] It was almost certainly shortly after the expulsion of Piero di Lorenzo de' Medici in 1494 that Vespasiano wrote, in a *proemio* addressed to Bernardo Rucellai, that 'the most merciful God has returned the affairs of the city to the true path'.[35] His republican sentiments, combined with a probable long-term commitment to the exiled Filippo Strozzi, suggest that his picture of Palla was less than dispassionate. Like many other Florentines of the Quattrocento, Vespasiano believed that his century had witnessed a golden age of learning and culture. But significantly he placed this golden age before the advent of Medicean dominance:

In this time, from [fourteen] twenty-two to thirty-three the city of Florence was in the happiest condition, abundantly supplied with outstanding men in every branch of learning, and it was full of most excellent citizens, each of whom endeavoured to outdo the others in their abilities [*nella virtù*] and she was famous in all the world for her excellent government . . .[36]

To Vespasiano, Palla was the exemplar of this golden age, and he wished to display his hero's merits to the full. Yet he seems to have been influenced in his description by the attributes of the great patron of his own maturity, Cosimo de' Medici. It would appear that Cosimo was excluded from Vespasiano's golden age for reasons of political ideology rather than of historical judgement.

It has generally been accepted that Palla was born in 1372; but 1376,

---

[33] On Cosimo's commissions for the libraries at San Marco and at the Badia at Fiesole, see de la Mare, 'Vespasiano da Bisticci', ii. ch. 3.

[34] His attitude even to Cosimo was by no means completely uncritical; see, e.g., the Life of Ser Filippo, in Greco (ed.), *Le Vite*, ii. 257. For criticism of the regime under Lorenzo, see e.g., the Life of Donato Acciaiuoli (*Le vite*, ii. 36–8, 42–3.)

[35] Greco, (ed.), *Le vite*, ii. 460.

[36] Ibid., 144. In the *Life* of Benedetto Strozzi he drew a clear comparison between this 'golden age' and the present: 'E così come oggi . . . chi non ha danari, non è stimato nulla, et in quel tempo chi non sapeva lettere non era stimato fusse uomo . . .'

the date indirectly supplied by Giovanni Rucellai, seems nearer the truth.[37] He was the second son of Nofri Strozzi and Giovanna, or Nanna, Cavalcanti; Nofri had a third, illegitimate son as well, and five daughters who lived long enough to be dowered.[38] Nofri appears to have built up a very substantial fortune in the French and English wool trade. He achieved high office in the commune, and was Gonfalonier of Justice in 1385 and 1396. In 1403 his *prestanza*, or forced loan, contribution was assessed at 121 florins, the highest in the quarter of Santa Maria Novella and the seventh highest in the city.[39] An undated statement on the value of his assets in his son Palla's hand (which probably comes from 1403 and may well be a draft of a statement submitted to the commune seeking a reduction in his estimate) refers to '12,000 florins or more' spent since 1380 without any return.[40] Even the fragmentary records of his property purchases suggest the activity of a man with a great deal of spare cash. Particularly noteworthy was his accumulation of a large number of houses surrounding the family residence between the Via Tornabuoni and the Piazza Strozzi, a programme completed by his son.[41] Nofri married his younger legitimate son, Palla, to a daughter of the exiled archguelf Carlo Strozzi in 1397, when Palla was probably twenty-one, Marietta's dowry being 900 florins.[42] Nofri's best-known project is the burial chapel in Santa Trinita dedicated to his and his eldest son's patron saints, Honophrius and Nicholas.[43] Despite the difficulty in distinguishing Nofri's intentions from his son's execution of them, there seems little that was modest in this plan. Nor was there in the provisions for his funeral in Santa Trinita: the keeper of that church's accounts was moved to

---

[37] See above, n. 27.

[38] Lorenzo Strozzi (*Vite degli Strozzi*, p. 23) wrongly identifies Palla's mother as Alessandra Cavalcanti. For Palla's dispute with Marco over their father's estate, see Arch. Bent., lib. IV.1.2, fos. 21–2; for his five sisters, CS 3, 116, fo. 4ʳ (undated statement on the 'valuta dello stato' of Nofri di Palla Strozzi).

[39] On Nofri's business activities, see two account books in CS 3, 280–1; on his being Gonfalonier of Justice, see Priorista Mariani, i. fo. 94ʳ; as consul of the *arte della lana*, CS 3, 79, fo. 89; on his *prestanza* assessment, Martines, *The Social World*, App. 2, pp. 359–62.

[40] CS 3, 116, fo. 4ʳ. This had been spent chiefly on dowries (5,000 florins) and on taxes (more than 8,000 florins).

[41] Records of some of Nofri's acquisitions are in CS 3, 281, fos. 14ᵛ, 15ᵛ–16ʳ, and 3, 93, fos. 419, 421. For the very large site Palla had accumulated by 1427, see my thesis, 'A Florentine Family in Crisis', pp. 53–5.

[42] Belle, 'A Renaissance Patrician', p. 45.

[43] Davisson, 'Iconology', pp. 321–3.

comment, most uncharacteristically, that 'on the 17 April [1417] the funeral of Nofri di Palla was held, most magnificently'.[44] The lack of information about Nofri's life may well obscure what was a significant career as a builder, and one which may have influenced his son considerably.

From the little that is known of Palla's early life it appears that, as the younger son of a very rich man (his elder brother Niccolò did not die until 1411[45]), he enjoyed sufficient leisure to pursue the new humanistic studies seriously. According to Vespasiano, Palla was (with Niccolò Niccoli) personally responsible for bringing Manuel Chrysoloras to Italy in 1397. Palla, in referring to the occasion long after, was non-committal, stating only that the Greek 'was brought' to Italy in that year.[46] In 1404, Palla was one of twenty 'youths' sent by the Florentine commune as hostages to Pisa; he was knighted by the King of Naples in 1415, during one of his many ambassadorships. While he also held some internal offices, these were, with the exception of the *Dieci di balìa* during the 1420s, not partisan in nature, and even with the *Dieci* it seems likely that his presence was due to his unequalled diplomatic experience.[47]

During a career of thirty years in Florentine politics, Palla was not once a member of the *Signoria*, the city's leading magistracy, despite both the very large majorities which he received in scrutinies, and the frequent appearances as Prior by other prominent members of his lineage. This is not to suggest that he was a negligible figure in internal Florentine politics: Dale Kent has shown that he was one of sixty-four Florentine citizens requested to appear at between thirty and seventy meetings of the *consulte e pratiche*, or informal government

---

[44] Conventi Soppressi, 89, 10, fo. 31ᵛ. Six hundred *libbre* of wax were used at a cost of 268 lire; cf. the cost of the wax (18 lire) at the funeral of Vieri di Rinaldo Strozzi in Nov. 1414; ibid., fo. 36ʳ.

[45] CS 3, 280, fo. 117ᵛ; Conventi Soppressi, 89, 10, fo. 14ᵛ. He died on 25 July 1411, and was buried in Santa Trinita on 29 July.

[46] Greco (ed.), *Le vite*, ii. 140; Arch. Bent., lib. III, 34, fo. 27; 'messer Manuello Crisolora Greco di Constantinopoli, quando a Firenze venne condocto ad insegnar Greco nel mccclxxxxvii'.

[47] On the Pisan episode, Martines, *The Social World*, p. 51; on his knighting in Naples, CS 3, 103, fo. 26. Other offices included that of ambassador to the pope in 1424, to the Marquis of Ferrara in 1426, to Ferrara again in 1428, 1432, and 1433, of Florentine orator in Venice in 1428, and ambassador to Siena in 1433. In 1427 he was (with Rinaldo degli Albizzi) war commissioner to Volterra, and was appointed a member of the *Dieci di balìa* in 1423, 1424, 1427, and 1432 (CS 3, 103, fo. 54; 3, 112, fo. 112; 3, 132, fo. 220; 3, 146, fos. 3–5, 8–9; Belle, 'A Renaissance Patrician', pp. 264, 284, 286–7).

discussions, in the five-year period 1429–34.[48] This is all the more significant when it is remembered that he was absent from Florence on ambassadorial duties for long periods during these five years. While it is difficult to know precisely what conclusions should be reached about his career, it seems reasonable to suppose that he lacked the ambition or motivation for a career in Florence's internal politics, and that he was certainly not at the heart of the Albizzi faction up until 1434. However he clearly was a man of influence whose opinion was widely respected within the political class.[49] His surviving private letters make almost no reference to domestic politics, and on only one occasion do they include statements which could be construed as criticism of the regime.[50] In the context of a career from which factional politics appear to have been largely absent, it is perhaps not so surprising that he eventually failed to join the attempted *coup d'état* of September 1434, led by Rinaldo degli Albizzi, the Peruzzi, and others among their faction. Indeed he was originally elected a member of the pro-Medicean *balìa* or special council of 1434, which eventually (though apparently only with difficulty) secured his exile. It seems likely that he was exiled more because of his wealth and prominence, and the possession of a network of anti-Medicean kinsmen and marriage alliances, than because of any factional activity of his own.[51]

It is tempting to see Palla Strozzi as a merchant hero of the early Renaissance, fitting everything else into a life dominated by mercantile endeavour. Giovanni Rucellai described his father-in-law as he was when he and Jacopa were betrothed in 1428: 'the said Messer Palla was the most powerful and the greatest citizen of our land, and the richest, and it was believed that Christendom had no citizen richer than he.'[52] However it seems true that Nofri's great fortune began to

---

[48] In the scrutiny of 1433 Palla received 249 'yes' and 11 'no' votes—a larger majority than that gained by any other person in the district of the Red Lion: Tratte, 46, fos. 72–5; D. V. Kent, 'The Florentine *Reggimento* in the Fifteenth Century', *Renaissance Quarterly*, 28 (1975), 604–5.

[49] Hence Rinaldo degli Albizzi's desperate attempt to persuade him to join the Sant'Apollinare rising (Kent, *Rise of the Medici*, pp. 333–4).

[50] CS 3, 112, fo. 112—Palla Strozzi to Matteo Strozzi, Ferrara, of 3 Apr. 1433; written during protracted negotiations to end the war with Lucca, which he had always opposed.

[51] The sentences of exile are in Otto di Guardia e Balìa, 224, fo. 46ᵛ; for Palla's membership of the *balìa* of 1434, see Rubinstein, *The Government*, p. 251. He was exiled for only five years in the first instance. Lorenzo Strozzi records a romanticized tradition of the difficulty which the *balìa* had in securing his exile (*Vite degli Strozzi*, pp. 38–9). See also Kent, *Rise of the Medici*, p. 343, for Palla's continued appearance in *pratiche* in Oct. 1434.

[52] Perosa (ed.), *Il zibaldone quaresimale*, p. 63.

decline soon after Palla inherited it, and that its detailed administration
was always in the hands of others. By 1427, when it was recorded in
the tax returns, the bulk of his fortune was in the form of shares in
the *monte* or communal debt, country property and urban real estate,
none of it particularly profitable.[53] His main business enterprise was
the bank, officially a partnership between his son Lorenzo and Orsino
Lanfredini, but in practice conducted by Orsino. Writing from Arezzo
in January 1424, Palla told Orsino that Lionardo Bruni wished to
invest in the bank. After explaining how 'very discreetly and prudently,
as always' Messer Lionardo had expressed the wish that his money be
invested safely, and that he did not have a large appetite for profit, he
concluded:

I believe it will be best to use the money in honest matters. You know how
to lighten his conscience, always using a reasoned judgement in your dealings
with him . . . I do not understand these matters and I could make errors. You,
as one who both understands and practises such business, must make what
seems to you the best arrangements, for him and for us, and which will
maintain his friendship and brotherly feelings. He is happy to deal with our
bank, and we must be happy to deal with him. I do not know the sum . . .[54]

This extract illustrates very clearly the distance that Palla maintained
from what was, after all, his most important business enterprise.

It would not, however, be accurate to suggest that Palla inhabited
a rarefied world into which the sordid realities of Florentine economic
life did not obtrude. Indeed, a large part of his surviving correspondence is concerned with financial matters. For example, he
wrote many letters in 1424 to his son-in-law, Neri Acciaiuoli, pleading
with him to come home from Romania to deal with urgent financial
concerns. The series begins calmly enough in January,[55] but by July
his tone had changed to one of urgency: after several more months of
war, and very numerous *prestanze*, it now seemed a matter of life and
death that Neri should return:

I have advised you to return here quickly for your own good, and so that you
can make provision for your financial position, which it seems to me, if not
provided for, will go to ruin. Such has happened to many others who have

---

[53] Molho, *Florentine Public Finances*, pp. 157–60.

[54] BNF Fondo principale, II, V, 10, fo. 218—Palla Strozzi to Orsino Lanfredini, Arezzo,
of 6 Jan. 1424. In 1433 Bruni was a creditor of the bank for 1026 florins (Catasto, 463,
fo. 344ʳ).

[55] Biblioteca Laurenziana, Ashburnham 1830, Carteggio Acciaiuoli, Casetta 2,
fo. 428—Palla Strozzi to Neri Acciaiuoli, Arezzo, of 6 Jan. 1424.

been badly treated with taxes. I have waited for you for some months, believing every day that you must return. And with this hope, and so that your property and everything doesn't go to ruin, I have paid the *prestanze* for you, borrowing for you at interest.[56]

Significantly for our understanding of Palla's financial position at this time, he added that he had borrowed money for Neri because 'it didn't suit me to borrow money again on my own account, which would have been awkward for me'. That Palla, as the *de facto* proprietor of a major Florentine bank, had had to raise money at interest to pay his own taxes—he noted in the same letter that the *prestanze* had been levied forty times since the present war had begun, and as many as five times in a single month—shows that he was already short of liquid assets, despite his apparently great wealth.

As early as 1422 Palla, then in Venice on urgent business matters ('I find myself here to make what provisions I can to stop our property, and more besides, going completely to perdition'), had written at length of the difficulties he faced in paying the taxes imposed on him, difficulties which would in normal circumstances have brought him back to Florence. Simone Strozzi, to whom this letter was addressed, was a close friend and kinsman, and Palla asked him to make what representations he could to the men of the district of the Red Lion on his account.[57] He went on to describe to Simone the expenses he had suffered in the previous five years:

At the present time, if I make a full account, between the funeral of Nofri and in building and decorating the chapel, and losses which I have suffered, and dowries which I have had to pay, and other things, since Nofri died to the present time, I am the worse off, and altogether thirty thousand florins have gone. This is certain, and doesn't take into account the properties and other possessions from the house which went to Marco. And if I am not treated with consideration, given the great amount which has gone under, and the unbearable expenses I have had, though I could not do less, I see no remedy for my affairs.

The interest of this statement is in proportion to its rarity. Unlike, for example, Giovanni Rucellai, Palla was not given to expansive remarks about his own patronage. While it is clearly necessary to accept his expressed desperation about financial affairs with caution, the sum mentioned (30,000 florins) is very substantial indeed. Almost equally eloquent of straitened circumstances was the fact that by March 1428 Palla devoted nearly all of a letter to Orsino Lanfredini to a discussion of the purchase of a single farm, commenting that 'I know I am in no position to buy, and that I should sooner wish to sell'.[58] Whatever the financial strains Palla had encountered during the earlier 1420s— and it seems they were at times considerable—his tax burden was intolerably increased from 1427 onwards, with the introduction of the *catasto*. Giovanni Rucellai tells us that Palla paid the sum of 160,000 florins in taxes between 1423 and 1433.[59]

When we come to the discernible motives for Palla Strozzi's artistic patronage, the best starting-point is the description given above of the great expense in which his building the Santa Trinita chapel, amongst other things, had involved him. This statement bears a passing resemblance to Lorenzo de' Medici's famous account of the money he, his father, and grandfather had spent on 'buildings, charities and taxes' between 1434 and 1471.[60] But in contrast to Lorenzo's rider, 'I think it gave great lustre to the state and this money seems to have been well spent', making clear the public and political connotations he associated with this big expenditure, Palla's statement places the expense to which the Santa Trinita sacristy had committed him firmly in the private domain, together with dowries, his father's funeral, and business losses. This impression may be confirmed by the fact that Palla makes no references to taxes in this estimate of expenses, even though the same letter describes in detail his current difficulty in paying them. For Palla, money spent on such patronage was less a public or civic duty or benefaction, than a private and family obligation: 'I could not do less.'

Palla's patronage falls into three main categories: his collection of Greek and Latin manuscripts, his friendship with, and in some cases sponsorship of, humanist scholars such as Bruni, Chrysoloras, Francesco Filelfo, and Tommaso Parentucelli (the future Pope Nicholas

---

[58] BNF, Fondo principale, II, V, 10, fo. 231—Palla Strozzi to Orsino Lanfredini, Ferrara, of 22 Mar. 1428; Orsino was to buy it 'per il meno che si può honestamente e ragionevolemente'. It is not identified.

[59] Perosa (ed.), *Il zibaldone quaresimale*, p. 63; Molho, *Florentine Public Finances*, p. 160, arrives at a similar figure, made up of forced loans and interest on loans taken to meet his tax assessments.

[60] Gombrich, 'The Early Medici as Patrons of Art', pp. 284–5.

V),[61] and his building projects. The latter include the chapel and perhaps a plan for a family palace. (This is not documented, but there is a record of property acquisition.)[62] If Palla's grandson, Alessandro di Giovanfrancesco Strozzi, was correct in stating in 1477 that his father's share of Palla's 'residual' manuscripts (those that remained after his bequest to Santa Giustina in Padua) included 'eighty-three . . . volumes of Greek works', Palla must have had one of the largest such collections of the early Quattrocento.[63] However its creation was essentially in the private domain, and there is no evidence that it was destined to form the nucleus of some public collection.[64]

After describing Palla's employment of scribes and purchase of books, Vespasiano stated that he had

the intention of making a most excellent library in S. Trinita, and of building there a most beautiful place for it. He wished that it should be public, and that everyone should have access to it, and that it should be in S. Trinita, because it is in the middle of Florence, a place very convenient for everyone. And in this library there were to be books on all subjects, sacred as well as secular, and not only in Latin but also in Greek.[65]

It is very tempting to view Palla's activity as a collector of manuscripts in what we might call a 'Medicean' light, and to assume that Vespasiano is correct here. However when we look more closely at this tradition, we find that there is nothing beyond Vespasiano's testimony

[61] For Filelfo's friendship with Palla Strozzi and his sons, see CS 3, 112, fo. 91—Nofri di Messer Palla Strozzi to Matteo Strozzi, Ferrara, of 22 Dec. 1431. A. Brown, 'The Humanist Portrait of Cosimo de' Medici', *Journal of the Warburg and Courtauld Institutes*, 24 (1961), 190, cites a letter of Filelfo to Cosimo in 1440, urging him to restore the exiles to Florence. We are mainly reliant on Vespasiano's account for our knowledge of Palla's friendship with Nicholas V, but there seems no reason to doubt that it is broadly correct; see, e.g., the account of Nicholas's patronage of Messer Carlo, Palla's youngest son, before Carlo's early death (Greco (ed.), *Le vite*, ii. 163; and my 'A Florentine Family in Crisis', pp. 223, 248).

[62] See above, n. 41.

[63] On Palla's collection, and Giovanfrancesco's share of it, see my article, 'A Further Note', p. 184; for the size of other fourteenth- and fifteenth-century collections, see M. Grendler, 'A Greek Collection in Padua: the Library of Gian Vincenzo Pinelli', *Renaissance Quarterly*, 33 (1980), 393-4. I am grateful to Dr M. Sosower for his suggestion that, given this high number, Alessandro's enumeration of these volumes may not be completely trustworthy.

[64] It is clear that the volumes in Palla's collection were privately circulated; see the list of volumes lent to friends in his fragmentary *ricordo* of c.1418, now published by R. Jones, 'Documenti e precisazioni per Lorenzo Ghiberti, Palla Strozzi e la sagrestia di Santa Trinita', in [Ghiberti], *Lorenzo Ghiberti nel suo tempo* (2 vols., Florence, 1980), ii. 509 n. 7.

[65] Greco (ed.), *Le vite*, ii. 146.

and a certain amount of circumstantial evidence, to support it. It has already been noted that Vespasiano seems consciously to have created a resemblance between Cosimo and Palla, with respect to their personal style, their political deportment, and their patronage.[66] That he should have credited Palla with the intention of founding a library, as had Cosimo, is almost in itself suspicious, as certainly is his emphasis on the superiority of Santa Trinita as a location, because it was 'in the centre of Florence, a place very convenient for everyone'. There is a good deal of partisanship being displayed by the biographer here. Vespasiano's assertion is supported only by the fact that Palla possessed a noteworthy collection of Greek and Latin manuscripts, and that he and his father had an established record of patronage at Santa Trinita.

Palla's actual disposition of his collection of manuscripts tends to confirm suspicions about Vespasiano's accuracy. Best known is his bequest of part of his collection to the monastery of Santa Giustina in Padua. In the will of 1447 there were thirteen volumes thus designated, in 1462 there were eighteen. It must be stressed that these works made up only a small part of his collection, which may have contained as many as 400 volumes.[67] Palla placed great emphasis on the obligation of the monastery, and in particular its abbot, to preserve these volumes,[68] several of which were in his own hand, and written during his exile in Padua; another, in the hand of Giovanni Argyropoulos, dated from the latter's visit there in 1441. While there was one work in the collection which was definitely 'Florentine' in provenance (a Greek manuscript of the Gospels which came from Chrysoloras), there is in general nothing which suggests that this represented the transposition to Padua of a plan which was Florentine in conception. Nor is there any suggestion that the volumes should form a public library at Santa Giustina, although Palla stated that any monk who wished to learn Greek was welcome to use them.[69]

Palla changed his mind during the last fifteen years of his life about the disposition of the larger part of his collection. In 1447, some years before he finally resigned himself to the fact that he would never

---

[66] Davisson has noted this similarity ('Iconology', p. 323).
[67] On the 1447 bequest, see Arch. Bent., lib. IV.1.2, fos. 23–4; on the bequest of 1462, Fiocco, 'La casa di Palla Strozzi', pp. 375–7; on the possible size of his collection by the time of his death, see my article 'A Further Note', pp. 183–4.
[68] Arch. Bent., lib. III.34, fo. 21.
[69] Ibid.

return to Florence, and in the same will in which he showed a strong continuing attachment to Santa Trinita, he decreed that the residual portion of his collection should be sold, and that the proceeds be combined with his common estate. He added the somewhat pathetic rider that the Greek volumes should be sold together if possible.[70] By 1462 he had decided that these residual volumes should stay with his descendants: 'And also, because there are some which have been in the house for a very long time ... and because there are some in my hand, in Greek and Latin, either in whole or part, I believe it cannot be other than good that they should not be sold or alienated.'[71] He referred specifically to his two copies of the *Cosmographia* of Ptolemy, particularly enjoining his heirs not to sell them. Manuel Chrysoloras had brought one copy from Constantinople, the first known in Italy; the second was in Chrysoloras's own hand. About the latter Palla wrote: 'it seems to me that this should not be alienated by my sons and grandsons, but kept in the house in memory of he who made it.'[72] All of his writing about his manuscripts emphasizes their character as personal possessions, almost—in the case of those in his own hand— as an extension of his own personality. There is no hint here that they had ever been intended to form a public collection.

Darrell Davisson has advanced a number of hypotheses about the Strozzi chapel in Santa Trinita, among which is the assertion that Gentile da Fabriano's *Adoration of the Magi* belonged not on the main altar in the major sacristy, but in the minor sacristy.[73] This argument, if accepted, has significant implications for our understanding of the

---

[70] Arch. Bent., lib. IV.1.2, fo. 25.

[71] Arch. Bent., lib. III.34, fo. 26.

[72] Ibid., fo. 27.

[73] See Davisson, 'Iconology', p. 330, for the suggestion that the Abbot of Santa Trinita, Don Bonamico da Prato, acted as artistic and intellectual adviser on the chapel. In addition to the fact that virtually nothing is known of Don Bonamico, the suggestion ignores both Palla's likely status as an expert in such matters (see A. Middeldorf Kosegarten, 'The Origins of Artistic Competitions in Italy', in [Ghiberti], *Lorenzo Ghiberti nel suo tempo*, i. 184–5), and the now established fact that Ghiberti acted as Palla's artistic adviser during this period. On Ghiberti, and his connection with Palla Strozzi and the Santa Trinita chapel, see R. Krautheimer, *Lorenzo Ghiberti* (Princeton, 1956), p. 261; U. Middeldorf, 'Additions to Lorenzo Ghiberti's work', *Burlington Magazine*, 113 (1971), 72–9; J. Russell Sale, 'Palla Strozzi and Lorenzo Ghiberti: New Documents', *Mitteilungen des Kunsthistorischen Institutes in Florenz*, 22 (1978), 355–8, and Jones, 'Documenti e precisazioni', pp. 507–22. The notion that Francesco Zefiro, or Franciscus Zephyrus (not Franciscus Zephyrus Strozzi, as Davisson calls him) only recorded, rather than composed, the dialogue *De quiete animi*, raised by Davisson (p. 332), has been examined and convincingly dismissed by Baron, in 'The Year of Leonardo Bruni's Birth', pp. 621–3.

motives of Palla as the patron of the chapel. The main reason Davisson advances is that it would have been inconceivable for a chapel co-dedicated to its founder's patron saint, Honophrius, to have as its major altar-piece a painting making no reference to that saint.[74] But, unless we suppose (and there is no evidence) that Palla's wishes were not heeded in the commissioning of Fra Angelico to paint the second altar-piece for the chapel (the *Deposition*), it seems he had ultimately no wish to devote either of the two altar-pieces in the chapel to this purpose.[75]

Davisson's argument also misinterprets Palla's role as the dominant patron of the chapel. Even though his father Nofri had conceived the idea of the sacristy chapel, it was very much Palla's creation. In his will of 1447 Palla wrote that he wished his body to be taken from Padua to Florence, and buried in the chapel there, which he described as 'la capella nostra nuovamente [and here 'facta' has been scored out] per Nofri mio padre ordinata e facti e fondamenti [*sic*] e per me messa ad executione e compiuta come lasciò per suo testamento et ultima volontà'.[76] This very precise description is psychologically revealing, as is his scoring out of the word 'facta'. I understand it to mean: 'our new chapel, ordered and planned and begun by Nofri my father, and carried out and completed by me.' While noting that the chapel was planned and begun by Nofri, he makes clear his own very considerable role. He referred to the origins of the chapel again, when describing how one of his garments, of red velvet, was to be made into a chasuble to be used there: '... our new chapel, which Nofri my father willed should be made, and thus I did. And there it [the chasuble] is to be, together with the other objects and furnishings which I have continually ordered to be made for the ornamentation of that chapel.'[77] Palla here wished to emphasize his own role in the chapel's creation over an extended period of time. It may indeed have been an oblique acknowledgement that, while his father had conceived the idea for the chapel, the way in which it had been carried out was virtually all his own. Certainly this second statement makes clear that Palla knew that he, rather than Nofri, was responsible for its ornamentation. To look,

[74] Davisson, 'Iconology', pp. 320–3.

[75] The Fra Angelico *Deposition* has been variously dated within the period 1430 to 1445. See S. Orlandi, *Beato Angelico* (Florence, 1964), pp. 45–51; J. Pope-Hennessy, *Fra Angelico* (2nd edn, London, 1974), p. 210; and D. Cole Ahl, 'Fra Angelico: A New Chronology for the 1430s', *Zeitschrift für Kunstgeschichte*, 44 (1981), 140ff.

[76] Arch. Bent., lib. IV.1.2, fo. 5.

[77] Ibid., fo. 16.

therefore, for an arrangement of the paintings within the chapel which reflects in some way a concentration on the patron saints of Nofri and his elder son, Niccolò, is a mistake. While Palla was not an obviously undutiful son or brother, none of his writings on the chapel makes mention of its patron saints, and neither altar-piece, as completed, alludes to them. This must have been a deliberate choice, and may have been one which contravened his father's wishes, implicit or explicit.

It has also been suggested that the Santa Trinita chapel was such a public, indeed such a political, statement about Palla's wealth, power, and prestige, that it had somehow to be 'adjusted' or modified by the Medici regime after his exile. But there seems to be no evidence to support this view.[78] If, indeed, the function or the contents of the chapel had been interfered with, it is difficult to believe that Palla would not have referred to this fact in his wills, as he mentioned, for example, the inequitable disposal of certain of his properties to pay what he believed were unjust taxes.[79] It is true that in 1462 Palla discarded the provision of 1447 that he should be buried in the chapel, beside his mother; but this seems to have been a purely practical admission of changed circumstances.[80]

Palla Strozzi does not seem to have been a particularly ambitious man, so far as either his political or economic status was concerned. Nor is there any reason to believe that his patronage had a consciously political motivation. It was not designed deliberately to raise his status in the political class, and lead him to a more powerful position in Florentine politics. However it is necessary to make a distinction here. Even patronage such as Palla's, which was undertaken to meet his intellectual, spiritual, and family interests, inevitably had a public

---

[78] Davisson, 'Iconology', p. 323. In connection with continued activity in the chapel, Conventi Soppressi, 89, 1, fo. 17^r, refers to financial provision for saying mass there, on 27 Feb. 1435. Ibid. 89, 65, fo. 32^r, Apr. 1481, refers to the fact that 'detto Pagholo [Strozzi] à nelle mani trecento fiorini di sugello per comprare beni immobili per la cappella degli Strozzi posta in Sancta Trinita'. Pagolo di Benedetto Strozzi was one of the three executors of Palla's will. However there were two Strozzi chapels in Santa Trinita, and it is unclear which of them is referred to here.

[79] Arch. Bent., lib. III.34, fo. 53: 'da poi ch'io fu confinato, perchè proprio per privarmi d'ogni mia sustantia, mi fu posto allora grandissima et incomportabile graveza. Si chè per quella via ogni mio bene e sustantia avesse ad entrare in commune ... entrò e preselo il commune e concedectele a chi ne volle per piccolissimi pregi.'

[80] Until 1458 only Palla and his son Nofri were legally exiled. In that year the sentences were extended to all sons and grandsons of those Strozzi originally exiled; see Rubinstein, *The Government*, p. 110.

dimension and made a public impact. We may briefly take three examples. It is quite possible that Palla's eminence as a builder, collector, and sponsor of humanists contributed significantly to the desire of the new Medici regime in 1434 to remove him from the city. It is also probable that his example later influenced his kinsman Filippo Strozzi in the employment of his formidable energy as a builder.[81] Finally, Palla's example may have exercised some influence on the direction of Medici patronage, though the only tangible link between the two, the use of the Magi theme,[82] seems rather a slender basis on which to build a theoretical edifice. But it is also necessary to reiterate that the motivation and intentions of the patron are one thing, and the influence and repercussions of his activity are another.[83]

---

[81] On the 'family' dimension of Filippo Strozzi's building activity, see F. W. Kent, ' "Più superba de quella de Lorenzo": Courtly and Family Interest in the Building of Filippo Strozzi's Palace', *Renaissance Quarterly*, 30 (1977), 311–25.

[82] Davisson, 'Iconology', p. 323. On Medici patronage of the Compagnia de' Magi, see R. Hatfield, 'The Compagnia de' Magi', *Journal of the Warburg and Courtauld Institutes*, 33 (1970), 107–61.

[83] After this chapter was completed my attention was drawn to the study by Roger Jones of Palla Strozzi's involvement with the Santa Trinita sacristy and related matters, 'Palla Strozzi e la sagrestia di Santa Trinita', *Rivista d'Arte*, ser. 4, 37 (1984), 9–106. Jones's conclusions regarding the motivation behind Palla's activity appear similar to those advanced here. He also publishes at length many of the documents cited more briefly here.

12

Patronage in the Tornaquinci Chapel, Santa Maria Novella, Florence

PATRICIA SIMONS

OUR habit often has been to approach the patronage of art with a series of binary oppositions in mind: artist against patron, aesthetic sensibility and even 'freedom' against adviser and programme, style against subject.[1] But a more coherent, fluid picture of patronage can sometimes be discerned in both the process whereby patronage rights are acquired and in the visualization of certain associated themes. In the main chapel of Santa Maria Novella, Florence, Dominican friars and patrons engaged in mutual manipulation to achieve, through the artist, the honourable decoration of a prestigious site. He rendered visible certain values that declare the magnificence of the patrons. And an interchange between the various parties and an equality of contribution is more notable here than any hierarchy of relationship between friars, patron, and artist.

Usually called the Tornabuoni chapel because Giovanni Tornabuoni signed a contract with Domenico and David Ghirlandaio on 1 September 1485 for its frescos, the *cappella maggiore* in the Dominican friary has more title to be called the Tornaquinci chapel, for important reasons. It was to Giovanni Tornabuoni's entire *consorteria* or lineage, the Tornaquinci, that patronage rights were ceded by the Dominicans

---

[1] In particular, several recent writers have stressed that artists were 'freer agents than might be supposed' (so D. S. Chambers (ed.), *Patrons and Artists in the Italian Renaissance* (London, 1970), p. xxviii). See also C. E. Gilbert, *Italian Art 1400–1500: Sources and Documents* (Englewood Cliffs, 1980), pp. xviiiff., esp. pp. xxv, 8, 124; C. Hope, 'Artists, Patrons, and Advisers in the Italian Renaissance' and H. W. Janson, 'The Birth of "Artistic License": The Dissatisfied Patron in the Early Renaissance', both in G. F. Lytle and S. Orgel (eds.), *Patronage in the Renaissance* (Princeton, 1981); cf. W. L. Gundersheimer, 'Patronage in the Renaissance: An Exploratory Approach' in the same volume, esp. pp. 5, 16, 18–19, where it is pointed out that attention to 'the central binary relationship' between patron and client 'begins to lose sight of the networks of mental attitudes and social connections that provide its supportive structures'.

on 13 October 1486.[2] Giovanni's role in engineering this legal control, his determination and interest in the project, evident in the contract and still uppermost in his will of March 1490, as well as his payments, ensure his fame. But the legal ownership, signified by his own choice of *arme* and portraiture, each of which represented within the chapel every branch of his *consorteria* (Plate 17), justifies our calling it the Tornaquinci chapel.[3]

Perhaps the chapel is best known for Warburg's vivid image of a piqued Francesco Sassetti abandoning it for one in Santa Trinita, an image delightfully augmented by Vasari's account of the 'gran romore' when the Ricci rushed off to their lawyers on opening day since their *arme* or coat of arms on the tabernacle was too small.[4] Other machinations over the chapel's patronage concern us here, those whereby a long-standing family association with the church and particularly its *cappella maggiore* enabled, possibly required, a virtual mythology of patronage to form one of Ghirlandaio's central themes. (Such an interpretation has been aided immeasurably by the recent archival research of Rab Hatfield, to whose generosity I owe several important documentary references.)

What the legal action of 1486 did, from a Tornaquinci point of view, was no more than reassert that *consorteria*'s prestige as the most generous founders of Santa Maria Novella. In 1221 the Dominicans, newly arrived in Florence, received 'a little church [*chiesetta*] built by a certain Jacopo Tornaquinci ... amongst the vineyards', as was

---

[2] Archivio di Stato, Florence, Notarile Antecosimiano (henceforth NA), M 237, fos. 159^r–160^r for the contract; fos. 192^r–3^v for patronage rights. (All manuscript references are to collections in the Florentine State Archives, unless otherwise indicated.) The contract was published by G. Milanesi, *Nuovi documenti per la storia dell'arte Toscana dal XII al XV secolo* (Florence, 1901), pp. 134–6.
This chapter is drawn from Chapters 5, 6, and 7 of my doctoral thesis, 'Portraiture and Patronage in Quattrocento Florence with special reference to the Tornaquinci and their Chapel in S. Maria Novella' (University of Melbourne, 1985). For a brief history of the *consorteria*, see G. Pampaloni, 'I Tornaquinci, poi Tornabuoni, fino ai primi del Cinquecento', *Archivio storico italiano*, 126 (1968), 331–62.

[3] NA C 644, fos. 47^r–50^r for the will. This and numerous other documents on the chapel have been unearthed by Rab Hatfield, who is also to be thanked for reading a first draft of this chapter. For the now lost *arme*, which even represented defunct branches, see G. Vasari, *Le vite de' più eccellenti pittori, scultori ed architettori*, ed. G. Milanesi (Florence, 1878–81), iii. 261–2 (henceforth cited as Vasari-Milanesi), and S. Rosselli, *Sepoltuario* (Manoscritti, henceforth MSS), 625, II, p. 679.

[4] A. Warburg, 'Le ultime volontà di Francesco Sassetti' (1907), in his *La rinascità del paganesimo antico* (Florence, 1966), pp. 211–46; Vasari–Milanesi, iii. 260, 262.

recognized by the Dominican prior Fra Niccolò Sermartelli in 1617.[5] Our earliest source for this foundation comes from the Trecento and speaks in part of 'a small church, which a Jacopo Tornaquinci had had built, which was where is today the sacristy of the friars'. This *ricordo* of c.1376 by an anonymous Tornaquinci is a detailed and clear family remembrance, whereas by Vasari's time the site donated by Jacopo's sons is legendary and vague, simply 'the major part of the site of the church and convent'.[6] Ghirlandaio's frescos themselves had contributed to this enlarged but generalized legend. The artist, in relaying the family's awareness of its generosity, made a grand and idealized addition, which granted visual potency to a history which was becoming 'mythology' or aggrandized legend.

Even in the late 1470s a rather vague memory was current: Fra Giovanni Caroli, who later witnessed the document of 1486, wrote of the early donation only briefly, crediting it to Messer Jacopo's sons and concluding: 'Perhaps thanks to this, the altar was first assigned to the family of the Tornaquinci.'[7] In the sixteenth century Vasari and soon thereafter another Dominican chronicler, Fra Modesto Biliotti, ensured that only a general awareness of the Tornaquinci's donation entered the dim annals of the convent's early history.[8] Within the

---

[5] The original is at Santa Maria Novella and is here quoted from its earliest surviving copy, made by Cavalcanti in the seventeenth century: MSS 621, fos. 3ʳ–4ᵛ. The Martini copy of 1729 agrees (Biblioteca Riccardiana, Codex 1935, fos. 11ᵛ–14ʳ); another eighteenth-century copy inserts a quotation from the ancient Tornaquinci *ricordo* (see n. 6 below): MSS 812, pp. 2–3. The *ricordo*, Caroli (see n. 7 below) and Sermartelli are the three most precise but previously unrecognized sources on this 'piccola chiesetta fatta da un certo Jacopo Tornaquinci ... in mezzo a molte vigne'.

[6] Biblioteca Riccardiana, Codex 1885, fos. 4ʳ–5ʳ; Santi Arrighi O.P., *Memorie del Convento di S. Maria Novella* (of the 1620s), Biblioteca Nazionale, Florence, Conventi Soppressi, D.8. 96, fos. 340ʳ–5ᵛ contains a copy of this *ricordo* as a vellum insert; Vasari–Milanesi, i. 351.

[7] S. Orlandi, *Necrologio di S. Maria Novella* (Florence, 1955), ii. 389, published the text from the presentation copy still at Santa Maria Novella, which agrees with Caroli's autograph copy (Biblioteca Laurenziana, Plut. 89 inf. 21, fo. 24ʳ). For these versions and the date, see S. Camporeale, 'Giovanni Caroli e le "Vitae Fratrum S.M. Novellae": Umanesimo e crisi religiosa (1460–1480)', *Memorie Domenicane*, NS 12 (1981), 141–267, esp. 163–8. In Nov. 1221 Lotterio di Jacopo Tornaquinci was one of the witnesses, *in coro*, of the friars' receipt of Santa Maria Novella; see G. Richa, *Notizie istoriche delle chiese fiorentine* (Florence, 1755), III. i. 96–7.

[8] M. Biliotti, 'Venerabilis Coenobi Sanctae Mariae Novellae de Florentia Chronica', in *Analecta Sacri Ordinis Fratrum Praedicatorum*, ser. III, i (1893–94), 41–2, 49–52 (hereafter cited as Biliotti, *Chronica*). The convent's early history and building campaigns are still unclear: see J. Wood Brown, *The Dominican Church of Santa Maria Novella* (Edinburgh, 1902); W. and E. Paatz, *Die Kirchen von Florenz* (Frankfurt-am-Main, 1952), iii. 663ff.; K. Giles Arthur, 'The Strozzi Chapel: Notes on the Building History of Sta. Maria Novella', *Art Bulletin*, 65 (1983), 367–86.

consorteria itself, the *ricordo* preserved a clearer tradition and in the Cinquecento Bishop Niccolò di Donato Tornabuoni commemorated his family's honour and antiquity by having its original donation visually portrayed in a lunette of the convent's Great Cloister. According to Fineschi, the fresco contained Niccolò's portrait and 'in the architecture of the Church one sees the arms of the Tornaquinci, Tornabuoni and of the Consorteria'.[9]

The strict accuracy or historical validity of the Tornaquinci's claim to a generous act of donation is not at issue here. The point is that from at least the Trecento to the Cinquecento, with the *cappella maggiore* scheme included, the *consorteria* believed itself to have been 'padroni' of the original benefice, donors to the Dominicans and thereafter practitioners of a 'singular reverence to that church and those friars'.[10] Acting on a sincere belief which required proclamation and assertion, the family more than once resorted to visual propaganda, containing *arme* and portraits, to stake its claim both to the chapel and to the honour owed to its magnificence.

Rights over the chapel would also have been ceded to the Tornaquinci because their *arme* had been placed there by 1348, after a maternal relative, the famous Fra Jacopo Passavanti, had apparently encouraged their payment for frescos executed in the chapel by Orcagna. So, at least, runs the record of the convent's *Liber novus* from the 1360s which copied an older chronicle.[11] On the other hand, by the sixteenth century Giovanni Tornabuoni had long since replaced those *arme* with ones representing the Tornaquinci and all its branches, and the document of 1486 had been forgotten, only to be briefly cited by Glasser in 1965.[12] Deaths, and the confiscation of Tornabuoni

---

[9] V. Fineschi, *Il forestiero istruito in S. Maria Novella* (Florence, 1836 edn), p. 54; Wood Brown, *Santa Maria Novella*, p. 11 n. 1. Alinari 31212, which includes the kneeling donor portraits of a man and woman, reproduces a fragment of what the bishop believed to be the original portal. For a reproduction of the fresco, see D. Mignani, 'La scuola Sottufficiali Carabinieri nell'ex convento di Santa Maria Novella', in U. Baldini (ed.), *Santa Maria Novella, la basilica, il convento, i chiostri monumentali* (Florence, 1981), p. 342.

The first major ancestor at the head of a family tree, prepared for Matteo Tornaquinci in 1619–20, was Messer Jacopo di Tornaquinci di Alberto di Tornaquinci; he, it is said, 'edifica la chiesa di S. Maria Novella' (Carte Strozziane, ser. 2, 135, fo. 43').

[10] See the Tornaquinci *ricordo* (n. 6 above). The family's long involvement with the church, including regular burials and masses and the patronage of three other chapels, is documented in Chapter 5 of my thesis.

[11] Orlandi, *Necrologio,* ii. 434.

[12] H. Glasser, *Artists' Contracts of the Early Renaissance* (New York, 1977), pp. 53, 112 n. 1, who nevertheless states that rights were 'conferred on Giovanni Tornabuoni'.

property in 1497, had led to the family's decline. Vasari and Biliotti, then, were able to distort their histories so much as to attribute the patronage of Orcagna's frescos to the Ricci, a tradition never subsequently questioned.[13]

In 1486 no specific mention was made of the Tornaquinci *arme*, nor was any previous holder of rights named. Instead the document cited the 'many worthy [works], obsequies, benefits and favours exhibited' towards the convent by the *consorteria*'s male and female members. To them were translated and donated the 'indubitable and perpetual patronage rights of the said chapel and altar'.[14] In 1470 Francesco Sassetti had been granted patronage rights over the altar, but more venerable, generous (and, one suspects, more assertively made) claims seem to have led to his defeat, such that the Tornaquinci were emphatically granted rights over both the 'major chapel with the major altar' in 1486. When, less than a decade later, the chapel's new window depicted the *Founding of Santa Maria Maggiore* (Plate 19), its reference to the selection of land for the construction of a major church dedicated to the Virgin was most apposite.

The well-known contract of 1485 between Giovanni and the Ghirlandaio, which claimed 'indubitable' rights of patronage, was only the patron's first step in his reassertion of ancestral generosity and his total, magnificent refurbishment of his family's chapel. Any wrangles between the Sassetti, Ricci, Tornaquinci, and Dominicans over patronage of various elements within the *cappella maggiore* are of lesser importance beside this statement of Tornaquinci primacy.

Failing to realize that patronage rights within the area were juridically divided, and that Francesco Sassetti was able to profess patronage only of the altar, Warburg gave that Medicean banker more stature in relation to the Dominicans than is warranted.[15] Admittedly

---

[13] Biliotti, *Chronica*, i. 49–52; Vasari–Milanesi, i. 594; followed, for instance, by Borghigiani's chronicle in the eighteenth century (Orlandi, *Necrologio*, ii. 399, and reported from a different passage by E. Borsook and J. Offerhaus, *Francesco Sassetti and Ghirlandaio at Santa Trinita, Florence: History and Legend in a Renaissance Chapel* (Doornspijk, 1981), Doc. 17). Ghiberti first attributed the frescos to Orcagna, but did not name the patron: see A. Busignani and R. Bencini, *Le chiese di Firenze: quartiere di Santa Maria Novella* (Florence, 1979), p. 32.

[14] NA M 237, fos. 192ᵛ–3ʳ, which further uses the phrase 'cappelle et altaris' twelve times.

[15] Warburg, 'Le ultime volontà', was confused by the word 'hedificium' in the document of 1470 (n. 18 below) which refers to the frame and structure of the altar only. While J. Offerhaus (*Motief en achtergrond: Studies over het gebruik van de architektuur in de 15e eeuwse florentijnse schilderkunst* (Utrecht, 1976), p. 115) recognized the division of patronage rights, he incorrectly claimed that the Ricci had

Francesco himself took an offended stance against the friars' 'villainy' in his now lost 'last wishes' of April 1488, although he still hoped to regain 'authority' there and endowed Santa Maria Novella with a locksmith's shop as late as October 1485.[16] He is last mentioned in that convent's records in November 1485 when he again purchased 2 *libbre* of wax for the feast-day 'of the dead', as he had done regularly since at least 1480, although he had officially acquired his chapel at Santa Trinita early in that year at the latest. Recognized, like Giovanni Tornabuoni, as an important patron by the convent's donation of candles on the feast-days of the Virgin's Purification for 1480–5, Francesco Sassetti does not appear there for the ceremony on 2 February 1486.[17] Hence the act which so infuriated and insulted Francesco, the removal of the Sassetti arms from the altar, had probably occurred after the Tornabuoni contract with the Ghirlandaio and not long before the Tornaquinci were granted the chapel and altar in October 1486, close to the time when the Santa Trinita chapel was operational.

Yet on 22 February 1470, the convent had with 'unqualified, complete and gratuitous liberality' granted Francesco patronage of the high altar, nevertheless omitting to note the deed's irrevocable nature.[18] What seems most important to the friars is that Francesco 'intends' to rectify past neglect—a plan not fulfilled if we are to judge by the apparent fragility of the altar-piece in the early 1480s.[19] Francesco had promised the 'rebuilding' of the old-fashioned altar-piece in 1468 and its 'ornamentation' in 1470, but his virtual adoption of a bequest for its new 'cover' made in 1430 by Fiondina Sassetti similarly produced

---

burial rights. An anonymous eighteenth-century Dominican (novice?) was also clear on the division, although incorrect about the Ricci and desirous of proving the friars' primacy: see Conventi Soppressi (henceforth Conv. Soppr.), 102, 103, insert 87.

[16] Warburg, 'Le ultime volontà', published the 'ultima voluntà' of 1488 but the document cannot now be traced. Borsook and Offerhaus (*History and Legend*, Doc. 24) give a brief version from the Strozzi *Spogli*. The act of 1485 has been found by Rab Hatfield.

[17] The Nov. payments are in Conv. Soppr., 102, App. 84, fos. 5ᵛ, 10ʳ, 18ᵛ, 22ᵛ, 26ᵛ; the Feb. actions are at fo. 60ʳ and later unnumbered folios. For Santa Trinita, see Borsook and Offerhaus, *History and Legend*, Doc. 8.

[18] NA B 398, fos. 153ʳ–4ʳ; partly in Offerhaus, *Motief en achtergrond*, pp. 229–30 and Borsook and Offerhaus, *History and Legend*, Doc. 21. Several features of the document may be unusual. The use of the word 'pretendit' and the suggestion that Francesco has done the claiming, are not in the usual cool, legal, spirit of such documents. Unusual, too, is the very late mention of Sassetti heirs, without elaboration as to the masculine line.

[19] Conv. Soppr., 102, App. 16, fos. 93ʳ, 100ʳ, 115ʳ lists repairs to the altar-piece by the friars in 1483 and 1484.

no action.[20] Litigation concerning the bequest of Fiondina, a woman who enjoyed only remote kinship with Francesco, was largely settled by these notarial acts of 1468 and 1470. In effect owing the Sassetti money from Fiondina's unfulfilled bequest, the friars may have been responding to financial duress, and so have granted rights liberally to avoid mention of any outstanding obligation on their part. Their mention of 'any instance in which he did not possess any right' might also suggest that Francesco was creating a right which his ancestors had not held in any formal or widely recognized sense.[21]

Sassetti claims to patronage seem to have developed gradually, by default and more by promise than execution, and to have been assertively shaped into a legal right by Francesco in 1470. His beneficence was recognized in 1470, but not as warmly as were those gifts of Giovanni Tornabuoni and the Tornaquinci in 1486. At some stage Francesco did donate embroidered vestments; but little else is known of his patronage there, other than the purchase of wax for masses

[20] Borsook and Offerhaus (*History and Legend*, pp. 10–14 and Docs. 13–22, 24) publish extracts from documents concerning Fiondina Sassetti's bequest to the altar in 1430 and Francesco's attempt to take over and augment the troubled bequest in 1468 and 1470.

The protracted litigation concerning Fiondina's designation of the convent as her heir is covered by several instruments in Diplomatico, Santa Maria Novella, for the early 1430s. An unnumbered insert near the beginning of Conv. Soppr., 102, 94, pt II, is an unfinished summary of 1583 which contains twenty long and complex items covering matters relating to Fiondina's property and Sassetti actions for the years 1324 to 1454. A few other Sassetti gifts to Santa Maria Novella are mentioned, but the altar is not, land being virtually its sole subject.

[21] It is often thought that in the early 1320s Fra Baro Sassetti commissioned an altar-piece for the high altar; but his death notice mentions only his donation of embroideries to the sacristy and a 'tabulam altaris'. The account is in Orlandi, *Necrologio*, i. 40, and all citations of this document since Biliotti (see *Chronica*, i. 51; ii [1895–6]. 238) take the words 'tabulam altaris' to refer, not to an altar-piece for the sacristy, but to a 'tabulam maioris altaris'. Vasari, though, does not connect the Sassetti family with the high altar-piece (which was then located in the chapter house—see Vasari–Milanesi, i. 454); but subsequent writers conflate his account with the altered *Necrologio* to hypothesize a Sassetti altar-piece from the Trecento, some of the suggested topics of which conform to 'Unam Immaginem ... Marie Virginis de Angelo', housed in the original sacristy in 1351 (see Conv. Soppr., 102, 94, pt I, second *filza* of *Inventari*). Francesco's great grandson relied on Vasari, on Biliotti, and on Francesco's angry statement of 1488 when saying that this ancient Sassetti *tavola* was removed from the high altar around 1485 (see F. Sassetti, *Lettere*, ed. E. Marcucci (Florence, 1855), pp. xxix–xxx). Even if Baro were the patron of the earlier high altar-piece, it is probable that his donation was the act of a Dominican (possibly a sacristan) rather than a family representative. Previous ancestral actions at the high altar are first mentioned, vaguely and briefly, by Francesco in 1468, and this refers mainly, if not wholly, to Fiondina's bequest.

which was only half as generous as Giovanni's expenditure.[22] A patron whose energy and reliability at Santa Maria Novella was over-shadowed during the early 1480s by his commitment to the Santa Trinita ensemble, Francesco was never as generous to the Dominicans as was Giovanni Tornabuoni.

Both Francesco and the friars appear to have ignored the document of 1470, Francesco doing little about his promise and the convent implicitly revoking it when the altar was granted to the Tornaquinci in October 1486, the Sassetti arms by then probably having been removed from it. Similarly, the friars had earlier negated Baldesi rights over the church's façade when Giovanni Rucellai entered the convent's ken as a much richer and more determined patron; the 'friars have removed our arms', reported a Baldesi by 1458. Ten years earlier the Archbishop Antoninus and three other arbiters had judged Minerbetti claims against the Rucellai regarding the pulpit at Santa Maria Novella as being too weak, and had given greatest priority to the 'utility and ornamentation' of the church. By the later 1480s, again, the friars had probably assessed their needs, judged the merits and magnificence of counter-claimants, consulted the Master General of their Order, seen Giovanni's promised 'enhancement of the said church and chapel' begin and, having made their decision, removed the *arme* of the loser.[23]

In 1470 Francesco made of a relatively meagre and litigious ancestral tradition a legal privilege but, because he did not follow this through with adequate action, his 'authority' was never high. Of all the masses he ordered at Santa Maria Novella until 1485, the location of only one is specified: that for a special mass commemorating the dead friars in 1481, candles being placed 'on the altar and two at the sepulchre' of Francesco. That same mass was more generously aided by Giovanni

[22] On the vestments, see Biliotti, *Chronica*, i. 51, and ii. 238–9 (partly in Borsook and Offerhaus, *History and Legend*, Doc. 15); also Sassetti, *Lettere*, p. xxxviii. Francesco's recognition at Candlemas and his purchases of wax are cited in n. 17 above; Giovanni's gifts are mentioned liberally throughout the extant sacristy books. See also a sixteenth-century record of the convent's obligations to conduct anniversary masses (Conv. Soppr., 102, 81, unnumbered insert). Francesco had also intended to place at Santa Maria Novella (probably in an *avello*) a marble sepulchre for his father; see Warburg, 'Le ultime volonta', p. 228.

[23] The quotation is from Giovanni's contract of 1485 with the Ghirlandaio (tr. in Chambers, *Patrons and Artists*, p. 173). For the Baldesi case, see F. W. Kent in F. W. Kent (*et al.*) *Giovanni Rucellai ed il suo zibaldone*, II: *A Florentine Patrician and his Palace* (London, 1981), pp. 60 n. 7, 63; for the Minerbetti, see the references cited in n. 34 below. The Master General is explicitly cited in Oct. 1486 (see NA M 237, fo. 193ᵛ). Giovanni's familiarity with the papal curia may have aided his possible campaign on the Roman front.

Tornabuoni, whose *candellieri* were placed precisely 'at the high altar and two at [Giovanni's] sepulchre'.[24] Despite his legal acquisition of rights over the high altar in 1470, Francesco did not receive ritual access to it often enough or for his own commemorative purposes; and while his rights of recognition were met at the yearly Candlemas, his more particular prestige in relation to the high altar was not visibly proclaimed. At Santa Trinita, Francesco achieved what he had no likelihood of attaining at Santa Maria Novella—a properly intramural and prestigious chapel and burial site.[25]

Now publicly committed to another and splendid place, and having shown himself to be disappointing as a patron of the Dominican high altar, Francesco probably was rejected by the friars as a 'bad bet', with Giovanni Tornabuoni so much more assiduous.[26] Giovanni knew by which rules to play, and what strings to pull, expending more on the purchase of wax, more quickly and firmly acting on his intentions to decorate, involving himself in a key confraternity, standing on his ancestral heritage and personal commitment to the Dominican Order and to Santa Maria Novella. He belonged to a family not only of far greater civic and historical prestige, but also one far more active and renowned within the convent's precincts. Francesco was convinced utterly of his claim's legitimacy and of a family 'mythology', probably largely of his own making; but, despite the deed of 1470, he had inadequate documentary or active proof, let alone family tradition, to

[24] Conv. Soppr., 102, App. 84, unfoliated.

[25] Since I argue that Sassetti prestige had never been really high at Santa Maria Novella, I would also see the issues of intramural burial and unfulfilled ambition as the principal causes for Francesco's migration to what was his 'cappella et altare et sepultura' (Warburg, 'Le ultime volonta', p. 228), at Santa Trinita.

In Mar. 1490 Giovanni Tornabuoni's will in the presence of nine leading friars including the prior, elaborately planned four tombs above the steps 'in dicta cappella, et iuxta dictam altare'. His grandson's testament of September 1540 desired a similar arrangement 'que fiat ad instar Sepulture Cosmi de Medicis' (Conv. Soppr., 102, 106, 1, no. 11, fos. 68ʳ–72ʳ). Restoration has uncovered a roughly plastered surface behind the choir stalls which indicates that at least one Tornabuoni did fulfil a desire for burial in that chapel (Gabinetto Fotografico, Soprintendenza alle Gallerie, Florence, nos. 152754–5). Crudely inscribed '1566/IOANNES TORNABON' HIC IACET/HIC MEMBRA JOHANNIS DE TORNABONIS TRANSLATIO SUA', the removal surely resulted from Vasari's remodelling, begun in 1565, which included bringing the altar forward and changing the arrangement of tombs (see the document in M. Hall, *Renovation and Counter-Reformation: Vasari and Duke Cosimo in Sta. Maria Novella and Sta. Croce, 1565–1577* (Oxford, 1979), p. 168).

[26] The Sassetti were not politically or financially strong before Francesco's managerial position in the Medici Bank. None of their five burial sites at Santa Maria Novella was inside the church (see Borsook and Offerhaus, *History and Legend*, p. 13).

give him power and 'authority'. As Borsook and Offerhaus have argued for different reasons, Francesco did manage to assert his status at Santa Trinita; the Tornaquinci were able to do so with more confidence and ease on their home ground at Santa Maria Novella.

Giovanni Tornabuoni also ensured that another family did not oppose his encroachment upon the domain. It is no longer at all clear just what rights, over which element in the chapel, the Ricci deserved, although Vasari's story of the dispute created by the small size of Ricci *arme* on the tabernacle has been confirmed by Hatfield's discovery of a fragmentary 'Licence' of February 1495. In this Giovanni, with certain 'pacts, conditions and limitations and . . . reservations', granted the Ricci the right 'to place their arms in and above the tabernacle of the Corpus Christi'.[27] Sermartelli followed Vasari and Biliotti in asserting that the Ricci were Orcagna's patrons, but in singling out Messer Rosso de' Ricci, the man buried near the altar in 1383, he probably indicates one of the chief causes of the misunderstanding.[28] Rosso's tomb slab, prominently placed 'at the foot of the high altar' (a singular honour), was perhaps noticed and utilized in later discussions as to family rights there. The presence of the tomb slab and of the same Ricci *arme* on the tabernacle required an explanation which Cinquecento writers supplied by suggesting Ricci patronage of the chapel in the Trecento. Recently, Offerhaus has taken the tomb slab as an indication that all the Ricci had burial rights at the chapel,[29] but Rosso's own will never refers to the chapel as under his family's control, and no other Ricci burials there are recorded.

The existence of the 'Licence' suggests that the Ricci merited some recognition as one-time patrons, probably over the tabernacle, or perhaps in relation to the window, stalls, or altar. But in the late Quattrocento, as Vasari and Sermartelli knew, the family was in economic, political, and numeric decline, unable to pursue vigorously whatever responsibilities and rights it held in relation to the poorly

---

[27] NA B 910, insert 1, fo. 299ᵛ; Vasari–Milanesi iii. 260, 262.

[28] For Vasari and Biliotti, see n. 13 above; for Sermartelli, see MSS 621, fo. 14ʳ⁻ᵛ. A seventeenth-century summary of Rosso's will records the agreement he had reached with the convent to be buried 'a piè della Altar Maggiore' (Conv. Soppr., 102, 94, pt I, second *filza* of *Inventari*).

[29] For Offerhaus see n. 15 above. The Ricci *arme* on the tabernacle are reproduced in MSS 812, fo. 45ʳ, and are the same as those seen today on Rosso's tomb: (yellow) stars and three hedgehogs over a (blue) ground. This differs slightly from the arms used by another branch of the Ricci (e.g. in the oculus donated by Tebaldino de' Ricci).

maintained chapel and its accoutrements.[30] Active patrons at the convent during the Trecento, the Ricci could have appealed to a stronger ancestral tradition than could Francesco Sassetti, but given their later lack of power they could not have competed with Giovanni Tornabuoni's campaign. Whatever claims Giovanni was appeasing, he was engineering the acquisition of complete and unconditional rights over the entire area.

Probably one man enabled the Ricci to stake a claim in the 1480s. That man, one of many Ricci Dominicans at Santa Maria Novella through the centuries, was Fra Domenico di Gherardo Ricci. He could have kept his family's traditions alive forcibly in the halls of the convent. It could have been he who extracted the 'Licence' from Giovanni and a few months later, for whatever reason, he did pay a poor woman the large sum of 20 florins 'to exonerate the conscience' of Lorenzo di Giovanni Tornabuoni.[31] Nevertheless, as one of the witnesses to the document of October 1486, Fra Domenico had long known and agreed to Giovanni's actions: the precise placement of *arme* was the matter under negotiation, rather than conflicting claims to current patronage rights.

Indeed, at the inception of the frescos, around May 1486 at the earliest, Fra Domenico may have been placated, and his fellow-friars wooed, by visual means, for it is possible that his is the tonsured portrait, standing in profile near the Virgin's bier in her *Dormition*, while the two other clean-shaven and tonsured men with individualized faces may also be portraits of Dominicans.[32] Further, the frescos were

---

[30] Sermartelli (n. 28 above); Vasari–Milanesi, iii. 260. For the family's 'rovescio', see esp. the *memoria* of the late fifteenth century by Agnolo di Giovanni di Francesco di Messer Rosso de' Ricci, the last of his line (*Delizie degli eruditi Toscani*, ed. Ildefonso di San Luigi (Florence, 1770–89), XIV. i. 213–30; hereafter cited as *Delizie*).

[31] NA A 300, fo. 437^{r-v}. The nuns who executed Botticelli's designs for Tornabuoni embroideries were paid by Fra Domenico on 22 June 1495 too (Conv. Soppr., 102, App. 19, fo. 110^v). The documentation of both events was discovered by Rab Hatfield. For Fra Domenico at the convent, see Orlandi, *Necrologio*, ii. 368–9, 587; G. Pomaro, 'Censimento dei Manoscritti della Biblioteca di S. Maria Novella', *Memorie Domenicane*, NS 11 (1980), 333ff., 427; P. Ricozzi, 'Necrologio di S. Maria Novella (1505–1665)', ibid. 230.

[32] The portrait bears a plausible resemblance to Fra Domenico's medal (see G. F. Hill, *A Corpus of Italian Medals of the Renaissance before Cellini* (London, 1930), no. 1009). Nearby, a plump tonsured man turning to the right is suggestively similar to another friar of learning and importance to the chapel, Fra Giovanni Caroli: see his portrait in the presentation copy of his *Vitae*, reproduced by Camporeale, 'Giovanni Caroli', Tav. I. A third (and again tonsured) portrait in the *Dormition* is of a man kneeling in the left foreground, perhaps Fra Gabriele Narucci, who was prior at the

described by the friars in October 1486 as 'for the major part perfected'. This is a patent untruth, but it could suggest that at least the vault and the lunette containing their portrayed representatives were complete and had impressed those who had climbed the scaffolding.[33] If either the identifications offered here, or the dating suggested, is plausible, then Giovanni Tornabuoni seems to have been using art as an instrument of flattery and for the ends of a greater patronage goal—control over the chapel's entire refurbishment. Perhaps Fra Domenico Ricci was a self-appointed *mezzano*, or middle-man, on behalf of his family's honour inserting himself in a process which Tornabuoni knew better how to manipulate than did Sassetti.[34]

Further complications need not detain us here. What can be said with the greatest certainty is that no one family had secure and total rights over the chapel and its altar until the Tornaquinci legally obtained them in 1486, and that later confusions have arisen because the act of 1486 and the history of the 'chiesetta' have been unknown. It also seems clear that the Dominicans retained certain privileges and controls over what Sermartelli termed this 'site of the Fathers and not of others'.[35] The complications and obscurities bear witness to an extremely active competition over one of the most prestigious sites of patronage in later Quattrocento Florence.

Giovanni Tornabuoni claimed the 'indubitable rights' held over the 'major chapel' in September 1485 (surely because the arms of his *consorteria* had been placed there by 1348), but the document of 1486 seemed legally to confirm and clarify the issue. Only able to plan murals for the walls in 1485, his will of 26 March 1490 could outline detailed plans for the window, altar-piece, choir-stalls, embroideries, candlesticks for the altar, and intended tombs. Like the document of 1486, the will too spoke of 'indubitable' patronage over the 'major

time the frescos were begun (after May 1486) and when patronage rights were ceded in Oct. of that year (Orlandi, *Necrologio*, i. 198–9; ii. 335–44).

[33] NA M237, fo. 193ʳ: 'precipue per magnificum et generosum virum Johannem … qui, ut ad presens oculata fide inspicitur, cappellam maiorem eiusdem ecclesie egregiis ac splendidis et ornatis picturis, eiusdem Johannis magna impensa, decorare ac ornare conatur—et iam in fieri opus ipsum pictarum apparet pro maiori parte perfectum.'

[34] Compare how, in the mid-fifteenth century, Fra Andrea Rucellai had been an acknowledged *mezzano* in the affair of his family's pulpit at Santa Maria Novella (S. Orlandi, *S. Antonino* (Florence, 1960), ii. 308–10; idem., *Necrologio*, i. 168; ii. 258–9; F. W. Kent, *Household and Lineage in Renaissance Florence: The Family Life of the Capponi, Ginori and Rucellai* (Princeton, 1977), pp. 282–3).

[35] MSS 621, fo. 14ʳ⁻ᵛ, discussing the council of 1348 (n. 11 above). Certain payments after Oct. 1486 by the friars suggest that they never relinquished all responsibilities, let alone control, over the high altar.

Chapel with the high altar'. Nevertheless, Giovanni envisaged an expensive altar-piece, if and when the friars handed over the rights to the major altar without any 'contradiction or molestation'.[36] So, despite the grant of 1486, Giovanni could not presume automatic patronage of the altar-piece, Francesco Sassetti's legal claim of 1470 over the altar (and his subsequent anger) being still a potential obstacle, even if the visible sign, his arms, were no longer in place. Giovanni was surely remembering Francesco's public ire when the *arme* were removed, for these colleagues in the Medici Bank were well-known rivals.[37] Tornabuoni's will shows an awareness of lingering illfeeling and of the need to tread carefully, for Sassetti had the power to make legal difficulties.

Although Giovanni was optimistic and determined that he would acquire that right before his own death, he carefully inserted plans in his will to ensure that every detail of his desire regarding the chapel would be fulfilled. Past and future 'molestation', or what Francesco called 'villainy', were to be overcome by careful organization and resolution, so that the act of 1486 would be totally and visually confirmed. Only five days after the will's formulation Francesco Sassetti died (Giovanni must have known of the man's stroke, which occurred on 21 March), and by May 1494 the Tornabuoni altar-piece was in place.[38] Changes to the fresco cycles' programme, as it was originally described in the detailed contract, occurred after November 1487, and some of those changes foresaw the transfer of subjects from the walls to the altar-piece and/or the window.[39] Francesco Sassetti's anger in April 1488 may well have been aroused by this further intended

[36] NA C 644, fos. 47ᵛ–50ʳ.

[37] Borsook and Offerhaus, *History and Legend*, pp. 14–15, 51; R. de Roover, *The Rise and Decline of the Medici Bank 1397–1494* (Cambridge, Mass., 1963), esp. pp. 223, 301ff, 333, 345.

[38] For Francesco's illness and death, see de Roover, *Medici Bank*, p. 363. The 'tavolla nuova' is first mentioned in the sacristy books on 14 May 1494 (Conv. Soppr., 102, App. 19, fo. 103ᵛ). Baccio d'Agnolo may have begun the frame as early as 1 Jan. 1492, when he was paid 'per manifattura della residentia dell'altar magiore' (fo. 86ʳ).

[39] The first change to the cycle occurred on the register immediately below the *Dormition*, where the Virgin's Purification and Christ Disputing with the Doctors were, in the first instance, transferred to the window and, in the latter case, deleted. Instead, Ghirlandaio produced the *Adoration of the Magi* and the *Massacre of the Innocents*. The naturalistic precision of a giraffe in the *Magi* fresco dates it to after the arrival in Florence of an actual giraffe in Nov. 1487 (Luca Landucci, *Diario fiorentino*, ed. I. Del Badia (Florence, 1883), pp. 52–3). All six saints planned for illustration on the window wall in 1485 were also moved to the altar-piece and/or window. For 'Giovannino' Tornabuoni's birth in late 1487 affecting the Baptist's cycle, see n. 45 below.

intrusion upon his legal preserve. Well before Giovanni's will in 1490, the enlargement of the chapel's decorative programme had prefigured his family's triumph.

Whatever the full extent of claim and counter-claim, with varying degrees of documentation and assertion available to the contenders and placed before the harried (or harrying?) Dominicans, Giovanni Tornabuoni overcame any disputes with decisive results, proclaiming his family's heritage, possibly mollifying Fra Domenico Ricci more than once, outbidding Francesco Sassetti, pursuing the salvation of his ancestors' souls by regular masses, expending generous amounts on the purchase of such things as wax and vestments, convincing the Dominicans of his pious, solvent, and firm intentions. Perhaps the final coup was engineered through another patronage access route, the Confraternity of St Peter Martyr or *dei Laudesi*, which had long occupied a prestigious and key administrative position in the convent and seems to have had special authority over the high-altar area.[40] Elected one of its four captains by the friars, on the anniversary of the church's latest consecration, 1 September 1486, Giovanni marked his entrance and the convent's feast-day with a blaze of light, purchasing the enormous amount of 203 *libbre* of 'courtier's torches'.[41]

Neither his administration nor his wealth went unnoticed, for on precisely the day when he also became the confraternity's provost, 13 October 1486, the friars singled out the 'magnificent and generous man Giovanni' and granted his entire *consorteria* patronage rights over the chapel and altar. On 18 February 1487, precisely when he again became provost, Giovanni left the confraternity a wool shop which later provided his commemorative masses and was, indeed, the chapel's dowry.[42] He was captain once more in the March to September term of 1490, appointed shortly before he drew up his will with its optimism, detail, and determination about the chapel's entire decoration and its designation as a burial site. The competitors had been shrewdly outmanoeuvred and Giovanni had played a winning game.

With the 'mythology' of the *consorteria*'s generosity restored and

[40] See esp. Orlandi, *Necrologio*, i. 314–15 n. 27, 322, 639; ii. 299, 403–4, 502, 538, 576, and R. Hatfield, *Botticelli's Uffizi 'Adoration': A Study in Pictorial Content* (Princeton, 1976), pp. 16, 25.

[41] See NA C 183, booklet 15 (1476–89), fos. 19ʳ, 20ᵛ, for all Giovanni's offices as mentioned herein; and Conv. Soppr., 102, App. 16, fo. 39ᵛ and App. 84, after fo. 61ᵛ, for the 'torchi alla cortigiana'.

[42] *Decima Repubblicana*, 25, fo. 607ᵛ (Giovanni's tax report of 1495). Rab Hatfield has discovered the notarial documentation for the bequest.

even enhanced, Giovanni's own magnificence recognized and disparate rights gathered under the one title, Giovanni from October 1486 could move toward the inclusion of an altar-piece, stained glass, intarsia work, vestments, and so on, in the chapel's scheme. Here we are concerned with only three changes to the chapel's programme as it had been outlined in September 1485 but (as stated in Ghirlandaio's contract then) not begun until May 1486. Firstly, the *Virgin's Purification* was moved to the window, a new decorative arena which also contained the vital insertion of the miracle of the *Madonna of the Snow* (Plate 19). Secondly, the *Expulsion of Joachim* (Plate 18) formed an entirely new opening to the Virgin's cycle. Thirdly, the *Annunciation to Zacharias* (Plate 17) remained as the initiating scene opposite, in the Baptist's cycle, but with important changes made to the presentation drawing that had been required by the contract.

From its inception, when a marginal addition was made to the contract, adding an informed catalogue of the sorts of architecture to be depicted, the chapel's decoration was subject to innumerable alterations.[43] The Dominicans were coaxed towards their settlement of conflicting privileges, allowing expansion of the programme and, eventually, burial rights for Giovanni and his ancestors. Changes were made to Ghirlandaio's drawings by artist and patron alike. By the time of the testament in March 1490, well before the frescos' unveiling in December,[44] other media and subjects had been added to the scheme, including the *Naming of the Baptist* which was most probably Giovanni's proud response to the birth on 11 October 1487 of his first grandson, whose name remade his own image.[45]

Giovanni Tornabuoni and other relatives; Domenico Ghirlandaio and his workship; the friars, including one or two key Dominicans

---

[43] NA M 237, fo. 160ʳ: 'hedifitia, castra, civitates, villes' (the last word being omitted from all publications).

[44] Landucci, *Diario fiorentino*, p. 60 (22 Dec. 1490).

[45] Giovanni di Lorenzo di Giovanni Tornabuoni's birth is recorded in Libro dell'Età, 443 bis, fo. 140ʳ and 444 bis, fo. 162ʳ. For the Florentine practice whereby nomenclature could 'remake' a usually dead relative, see Kent, *Household and Lineage*, pp. 45–7 and C. Klapisch, 'Le nom "refait": La transmission des prénoms à Florence (XIVe–XVIe siècles)', *L'Homme*, 20 (1980), 77–104. Several writers have instead seen the fresco as a reference to Giovanni di Lorenzo de' Medici's baptism in 1475 (G. Davies, *Ghirlandaio* (London, 1909), pp. 122–3 and E. Barfucci, *Lorenzo de' Medici e la società artistica del suo tempo* (2nd edn, Florence, 1964), p. 131). R. van Marle, *The Development of the Italian Schools of Painting* (The Hague, 1931), xiii. 86 n. 1, ably refuted Davies. More positively, it can be stated that religious and dynastic significations are uppermost in this scene and in the chapel. Unlike the Sassetti chapel, the Tornaquinci domain is conspicuous for the absence of the Medici.

such as Giovanni Caroli and Domenico Ricci—all could have engaged with curiosity and excitement in a proceeding that resulted in what is today a deceptively static but still relatively intact ensemble. One senses that Giovanni Tornabuoni in particular had a growing awareness of how to insert himself into more than one process, whether it was encouraging the friars or the artist to share his convictions. He almost acted as a *mezzano* himself, in that his position as representative donor on behalf of his family and *consorteria* made of him a point at which the bonds of patronage were brought to focus.

Ghirlandaio's previous experience of changes in the Sassetti chapel, which he had completed recently,[46] may have inured him to change and to a patron's whims. But those exasperations, let alone Giovanni's control as stipulated in the contract, probably motivated the artist to consult frequently with the patron and the friars, so that the wet plaster only received images already well discussed. Thereby Ghirlandaio, too, would have had the opportunity both to give and to gain advice. In fact, on at least eight other occasions the artist produced work for Giovanni and his son Lorenzo: the relationship surely was one of trust and satisfaction. Warburg divided his 'drei K [*Kirche, Künstler und Kaufmann*]' into rather isolated, even warring worlds;[47] but the notion of patronage available to us now need involve no such alienation of one category from another.

On the lowest register of the wall, closest to a viewer at the entrance

---

[46] W. Welliver, 'Alterations in Ghirlandaio's S. Trinita Frescoes', *Art Quarterly*, 32 (1969), 269–81; A. Rosenauer, 'Ein nicht zur Ausführung gelangter Entwurf Domenico Ghirlandaios für die Cappella Sassetti', *Weiner Jahrbuch für Kunstgeschichte*, 25 (1972), 187–96; Borsook and Offerhaus, *History and Legend*, pp. 69–70, Pls. 4 and 5, figs. M–R, U–W.

[47] E. H. Gombrich, *Aby Warburg: An Intellectual Biography* (London, 1970), p. 115. Ghirlandaio also decorated Giovanni Tornabuoni's chapels in his villa at Chiasso Macerelli and in Santa Maria sopra Minerva, Rome, and portraits of himself and his son were painted in the Sistine Chapel by Ghirlandaio too (Vasari–Milanesi, iii. 258–61, 269, 276). Vasari also stresses 'l'amicizia e la familiarità' between artist and patron. Ghirlandaio painted at least three panels which were present in the Tornabuoni palace in 1498: portraits of Lucrezia Tornabuoni (National Gallery, Washington) and Lorenzo's wife, Giovanna Albizzi (Thyssen–Bornemisza Collection, Lugano), and an *Adoration of the Magi* tondo (Uffizi, Florence): Pupilli avanti il Principato, 181, fos. 147^v, 148^r. Lorenzo Tornabuoni's chapel at Cestello contained an altar-piece and window designed by Ghirlandaio: see A. Luchs, *Cestello: A Cistercian Church of the Florentine Renaissance* (New York, 1977), esp. pp. 42, 44–5, 67–8, 86–8, 116, 283f., 348. Four narratives in stained glass donated by Giovanni Tornabuoni to Santa Maria delle Carceri were also of Ghirlandaio's design: see P. Morselli and G. Corti, *La chiesa di Santa Maria delle Carceri in Prato: Contributo di Lorenzo de' Medici e Giuliano da Sangallo alla progettazione* (Florence, 1982), pp. 69–70, 117, 119, figs. 33–6.

who had passed through the *tramezzo* or choir screen, the *Annunciation to Zacharias* (Plate 17) is the chapel's most important and last scene, bearing three inscriptions including the dedication with its date of 1490. Presenting twenty-one male portraits of the *consorteria* and its notable associates, it is an extended patron portrait whose inscriptions further attest to its mythologizing or idealized grandeur. The wealth of portraiture, which resulted from the patron's contractual examination of the presentation drawing, made for an overcrowded scene; but even the drawing probably indicates, by name, and by style and placement, ten portraits. Only two of the four names have been noticed: 'Messer Giuliano' and 'Giovanfrancesco' clearly stand full length to the right; but it is equally clear that a 'Messer Luigi' is the outer left figure opposite, while next to him and nearest to the angel is an unclear designation which might read 'Lorenzo'.[48]

At least the three legible names match those given in 1561 by the eighty-nine-year-old Benedetto di Luca Landucci, called in by Vincenzo Tornaquinci, who wished to record his family's history. Son of a tenant who leased property owned by the Popoleschi and later Tornabuoni, Benedetto's memory appears acute, or at least well aided by Vincenzo's research and, except for one minor slip, the twelve Tornaquinci men identified in the *Zacharias* scene are present in the family tree, with both age and costume (as far as these can be determined), also suggesting that Landucci was accurate.[49]

In the fresco the younger Tornabuoni with their associates in the drawing are now joined by several other men, in particular four elders representing the extant branches of the Tornaquinci *consorteria*: the Tornabuoni, Popoleschi, and Giachinotti. Featured in the most prominent and honourable position, adjacent to the angel, we see from left

---

[48] The only texts to notice the two names are A. Stix and L. Fröhlich-Bum, *Beschreiben der Katalog der Handzeichnungen in der graphischen Sammlung Albertina* (Vienna, 1932), iii. 6–7, 92; O. Benesch, *Meisterzeichnungen der Albertina* (Salzburg, 1964), p. 321; C. Gilbert, 'The Drawings Now Associated with Masaccio's Sagra', *Storia dell'Arte*, 3 (1969), 269 n. 15, and Glasser, *Artists' Contracts*, pp. 142–3. See, most recently, *Old Master Drawings from the Albertina* (exhibition catalogue, Washington, 1984), no. 45, with a clear reproduction. Neither Dale Kent nor I was able to come to a clear conclusion on the fourth name when the drawing was on display in The Pierpont Morgan Library, New York, in April 1985.

[49] The Landucci list was first published in part by D. M. Manni, *Osservazioni istoriche sopra i sigilli antichi de' secoli bassi* (Florence, 1746), xviii. 130–1 and is most readily available in Vasari–Milanesi, iii. 266–7 n. 1. Warburg's adaptation of the list is unsatisfactory, as he seems to have admitted (Gombrich, *Aby Warburg*, pp. 116–17). In a few instances only we have independent portraits in other media to verify the identifications.

to right, 'Giovanni [di Francesco di Messer Simone] Tornabuoni' (1428–97), 'Piero [di Niccolò di Piero] Popoleschi' (1427–1507), 'Girolamo [d'Adovardo di Cipriano] Giachinotti' (1426–97?) and 'Lionardo [di Francesco di Messer Simone] Tornabuoni' (1422/5–92). Witnesses, performers, donors, they are 'signatories' in a 'religious foundation charter', as Warburg perceived.[50]

Besides the granting of patronage rights to the *consorteria* in October 1486, another document further explicates the presence of men outside the Tornabuoni branch and, in this instance, particularly of the four elders. In December 1487 the Tornabuoni, Giachinotti, and Popoleschi (but not the Tornaquinci, for they were renowned as magnates, without access to civic office) had petitioned the *Signoria*, with some success, to break the *divieto* which restricted their separate access to high office. For political reasons alone the elders stated that their families were 'divided'. In doing so they were motivated by the same desire that had caused their ancestors to form new branches from the Tornaquinci stem in the second half of the fourteenth century.[51] That the social and cultural reality was otherwise is suggested not only by the continuation of the *divieto* for the *Tre Maggiori* and the narrow margin by which their petition was passed, but also by this group of elders in the *Zacharias* fresco, where the same three heads, or in the case of Lionardo and Piero their successors in 1488 and 1489 respectively, stand united and dignified.

They wear sober gowns which remind us that they were honourable citizens who had attained the priorate—or, in Giovanni's case, the Gonfaloniership—standing as statesmen and patrician elders in a pub-

---

[50] Gombrich, *Aby Warburg*, p. 119. A genealogy of the family is in P. Litta, *Le famiglie celebri italiane* (Milan, 1819 ff.), s.v. Tornabuoni, Tav. I and II, but frequent inaccuracies require it to be used with care. There is more information in the anonymous *ricordo* (n. 6 above); a Tornaquinci family tree in Biblioteca Riccardiana, Codex 1859, fos. 72ᵛ–74ʳ; accurate notes in Biblioteca Nazionale, Florence, Poligrafo Gargani and (less reliably) those in Collezione Genealogica Passerini; death notices in *Delizie*, ix. 123–217 and C. Calzolai, 'Il "libro dei morti" di Santa Maria Novella (1290–1436)', *Memorie Domenicane*, NS 11 (1980), 15–218; and several collections in the Florentine State Archives, esp. the Catasto, Decima and Libro dell'Età.

[51] For the actions in the Trecento, see esp. *Delizie*, xiv. 256–73 and Manni, *Sigilli*, xviii. 126–30. The petition of 1487 is in Diplomatico, Strozzi-Uguccione, 20 dicembre 1487 (my thanks to F. W. Kent for this reference). It mentions that the Tornaquinci were made *popolani* in 1434, when twenty other magnate families were also freed from this restriction (see D. Kent, *The Rise of the Medici: Faction in Florence 1426–1434*, Oxford, 1978, pp. 346–7). Nevertheless, no Tornaquinci name entered a *priorista*, nor is the family listed as one of the petitioners in 1487: its reputation was too well known, it seems.

lic piazza-cum-religious sanctum, surrounded by their clients, associates, and Florentine worthies. Past unity is commemorated and its future proclaimed; continuum and solidarity rather than change or division is the assurance, addressed to their audience and their successors. Hope for yet more political offices required one kind of rhetoric in the petition; hopes for the family's future and dignity another. In some ways the fresco is a visual response to the documented actions of 1486 and 1487. The Tornaquinci as a *consorteria*, of proud ancestry and noble stature, 'padroni' of the 'chiesetta' and now of the entire *cappella maggiore* and its altar, are proclaimed as generous patrons and worthy citizens, united in the face of political contingency.

A civic and religious proclamation, again of a self-consciously public nature, is also made by the inscriptions. The one most visible today uses language common to the learned and Medicean circles who share the Tornaquinci's space, speaking as would a Landino or a Poliziano: 'In the year 1490, when the most beautiful city, graced by treasures, victories, arts and buildings, enjoyed wealth, health and peace.'[52] Both this phrasing and the architecture idealize Florence not only into a New Rome but, beyond that, into a generalized City of God in which the Triumphal Arch and its military reliefs bear a double reading as both civic and Christian.

A second inscription runs along the entablature on either side of the central apse: DOMINVS AB VTERO VOCAVIT ME DE VENT[RE] or 'The Lord called me from the womb ...' (Isaiah 49: 1).[53] Like virtually all the Biblical passages employed in the chapel, this text comes from the Missal, here the feast-day of the Baptist's Nativity. In the opening scene of his cycle, it announces John's mission, his fulfilment of prophecy and his sanctification even before birth—a meaning which reverberates with John's position as patron saint of Florence. But it is a third inscription, contained by the apse's entablature, which interests us most here: ORATIO MEA SICVT INCENSVM IN CONSPECTV TVO, for it is a donor's petition: '[Let] my prayer [be counted] as incense before thee'

[52] Adapted slightly from the translation in Gombrich, *Aby Warburg*, p. 117. The original reads: 'AN. MCCCCLXXXX QUO PULCHERRIMA CIVITAS OPIBUS VICTORIIS ARTIBUS AEDIFICIIS QUE NOBILIS COPIA SALUBRITATE PACE PERFRUEBATUR.' Usually attributed to Poliziano, the inscription has many conceptual and verbal parallels in Landino's *De vera nobilitate*, written around 1487 (ed. M. T. Liaci, Florence, 1970).

[53] D. A. Covi, 'The Inscription in Fifteenth-Century Florentine Painting', PhD diss. (Institute of Fine Arts, New York University, 1958), pp. 114, 426–7; Offerhaus, *Motief en achtergrond*, p. 136.

(Ps. 141: 2).[54] Part of the Offertory Rite, it was recited as the priest, like Zacharias, incensed the altar, before performing the same ritual over the 'whole multitude of the people' (Luke 1: 10) who thereby participate in the eucharistic sacrifice. No more appropriate inscription could accompany this 'patron portrait', where the offering of the *consorteria*'s donation (both 'chiesetta' and chapel), and its prayer for eternal salvation, are forever visualized.

In one liturgical inscription the humble petitioner calls for salvation, in the other the Lord summons, as he begins the path towards Incarnation: the donor's prayer to be heard is indeed answered. 'Victories' or triumph is in many ways the fresco's central meaning, incorporating what Francesco Guicciardini later termed 'the perpetual triumph of the city' and 'the glory of our house . . . for ever',[55] a theme inextricably tied to John's coming and the promise he brings, along with the triumph of the Christian soul over death. The very form of the inscribed arch embodies such a multivalent signification, since it is both Triumphal Arch and apse. Ghirlandaio innovatively includes a central apse reminiscent of the architecture of contemporary chapels, hence transforming the Arch of Constantine into the flanking arms of a Greek Cross church. The 'piazza' occupied by the congregation or *corpo* of the church replaces the fourth chapel of a centralized temple so that the Tornaquinci stand figuratively, as well as literally, within the confines of a family chapel.

Amongst *parenti* the Tornaquinci take part in a family gathering; amongst *amici* a peaceful *passeggiata*, or *convivio*; amongst *vicini* a civic ceremonial occasion. As donors to a Dominican church, and as the *corpo* of the church, they stand as observers of or participants in— the ambivalence I believe is a deliberate one—what Warburg called 'a miracle play'.[56] Noble and elect on earth, members of a city and a family of proportions approaching the mythological, the Tornaquinci also prefigure, *in perpetuo* like their family masses, their desired elec-

---

[54] Covi, 'The Inscription', pp. 114–15, 421, 426; Offerhaus, *Motief en achtergrond*, p. 152. Jacopo da Voragine, *The Golden Legend*, tr. and adapted from the Latin by G. Ryan and H. Ripperger (New York, 1969), pp. 87–8, 774, citing Ps. 141: 2, speaks of incense as a sign of 'piety and prayer', for which other Biblical references include Rev. 5: 8, 8: 3–4. The image is placed in an illuminating context by Pier Filippo Pandolfini's sermon delivered to the Compagnia de' Magi in 1476 (see Hatfield, *Botticelli's Uffizi 'Adoration'*, p. 53).

[55] C. M. Ady, 'Morals and Manners of the Quattrocento', *Proceedings of the British Academy*, 28 (1942), 181.

[56] Gombrich, *Aby Warburg*, p. 116; cf. C. Gilbert, 'The Renaissance Portrait', *Burlington Magazine*, 110 (1968), 284: 'citizens seeing a mystery play.'

tion to paradise. Magnificent donors, worthy citizens, men with honourable ancestors and associates, they stand in a group portrait as representatives, not individuals, proclaiming their Christian as well as their humanist *virtù*.[57] Their heritage, good works, and reputation allow them a place in a patron portrait.

That such a multivalent but consistent reading is possible, even necessary, is suggested by Giovanni Tornabuoni's description of his motives in the contract of 1485, selecting certain but several links in what Lorenzo de' Medici called 'the solid chain'.[58] Giovanni commissioned the chapel's restoration 'to decorate the said chapel with noble, worthy, exquisite and decorative paintings ... as an act of piety and love of God, to the exaltation of his house and family and the enhancement of the said church and chapel'. City and self (often 'links' in such descriptions) are subsumed in the chapel, the former under its guise as a City of God, the latter under a family identity and a religious humility. Giovanni's two donor portraits suggest just this multivalent and corporate identity: in the *Zacharias* he stands in civic gown proudly amidst his *parenti*, in a window wall fresco he kneels in simpler garb opposite a posthumous portrait of his wife, making a gesture connoting supplication and humility.[59]

Portrait identification is not so easy for the *Expulsion of Joachim* (Plate 18), but we are sure that Domenico Ghirlandaio included himself with his own chosen retinue, drawn largely from his workshop and family, on the right. His costume, gaze, posture, and gesture rather mirror those of Lorenzo di Giovanni Tornabuoni on the other side of the temple and all bespeak an artist of growing confidence, aware of the viewer and his relationship with that eye as it observed his full-

[57] Too often the Christian nature of magnificent patronage and *virtù* is forgotten in discussions of Renaissance art, including portraiture. Individualism and worldly aggrandizement are more usually cited as the patron's motivations. For the importance of good works and one's worthy actions in this world in earning a place in the next, see for instance, P. Ariès, *The Hour of Our Death* (Harmondsworth, 1981), pp. 214–15 and J. O'Malley, *Praise and Blame in Renaissance Rome* (Durham, 1979), ch. 5.

[58] J. Ross, *The Lives of the Early Medici as told in their Correspondence* (London, 1910), p. 334. Similar comprehensive explanations of motives include Lorenzo in 1490 as quoted by J. Gage, *Life in Italy at the Time of the Medici* (London, 1968), p. 97; Leon Battista Alberti, *Ten Books on Architecture*, tr. J. Leoni (London, 1955), Pref. p. x, and A. Perosa (ed.), *Giovanni Rucellai ed il suo zibaldone*, I: *Il zibaldone quaresimale* (London, 1960), p. 121. The contract's translation here is from Chambers, *Patrons and Artists*, p. 173.

[59] For the gesture, see M. Baxandall, *Painting and Experience in Fifteenth-century Italy* (Oxford, 1972), pp. 55, 65; L. Gougaud, *Devotional and Ascetic Practices in the Middle Ages* (London, 1927), pp. 19–20.

bodied possession of space on a two-dimensional surface.[60] Standing with one hand on his hip so that his elbow projects his presence beyond the picture plane, his active pose confirms a contemporary assessment of him as 'an expeditous man and one who gets through much work'.[61]

Domenico's right hand moves towards his chest, indicating himself as the artist responsible for what was possibly the largest fresco cycle completed by the one shop in Florence during the fifteenth century, overseen by an artist at the peak of his skill and prestige. The gesture also echoes that of a faithful female in the midground nearby who brings her offering to the altar, a gesture used elsewhere to connote humble adoration.[62] Domenico is self-consciously alluding to the donation of his artistic skill in a church which was the site of his family's burials.[63] In the adjoining scene, depicting the Virgin's birth, Domenico placed elaborate signatures of a verbal sort, BIGHORDI and GRILLANDAI, visible amidst the innovative, modern *grottesche* work painted in gold on the panels in St Anne's bedroom. Visual consciousness, religious sensibility, and familial commemoration were each understood by Ghirlandaio in his own portrayal, as well as in that of his patrons.

Neither Giotto's personal intensity, nor Giovanni da Milano's stern rejection which Meiss read as 'institutional', are chosen by Ghirlandaio in his *Expulsion of Joachim*.[64] Joachim moves, not towards an isolating

---

[60] Vasari–Milanesi, iii. 263 for Ghirlandaio (cf. his self-portrait in the Sassetti chapel, Santa Trinita—see Borsook and Offerhaus, *History and Legend*, p. 41, Pl. 37); V. Follini, *Firenze antica e moderna illustrata* (Florence, 1795), vi. 323 for the first clear proposition that Lorenzo Tornabuoni is present (cf. his medal in Hill, *Corpus of Italian Medals*, no. 1068).

[61] Baxandall, *Painting and Experience*, p. 26.

[62] Ibid., pp. 51, 65. The gesture is used in other works by Ghirlandaio, including the 'Simonetta Vespucci' figure in the *Madonna della Misericordia*, Ognissanti, Florence, one of the adoring shepherds in the Sassetti Altar-piece, Santa Trinita and one of the Magi in his Innocenti altar-piece. Lippi uses it in several other but related contexts—for St Jerome, for the two actors in the Annunciation, and a donor in the Barberini Annunciation (G. Marchini, *Filippo Lippi* (Milan, 1975), Pls. 35, 37, 39, 57, 62, 66, 144, 154, 155, 171).

[63] Rosselli, *Sepoltuario*, p. 768. Domenico's burial at S. Maria Novella in 1494 is well known (see Orlandi, *Necrologio*, ii. 588) but Rab Hatfield has found other instances where the Bighordi dead were buried or commemorated there.

For an artist alluding to his own donation, esp. by means of signature or self-portraiture, see the issue of *Revue de l'art*, 26 (1974) on 'Art de la signature', esp. 18–20, 89; and J. H. Stubblebine, ' "The Face in the Crowd": Some Early Sienese Self-Portraits', *Apollo*, 108, no. 202 (1978), 388–93.

[64] M. Meiss, *Painting in Florence and Siena after the Black Death* (New York, 1964), pp. 29ff.; J. Lafontaine-Dosogne, *Iconographie de l'enfance de la Vierge dans l'Empire byzantin et en Occident* (Brussels, 1965), ii. 62–6.

void, but in the direction of the adjacent *Birth*, his momentum following on from the priest (who is not at the usual expelling distance) and integrating with the nearby group of witnesses. No longer isolated or forlorn, Joachim clings to the lamb in a protective but not desperate manner, soon to be assured and childless no more. The narrative moment and the rejection is contrasted with the acceptable offerings from now very young supplicants who approach the altar from the side at which Lorenzo Tornabuoni and his associates witness the donation. This acceptance, and the hope it offers for the future, is emphasized by an unprecedented spatial tunnel and architectural centralization which indicate that it is a visible and normal occurrence. The physical focus for this ritual, the altar itself, contains four reliefs of Old Testament heroes: Judith victorious over Holofernes; a Jewish sacrifice scene; a king, probably David, praying to Jehovah; and a youthful David victorious over Goliath.[65] So the two central reliefs aptly represent supplication and sacrifice while those on each flank celebrate victory.

Another unusual feature is the woman carrying doves in a basket, bringing to the temple her offerings after childbirth, just as the Virgin will at her Purification, offering 'a pair of turtle doves'.[66] The same basket with its doves is held by Joseph in the chapel window's *Purification* designed by Ghirlandaio. This visual reference to the Purification is made more explicitly by an inscription running across the temple's frieze in the fresco, VENIET AD TEMPLVM SANCTVM SVVM DOMINATOR, which occurs in the liturgy for the feast-day of the Purification.[67] This prophecy of future grace (Malachi 3: 1) refers to the advent of Christ, who was presented to the temple in the same ritual, borne by Mary who was the tabernacle, after which 'right offerings to the Lord' (Malachi 3: 3) will be acceptable from a purified nation. Joachim need show little perturbation since 'presently the Lord, whom you seek ... shall come to His temple'. So too the Tornaquinci could be confident that their offering will be accepted and salvation assured.

The Expulsion takes place before a structure which has long been

[65] The first three scenes are identified by T. M. Thomas, 'Classical Reliefs and Statues in later Quattrocento Religious Paintings', PhD diss. (Univ. of California, Berkeley, 1980), p. 128. The winged Victories on either side of the central arch also suggest the Lord's imminent advent in the Temple, as does the inscription (see n. 67 below).

[66] Jacopo da Voragine, *Golden Legend*, p. 150; Luke 2: 24.

[67] Offerhaus, *Motief en achtergrond*, pp. 134–5 could not identify the source. It was the text chosen by the Dominican Archbishop Antoninus when he discussed the Purification (*Lettere di S. Antonino* (Florence, 1859), pp. 128–31).

associated with San Paolo's loggia opposite Santa Maria Novella, but a study by Goldthwaite and Rearick gives due credit to Ghirlandaio's imaginative reinvention of 'the still abuilding loggia'.[68] The artist places probably more than one younger Tornabuoni donor in the idealized piazza of the church their *consorteria* 'founded', just as their elders stand, opposite, in or near an idealized piazza-cum-temple which is also based on a Greek Cross plan (Plates 17, 18). Nowhere in the Tornaquinci chapel does Ghirlandaio employ topographically accurate views of Florence; instead his patrons are present on an idealized stage, here depicted in the most up-to-date Sangallesque idiom, amidst airy portals and classicized features which represent the 'Sacred Temple'. An addition after the contract, the *Expulsion of Joachim* was a fitting mirror image to the *Zacharias* scene, each treating the fertility and continuity of a family, the narrative of offering and prayer before an altar, the implicit message of hope and future salvation, and each allowing the presence of many witnesses or patron portraits in idealized spaces. Both frescos have patronage at the heart of their content and form.

The third scene I wish to single out was in the central lancet of the stained-glass window, again in the lowest register of its setting but probably more visible from a distance. The *Madonna della Neve* (Plate 19) was surmounted by the *Purification* and then the episode during the Virgin's *Assumption* when she passed down her girdle to Thomas as tangible proof of her purity. The founding of a church, Santa Maria Maggiore in Rome, by the Madonna of the Snow, refers to the consecration and purification of *ecclesia*'s edifice, to the Virgin's protective and symbolic link with the church and to the Tornaquinci as original *padroni* of a church's site. Ostensibly showing the establishment of the church in its physical and temporal aspect, the scene would be easily read by Dominican and layman alike as a multivalent image.

An unusual subject of rare currency in Florence, one of its few instances executed by Florentine artists in the Quattrocento was an altar-piece painted by Masolino and Masaccio for the Colonna chapel itself in Santa Maria Maggiore, Rome.[69] No doubt the same basic

---

[68] R. A. Goldthwaite and W. R. Rearick, 'Michelozzo and the Ospedale di San Paolo in Florence', *Mitteilungen des Kunsthistorischen Institutes in Florenz*, 21 (1977), 250–1; cf. H. Hauvette, *Ghirlandaio* (Paris, 1907), p. 113 n. 1 and Offerhaus, *Motief en achtergrond*, p. 151.

[69] Other than H. van Os, 'Schnee in Siena', *Nederlands kunsthistorisch jaarboek*, 19 (1968), 1–50, the literature mainly treats Masolino's scene, for which see esp. M. Meiss,

meaning lay behind both Masolino's work and Ghirlandaio's—the foundation of the Universal Church; although if a sense of the church restored physically and morally after the Schism imbued the earlier painting, at the end of the century any sense of restoration suggested by Ghirlandaio's design presumably referred instead to the reconciliation between Florence and the Papacy after the Pazzi war.[70]

Ghirlandaio's depiction contains the most explicit portrayal of an emperor within this scene by any Renaissance artist. While the presence of the pope and a modern secular palace behind him are not unusual, the emperor's uniqueness is matched by the backdrop to his retinue, which can only be an idealized view of another church dedicated to the Virgin (and whose building began on the feast-day of Purification):[71] Brunelleschi's *cupola*, covered in terracotta tiles and topped by its lantern with gilded sphere. As in the convent's chapter house painted over a hundred years before, we find church and state in peace and harmony with pope and emperor before an idealized depiction of the Florentine cathedral.[72] But now a legendary narrative is the less allegorical garb, and Rome has become Florence, or rather an idealized City of God, just as contemporary illustrations of Augustine's famous

'The Altered Program of the Santa Maria Maggiore Altarpiece', in W. Lotz and L. Mötler (eds.), *Studien zur Toskanischen Kunst: Festschrift für L. H. Heydenreich* (Munich, 1964), pp. 169–90, and A. Braham, 'The Emperor Sigismund and the Santa Maria Maggiore Altar-piece', *Burlington Magazine*, 122 (1980), 106–12. Lorenzo Monaco's semi-ruined fresco in the Bartolini–Salimbeni chapel, Santa Trinita, is reproduced (but with little comment) by C. Gardner von Tueffel, 'Lorenzo Monaco, Filippo Lippi und Filippo Brunelleschi: die Erfindung der Renaissancepala', *Zeitschrift für Kunstgeschichte*, 45 (1982), 1–30, fig. 1.

[70] Vasari–Milanesi, ii. 294; Braham, 'The Emperor Sigismund'; B. Kery, *Kaiser Sigismund: Ikonographie* (Vienna, 1972), pp. 78–83. The end of the Pazzi wars has been connected with Ghirlandaio's *Confirmation of the Rule of St Francis* in the Sassetti chapel, Santa Trinita, particularly by Borsook and Offerhaus, *History and Legend*, pp. 49ff. 'PACE' is celebrated in the dedication inscription of 1490 in the Tornaquinci chapel.

[71] M. Franceschoni, *Firenze sacra ovvero feste, devozioni, e indulgenze che sono nelle chiesa della Città di Firenze* (Florence, 1739), p. 29 and C. Guasti, *Santa Maria del Fiore* (Florence, 1887), p. 8, which also documents the city's offering at the cathedral on this feast-day (pp. 310–13, 316–18). One of the few notices we have of the day's public observance treats the city's welcome to Emperor Frederick III in 1452 at the cathedral (Orlandi, *S. Antonino*, ii. 301–2 and R. Trexler (ed.), *The Libro Cerimoniale of the Florentine Republic* (Geneva, 1978), pp. 72–3).

[72] E. Borsook, *The Mural Painters of Tuscany* (2nd edn, Oxford, 1980), p. 50; J. Gardner, 'Andrea di Bonaiuto and the Chapterhouse Frescoes in Santa Maria Novella', *Art History*, 2 (1979), 123; P. Watson, 'The Spanish Chapel: Portraits of Poets or a Portrait of Christian Order?', *Memorie Domenicane*, NS 11 (1980), 471–87.

text used Florence instead of Rome as the City seen by Augustine, so that Florence was 'simultaneously city of man and city of God'.[73]

Local legend, dating at least from Villani's time, encouraged this transfer of location, since it claimed that Florence's own Santa Maria Maggiore was built, 'as at Rome', during the city's reconstruction, and it was also believed to have been directed by a pope.[74] The young Baptist's presence at the *Purification* in the window above this scene may also have intended a patriotic reference, for there the city was present in the Temple of Jerusalem through her chief patron saint and advocate. In both cases any Florentine reference is making of that city a remaking of another city, the exemplary site of a new temple or New Jerusalem. Similarly, no matter which emperor Ghirlandaio's scene represented (Charlemagne or Augustus, both imperial rebuilders of Florence), his presence gives further point to the chapel's classicizing presentation of 'the most perfect city' as 'another new Rome'.[75] A Florence inhabited by the Tornaquinci is an ideal and renovated *polis*, a City of God in its earthly form.

This rare scene, which in liturgical terms celebrates the consecration of a major Mariological church, may also allude to the donation of the original 'chiesetta' and land to the Dominicans by the Tornaquinci, a generous act of patronage already assuming vague but aggrandized dimensions at this time when Giovanni Tornabuoni had successfully asserted the claims of his *consorteria* to the chapel. The sixteenth-century representation in the convent's cloister of that donation seems to have followed a visual pattern similar to that of the *Neve* scene: the Dominican prior and the Tornabuoni bishop who was the fresco's

---

[73] A. Chastel, 'Un épisode de la symbolique urbaine au XVe siècle: Florence et Rome, Cités de Dieu' in *Urbanisme et architecture, études écrites et publiées en l'honneur de Pierre Lavedan* (Paris, 1954), pp. 75–9, repr. in A. Chastel, *Fables, formes, figures* (Paris, 1978), i. 516–24. The quotation here is from C. Trinkaus, 'The Religious Thought of the Italian Humanists and the Reformers: Anticipation or Autonomy?', in C. Trinkaus and H. Oberman (eds.), *The Pursuit of Holiness in Late Medieval and Renaissance Religion* (Leiden, 1974), p. 341 n. 2.

[74] See Busignani and Bencini, *Quartiere di Santa Maria Novella*, pp. 105–7, which discusses Santa Maria Maggiore, Florence.

[75] Benedetto Dei, portrayed in the *Zacharias* scene, called Florence 'un' altra Roma novella' (F. W. Kent, *Household and Lineage*, p. 101). For the imperial reconstruction of Florence, including Poliziano's recent discovery of 'evidence' indicating Augustus' role, see esp. Borsook and Offerhaus, *History and Legend*, pp. 53–4, and N. Rubinstein, 'Il Poliziano e la questione delle origini di Firenze', in *Il Poliziano e il suo tempo* (Florence, 1957), pp. 101–10.

patron are depicted against an architectural backdrop.[76] But it may be that Giovanni Tornabuoni also chose the *Neve* scene as a Roman miracle involving another Giovanni, familiar to him after his years in that city and applicable in a remade form to his own Florentine magnificence. The legend was most apposite because in 1478 Giovanni Tornabuoni had rented the benefice at Florence's own Santa Maria Maggiore,[77] and his responsibility for services and maintenance at that church not far from his palace made of him an unusual patron closely associated with the Madonna of the Snow. Whether referring to an ancient family action or to Giovanni's beneficent remodelling and enlarging of that heritage at several Tuscan sites, or more probably to both, the scene makes an explicit and appropriate reference to patronage and to a harmony between secular and religious worlds guided by the Virgin's intercession.

We are in a sense presented with the founding of Santa Maria 'Novella' anew, and the Dominicans also had some reason for associating themselves with the legend of the snow. Their dedication to the church and the Virgin found joint expression there. Further, until the late Cinquecento, the feast-day for the *Madonna della Neve* fell on the same day in August as St Dominic's.[78] More particularly, the same pope who commissioned Masolino's altar-piece, Martin V, had consecrated 'the church and the high altar' of Santa Maria Novella on 1 September 1420, and thereafter it was this day of 'foundation' which was celebrated annually at the high altar. The massive weight of

[76] See n. 9 above. Martin V's own choice of the subject may also have been affected by his family's role as early patrons of the rebuilt Santa Maria Maggiore and by his own activity in Rome as a 'great builder' (see Meiss, 'The Altered Program', pp. 178, 182, who does not, however, make this connection). The patron of Matteo di Giovanni's *Madonna della Neve* altar-piece of 1477 was another Giovanni, Bishop of Pienza, who also founded the Oratory dedicated to the Madonna of the Snow in Siena wherein resided the altar-piece. Van Os, 'Schnee in Siena', p. 16 and n. 22, suggests that family portraits are present in the *predella*.

[77] G. Brucker, 'Urban Parishes and Their Clergy in Quattrocento Florence: A Preliminary *Sondage*', in A. Morrogh, F. Superbi Gioffredi, P. Morselli, and E. Borsook (eds.), *Renaissance Studies in Honor of Craig Hugh Smyth* (2 vols., Florence, 1985), i. 22.

[78] Van Os, 'Schnee in Siena', p. 26, briefly mentions Dominican association with the legend. It may be pertinent that Gregory the Great compared the snowfall to the word of preachers (Y. Hirn, *The Sacred Shrine* (London, 1912), p. 544 n. 1). Antoninus disliked 'apocryphal tales' (Gilbert, *Italian Art*, p. 148), but in 1445 he approved the *capitoli* of the *Madonna della Neve* confraternity which gathered at Sant Ambrogio (Capitoli, Compagnie Religiose Soppresse, 606, fo. 50ᵛ). A certain link between the miracle and the Virgin's Assumption (depicted for instance on the reverse of Masolino's altar-piece) may have been relevant in this Florentine chapel dedicated to the Assumption.

'courtier's torches' purchased by Giovanni Tornabuoni on 1 September 1486 may have been for this very purpose.[79] Because the *Madonna della Neve* was honoured on the same day as their founder, and since they too commemorated the 'founding' or consecration and remaking of their church, the friars could have been pleased to have this scene commemorating *ecclesia* and a miracle of the Virgin near the very altar where they celebrated both days.

It may not be a coincidence that Giovanni Tornabuoni signed his contract with the Ghirlandaio brothers on 1 September, the sixty-fifth anniversary of Santa Maria Novella's consecration. Perhaps he was aware, too, that not only was the builder of Santa Maria Maggiore another Giovanni but that one of his city's rare *Neve* scenes was presented in the medium of stained glass at Or San Michele. It is only there and in a fresco at Pistoia (both from the Trecento) that a middle-aged married couple kneel below the patriarch Giovanni, adoring the miracle and offering their faithful prayers, as if they were donors.[80]

In Santa Maria Novella, Giovanni and his dead wife kneel eternally either side of the window, using the same variation in prayer gestures as occurs at Or San Michele. The Tornabuoni couple knelt in paradisal settings on the *Neve* level, addressing the reverse of the altar-piece where the *Resurrection* was a clear reference to eucharistic salvation, and this on the very altar which often saw a special celebration of the Corpus Christi cult.[81] They adore the whole miracle of Christianity and pray that they, as representatives of the *consorteria*, will be accepted as purified souls who have contributed greatly to the church's 'foundation' and decoration.

As the window rises towards the 'dome of heaven' and the lunette where the *Coronation of the Virgin* shows the elect in Paradise, its images move through a hierarchy of donation, from man as donor to man as recipient of the church's blessing and to man's ultimate reward

[79] See n. 41 above for 1486; G. O. Corazzini (ed.), 'Diario fiorentino di Bartolommeo di Michele del Corazza (1405–38)', *Archivio storico italiano*, ser. 5, 14 (1894), 270–1, and Biliotti, *Chronica*, ii. (1895–96), 178ff. for 1420.

[80] W. Cohn, 'Zur Ikonographie der Glasfenster von Orsanmichele', *Mitteilungen des Kunsthistorischen Institutes in Florenz*, 9 (1959–60), 8–9, fig. 8; van Os, 'Schnee in Siena', Pl. 14 reproduces the damaged fresco in Pistoia.

[81] C. von Holst, 'Domenico Ghirlandaio: L'altare maggiore di Santa Maria Novella a Firenze ricostruito', *Antichità viva*, 8, 3 (1969), 36–41. On the Corpus Christi cult, see esp. V. Fineschi, *Della festa e della processione del Corpus Domini in Firenze* (Florence, 1768); an extract from Borghigiani's chronicle in M. Hall, 'The "tramezzo" in S. Croce, Florence, reconstructed', *Art Bulletin*, 56 (1974), 340 n. 1; and Hatfield, *Botticelli's Uffizi 'Adoration'*, esp. pp. 50–2.

from the supreme Patron. Divine grace and eternal salvation are the supreme Patron's alone to give, the most extreme instance of that 'inequality of power or resources' (to use Weissman's summarizing phrase at the beginning of his chapter) which binds patron to donor along the patronage spectrum.[82] The Virgin, as broker or intercessor—particularly in her earthly guise as the church who facilitates the client's access to the spiritual—is the window's subject. Patronage and its mythologizing therefore informs the chapel's iconography on several levels.

Both in the figures of the Lord God and of the Tornaquinci 'padroni', the patron and his patronage are celebrated and idealized, not only through the choice of subject and the contextual interplay between scenes but also by various visual or stylistic means. Arrangement in relation to the viewer or in relation to the setting, either at the initiation of a cycle or graded in the window's hierarchy, are formal placements then reinforced and augmented by careful spatial and compositional decisions only briefly touched upon here.

Like all Renaissance artists, Ghirlandaio manipulated both naturalism and idealism into the one non-contradictory style, making of his mythologies a persuasive reality which could be characterized as 'rhetorical realism'. He demonstrated and praised the ideal through the particular, celebrated the substance of the Incarnation through the truthful depiction of its superficial appearance,[83] idealized the 'pulcherrima civitas' through the presentation of the latest architectural fashions, portrayed his patrons in recognizable costumes moving in stately dignity through universal spaces, made of the invisible vision a tangible panorama.

Instead of style, iconography has here been our subject; yet even so, an investigation of donor portraiture, and of certain scenes and their emphases, could repay attention in our investigation of patronage. Thematic as well as instrumental realms of patronage could be questioned anew if we worked with a more fluid, less deterministic, sense of how patron and client operated. At Santa Maria Novella friars,

[82] God was the 'donatore d'ogni bene e d'ogni grazia' according to Giovanni di Pagolo Morelli (*Ricordi*, ed. V. Branca (Florence, 1969), p. 542); a possible 'patron' according to a Romanesque manuscript; a feudal 'Master' in an inscription on an Italian altar-piece of 1365 (B. Lane, 'The Development of the Medieval Devotional Figure', PhD diss. (Univ. of Pennsylvania, 1970), pp. 72, 138). Suggestive remarks are made by R. Trexler, *Public Life in Renaissance Florence* (New York, 1980), ch. 3: 'Exchange'.

[83] Naturalism is treated by L. Steinberg, 'The Sexuality of Christ in Renaissance Art and in Modern Oblivion', *October*, 25 (Summer 1983), 1–222.

artists, and patrons were all engaged in a shifting process, in both the manipulation of patronage rights and the production of art. This makes of the 'programme', the existence of which art historians have long assumed, and lately queried,[84] not something non-existent but rather a more flexible dialogue, as it operated in the Renaissance, and a more usable tool as we apply it today.

In such a common-sense scheme the artist is rescued from the role of mere illustrator, yet not isolated in some aesthetic prison. Domenico Ghirlandaio presents us with a world reinvented and shaped anew, which also accorded with the patron's less visually skilful desires and with the beliefs and demands of the friars. This nexus between artist, patron, and friars, sharing a mutual comprehension, contributed to a continuous flow of production which proceeded in harmony, not by the exclusion of one agent from another.

---

[84] Gilbert, *Italian Art*, pp. xviii–xxvii; Hope, 'Artists, Patrons, and Advisers'.

The Priority of the Architect: Alberti on Architects and Patrons

JOHN OPPEL

ALBERTI, it is usually said, raised architecture to the status of one of the liberal arts. It would be at least as true and historically more appropriate to argue that he did just the reverse, that he brought the liberal arts down to the level of the mechanical ones, that his career—his intellectual career—can be seen as one of condescension in the sense of moving away from the culture of the *litteratus* and towards that of the ordinary, educated, intelligent, intellectually alive and curious member of the Italian or Florentine political élite. Alberti accommodated himself more and more to the condition of life in the city-state, at least after the early 1430s, putting his gifts, such as they were, at the service of the community; and, as we shall see, he also thought of architectural patronage not in terms of individual self-promotion but as a form of public service. The model for Alberti's architect may be drawn from Vitruvius but closer to home were the traditions of the master builders and, in Italy, of the city-sponsored 'architects' on whose achievements, both as artists and engineers, Alberti confers the legitimacy of his own noble birth and of his initiation into the disciplines of classical literature. Condescend as he might, however, Alberti preserves his own detachment, compensating for the decline of his family and his own relative loss of status by the intellectual authority which he came to enjoy and which he did think of as just that—as a real form of authority.

This matter of the division between the liberal and the mechanical arts—and, as I have suggested, of Alberti's moving from a basis in the former towards the latter—requires some looking into, and it is clear that to divide the one sphere from the other, neatly and clearly, as Hugh of Saint Victor did in the twelfth century will not do for our purposes. Closer to Alberti in spirit is another twelfth-century writer, Dominicus Gundissalinus. He extends the traditional Greek division of the sciences into two sorts, the theoretical and the practical: under the heading of the latter he includes 'politics, or the art of civil government', and 'the art of family government'. Subordinated to these and in their sphere of influence were the 'fabrile and mechanical arts'. 'Through the mechanical arts resources were acquired which provided for the needs of the family.'[1] This division suggests a continuity in Alberti's intellectual development; it suggests how he moved from his first major work, the treatise on the family, to his second and last, the *Ten Books on Architecture*, written between 1444 and 1450. The continuity between these two works is, in any case, apparent, since one of the overriding purposes in both is to preserve the family (defined as parents, grandparents, children, in-laws, and dependents) from the forces which threaten it with decay and dissolution in what Alberti sees as (for families) dangerous times: 'How many noble families, reduced by the calamity of the times, had been utterly lost, both in our own native city, and in others, had not their paternal habitations preserved and cherished them, as it were, in the bosom of their forefathers.'[2] The architect becomes, then, a kind of family friend—or a supportive uncle—somewhat like Lionardo Alberti in Alberti's *Books on the Family*. The ethics which are promoted in the work on architecture, too, are very like those we identify with Giannozzo Alberti in Book III of *The Family* (which enjoyed great popularity in Florence)— the pursuit of the mean in the true Aristotelian sense seen not as some comfortable middle ground, an easy option, but more like walking a tightrope or hitting the centre of a target, a life of continual alertness and awareness, both practical and moral.

The early 1400s see the emergence of two new social or intellectual types, the architect and the patron. Alberti has a major role in defining these two and in giving them more specific identities. In the cases of both the architect and the patron, to speak of an 'emergence', or to make a claim for novelty, is to raise what is, at least in part, a question of definition. By an 'architect' I mean a professional—that is, a specialist—who is responsible for the idea or, more precisely, the design of a building but not for its execution. By a 'patron' I mean a

---

[1] See A. C. Crombie, *Augustine to Galileo: Science in the Middle Ages* (London, 1952), p. 179

[2] Leon Battista Alberti, *Ten Books on Architecture*, tr. into Italian by C. Bartoli and into English by J. Leoni (London, 1965), p. ix (henceforth, Alberti). The English translation is used here for convenience, in preference to the critical edition, *L'architettura (De re aedificatoria)*, G. Orlandi, and P. Portoghesi (eds.) (2 vols., Milan, 1966).

person who, acting more or less as a free agent, not only pays for but determines the initial conception and oversees the actual construction of a building. Architecture and patronage had existed before but not architects and patrons in this sense or, at least, both had considerable novelty in the early 1440s. Patrons had acted before but, especially in Florence, their individualities were submerged as members of collectivities. Alberti himself gives a good example of this when, in Book III of *The Family*, he refers to his ancestor 'Alberto the son of Sir Iacopo, the lawyer', who was a member of the *Signoria* which undertook the founding of the public palace.[3] Alberti, as we shall have occasion to observe, comes from a family with a long republican tradition. 'Architects' were masters in the building trades or, in Florence, the term had been reserved for city planners.

Alberti is concerned with defining the proper spheres of action of architect and patron and, I think, with subordinating the latter to the former, not in the sense of any formal hierarchical arrangement but in that of bringing him under the sway of a pervasive moral and social influence like that of teacher over student or, perhaps, master over disciple. The architect certainly sacrifices very little of his intellectual independence to the patron. He waits to be called upon, never calls first. Indeed, the emergence of the patron as a freely acting individual is something of a pretext by which the moralist/architect whom Alberti favours can get his way. If Alberti's elusive social and political theorizing has any content, if it gives rise to any notion of an ideal or especially desirable social order, that ideal might be described as an (insidious) despotism of the intellectuals. In the opening chapter of Book IV of *On Architecture*, Alberti attempts to define social roles in terms of the degree to which various categories of people participate in the faculty which separates human beings from the brute beasts— reason, and the good arts which he sees as reason's necessary consequence.[4] Alberti, I think, is serious here. As far as possible he wants to realize this objective: a community where intellectuals can be kings or, at least, princes. Promoting the architect, as a new type of intellectual, is a way to realizing this end. Alberti always associates intellectuality with authority.

Architecture was attractive to writers in the early Quattrocento, partly for its intrinsic intellectual satisfactions but also because it

---

[3] R. N. Watkins, *The Family in Renaissance Florence* (Columbia, SC, 1969), p. 168; see, too, the edition of Cecil Grayson, in Alberti's *Opere volgari*, i (Bari, 1960).

[4] Alberti, p. 65.

opened up ways to wealth, status, and power. In some ways, to be sure, the opportunities for architects to participate in these goods of Fortune were narrowing rather than broadening,[5] but this development is not necessarily germane to the ideal which Alberti and his contemporary Filarete (the author of another treatise on architecture) had in mind. They looked to a past when, especially in the Italian cities, master builders had enjoyed special privileges and a high degree of social visibility (privileges which suggestively resemble those held by a few humanists, especially the official historians, in the 1400s); they had been a sort of aristocracy among the practitioners of the manual arts.[6] Indeed, in opening his treatise on architecture by sharply distinguishing between architects and mere craftsmen who simply work on building projects, Alberti might have been echoing the claim of the thirteenth-century preacher Nicholas of Biart, who distinguishes between the master builder, with rod and gloves, and the ordinary manual workers who follow his instructions.[7] The special status of the architect—once again, as city planner—had been particularly apparent in Italy. Architects, although not counted as such, had been among that small category of intellectuals who had conversed on a level of complete social and civil equality with their counterparts in the social hierarchy. If, as I have suggested, Alberti aims for a complete fusion of the social and intellectual élites—at least in his own person—then the architectural profession has for him an extraordinary attraction. Nor did Filarete and Alberti need to look only to the distant past; they could also note the revival of these traditional privileges in Brunelleschi—*Philippus Architectus.*

But perhaps this is to make too much of a rather pragmatic attitude of mind. Alberti was a man of letters, a poet; and in considering the

[5] Both Richard Goldthwaite, in his 'The Building of the Strozzi Palace: the Construction Industry in Renaissance Florence', *Studies in Medieval and Renaissance History*, 10 (1973), 99–194 and J. Ackerman, 'Architectural Practice in the Italian Renaissance', *Journal of the Society of Architectural Historians*, 13, (1954), 3–11 suggest diminishing material returns.

[6] On the position of architects in Italy, and more generally in the later medieval world, see L. R. Shelby, 'The Role of the Master Mason in Medieval English Building', *Speculum*, 39 (1964), 387–403; idem. 'The Education of Medieval English Master Masons', *Medieval Studies*, 32 (1970), 1–26; J. Harvey, 'The Masons' Skill: The Development of Architecture', in J. Evans (ed.), *The Flowering of the Middle Ages* (London, 1966), pp. 82–132; on Italy, very briefly and usefully, J. Larner, *Culture and Society in Italy: 1290–1420* (London, 1971), pp. 303–9.

[7] See N. Pevsner, 'The Term "Architect" in the Middle Ages', *Speculum*, 17 (1942), 561.

attraction of the profession of the architect for such a person—a man who is also concerned to recover something of the lost prestige and status, the honour, of his family line—we should not discount altogether the power of metaphorical thinking. In Alberti's mythological fantasy, *Momus*, Jupiter rebukes himself for not calling on architects—rather than philosophers—for assistance in the task of designing a new order for the world.[8] In medieval manuscript illuminations, as Harvey points out, God is occasionally depicted in the attitude of an architect, rule and compass in hand, busily creating: the architect—god/man.[9] Or, again, architecture and philosophy (the nature of which was one of Alberti's continuing preoccupations) appear to have something in common. They both have co-ordinating, directing functions within the circle of subordinate sciences or skills. L. B. Shelby, in his study of the English master masons, argues that 'ultimately every craft which was represented on the project touched in one way or another on the work of the masons'.[10] The master builder has a central, co-ordinating function. He passes judgement on the contributions of the masters in each of the other trades. Vitruvius says something very similar: 'The architect should be equipped with knowledge of many kinds of study and varied kinds of learning, for it is by his judgement that all work done in the other arts is put to the test.'[11] If one thinks about this sentence and what it might have meant to Alberti—and to Filarete—in connection with what we know about the way in which the medieval master builders had, in a sort of metaphorical way, already achieved this objective, it leads to fascinating results. It makes the architect a sort of master of everything.

If we look at Filarete thus, we observe the architect as despot, as prince. The architect, for Filarete, is Xenocrates or—it amounts to almost the same thing—Alexander. Absolute access, which is what Filarete's 'architect' seems to enjoy, is absolute power; and when we consider the difficult question of the 'status' of the various intellectual trades—or arts (to use Alberti's phrase as well as that of the medieval universities)—we have to think in terms of such things as proximity to the location of wealth and power, wherever these may be situated, and we can see that the 'status' of the various arts (in so far as it makes

---

[8] Leon Battista Alberti, *Momus o del Principe*, ed. G. Martini (Bologna, 1942), p. 150.
[9] Harvey, 'The Mason's Skill', ill., p. 83.
[10] Shelby, 'The Role of the Master Mason', p. 403.
[11] Quoted from W. L. McDonald, 'Roman Architects', in S. Kostof (ed.), *The Architect: Chapters in the History of the Profession* (New York, 1977), p. 38.

sense to think in this way) cannot be decided simply in terms of their intrinsic worth. And we shall see also, of course, that the status of architecture has to be broken down further into the question of the relative importance of the various activities in which architects engage. Thus Alberti fundamentally sees the architect in the role of a friend of the family; architecture in the service of the family might be his motto.

Alberti's conception, however, is fundamentally different from Filarete's. Alberti's idea of the architect, of architecture, as we might expect of a person of his family background, is profoundly republican. To say this is not to suggest that he is so committed to republican values that he is blinded by them to the point of being incapable of political relativism; but one has only to consider the distaste with which Alberti speaks of despotism in the first part of Book IV of *On Architecture*, when he speaks of various kinds of civil constitution, and the almost perverse pleasure which he takes in describing the tyrant's palace or fortress within the city—in every way seen as repressive of the liberties of the inhabitants of the place, based, that is to say, on pure force—to recognize the nature of his true feelings. Surely Alberti is committed to some notion of a *regimen politicum* in the sense, say, in which it had been defined by Ptolemy of Lucca. His whole intellectual orientation simply does not make sense otherwise; and neither, for that matter, does his idea of how architects operate. Alberti's unbending—or, as I put it earlier, his 'condescension'—does not make sense in any other terms. As I have argued elsewhere,[12] Alberti moves from the ethical posture (it may have been a pose) of the cloistered melancholic confronted, in very 'medieval' fashion, with the temptations of the world, to, at least, the 'mask' of a happy man— and this means, to speak colloquially, rejoining the human race. Moral philosophy, as Alberti conceives it, is a matter of continuously consoling oneself, and the movement which one detects in his general attitude is one towards a more affirmative view of life in the community, away from sequestration. Just so in his view of the architect: it might be said that as, in a republican framework, what one has is not so much government by vote as government by counsel,[13] so the

[12] In a paper on 'Leon Battista Alberti: a New Type of Intellectual?' given in Sydney, in July 1982, at the Frederick A. May Foundation's Conference on Italian Studies.

[13] On consultation as the basic principle of Florentine government in the early 1400s, see G. Brucker, *The Civic World of Early Renaissance Florence* (Princeton, 1977), pp. 246–65.

Albertian architect is nothing more nor less than the most ubiquitous of all possible counsellors. In this sense he is, too, the model of the perfect citizen.

Now patronage is, itself, a matter of continually asking for and accepting advice. It is wrong, therefore, to think of the patron as acting alone, although his isolation as an individual is nevertheless what I here take to be his defining characteristic. Indeed, both Alberti and Filarete conceive of the patron as exercising a kind of temporary dictatorship in that republic of incipient intellectuals (and an 'intellectual', for these people, is somebody who has a humanistic education) which is the world of the architect. The intellectual *raison d'être* for patrons, in other words, is because architects cannot agree. It is a sort of *balìa*, or special council. In fact, from all the accounts we have, the 'typical' building site in the early Renaissance is a place of almost continuous dissension, but this is, in microcosm, itself a sort of image of the civic life and, to that extent, healthy. Intellectual—like political—life thrives on disagreements.

But the Vitruvian programme—just like the central or directing position of the architect in the making of the medieval cathedral—has other implications as well. By saying that it is 'metaphorical' I mean to suggest that it captures the imagination; and what image could be more captivating to the intellectually ambitious person than that with which Vitruvius describes the education of the architect—an education, that is, not an apprenticeship? He writes as follows: 'only persons can justly claim to be architects who from boyhood have mounted by the steps of their studies and, being trained generally in the knowledge of arts and sciences, have reached the temple of architecture at the top'.[14] The temple of architecture: Wittkower has shown how Alberti thinks of building in terms of a hierarchy of structures in which the religious edifices come first and, indeed, his whole intellectual orientation is nothing if not deeply hierarchical.[15] Still it is interesting to reflect on this passage. Alberti shows a certain scepticism concerning Vitruvius' claims about what the architect should know. Vitruvius, he thinks, goes much too far. Despite this, however, Alberti himself realizes the Vitruvian synthesis. His *On Architecture* is itself a sort of encyclopaedia, somewhere between Vincent of Beauvais and Villard de Honnecourt. To overcome the

---

[14] McDonald, 'Roman Architects', p. 38, quoting Vitruvius I. i. 11.
[15] R. Wittkower, *Architectural Principles in the Age of Humanism* (London, 1962).

distinction between mechanical and liberal arts, of course, simply means to overcome that between the eye and the mind, and Alberti had done this already, in his work on painting. In a way the intellectual as well as the social aspirations of the French master builder are realized in the Italian city-state of the early Quattrocento.

Alberti wants to reform both the education of the architect and that of the citizen—for whom, of course, one can also read patron. Patronage, in Quattrocento Florence, legitimizes wealth. To speak of the 'temple' of architecture, however, suggests a further line of thought. Architecture is, for Alberti, a profoundly religious conception: the intimacy between architect and patron is rather like that between priest and laity. Alberti is continually assimilating intellectuals to clergy and vice versa. And another question might be asked here, though in passing. What is the connection between the preoccupation with number—with measures—in the fifteenth-century architect and the Florentine (or Italian) patrician? Filarete begins his treatise (in a passage which must delight Michael Baxandall) with a definition of architecture as a science of *misure*, and he proceeds to look, in the most literal-minded way, at the meaning of the *braccia* as a unit of measurement. The patrician, that is, makes use of the same measuring rod in appreciating the proportions of the façade of Santa Maria Novella as is used in measuring a piece of cloth. I mention this consideration here because it is another dimension of the encyclopaedic character of Alberti's treatise on architecture. The point to make about this work is that it tells not only the architect but also the Florentine patron—that is, the patrician—everything that he needs to know; it is, thus, a humanistic education as well as a technical one. After reading Alberti on architecture you do not need Cicero. The *On Architecture* is, truly, a lifetime's work, a book into which the author has put his very self. To see it as defining and calling forth a single specialization is a misunderstanding.

Architecture, thus, metaphorically takes on a synthesizing role, sitting in judgement on the contributions of the other sciences. It occupies the position of theology at the entrance to the temple. Alberti takes this idea very seriously. The only other model which he might have known of comparable universality is that of Cicero's ideal ora-tor—a figure it was precisely the aim of the humanistic education of the early Quattrocento to try to produce and who, perhaps, bears the same relation to the mere specialist in words—for persuasion as well as for ornament—as the master builder does to the artisan. Somewhere behind Alberti's idea of architecture, though it is hard to say where, lies the idea of persuasion; it is the fundamental notion in Renaissance culture.[16]

Filarete, too, takes the claims of architecture to be considered as a kind of universal science quite seriously. He too emphasizes the synthesizing, co-ordinating role of architecture and the dignity—the honour—which consequently attaches to the architect. One of the many socio/architectural fantasies in Filarete is a house of the virtues and vices in which are offered all the skills that lead a person to the possession of the cultivated laurel and which make of him a scholar and a gentleman. Architecture is not one of these disciplines (it never is; nobody ever knows quite where to put it), and the architect has a place apart, set aside from the other *bonae artes*. Here, indeed, we might note the first example of that pleasing fantasy of the architect's— or, if you prefer, the artist's—house. Mantegna, in fact, was the first person to inhabit such a dwelling, in Mantua, designed for him by Luca Fancelli, Alberti's assistant.[17] And we might note, too, that Mantua was, of all places in Italy, the one where architecture was valued at its real worth. Alberti therefore had no difficulty in convincing Ludovico Gonzaga that his drawings were superior to any other submission in terms of the Vitruvian properties of durability, convenience, and beauty. Indeed, in Mantua Alberti broke one of his own cardinal rules, never to build anything fantastic. The church of San Sebastiano was something which could not be described as either church, mosque, or synagogue.[18] It was too original, too out of the ordinary; something which never could be, never was, built—not, that is, in the way Alberti had designed it. One of the reasons for building, of course, is to achieve a sort of secular equivalent for immortality— fame or glory. This is one of the considerations which moved Giovanni Rucellai, just as, in the mid-Trecento, it had moved Nicola Acciaiuoli. Men immortalize themselves in bricks and mortar just as they do in children.[19] In order for a building to last it is not enough that it be able to withstand the hostility of the elements, the weathering effects

[16] On 'persuasion', see J. E. Seigel, *Rhetoric and Philosophy in Renaissance Humanism: The Union of Eloquence and Wisdom from Petrarch to Valla* (Princeton, 1968).

[17] L. H. Heydenreich and W. Lotz, *Architecture in Italy, 1400 to 1600* (Harmondsworth, 1974), p. 82.

[18] Ibid., pp. 34–5.

[19] On Giovanni's urge 'to reproduce and to build', see F. W. Kent, 'The Making of a Renaissance Patron', in F. W. Kent *et al.*, *Giovanni Rucellai ed il suo zibaldone, II: A Florentine Patrician and his Palace* (London, 1981), p. 13.

of time. Life as a race with time is one of the major themes of *On Architecture*, just as it is in the work of Petrarch who, unlike Alberti, did not spend much of his time imagining buildings. Ageing is just one of the reasons why buildings fall into decay. A more important reason is the absence of building materials and it was, of course, one of the ironies of the Renaissance 'building boom' that one way to create new buildings was out of materials taken from old ones; in order to recreate the pást, that is, one tore it down. People preserve and maintain buildings they like and feel at home with. San Sebastiano, for this reason, did not stand the test of time.

Filarete imagines the house of the architect, if not in Mantua, then near it.[20] It is frescoed with images of the inventors of the most useful human skills, the builders of great, legendary buildings. Why put the architect aside like this, in a place apart? 'There was also a place here appointed for the architect, where he who had built this entire building was to live.'[21] Or again: 'all these noble masters and inventors were painted in this house [of the architect].'[22] Perhaps between the Vitruvian ideal of a universal competence at one remove from actual technical skill, and the Albertian, modified version of it, there is something like the relationship between the Platonic ideal of how things ought to be and Socrates' remark (quoted by Alberti) that we should settle for the best that we can possibly get.

While discussing the metaphorical associations of architecture (which are practically endless) it seems appropriate to mention the most famous of them all. St Paul (1 Cor. 3: 10) describes himself as follows: 'ut sapiens architectus fundamentum posui.'[23] An architect is someone who lays foundations. Brunelleschi is described by Toscanelli—at least according to Vasari and, presumably, on the basis of some sort of tradition—as St Paul reborn. But, oddly, there are no associations of this sort in either Filarete or Alberti.

The architect, says Alberti, is a public servant. He did not have to look far afield for examples of architects who had achieved greatness and worldly success and had been of special service to the general public. Architects, for example, win wars as much as generals: 'I am really persuaded that if we were to enquire of all the cities which,

---

[20] On the milieu of which Filarete's treatise is a product, see the editor's introduction to his translation of Filarete's *Treatise on Architecture*, ed. J. R. Spencer (New Haven and London, 1965), pp. xvi–xxxvii.

[21] Ibid., p. 257.

[22] Ibid., p. 267.

[23] See Pevsner, 'The Term "Architect"', for the history of this phrase.

within the memory of man, have fallen by siege into the power of new masters, who it was that subjected and overcame them, they would tell you the architect.'[24] One can learn this from Vegetius, or one could simply look there to find confirmed what one already knew. In the Sienese public palace there was a famous fresco, by Simone Martini, of Guidoriccio of Foligno and his seizure of Montemassa. The real hero on this occasion had been the architect Lando di Pietro, and he had been appropriately honoured by the commune.[25]

Braunfels, in his book on thirteenth-century city planning, has a chapter on the status of the architect and what he needed to know in order to exercise his profession: 'to conceive of craftsmanship as a form of learning', he notes, 'is medieval.'[26] If this is true, then Alberti is certainly a medieval and not a renaissance man. The craftsman, according to Braunfels, is a *docta manus*. As depicted in French gothic tombs, architects are master builders in the robes of university professors. They certainly had intellectual pretensions.[27] 'Learning' is an important concept for Alberti, but in and of itself he thinks that it is of little value. In Book IV of *The Family* one speaker rebukes another for being content with mere booklearning: learning, it is argued here, is of no value if it is without some connection with experience. Alberti is very suspicious of all kinds of learning, just as he is very suspicious of all kinds of ignorance. The final test, as Giannozzo puts it, is practice, or *pruova*, but the notion of the *docta manus* leads us to the vexed issue of Alberti's technical interest and competence.

Alberti, it is sometimes suggested, was not interested in the mundane details of how buildings are built.[28] But it is difficult to see how the treatise on architecture could convey this impression, unless to one with a preconception about the incompatibility between the liberal and the mechanical sciences, and a fixation about the aristocratic, anti-popular character of the Renaissance, of which Alberti was somehow a representative. Alberti, it would be argued, likes villas; therefore he is an élitist.[29] But the treatise on architecture is a practical book which

---

[24] Alberti, p. x.

[25] W. Braunfels, *Mittelalterliche Stadtbaukunst in der Toscana* (Berlin, 1953), p. 234.

[26] Ibid., p. 226.

[27] See the illustration in his contribution, 'The Architect in the Middle Ages, East and West', in Kostof (ed.), *The Architect*, p. 78.

[28] See, for example, L. D. Ettlinger, 'The Emergence of the Italian Architect', in Kostof (ed.), *The Architect*, p. 111; 'he never pretended to any interest in the practical side of architecture.'

[29] I believe this summary does not do too much violence to the argument of M. Petrini, 'L'uomo di Alberti', *Belfagor*, 6 (1951), 665–74.

tells its readers how to do things. The range and insight in the whole of the second book on building materials is striking. Alberti far surpasses Filarete here, on what might have been taken to be Filarete's home territory. But this is not, perhaps, surprising, since they are trying to win the confidence of different publics. Alberti addresses himself to master builders as well as to patrons. He says as much, and why should we doubt him?[30] Similarly, why should we doubt that, in the work on painting, he addresses himself to actual practitioners of the craft? I want to be read by builders, he says, therefore I shall tell them only so much about the Aristotelian science of movement as they need to know to move heavy objects.

Indeed, for Alberti, the whole of architecture is based on mechanics. Thence derives much of its intellectual dignity. From this derives the otherwise rather perplexing claim, repeated at various times in the course of the book, that architecture is the science of how heavy things are lifted and moved. According to Ackerman, Milanese builders— neophytes—responded to the gibes of their northern European critics that *ars sine scientia nihil est* by claiming that, at the very least, they knew their Aristotle.[31] This retort was an attempt to confuse the issue, according to Ackerman and, in any case, it was manifestly false. Perhaps it was so in early Quattrocento Milan, but it was not the case with Alberti, who certainly knows his Aristotle and who effects a beautiful synthesis of book learning and practical lore throughout the treatise on architecture. Renaissance architects, we are repeatedly told, did not know what made buildings stand up. Gothic architects, the implication is, did, even though, because they were illiterate, they were unable to put it into words. But the charge is clearly not true of Alberti. Read his description of a wall.[32] He knows as well as anybody ever has, before or since, what makes a wall a wall, and he also makes the uninitiated reader aware for the first time that he does not. A wall, the uninitiated is likely to think, is just one stone piled on top of another. Not so, says Alberti. It is a skeleton, a frame. It has a nervous system. It has muscles and ligaments. It is an organic unity, a whole. Alberti's buildings are alive: they are full of dynamic forces.

[30] Because, Richard Goldthwaite suggested in discussion, the master builders of Alberti's time could not read Latin: the simple answer to this question is that Alberti was trying to call into being a class of master builders who could do so.

[31] J. S. Ackerman, ' "Ars sine scientia nihil est": Gothic Theory of Architecture at the Cathedral of Milan', *Art Bulletin*, 31 (1940), 84–111.

[32] Alberti, pp. 47–53.

In his autobiography Alberti, speaking of himself, tells us that: 'From craftsmen, architects, shipbuilders, and even from cobblers he sought information to see if by chance they preserved anything rare or unusual or special in their arts; and he would then communicate such things to those citizens who wished to know them.'[33] 'Even cobblers'—this is not merely a literary trope. Alberti not only paid close attention to what craftsmen—among them architects—were doing; he publicized their professional secrets. Of course, like Brunelleschi, Alberti had little use for the guild of master masons. He would rather have had a seat on the *Signoria*—at least in the ideal republic of which he dreamed and towards which, as a private person, he worked. But none the less he was not hostile to the manual professions. At the end of Book II of *On Architecture* he even cites at length what I can only imagine to be one of the rules of the master masons (though I am unable to identify its source).[34]

Filarete, likewise, is concerned with bridging the gap between liberal and mechanical skills—like Alberti, in the name of some sort of architectural science, though they are working towards the same goal from different ends. One of the reasons why architects, in the Renaissance, need to be literate is so that they can read books like those of Alberti and Filarete. Alberti is, of course, much more systematic than Filarete. He wants to get people away from the simple imitation of other buildings, whether they are ancient or modern—that is not architecture—and move them towards an understanding of the principles on which they are based, which can then be applied as occasion offers: originality within a framework of tradition.[35] Filarete has no such aspiration or, if he does, he is incapable of achieving it, and the difference is plain between Filarete's common-sense account of why a curved arch is strong and Alberti's much more theoretically informed discussion of the same point.[36] Both, however, are educational reformers with a serious intent. Filarete, thus, proposes a new sort of educational institution. In it the highest branches of liberal learning will be taught but, along with them, also the practical skills. 'Good. This would be like a school,' says his interlocutor. 'Yes, my lord, but

---

[33] Translated in J. B. Ross and M. M. McLaughlin (eds.), *The Portable Renaissance Reader* (New York, 1953), p. 487.

[34] Alberti, p. 54.

[35] This spirit of innovation within tradition is captured by J. Summerson, *The Classical Language of Architecture* (London, 1964).

[36] Alberti, p. 57; Spencer (ed.), *Treatise on Architecture*, p. 103.

you still have not understood me, because I want it to be more than a school. I say more, because there would be many faculties. Although it is not so dignified, I intend that some manual arts should be taught here by their practitioners.'[37] It would be interesting to compare this project with that of Vittorino da Feltre. Various schemes for educating children were in the air in the early fifteenth century and other skills were offered to the children of the rich and powerful than parsing Latin verbs and orthography.

Alberti's intellectual model in this matter of the fusion between the practical and the theoretic is Plutarch's Archemides. Plutarch writes of a certain kind of Hellenistic intellectual:

For the art of mechanics, now so celebrated and admired, was first originated by Eudoxus and Archytas, who embellished geometry with its subtleties, and gave to problems incapable of proof by word and diagram, a support derived from mechanical illustrations that were patent to the senses. For instance, in solving the problem of finding two mean proportional lines, a necessary requisite for many geometrical figures, both mathematicians had recourse to mechanical arrangements, adapting to their purposes certain intermediate portions of curved lines and sections. But Plato was incensed at this, and inveighed against them as corrupters and destroyers of the pure excellence of geometry, which thus turned her back upon the incorporeal things of abstract thought and descended to the things of sense, making use, moreover, of objects which required much mean and manual labour. For this reason mechanics was made entirely distinct from geometry, and being for a long time ignored by philosophers, came to be regarded as one of the military arts.[38]

The model for this sort of thing in the Quattrocento was, of course, Brunelleschi, who in addition to being a St Paul was also an Archimedes.

The heart of my topic is the relation between patron and architect. I have already suggested that the architectural theorists of the early Renaissance regarded the seizing of the initiative in planning and implementing works of architecture by the patrons (not just by princes but by people in city-states who affixed their family coats of arms to the buildings they had commissioned) as a kind of temporary measure, a *balìa*. A passage in Vitruvius throws some light on Alberti's ideas on this matter and on the patron/architect relation in the first half of

---

[37] Spencer (ed.), *Treatise on Architecture*, p. 228.
[38] *Plutarch's Lives*, tr. Bernadotte Perrin (Loeb edition, xi. 471, 473): Life of Marcellus, xiv. 5–6.

the Quattrocento. Vitruvius seeks to excuse himself for being relatively obscure as a practitioner of his craft:

Other architects beg and wrangle to obtain commissions; but I follow a rule laid down by my masters: not to seek employment but to be sought out; since an open countenance changes for shame when a request is made of a doubtful character ... Therefore our forefathers used to entrust commissions to architects of approved descent in the first place; in the second place they inquired if they were well brought up, considering that they should employ men with a sense of honour, rather than persons of a bold and insolent turn ... But while I observe that an art of such magnificence is professed by persons without training and experience, by those who are ignorant not only of architecture but even of construction, I cannot refrain from praising those owners of estates who, fortified by confidence in their own erudition, build for themselves, judging that if inexperienced persons are to be employed, they themselves are entitled to spend their own capital to their own liking rather than to that of anyone else. For no one attempts to practise any other calling at home, such as shoe-making or fulling or any other easy occupation, with the one exception of architecture, because persons who profess it are falsely called architects in the absence of a genuine training.[39]

While this passage justifies the intervention of patrons until, in the event, the true architects do present themselves, it does not tackle the socio/economic and moral questions raised by this flourishing in the early fifteenth century of owner–builders.

How a person spent his money then was everybody's business; money, it was thought, was to be used. Its use justified and legitimated its acquisition. There was an art of spending money, of using it properly. Important here, too, was the whole debate about magnificence.[40] It is hard to see how magnificence is a virtue at all, according to Thomas Aquinas. It certainly is not enough simply to do things on a big scale. One has to employ reason and calculation. One has to hold in check the irresistible urge to spend, to throw it all away, an urge which, on the contrary, Filarete thinks one should indulge freely, shamelessly. The difference between Filarete and Alberti on this point is that, while both conceive of the relationship between patron and architect as akin to that between husband and wife,[41] Alberti's pair

[39] Vitruvius, *On Architecture*, tr. Frank Granger (Loeb edition), Preface to Book VI, secs. 5–7.

[40] See A. D. Fraser Jenkins, 'Cosimo de' Medici's Patronage of Architecture and the Theory of Magnificence', *Journal of the Warburg and Courtauld Institutes*, 33 (1970), 162–70.

[41] Spencer (ed.), *Treatise on Architecture*, p. 15.

are a good homely couple while Filarete's 'wife' is a shameless hussy and her 'husband' a libertine. What the architect and the patron really need, according to Alberti, is a sense of *massarizia*, of domestic economy. They need, he is saying in effect, to read my other book on the family—or would if everything were not already in this one. At the end, when Alberti gives us the moral portrait of the architect, his virtues seem to be very close to those of the good householder: 'indeed his invention must be owing to his wit, his knowledge to experience, his choice to judgement, his composition to study, and his completion of his work to his perfection in his art; of all which qualifications I take the foundation to be prudence and mature deliberation.'[42] One wonders, on occasion, when Alberti is preaching or rationalizing, whether there is any bite to his moral philosophy. At one point he attempts a kind of moral history of architecture. The Romans come off particularly well in this sketch: 'Italy, in her first beginnings, having regard wholly to parsimony, concluded that members in buildings ought to be contrived in the same manner as in animals; as, for instance, in a horse, whose limbs are generally most beautiful when they are most useful for service, from which they inferred that beauty was never separate and distinct from conveniency.'[43] A good building, they liked to say, was like a good horse! After a time, however, the Romans overcame this rustic way of looking at things:

But still though the condition of their state was thus flourishing they thought it most laudable to join the magnificence of the most profuse monarchs to the ancient parsimony and frugal contrivance of their own country; but still in such a manner that their frugality should not prejudice conveniency nor conveniency be too cautious and fearful of expense; but that both should be embellished by every thing that was delicate or beautiful.[44]

He seems here to be talking not about the Romans, but about the Medici.

Alberti does, however, really want his Florentines to embody their ancestral virtues. His ideal seems to be one of public munificence and private restraint. Aristotle gives a very good idea of just when magnificence can be a virtue and when it is mere ostentation.[45] Spending money on architecture is a way of sublimating the acquisitive instinct. By doing so the individual transcends his own egoism. Both

---

[42] Alberti, p. 205.
[43] Ibid., p. 114.
[44] Ibid., p. 115.
[45] *Nicomachean Ethics*, IV. ii.

Giovanni Rucellai and Abbot Suger—who otherwise had little enough in common—were getting out of their own limited selves by signing their names all over their buildings.[46]

Ten Books on Architecture was a book written for Florentines—certainly not, as Cecil Grayson seems to think, for Nicholas V, who was, in any case, a Florentine by adoption.[47] It has nothing to do with Alberti's abandoning a commitment to the civic life. To argue that way is to draw the most far-reaching conclusions from the external details of an author's life, without paying attention to the spirit of the work itself. Let us imagine that Alberti had a certain audience in mind—a person that he did not know but whom he observed and whose behaviour and psyche he had studied from afar—with approval. Let us imagine that this person was Giovanni Rucellai. What other books did Rucellai know? Very possibly Lionardo Bruni's *Laudatio Florentinae urbis*, written fifty years before. The *Laudatio* begins with a physical evocation of the city of Florence that pays particular attention to its buildings. The spirit of this is pure Vitruvius, whether or not Bruni knew the *De architectura*. Private palaces are singled out for special mention. So too is the pervasive character of 'ornament' which runs like a bloodstream throughout the whole. If Giovanni Rucellai had not read this work, Alberti certainly had; it was his inspiration. At the beginning of the last book of his eulogy of Florence, Bruni asks what is the single principle which holds the whole thing together, which gives it its unmistakable character. It is, he argues, *concinnitas*, harmony, a sort of musical quality of the whole in which nothing can be altered without changing the total order for the worse. This idea is, really, the aesthetic equivalent of the idea of justice, and it is Alberti's key concept: 'Nusquam tantus ordo rerum, nusquam tanta elegantia, nusquam tanta concinnitas.'[48]

---

[46] On Rucellai, see F. W. Kent, *A Florentine Patrician*; on Suger, see Erwin Panofsky, 'Abbot Suger of St Denis', in *Meaning in the Visual Arts* (Garden City, NY, 1955), pp. 108–45.

[47] C. Grayson, 'The Humanism of Alberti', *Italian Studies*, 12 (1957), 33–56.

[48] Lionardo Bruni, *Panegirico della città di Firenze*, ed. G. De Toffol (Florence, 1974), p. 82. Bruni's phrase is translated as: 'Nowhere else do you find such internal order, such neatness, and such harmonious co-operation,' in B. G. Kohl and R. G. Witt (eds.), *The Earthly Republic: Italian Humanists on Government and Society* (Manchester, 1978), p. 168. [See now, on the themes of this essay, M. Hollingsworth, 'The Architect in Fifteenth Century Florence', *Art History*, 7 (1984), 385–410. Eds.]

14

Patronage and Diplomacy: The North Italian Residences of the Emperor Charles V

WILLIAM EISLER

DURING the period immediately following the Sack of Rome, the Eternal City temporarily lost its dominant position as an artistic centre. Artists active there during the 1520s gravitated towards the court of France or to other Italian cities under the control of the Emperor Charles V, who had displaced the French king as the dominant foreign ruler in the peninsula. Charles entered Italy as a conqueror in August 1529, and was crowned as Holy Roman Emperor on 24 February 1530 in Bologna.[1] His presence in Italy had a significant impact upon the patronage of the visual arts, particularly in cities controlled by close allies, who were required to receive him in a manner appropriate to his imperial dignity. Here I focus upon three cities whose rulers were dependent upon imperial patronage: Genoa, Mantua, and Trent. In each case the necessity to pay homage to the emperor affected the form and content of the palatial structures built by the local prince. The external decorations, the internal division of space, and the iconography of the rooms clearly reflect a preoccupation with the creation of an appropriate environment for the imperial guest, representing in visual terms the obligation of fealty to the new overlord of north Italy. At the same time, pro-imperial statements had to be tempered by political reality. Since past history indicated that the situation was subject to sudden and drastic change, those princes who associated themselves with one ruler to the exclusion of all others faced the possibility of retribution. Prudence argued against the humiliation of the Emperor's enemies—the pope and the king of France—with whom

---

[1] A day-by-day account of the emperor's travels can be found in M. de Foronda y Aguilera, *Estancias y viajes del Emperador Carlos V* (Madrid, 1914).

the princes under consideration were obliged to maintain correct diplomatic relations. Moreover, the possibility of a radical shift in the
balance of power, such as had occurred throughout the early Cinquecento, discouraged Charles's allies from developing an unam-
biguously pro-imperial iconography.

The first Italian city to receive the emperor in a sumptuous manner
was Genoa.[2] During his initial sojourn in that city (12–29 August 1529)
he was accommodated in the Palazzo Ducale. Upon his return to the
city after four years, the new Palazzo Doria in the suburb of Fassolo,
west of the city walls near the Porta San Tommaso, was ready for
occupancy (Plate 20).[3] The palace was the residence of Andrea Doria,
de facto ruler of the Republic. During the early 1520s Andrea had
served as admiral of the papal fleet while his native city was occupied
by Charles V's troops. In 1528, with Genoa under French control, he
placed his ships in the service of the emperor, enabling the latter to
drive the French away from Naples and bring about the 'liberation'
of the Ligurian republic. Precisely why Andrea decided to change sides
is difficult to determine; purely economic factors may have played a
decisive role.[4] The strong personal relationship between Andrea Doria
and the emperor enabled the latter to establish a protectorate in
Genoa—a city-state which, unlike Mantua or Trent, did not have any
ties with the Holy Roman Empire or the Hapsburg family. For his
part, Charles could not hope to control the Mediterranean without
the aid of Andrea's fleet. Thus it is not surprising that the admiral was
elevated to membership of the Order of the Golden Fleece in November
1531, together with the Marchese del Vasto, Alfonso d'Avalos, and

[2] For a discussion of works of art associated with Charles's entries into Genoa in
1529 and 1533, see E. Gavazza, 'La cornice del polittico', in *Il polittico di Sant' Erasmo
di Perin del Vaga* (exhibition catalogue, Genoa, 1982); and my unpublished doctoral
dissertation, 'The Impact of the Emperor Charles V upon the Visual Arts' (Pennsylvania
State University, 1983), pp. 181–205.

[3] The most thorough studies of the Palazzo Doria are by E. Parma Armani, 'Il palazzo
del principe Andrea Doria', *L'arte*, NS 3 (1970), 12–63, and the unpublished doctoral
dissertation by G. Gorse, 'The Villa Doria in Fassolo, Genoa' (Brown University, 1980).

[4] The deference paid by the leader of the Genoese republic to the emperor was
probably affected by a pressing need for Sicilian grain, controlled by Charles, king of
Naples and the Two Sicilies. E. Grendi, in 'Traffico portuale, naviglio mercantile e
consolati genovesi nel Cinquecento', *Rivista storica italiana*, 80 (1968), 593–629, has
suggested that Genoa's dependence upon Sicilian grain was an important factor in the
forging of the alliance with Charles, and this is borne out by the instructions of the
Signoria to the ambassadors of the republic in Spain (1528–9), which requested them to
ask for large supplies of food from the island. See R. Ciasca (ed.), *Istruzioni e relazioni
degli ambasciatori genovesi*, i (Rome, 1951), 104.

the younger brother of the duke of Mantua, Ferrante Gonzaga—the only Italians to be so honoured on that occasion.[5]

The Palazzo Doria thus served as the residence of one of the three principal allies of the emperor in the peninsula, where he was received for a total of 54 days (in 1533, 1536, 1538, 1541, and 1543). The name of the architect is not known, although presumably Perino del Vaga— the former student of Raphael brought to Genoa to direct Andrea's artistic projects—contributed to the decisions regarding its renovation. The central portion of the *primo piano*—the part of the edifice which principally concerns us—consists of two large *saloni* and a cluster of subsidiary rooms.[6] The ceiling of the western room is decorated with Perino's masterpiece, the *Destruction of the Giants by Jupiter*. In the eastern room, the artist executed the shipwreck of Aeneas and the calming of the seas by Neptune (now lost but known to us through a preparatory drawing).[7]

After his initial entrance into Genoa in 1529, the emperor visited the city only after having been received at his official residence at Fassolo. The Palazzo Doria had become the 'royal palace' of Genoa, primarily because of its patron's association with the Emperor. This relationship was celebrated visually on the south façade by four frescos representing the story of Jason, begun by Pordenone and Beccafumi and subsequently completed by Perino. These lost paintings are now represented by two preparatory drawings made by Pordenone.[8] The employment of this myth must, clearly, be associated with Andrea's acceptance into the Order of the Golden Fleece.

Inside the palace, the relationship between Charles and his admiral is given visual form in the iconography of the grand *salone*; the iconography of the Sala di Giove refers to the emperor, that of Nettuno to Andrea. The identification of Doria with the sea god dates from the period immediately prior to the execution of the frescos, specifically to Bandinelli's projected nude statue of Doria as Neptune commissioned by the Genoese *Signoria* in 1528.[9] Literary and artistic works in which the comparison is made between Charles and Jupiter striking

[5] For a list of knights present at the Tournai Chapter meeting (29 Nov. 1531), see de Foronda y Aguilera, *Estancias*, p. 357.

[6] See the plan published in E. Parma Armani, *Villa del Principe Doria a Fassolo* (Genoa, 1977).

[7] Parma Armani, 'Il palazzo', p. 26, fig. 11.

[8] C. E. Cohen, 'Two Studies for Pordenone's Destroyed Jason Scene in the Palazzo Doria', *Master Drawings*, 10 (1972), 126–33.

[9] Parma Armani, 'Il palazzo', pp. 33–8.

down the giants date from a slightly later period—for example, an apparatus for the imperial entry into Naples in November 1535, and a letter written by Pietro Aretino to the emperor in May 1537, shortly after he had entered the service of the Hapsburgs. Aretino there affirms that, while the giants' transgressions were against nature alone, those of Charles's enemies were against both nature and God.[10]

The iconography of the two rooms would thus appear to express on a mythic level the relationship of *clientelismo* between Charles and Andrea, indicating that the Palazzo Doria was indeed an imperial palace, built by one prince in large part to house another. It was probably under the figure of Jupiter, beneath an imperial baldacchino that appears in later inventories of the palace, that Charles V held audience.[11] It is also probable that it was in this room that important documents were signed, such as the decree granting the fief of Monferrato to the duke of Mantua, Federico Gonzaga (dated 3 November 1536) which concludes with the words: 'pro tribunali sedente in camera superiori palatii sui Imperialis, domus Ill.i. Princ.is Andreae de Auria sita in suburbio Genuae Portae Sancti Thomae ...'[12]

The Palazzo Doria, then, should not be considered as a private commission, but as a manifestation of international politics. At the same time, it must be remembered that Andrea was the first citizen of the Genoese republic, which as a sovereign state was not subject to imperial authority. Hence no inscription glorifying Charles V, no imperial coat of arms, can be seen anywhere in the palace. One may therefore hypothesize that the exaltation of the emperor in the Genoese milieu—especially in the official residence of the leader of the republic—could only be couched in allegorical terms; the symbolism of the vault in the Sala di Giove was not only in accord with an accepted

---

[10] Ibid., pp. 44–9, 59–63 and P. Aretino, *Il primo libro delle lettere* (Bari, 1913), pp. 153–4. Gorse, 'The Villa Doria', pp. 67ff., concludes that the decor of the two rooms refers to both Charles and Andrea, since both gods—like the men they symbolize—brought about harmony and order while suppressing chaos and violence. But whereas Charles V was on at least one occasion associated with Neptune—in the decoration of the Porta Santa Felice, Bologna, for the imperial entrance of 5 Nov. 1529 (see G. Giordani, *Cronaca della venuta e dimora a Bologna del Sommo Pontefice Clemente VII per la coronazione di Carlo V Imperatore* (Bologna, 1842), p. 12)—Andrea was never connected with Jupiter. Parma Armani, *Villa*, views the division of the rooms as one of parity, with Charles V as the ruler of the land and Doria of the sea. It does not seem likely, however, that Andrea would represent himself as the equal of the Holy Roman Emperor.

[11] For this inventory, see E. Pandiani, 'Arredi e argenti di Andrea Doria', *Atti della Società ligure di storia patria*, 63 (1926).

[12] A. Neri, *Andrea Doria e la corte di Mantova* (Genoa, 1898), pp. 68–9.

artistic mode during the Cinquecento, but was entirely appropriate to a delicately balanced political structure.

While Andrea Doria was preparing to receive the emperor in Genoa, Federico Gonzaga, ruler of Mantua and brother of Ferrante—Doria's colleague in the Order of the Golden Fleece—was constructing the Palazzo del Tè for his own pleasure and to receive honoured guests, the most famous of whom was Charles V, in whose honour an elegant entertainment was held on 2 April 1530.[13] Unlike the case of Genoa, Mantua's association with the Empire had a well-established historical foundation. In 1433 Gianfrancesco Gonzaga received the insignia of marchese from the Emperor Sigismund in the Piazza San Pietro; ninety-seven years later his descendent Federico was there granted the title of duke by Charles V.[14] It is true that, owing in part to the relative weakness of the emperors during the fifteenth century, the Gonzaga gravitated towards the papacy, serving as *condottieri* for Rome; but by the 1520s they were closely allied to the Hapsburgs and participated in Charles's military campaigns, notably at the Battle of Pavia.[15] Hence the reception at the Isola del Tè represented the celebration of an alliance just as significant as that between Charles and Andrea Doria. Ferrante Gonzaga would prove to be one of Charles's chief generals, and would serve the emperor in all of his future campaigns. In addition he would serve terms as imperial viceroy of Sicily (1536–46) and governor of Milan (1546–55), thereby securing the Gonzaga a position in international politics.[16]

When the palace was viewed by the emperor in 1530, Giulio Romano, court painter and architect (and, like Perino, a former assistant of Raphael), had completed only the northern wing. The portion which primarily concerns us, the east or garden wing, was only partially finished. The rooms visited by the emperor during his initial sojourn in Mantua (he returned in November 1532) were the Sala di Psiche, the Sala dei Venti, and the Sala delle Aquile, completed in 1528. Whereas the central Loggia di Davide was shown to the emperor in an unfinished state, construction of the southern portion—the Sala

---

[13] The following discussion is a condensation of my thesis, 'The Impact', pp. 232–55.

[14] For the entrance of Charles into Mantua in 1530 and its historical context, see A. Belluzzi, 'Carlo V a Mantova e Milano', in M. Fagiolo (ed.), *La città effimera e l'universo artificiale del giardino* (Rome, 1980), pp. 47–62.

[15] See E. Verheyen, *The Palazzo del Tè in Mantua: Images of Love and Politics* (Baltimore and London, 1977), pp. 17ff.

[16] For Ferrante's patronage in Sicily and Milan, see G. Guarducci, 'Un architetto pratese del Cinquecento: Domenico Giunti', *Prato, Storia e Arte*, 5 (1965), 127–62.

degli Stucchi, the Sala del Imperatore, and the Sala dei Giganti—had not yet been begun. It is this wing of the palace which reflects in the most emphatic terms the pro-imperial turn of the Gonzaga.[17]

The exterior walls of the garden wing were decorated with victories, spoils of war, trophies, and images of captives which, like the contemporary paintings on the garden façade of the Palazzo Doria, have disappeared. Hartt has convincingly identified three drawings of barbarians and victories as *modelli* for the façade paintings; a fourth was published by Bertini.[18] Verheyen's interesting attempt to reconstruct the original appearance of the façade by superimposing reproductions of the *modelli* over a drawing by Hippolito Andreasi (*c*.1567) gives a very different impression from that of its present state, with its eighteenth-century plastered walls and triangular pediment (Plate 21).[19] Possibly the façade functioned as a triumphal arch during the visits of important personages. The impact of the ceremonial entrances of Charles V into the north Italian cities, with their rich decorative ensembles, may be reflected in these decorations. However, unlike the Genoese frescos of the legend of the Golden Fleece, no specific reference to the relationship between Federico and Charles is discernible.

Further parallels between the Palazzo Doria and the Palazzo del Tè can be observed in the internal structure and decoration of the two palaces. Both contain two apartments, consisting of a *salone* and several subsidiary rooms.[20] The Sala di Psiche in the Palazzo del Tè forms the nucleus of the north-east apartment. Below the cycle representing the story of Psiche is the Latin inscription which reads in translation: 'Federico II Gonzaga, Fifth Marquis of Mantua, Captain General of the Florentine Republic, ordered this place built for honest leisure after work, to restore strength in quiet.' In the contiguous Sala dei Venti is an abbreviated inscription: 'Federico Gonzaga II Marchese Mantovanus V Sanctissimae Romanae Ecclesiae Capitanus Generalis.' The two inscriptions refer to titles granted to Federico by the Medici

[17] The stages in the construction of the palace, and their relation to the visits of the emperor, are discussed in F. Hartt, *Giulio Romano* (New Haven, 1958). The decorations of the loggia, as well as those of the Sala dei Giganti, were restored (after the removal of the scaffolding) for the second imperial visit in Nov. 1532, which indicates that the emperor had visited both these areas (see C. d'Arco, *Istoria della vita e delle opere di Giulio Pippi Romano* (Mantua, 1838), p. xiv).

[18] Hartt, *Giulio Romano*, p. 100; A. Bertini, *I disegni italiani della Biblioteca Reale di Torino* (Rome, 1958), cat. no. 212.

[19] Verheyen, *The Palazzo del Tè*, fig. 21.

[20] Compare the plan published in Parma Armani, *Villa*, with the plan in Verheyen, *The Palazzo del Tè*, p. 9.

in 1521 in connection with his family's activities as papal *condottieri*. The following year the *cedola secreta* obligating him to defend the pope against Charles V was secretly burned by his mother, Isabella d'Este.[21] Thus what is explicitly proclaimed on the palace walls belies the actual political orientation of the Gonzaga during the late 1520s.

The sumptuous feast of the gods depicted on the south and west walls of the Sala di Psiche corresponded to the actual activity within the room during the reception of the emperor in 1530, according to the chronicle of Charles's Italian voyage attributed to Luigi Gonzaga:

afterwards he went into the large room and, seeing it, His Majesty remained totally amazed, and stayed there more than one half hour contemplating it, praising everything greatly. While everybody ate, His Imperial Majesty and the Reverend Cardinals had already eaten, and His Majesty retired into the Camera delli Venti, and talked publicly for an hour with Cardinal Cibo, greatly praising these rooms and thus the master and inventor of them and of so many things that were there; and thus His Majesty wished to understand everything minutely.[22]

A significant aspect of the account is that, while the feast was held in the Sala di Psiche, the emperor did not participate but dined separately, suggesting that another space would have been required for an imperial dining hall. This may well have been the intended function of the Sala dei Giganti, located in the south end of the garden wing. We know that during a later period this room, with its cycloramic representation of the Fall of the Giants, was the scene of a banquet held in honour of King Henry III of France during his visit to Mantua in 1574.[23] Since the decorations of the Sala dei Giganti, like those of the Sala di Giove in Genoa, are probably meant to refer to the emperor, we may postulate that the rooms in the southern portion of the garden wing were intended for his use, just as the northern apartment can be associated with Federico.[24] We would then have an analogous division of space between emperor and vassal.

[21] Verheyen, *The Palazzo del Tè*, pp. 17–18.

[22] G. Romano (ed.), *Cronaca del soggiorno di Carlo V in Italia, 1529–30* (Milan, 1892), pp. 266–7.

[23] A. Belluzzi and W. Capezzali, *Il palazzo dei Lucidi Inganni* (Florence, 1976), p. 43 n. 98.

[24] The iconographic link between the Genoese and Mantuan representations of the Fall of the Giants was first observed by Hartt, *Giulio Romano*, pp. 160ff., and is discussed in more detail in Parma Armani, *Villa*, pp. 44ff. The most recent study of the Sala dei Giganti, which likewise associates the paintings with the theme of punishment against those who defy God's law, is B. Guthmüller, 'Ovidübersetzungen und mythologische

The dividing zone between the two portions of the wing is the Loggia di Davide, shown in an incomplete state to the emperor in 1530. Its decorations, which include scenes from the life of David, have been associated with Federico by Verheyen, but may also refer to Charles.[25] On the occasion of the imperial entrance into Bologna in November 1529, a relief representing Samuel's anointing of King David—an obvious reference to the forthcoming coronation—was executed on a triumphal arch in front of the Palazzo Scappi by Alfonso Lombardi.[26] The same artist was subsequently commissioned to execute statues of famous military leaders to decorate the Loggia di Davide, including Gonzalvo Ferrante, conqueror of Granada and south Italy on behalf of Charles's grandfather, Ferdinand the Catholic.[27]

The decor of the two rooms through which one passes to reach the Sala dei Giganti is unquestionably 'imperial' in nature. The Sala degli Stucchi contains a stucco frieze depicting a procession of Roman

Malerei—Bemerkungen zur Sala dei Giganti Giulio Romanos', *Mitteilungen des Kunsthistorischen Institutes in Florenz*, 21 (1977), 35–68.

[25] Verheyen, *The Palazzo del Tè*, pp. 30ff., discusses a medal struck by Gonzaga to commemorate his service to the emperor against the French at Pavia, which represents, on the obverse, David playing the harp after slaying Goliath.

[26] Giordani, *Cronaca*, p. 7.

[27] Federico wrote to Paolo Giovio on 10 Mar. 1531 requesting portraits of Matthias Corvinus and Gonzalvo Ferrante to serve as models for Alfonso Lombardi (see Verheyen, *The Palazzo del Tè*, p. 142). Eight statues of famous military men were contemplated, but the project was never brought to fruition (see N. Gramaccini, *Alfonso Lombardi* (Frankfurt, 1980), pp. 66–8).

The probability that Federico wished to associate Charles V with Gonzalvo is strengthened by a passage in Giangiorgio Trissino's *La Italia liberata da Gotthi* (Rome and Venice, 1547–8), pp. 114–15. Belisarius, Justinian's Captain, while visiting the Sibyl, views several portraits in her gallery of famous men of the future, among them Ferdinand, king of Aragon:

> Ma dopo Federico, un Ferdinando
> Che sia Re di Aragona, e di Castilja
> Cacciati i Mori fuor de la Granata;
> Con suo Consalvo Capitanio excelso
> Torra quel Regno da le man di Francia
> Ch'acquistato n'havea la maggior parte,
> E reggerallo con prudenzia molta;
> Poi lascerello in mano a Carlo Quinto
> Nipote e successor d'ogni suo regno,
> A Carlo Imperator, che con gran forza,
> Cercherà sempre apporsi a li' Ottomani;
> Ma prima espedirà l'impresa santa
> Contra i Germani heretici, e ribelli
> De la fede di Christo, e de l'Impero.

troops, whereas the Sala del Imperatore is decorated with scenes from the lives of Scipio, Caesar, and Alexander the Great. Moreover, the designation of the latter room as the 'Sala de lo Imperatore' is contemporary with the construction of the building, appearing on an order of payment dating from the first half of the year 1533.[28]

If, however, one can detect an 'imperial' quality in the decorations of these rooms, serving as antechambers to the Sala dei Giganti, one is forced to observe that, as in the Palazzo Doria, there is no direct, unmistakable reference to Charles anywhere in the palace. Whereas Federico's allegiance to the papacy (which by 1530 would have appeared quite tenuous) is explicitly proclaimed in the inscriptions in the Sala di Psiche and the Sala dei Venti, his association with the emperor is referred to only in symbolic terms. Once again, as in Genoa, there are no portraits of the emperor, no coat of arms; in short, nothing which would specifically identify the Palazzo del Tè as an 'imperial palace'.

The reluctance of the patron to identify his new overlord explicitly is most tellingly revealed in a drawing by Giulio Romano in the Uffizi. It depicts a seated winged victory carving the letters CAROL on to a shield. This sketch was identified by Hartt as a preparatory drawing for one of the figures in the Sala degli Stucchi, adjacent to the image of Mars in the lunette over the inner wall. From this evidence he postulated that the frieze of Roman soldiers is to be associated with the triumphal entrance of Charles V into Mantua.[29] When we examine the actual lunette, however, we observe that the victory's slate is practically empty, and that she has only begun to write upon it. Verheyen has suggested, on the basis of the differences in the shape of the lunette from that depicted on the drawing, that the latter may not have been for the Sala degli Stucchi, but rather for a triumphal arch.[30] In any case, the reluctance of Federico (and Andrea Doria) to refer directly to Charles outside the context of the *apparati* for a triumphal entry is noteworthy. In the permanent decorations of a palace, homage was paid to the emperor in a type of code, presumably explained to him in his presence, or to his ambassadors in his absence. Perhaps Federico feared a sudden reversal of Charles's political fortunes, which would transform an explicit apotheosis of the emperor into an embarrassing reminder of a past mistake.

[28] Verheyen, *The Palazzo del Tè*, pp. 125ff.
[29] Hartt, *Giulio Romano*, p. 148.
[30] Verheyen, *The Palazzo del Tè*, p. 125.

Approximately one year after the initial visit of Charles V to Mantua, Giulio Romano lamented that the city was 'empty of painters and gilders, because many have gone to Trent'.[31] Their departure was the result of recruitment efforts by Bernardo Clesio, the first Italian prince–bishop of a city previously governed by German prelates. A close political adviser to Charles's grandfather Emperor Maximilian I, and to his brother King Ferdinand of Austria, Bernardo was engaged in the construction and decoration of the Renaissance-style Magno Palazzo within the confines of the medieval Castello del Buonconsiglio.[32] Bernardo's attempt to rival the artistic achievements of the Gonzaga included a determined but unsuccessful effort to acquire the services of Battista Covo, architect and close collaborator of Giulio Romano.[33]

The new edifice was begun in February 1528 by an unknown architect and was severely damaged by fire in January 1531 (Plate 22). Soon thereafter, decoration of the interior was begun by Girolamo Romanino, Marcello Fogolino, and Dosso and Battista Dossi.[34] Without question, the requirement of providing a suitable setting for the reception of the emperor and his brother was one of the factors which affected the internal structure and decoration, as was the case in Genoa and Mantua.

Unlike Andrea Doria and Federico Gonzaga, Clesio never had the opportunity properly to receive his imperial overlord. When the emperor visited Trent in April 1530 the programme of decoration had not been initiated; Clesio died in 1539, before the emperor's visits to the city in 1541 and 1543. Nevertheless, the expectation of an imperial visit was a demonstrably strong stimulus for work on the edifice. In August 1532, during the siege of Vienna by Turkish forces, Clesio anticipated that, following the conclusion of the campaign, the

---

[31] G. Gaye, *Carteggio inedito d'artisti*, ii (Florence, 1840), 239.

[32] The most comprehensive study of Clesio to date is R. Tisot, *Ricerche sulla vita e sull'epistolario del Cardinale Bernardo Clesio* (Trent, 1969).

[33] G. Gerola, 'L'architetto Battista Covo a Trento', *Tridentum*, 13 (1911), 176.

[34] This discussion is based on my thesis, 'The Impact', pp. 255–62. On the Castello under Bernardo, see G. Gerola, *Il Castello del Buonconsiglio e il Museo Nazionale di Trento* (Rome, 1934). On the decorations, the best general study remains A. Morassi, 'I pittori alla corte di Bernardo Clesio a Trento', *Bollettino d'arte*, 15 (1929–30), 241–61, 311–34, 355–75. On the Dossi, see F. Gibbons, *Dosso and Battista Dossi—Court Painters at Ferrara* (Princeton, 1968). For Romanino, see M.L. Ferrari, *Il romanino* (Milan, 1961); for Fogolino, see L. Puppi, *Marcello Fogolino* (Trent, 1966). The most complete published set of documents concerning the palace is C. Ausserer, Jr. and G. Gerola, *I documenti clesiani del Buonconsiglio* (Venice, 1924).

emperor would enter Italy, passing through Trent (Charles's actual route took him through the Veneto, bypassing the Alto Adige entirely). He expressed his concern in a letter written in German to the superintendent of the works:

Our construction should be accelerated according to our order and desire for several motives, and now we have finally decided, hoping that God wishes it so, to accomplish at least half the task. In any case, the conflict with the Turks will be settled in one way or another; thus, if there will be a bit of fortune on our part, His Imperial Majesty will certainly travel in our direction; and His Majesty has been extensively informed, in particular by Antonio de Leyva, concerning various things relating to our construction.

Thus, if the edifice is not completed upon the arrival of His Majesty, or rather if some imperfection is apparent, regardless of how minute it may be, this imperfection would displease not only us, but would render the entire construction less beautiful, and thus make it worse.[35]

Charles would not have depended exclusively upon reports from Antonio de Leyva, commander of imperial troops in Italy, for information concerning the palace; he had seen it himself two years earlier (24 April 1530), and presumably discussed its form and decoration with Bernardo. Probably the portion of the structure of greatest concern to him would have been the Sala delle Udienze, or audience hall, a rectangular room, accessible from the courtyard. Opposite the entrance is a window overlooking the fortress walls and the city beyond. Over the courtyard entrance, Romanino has represented Bernardo Clesio accompanied by his secretary, who is shown recording the statements of Charles V and Ferdinand I, depicted above the window engaged in an animated discussion. Facing each other across the width of the room are three unidentified Roman emperors and the forebears of Charles and Ferdinand: Maximilian I, Philip the Handsome, and Ferdinand the Catholic. Securely within the confines of territory dominated by the Hapsburgs, there was no necessity to resort to allegory or myth. The relationship between the patron of the palace and his superiors in the political hierarchy is made absolutely explicit. The presence—literal and pictorial—of Charles and Ferdinand is essential to the meaning of the decorations, for the authority of the commissioner of the works flows directly from them.

At the same time, however, Bernardo was a cardinal in the Church of Rome, having been put forward as the candidate of Ferdinand for

---

[35] Ausserer and Gerola, *I documenti*, p. 86, doc. 119.

the papal throne upon the death of Pope Clement VII in 1534.[36] There were limits to the extent to which he could express his fealty to the emperor, limits which apparently were not perceived by the artists employed by him, as we learn from a letter of Bernardo to the superintendent of the works:

We have read a copy of the letter from Master Dosso of Ferrara, to which we are responding chapter by chapter, and you can thus inform him concerning our intentions, returning his chapters to him.

And first of all, concerning his expressed desire to paint in that beautiful room the capture of Rome, of the king of France etc., as you will see we are of the contrary opinion for two reasons, one because it would be a work involving great time and money, the other because it would be a most hateful thing in relation to Rome; it could happen that, if the pope, or his legates, nuncios, orators or the king of France came here and saw their figures represented, their displeasure would be aroused, and also because you know that our idea is not to make too many figures in the space of the wall below the frieze, except for those which we described in our last letter.[37]

The battle of Pavia and the Sack of Rome—the two events which signalled the beginning of Hapsburg domination of north Italy—were not suitable pictorial subjects even for the closest allies of the emperor in Italy. To pay homage to Charles V by constructing a visual pantheon of his family was one thing, but to represent the crushing of his enemies was quite another. If Bernardo wished to celebrate the imperial dignity on a large scale, he was compelled to be more discreet. The decorations of the Stanza del Torrione executed by Marcello Fogolino must have been viewed as the only possible solution to the dilemma (Plate 23). On the ceiling the Vicentine painter represented scenes from the life of Julius Caesar: the First Triumvirate, with Caesar, Pompey, and Crassus seated in a tribune; Ptolomey presenting the head of Pompey to Caesar; and the receiving of tribute from vanquished enemies. Thus, like Federico Gonzaga in the Sala del Imperatore in the Palazzo del Tè, Clesio was able to allude to the *romanitas* of the emperor without damaging his diplomatic relations with France or the Papal States.

However, themes which could not be represented on a large scale on the walls of a palace were eminently suitable in another context. The very scene which Bernardo would not permit Dosso Dossi to depict—the capture of the king of France at Pavia in 1525—appears

[36] K. Ausserer, 'Kardinal Bernhard von Cles und die Papstwahl des Jahres 1534', *Mitteilungen des Instituts für österreichische Geschichtsforschung*, 35 (1914), 114–39.
[37] Ausserer and Gerola, *I documenti*, pp. 21–2, doc. 12.

in an extraordinary rock crystal medallion which he presented to the emperor, presumably in 1530 (Plate 24). The work is accurately described in the Brussels inventory of the emperor's possessions dated 1536, and is preserved in the Kunsthistorisches Museum in Vienna.[38] One observes in this tiny masterpiece—especially in the figure of the fallen king turning toward his captors—all of the pathos of the collapse of French aspirations in Italy.

The impact of the presence of Charles V upon the artistic language employed by Italian princes to celebrate his glory is most graphically apparent in the case of Bernardo Clesio; in Genoa and Mantua the situation was even more delicate, hence the relationship had to be expressed in a more oblique manner. Nevertheless, in each city we observe the phenomenon of a patron constructing a palace with the conscious purpose of providing a suitable space for the reception of one more powerful than himself. The necessity of satisfying not only the requirements of one's own family but those of a higher authority would have a perceptible impact upon palace building in the later sixteenth century. An important example in the vicinity of Rome is the Villa Mondragone at Frascati, built after 1573 by Martino Longhi the Elder for the Cardinal Altemps, expressly to provide a proper edifice for the visits of Pope Gregory XIII.[39] It consisted of a large central *salone* and two symmetrically disposed apartments of three rooms each; one was given over entirely to the pope, the other to the cardinal. The pope's apartment contained a loggia with a great vista towards the north, a terraced garden, and a garden casino for his private use.

The Villa Mondragone is the best example of an edifice built in large part to accommodate Pope Gregory XIII; but one may also include in this category the Villa Lante built by Cardinal Giovanni Francesco Gambara at Bagnaia. A fresco in the Palazzina Gambara there indicates that two identical garden casinos were planned from the outset. One was completed in the seventeenth century by Carlo Maderno, the other bears the date 1578, and (according to David

---

[38] It appears certain that the piece is identical with the object described in the inventory of 1536: M. Michelant, 'Inventaire des joyaux ... de Charles-Quint, dressé à Bruxelles au mois de mai 1536', *Academie Royale de Belgique, Commission d'Histoire: Compte Rendu des Séances*, 3rd ser., 13 (1872), 363. The work has been attributed to Giovanni Bernardi da Castelbolognese by E. Kris, *Meister und Meisterwerke der Steinschneiderkunst in der italienischen Renaissance* (Vienna, 1929), pp. 62ff.

[39] See D. Coffin, *The Villa in the Life of Renaissance Rome* (Princeton, 1979), pp. 54–6.

Coffin) commemorates the visit of Pope Gregory.[40] We may speculate that the earlier of the two edifices was constructed for the use of the pontiff, although the evidence is less clear than in the case of the Villa Mondragone.

The visits of Gregory XIII occurred during a period when the papacy was developing into an absolute monarchy. They can be viewed in relation to the growth of Hapsburg power internationally during the early Cinquecento. In a wider sense, however, the idea that private dwellings must serve as the residences of the powerful became more significant during the course of the century. Housing the retinue of visiting dignitaries was considered obligatory for the Genoese nobility towards the end of the Cinquecento. In 1588 the first 'description of all the fine houses in the city where princes and other lords must be accommodated' was prepared by the city fathers. Eleven years later, the list of palaces (twenty-seven in all) was divided into four categories: the first was reserved for 'cardinals and great independent princes and feudatories', the second for 'the viceroys of Naples and of Sicily and for the governors of Milan', the third for 'lesser princes', and the fourth for 'papal and imperial ambassadors, and those of other kings'.[41] Thus the degree of magnificence of a princely dwelling could be measured in relation to the class of visitor it was to accommodate. As the official residence of the emperor in Genoa, the Palazzo Doria belonged to the first category, and represented the initial step leading to the construction of the Strada Nuova at mid-century, and to the plans and elevations of Genoese palaces by Rubens at the beginning of the Seicento.

The impact of the north Italian voyages of Charles V upon the structure and decoration of palaces leads us to conclude that patronage in the region was to a large degree an expression of the patron's position within the new political structure created by the emperor. At the same time, the Italian *signori*, seeking to protect themselves against any eventuality, wished to maintain correct relations with all parties, and the complexity of the political situation is mirrored in the works they commissioned.

[40] Ibid., p. 340; for the visits of Gregory XIII to Caprarola and Bagnaia, see J. A. F. Orbaan, *Documenti sul barocco in Roma* (Rome, 1920), pp. 388–90.

[41] E. Poleggi, *Strada nuova: Una lottizzazione del Cinquecento a Genova* (Genoa, 1968), p. 51.

Patterns of Patronage: Antonio da Sangallo the Younger and the *Setta* of Sculptors

TILL VERELLEN

ANY comprehensive account of sixteenth-century sculpture faces the problem of evaluating a variety of lesser, often inadequately researched and apparently disparate, artistic phenomena. Many of these, when viewed entirely in terms of their interaction with the major, necessarily inescapable, although often intrinsically erratic, forces at work, seem to defy integration into any plausible stylistic system. A number of minor artists, dependent as they were on the dominant modes of expression, naturally followed different working patterns and reacted to external influences differently from their greater contemporaries. To determine their status within an artistic community, and in society at large, may throw new light on our perception of cultural hierarchies and of sixteenth-century—particularly of mannerist—art theory.

The study of patronage, besides being an indispensable aspect of the social history of cultural activity in general, also contributes to the methodology of attribution and iconographic interpretation. The mechanics of the patronage of sculpture in the sixteenth century has a bearing on workshop conditions, and hence on sculptural procedure and on the development of individual and collective styles.

In recent years work on such artists as Valerio Cioli, Lorenzetto, Raffaello da Montelupo, Giovanantonio Dosio, and others has provided some insight into a sizeable and little-known substratum of cultural activity. The Sack of Rome and the collapse of Medicean patronage led to increasing competition among those artists who had either survived the crisis, or who had returned to the city in the 1530s. Vasari is perhaps our most useful source as to how some artists succeeded in establishing positions of control, sometimes by subtle and devious, but generally accepted, means of securing patronage. As Vasari says, all commissions went in the 1540s to Perino del Vaga[1]

---

[1] G. Vasari, *Le vite de' più eccellenti pittori scultori ed architettori*, ed. G. Milanesi (Florence, 1878–81), v. 627 (henceforth cited as Vasari–Milanesi).

and, according to Mancini, Vasari himself was able to practise a similar monopolization at a later date.[2] Antonio da Sangallo the Younger, like del Vaga a member of Raphael's circle and moving in the orbit of Alessandro Farnese at an early date, had soon begun to practise a successful type of professional lobbying that prepared him for the situation after the Sack. He was then able to draw upon a plethora of lesser, unemployed artists who became dependent assistants and extended his influence. In this sense, Sangallo's position was that of a secondary patron who would subcontract work to artists not directly connected to the patron. I propose here to focus on some of the sculptors who worked with Antonio da Sangallo at various stages, forming a sculptural *setta sangallesca* and following a particular type of workshop practice.

Even two decades after Sangallo's death in 1546, the *setta* (sect or faction) was still effective as a corporation of individuals bound together by economic considerations and by a common artistic and 'national' heritage. The Arberino correspondence confirms the tenor of Vasari's biography, and supplies us with a detailed account of Michelangelo's struggle to obtain over the *fabrica* of St Peter's a degree of control commensurate with his appointment as its architect after Sangallo's death.[3] But despite his determined stance, which began with a frontal attack on the Sangallophile *deputati* of the *fabrica* whom he accused of corruption, Michelangelo's need to dismiss all the assistants active under his predecessor (not just Antonio Labacco who had built the great model), was never completely satisfied. Moreover, a number of influential persons aligned themselves with the Sangallesque cause: Cardinal Giovanni Salviati, an eminent patron of the *setta*; Bishop Ferratino, once friend, now foe; and Pirro Ligorio, who was finally appointed Michelangelo's successor in August 1564.[4] Nanni di Baccio Bigi, perhaps the most intransigent and megalomaniac of Michelangelo's antagonists, continued his contention even after Michelangelo's death; he seemed to exemplify the disheartening realization that an emulation of Michelangelo could hardly be postulated on any

---

[2] G. Mancini, *Considerazioni sulla pittura* (1620), ed. A. Marucchi (Rome, 1956), i. 263.

[3] See H. Saalman, 'Michelangelo at St Peter's: The Arberino Correspondence', *Art Bulletin*, 60 (1978), 483–93.

[4] See R. Wittkower, 'Nanni di Baccio Bigi and Michelangelo', in *Festschrift Ulrich Middeldorf* (Berlin, 1968), pp. 248–62.

but the master's own grounds. He nevertheless had a remarkable career in the 1540s, with many independent architectural commissions, even if he was, as Michelangelo contemptuously put it, 'a poor thing' and one of the 'meanest, most villainous peasants'.[5]

A major enterprise, that Antonio da Sangallo had begun to control from about 1517 onwards, provided work for a number of artists in the difficult years following the Sack of Rome. Work in Loreto—on the cathedral, the Santa Casa, and the Palazzo Apostolico there—had long been given priority and was resumed very soon after the Sack.[6] In its proximity to fortified Recanati, the Santa Casa symbolized divine protection from the infidel, and its considerable income from devotional sources also aided Pope Clement VII in his flight from Rome. In September 1527, when in financial straits, Clement ordered the confiscation of valuables worth 4,224 ducats, and in October of that year the alms collection yielded some 21,000 florins, partially repaid when the pope visited Loreto on his way to the coronation of Charles V in Bologna.[7] Loreto, however, was unpopular with artists, and had a climate that one of them described as being 'as beastly as can be'.[8] It was also far removed from the centre of patronage, and the leading artist there, Andrea Sansovino, soon came to feel the effect of its isolation. In a brief of 22 June 1513, composed by Bembo, he had been employed under generous conditions. This occurred about a year after Antonio del Monte, who hailed from the same town of Monte San Savino in Tuscany, had been appointed first Cardinal Protector of Loreto. Sansovino was given complete authority, not only over the sculptural and architectural projects, but over all admin-

---

[5] See A. Gotti, *Vita di Michelangelo Buonarroti narrata con l'aiuto di nuovi documenti* (Florence, 1875), p. 310; Saalman, 'Michelangelo at St Peters', p. 487. For a summary of Nanni's architectural commissions, see Wittkower, 'Nanni di Baccio Bigi', p. 260 n. 30.

[6] Also patronized and frequently visited by Agostino Chigi; see G. Buonafede, *I Chigi Augusti* (Venice, 1660), p. 171; Fabio Chigi, 'Chigiae Familiae Commentarii' (MSS published by Cugnoni, in *Archivio della Società Romana di storia patria*, ii [1879], 73). The connection of Raphael and his school with Loreto is also seen in the dedication of the Chigi chapel in Santa Maria del Popolo to the Virgin of Loreto and SS. Agostino and Sebastiano: Cugnoni, in ibid. iii (1880), 441; see also J. Shearman, 'The Chigi Chapel in S. Maria del Popolo', *Journal of the Warburg and Courtauld Institutes*, 24 (1961), 129.

[7] A. Pirri, 'Andrea Sansovino a Loreto', *Civiltà cattolica*, 83, 1 (Jan., Feb. 1932), 253 n. 3; F. da Morrovalle, *I papi a Loreto* (Loreto, 1959), pp. 29ff.

[8] 'Quanto tiene il tempo, bestialissimo quanto si può dire', quoted by J. Pope-Hennessy, *Italian High Renaissance and Baroque Sculpture* (2nd edn, London and New York, 1970), p. 66.

istrative affairs as well.[9] But the situation began to deteriorate when Sansovino's patron was succeeded by Cardinal Bibbiena on 8 December 1514. On 1 July 1515 Bibbiena also acquired the position of *procuratore generale* with absolute jurisdiction, the result of this change being that Sansovino henceforth shared responsibilities with the *camerlengo* and the *governatore*, while other offices, such as the *dispositorio* and the *cancelleria*, were assumed by the canons.

The situation had become disadvantageous to Sansovino and may have been exploited by Antonio da Sangallo who began to appropriate a dominant position in this lucrative project. It seems probable that Sangallo had approached Bibbiena and had questioned the competence of Sansovino, because in a further brief of 17 January 1517 Sangallo was furnished with the right to investigate all aspects of Sansovino's activity in Loreto and was ordered to make a thorough inspection.[10]

Sangallo's visit to Loreto was followed by a meeting with Bibbiena,[11] the result of which was that Cristoforo di Simone Resse da Imola was put in charge of architecture, while Sansovino's sphere of activity was restricted to sculptural work. Resse supervised the execution of Sangallo's plans, apparently enjoying the latter's, as well as Bibbiena's, confidence, in spite of his disastrous mismanagement. He eventually owed the *fabrica* some 2,299 ducats.[12] The professional architect Sangallo, who had given his technical assistance to Bramante and to Raphael, displayed his characteristically matter-of-fact approach in a laconic remark on the Uffizi drawing of the Portico of the Palazzo Apostolico in Loreto: 'S. Maria in the Marches, or rather the palace in front of the church, begun by Bramante and badly conducted by Sansovino; this must be corrected.'[13] In 1519 Sansovino's special benefits for himself and his personal *garzone* were cancelled and, in a brief issued by Leo X on 20 January 1521, he is referred to as 'capo maestro

[9] A. Pirri, 'Andrea Sansovino a Loreto', *Civiltà cattolica*, 82, 4 (Dec. 1931), 418, 427f., doc. 1; I. A. Vogel, *De Ecclesiis Recanatensi et Lauretana* (Recanati, 1859), p. 339.

[10] See G. H. Huntley, *Andrea Sansovino, Sculptor and Architect of the Italian Renaissance* (Cambridge, Mass., 1935), p. 71; Pirri, 'Andrea Sansovino a Loreto', pp. 421f., 428f.

[11] F. da Monte Casoni, *Il santuario di Loreto e le sue difese militari* (Recanati, 1919), p. 153.

[12] Pirri, 'Andrea Sansovino a Loreto', pp. 425f.

[13] 'Santa Maria de Loreto in la Marchia, cioè lo palazzo inanzi alla chiesa, principato per Bramante, guidato male per lo Sansovino: besogna corregierlo': Pirri, 'Andrea Sansovino a Loreto', pp. 17f. See also G. Clausse, *Les San Gallo*, ii (Paris, 1902), pp. 247f.; H. von Geymüller, *Die ursprünglichen Entwürfe für Sant Peter in Rom* (Vienna and Paris, 1875), p. 95.

dell' opera del scarpello'. A little later his salary and leave were reduced to two-thirds of what they had been in 1513.[14]

If Sansovino had run into difficulties in his architectural undertakings, he had certainly encountered problems in the sculptural embellishment of the Santa Casa. Shortly after work had started in 1517, Domenico Aimo and Baccio Bandinelli were sent to Loreto to assist him. Bandinelli in particular was entirely unwilling to subordinate himself. In fact, the right half of the *Birth of the Virgin*, which he executed, demonstrates a clear departure in style, and is one of the few contributions that fail to conform to the concept of the whole. He apparently instigated rebellion among the assistants and, if we give credence to Vasari's account, provoked the aged Sansovino to the point of apoplectic violence by alleging that he lacked *disegno*. He soon absconded to Ancona, taking his work with him.[15] Other reports confirm that Sansovino's working methods were, in fact, wilful and erratic and confounded the prescribed modes of payment.[16] In 1524 he made abortive attempts to extricate himself by offering his assistance to Michelangelo[17] and, although he seems to have regained temporarily something of his former status, he is last recorded in Loreto in June 1526, the year in which Sangallo presumably returned to the project.[18]

While Sansovino was officially succeeded by his own assistant, Ranieri Nerucci da Pisa,[19] the technical supervision of the work carried out on the dome of Santa Maria was given to Sangallo's worthy brother Battista ('il Gobbo').[20] But the beginning of the second sculptural campaign on the Santa Casa, under the ultimate supervision of Antonio himself, seems to mark a transition from the traditional

---

[14] Cardinal Bibbiena died in Nov. 1519 and his successor, the Prior of Capua (Giuliano Ridolfi), confirmed these arrangements in a letter of 20 Jan. 1521: Pirri, 'Andrea Sansovino a Loreto', pp. 19–21; Huntley, *Sansovino*, docs. VIII, IX; K. Weil-Garris, *The Santa Casa di Loreto: Problems in Cinquecento Sculpture* (New York and London, 1977), i. 45ff.

[15] See Vasari–Milanesi, vi. 142ff.; Pirri, 'Andrea Sansovino a Loreto', pp. 225ff.; Huntley, *Andrea Sansovino*, doc. VII.

[16] Payments were made in three stages for each relief; Sansovino was apparently working on several simultaneously, which irritated Giuliano Ridolfi (see Pirri, 'Andrea Sansovino a Loreto', p. 21).

[17] K. Frey (ed.), *Sammlung ausgewählter Briefe an Michelagniolo Buonarroti* (Berlin, 1897), pp. 202f., 239.

[18] Pirri, 'Andrea Sansovino a Loreto', pp. 227–35; Huntley, *Sansovino*, p. 75; cf. Weil-Garris, *The Santa Casa*, i. 44, 61, 63 n. 68.

[19] Weil-Garris, *The Santa Casa*, i. 65.

[20] Pirri, 'Andrea Sansovino a Loreto', pp. 234ff., but see also P. Gianuzzi, 'Documenti inediti sulla Basilica Lauretana', *Archivio storico dell'arte*, 1 (1888), 16.

workshop practice to a more rationalized approach directed at expeditious completion of Sansovino's sculptural programme. Of the nine huge reliefs that adorn the Santa Casa only two—the *Annunciation* and the *Adoration of the Shepherds*— had been completed by Sansovino, while three further reliefs had been begun by him, Bandinelli, and Aimo. Under Sangallo, in the period from about 1530 to 1533, these were finished and four more reliefs, the putti over the doors, and many ornamental features were executed. The artists that were summoned for this purpose, most of them Tuscans, were Francesco da Sangallo, Tribolo, Raffaello da Montelupo, Simone Cioli, Simone Mosca, Raniere da Pietrasanta, Francesco del Tadda, and Girolamo Ferrarese.[21]

At this stage Sangallo's choice was determined largely by kinship and regional patriotism. These sculptors quickly evolved a rationalized mode of production. They adhered to the monumental, narrative compositions laid down by Sansovino and practised a disciplined conformity of style that has exacerbated problems of attribution. As is to be expected, it is primarily with the stronger artistic temperaments of Tribolo, and particularly of Bandinelli, that individual expression prevails. Tribolo, Montelupo, and Francesco da Sangallo, however, also formed a joint work-force, described as a 'società' or 'compagnia' in the documents.[22] In this capacity they collaborated very closely, particularly on the *gionta* or addition to Domenico Aimo's *Dormition of the Virgin* and on the putti over the doors. Their individual contributions are more difficult to discern. The documentary evidence in some instances fails either to confirm or to refute previous attributions made to members of the *compagnia*. They are simply referred to as *compagni*; and the computation of 11 December 1533, which summarizes the accounts over the period 1530–3, shows that they shared responsibility for the projects undertaken by them as a team, and that they were paid jointly for a variety of often overlapping tasks.[23]

Sangallo's monopolization of patronage after the Sack of Rome allowed him to choose and co-ordinate collaborators who depended on the work that was delegated to them. The workshop procedure that these artists adopted had a marked influence on style and this

---

[21] Vasari–Milanesi, iv. 63, 302.

[22] See the summary computation of 1 Oct. 1533 (Weil-Garris, *The Santa Casa*, ii— Libro Maestro 'K', 1531–3).

[23] For problems of attribution on the basis of the documentary evidence see Weil-Garris, *The Santa Casa*, i. 85f. and ii. docs. 737ff.

may have some bearing on our understanding of stylistic criteria commonly associated with mannerism. While the effect of Sansovino's giant reliefs is felt in the subsequent work of the collaborating artists— in the *Epiphany* in the Cathedral of Orvieto by Montelupo and Simone Mosca and in Tribolo's large relief of the *Assumption* in San Petronio in Bologna—these works nevertheless display individual modes of expression. But the teamwork practised in Loreto had a levelling effect on style, a standardization of expression analogous to that known from the dissemination of Sangallesque architecture. This 'depersonalization' of the work is reminiscent of similar aspects of decorative sculpture observed by Carl Justi in connection with the Spanish tombs executed in Carrara by the temporary workshops of Domenico Fancelli and his successor, Bartolomeo Ordonez, in the early 1520s. Justi remarked that specialized *virtuosi* were responsible for the large eagles and griffins, the acanthus ornaments and garlands and that these were, stylistically, indistinguishable.[24] In the difficult years after the Sack, Tribolo, Montelupo, Simone Mosca, and others continued to be involved in collaborative sculpture.

Michelangelo's resistance to collaboration, and his need to complete the arduous task of carving stone personally, are expressed in many of his writings. They can also be observed in his use of assistants, or rather *servatori*—people of little artistic talent and content to relinquish any *disegno* they might possess. An example is Antonio Mini, who was with him from 1523 to 1531.[25] When Clement VII was satisfied that work on the Santa Casa was progressing, he turned his attention once more to the Medici tombs in the New Sacristy of San Lorenzo in Florence. Michelangelo had not taken up Sansovino's offer of assistance but, urged by his patron, he now made ready use of the *compagni*. They had demonstrated their ability to subordinate themselves stylistically to a prescribed mode. Another sculptor and one of Michelangelo's truest followers, Giovan Angelo Montorsoli, had previously worked at San Lorenzo to the master's satisfaction. Moreover, he had been restoring the *Apollo* and the *Laocoon* at the Belvedere in 1532–3, the practice of restoring antiques naturally requiring a similar propensity for stylistic self-abnegation. It was this ability to apply archaeological fidelity and competent craftsmanship to the principles of his art that allowed Michelangelo to use them.

[24] C. Justi, 'B. Ordoñez und D. Fancelli', *Jahrbuch der königlichen preussischen Kunstsammlungen*, 12 (1891), 98.
[25] Frey, *Sammlung*, p. 197.

Their task in the New Sacristy was to assist in the sculpture already begun, and to copy faithfully the models of SS. Cosma and Damiano that Michelangelo had provided.[26] In 1535 Tribolo and Montelupo were again hired by Antonio da Sangallo to work *in compagnia* on the imperial and ducal arms, supported by large Victories and once placed on the north-eastern and south-western bastions of the Fortezza da Basso in Florence.[27] Sangallo's organization of a workshop could not have been more different from Michelangelo's. Buddensieg has observed that in the Chigi chapel of Santa Maria del Popolo Raphael had already formulated an alternative to Michelangelo's monuments with their emphasis on statuary. The problems Michelangelo encountered with personal execution and consequently with his patrons were apparent in the project for the tomb of Julius II.[28] Antonio da Sangallo's co-operation with Raphael at St Peter's, and his probable participation in the Chigi chapel[29] would have indicated that his organizational skills could be directed at more efficient procedures. Many of the artists later in his entourage and part of the *setta* were recruited from Raphael's circle and had been directly or indirectly involved in Raphael's projects. (Vasari, in his life of Raphael, attests to collaboration among the members of Raphael's workshop: 'because of the death of Raphael, Giulio Romano and Francesco Penni often worked together; and so they finished, *in compagnia*, the works that Raphael had left incomplete.'[30])

The relationships generated by the workshop are demonstrated by the various alliances and connections that existed between the followers of Raphael. Perino del Vaga's marriage to the sister of Francesco Penni was apparently a professional arrangement, and in 1523 the sculptor Lorenzetto (Lorenzo Lotti) married Giulio Romano's sister. Lorenzetto's collaborative involvement with Peruzzi, Penni, and Giulio Romano on two major projects was the result of the friendship with Raphael. Lorenzetto was in charge of the execution of the *Madonna*

[26] T. Verellen, 'Cosmas and Damian in the New Sacristy', *Journal of the Warburg and Courtauld Institutes*, 42 (1979), 274–7.

[27] Vasari–Milanesi, iv. 544; B. Bottari and S. Ticozzi, *Raccolta di lettere sulla pittura, scultura ed architettura ... dei secoli XV, XVI, XVII* (Milan, 1822–5), iii. 334 (no. CLXI).

[28] T. Buddensieg, 'Raffaels Grab', in *Festschrift Hans Kauffman* (Berlin, 1968), p. 56; Vasari–Milanesi, i. 169f.

[29] See Shearman, 'The Chigi Chapel', p. 130 n. 7; G. Giovannoni, *Antonio da Sangallo il Giovane* (Rome, 1959), i. 237; Uffizi, Dis. Arch. 169.

[30] Vasari (1550 edn), p. 730; cf. Shearman, 'The Chigi Chapel', p. 152 n. 104.

del Sasso for the tomb of Raphael in the Pantheon, a statue based (according to instructions left by Raphael himself) on the figure of an antique Venus later converted to a nymph and now in the Giardino della Pigna in the Vatican. Lorenzetto also completed works in bronze and in marble for the two Chigi chapels in Santa Maria del Popolo and in Santa Maria della Pace, in this being assisted by Raffaello da Montelupo, who joined his workshop around 1523.[31] These projects were carried out under the supervision of the executors of Raphael's will, Branconio dell'Aquila and Baldassare Turini.[32] The latter, a papal chamberlain and secretary under Leo X and Clement VII, was later to act as ambassador for Paul III.[33] He owned the *Madonna del Baldacchino* which had pride of place in what is now the cathedral of his native town, Pescia, until it was appropriated by Ferdinando de' Medici in 1697. Turini's villa on the Gianicolo, the Villa Lante, was decorated by Giulio Romano and was a meeting place of *letterati*. His city residence in the Piazza Nicosia was designed by Sangallo.

In prosperous times, Lorenzetto and his connections provided an opening for Tuscan sculptors. In 1530, for instance, Nanni di Baccio Bigi joined the workshop and Lorenzetto and Nanni executed the copy of Michelangelo's *Pietà* for Santa Maria de Anima. Nanni had also worked for Montelupo, possibly in the early 1530s, and by 1540 he was a member of the architectural *setta sangallesca*.[34] In times of hardship when commissions were lacking, Lorenzetto and his assistants relied on restoring antiques and trading in ancient marbles; in this capacity Lorenzetto worked for the Palazzo della Valle, for Isabella d'Este, and for the Cardinals Cesi, Farrara, and Farnese.[35] Apart from being an additional source of income, this activity was also of importance for maintaining relations with former patrons, whose antique collections had to remain in competitive condition. It was a

[31] The antique statue of Venus was transformed into an Hygieia by Pirro Ligorio before 1568, and acquired its present appearance as a nymph after 1787: see Buddensieg, 'Raffaels Grab'. For the Chigi chapels in Santa Maria del Popolo and Santa Maria della Pace, see J. Shearman and M. Hirst, *Journal of the Warburg and Courtauld Institutes*, 24 (1961). For Lorenzetto as a sculptor, see N. W. Nobis, 'Lorenzetto als Bildhauer', PhD Diss. (Bonn, 1979), and for Montelupo's own account of his contribution, G. Gaye, *Carteggio inedito d'artisti dei secoli XIV, XV, XVI* (Florence, 1839–40), iii. 588ff.

[32] V. Golzio, *Raffaello nei documenti, nelle testimonianze dei contemporanei e nella letteratura del suo secolo* (Città del Vaticano, 1936), p. 118.

[33] L. Pastor, *Die Geschichte der Päpste seit dem Ausgang des Mittelalters* (Freiburg i. Br., 1901–31), iv. 353, 279.

[34] Wittkower, 'Nanni di Baccio Bigi', pp. 249f., 258 n. 6.

[35] Gaye, *Carteggio*, iii. 590; Vasari–Milanesi, iv. 579; Nobis, 'Lorenzetto als Bildhauer', pp. 20, 26.

legacy that Lorenzetto passed on to his pupils, such as Montelupo, who later used it to help and train his own protégés. Valerio Cioli's entry into the Roman art world was thus effected by the protection of Montelupo, who introduced him to the Marchese Giuliano Cesarini, for whom he worked as a restorer.[36] According to Aldrovandi's description, Cesarini's extensive collection included a room of busts without heads and another of heads without busts.[37] Another pupil of Montelupo, Giovanantonio Dosio, whose career in Rome has been reconstructed on the valid assumption that the patronage enjoyed by the master would be extended to the protégé, was similarly involved in trading antiques, particularly at the Villa Giulia in the 1550s.[38]

Lorenzetto, however, had become a victim of the Sack of Rome. With the confusion of war his workshop had ceased to function and by the 1530s he had to be rescued from impoverishment by Sangallo. Like Vasari in Florence, Sangallo had acquired a large measure of control over the preparations for the entry of the Emperor Charles V in 1536. As one of the two *stimatori deputati* he was in a position to give Montelupo and Lorenzetto a prominent part in the decoration of the Porta San Sebastiano, of San Marco, and of the Ponte Sant' Angelo.[39] Lorenzetto had now lost his independent workshop and he remained a member of the *setta* until his death five years later. Sangallo also assumed control of a sculptural project completed in the early 1540s that may have been, at least temporarily, the focus of a political struggle involving the city of Florence. This was the commission for the tombs of the Medici popes Leo X and Clement VII. While the latter was still alive, Bandinelli had secured the commission for the tombs (then intended for Santa Maria Maggiore) and had made some preliminary models. Their execution was supervised by the Cardinals Ippolito de' Medici, Innocenzio Cibo, Giovanni Salviati, and Niccolò Ridolfi. The administration of the project was in the hands of Baldassare Turini, also a prominent member of the Medicean circle.[40]

---

[36] R: Borghini, *Il riposo* (Florence, 1584), p. 599.

[37] Aldrovandi, *Delle statue antiche* (Venice, 1558); for Valerio Cioli, see B. G. Thompson Fisher, 'The Sculpture of Valerio Cioli, 1529–1599', PhD Diss. (Michigan, 1976).

[38] See C. Valone, 'Giov. Antonio Dosio and his Patrons', PhD Diss. (Evanston, Ill., 1972), ch. 1.

[39] A. Bertolotti, 'Speserie segrete e pubbliche di Papa Paolo III', *Atti e memorie delle R. R. Deputazioni di Storia patria per le Provincie dell'Emilia*, iii (1878), 176ff.; Nobis, 'Lorenzetto als Bildhauer', pp. 20, 26; Giovannoni, *Sangallo*, i. 327.

[40] For Turini's correspondence with Lorenzo de' Medici, see Gaye, *Carteggio*, i. 138ff.; for a summary of the Medicean tombs in Santa Maria sopra Minerva after the death of Clement VII, see G. Vasari, *Le vite* (Novara, 1962–6), vi. 43ff.

The young Ippolito de' Medici kept an exotic court; in it some twenty different 'barbaric' languages were spoken by Indian divers, North African wrestlers, Mongolian archers, Armenian acrobats, and so forth.[41] It also provided a forum and a refuge for the Florentine exiles who opposed the regime of Alessandro de' Medici. For Ippolito (an illegitimate son of Giuliano, Duke of Nemours) this court may have been a substitute state. It would seem natural that, in order to further his cause, he should assume dynastic responsibility for the erection of the papal tombs that were to commemorate two of the most prominent members of his family. But apparently Ippolito could not command a group of respectable Florentine artists and he may have persuaded a sympathetic commission to hand over the project to his own protégé, the Ferrarese sculptor, Alfonso Lombardi.[42] Possibly with the connivance of Michelangelo who, according to Vasari, supplied Alfonso with designs, the bid was successful and Bandinelli was ousted. Alfonso made a highly praised model and was in Carrara choosing marble when his prospects were ruined by another turn of events. Ippolito, seeking the emperor's intervention in his favour, had travelled south in order to intercept Charles V in North Africa before his arrival on Italian soil. But on 10 August 1535, in Itri, he succumbed to a fever (or possibly to poison) and died.[43]

Lombardi never fully recovered from the loss of his patron and the fortunes of the exiles were also confounded when the political issue was resolved early in the following year with the announcement of the forthcoming marriage of Alessandro de' Medici to the emperor's daughter, Margarita of Austria. No contract had been signed with Alfonso and, on hearing of Ippolito's death, Bandinelli immediately left for Rome. Since the Florentines there regarded him with some suspicion, he chose a characteristically oblique course of action by approaching Lucrezia Salviati, a sister of Leo X, whom he persuaded to influence Cardinal Salviati by stressing Lombardi's inadequacies, who was lacking, as Bandinelli claimed (with recourse to contemporary theory) in *disegno*, *pratica*, and *giudizio*.[44]

Bandinelli's ploy was, of course, successful. He subsequently aban-

---

[41] See J. Burckhardt, *Die Kultur der Renaissance in Italien* (Stuttgart, 1976), p. 273 (P. Jovius, *Elogia*, pp. 307ff.).

[42] For Alfonso Lombardi and a summary of the political situation, see N. Gramaccini, 'Alfonso Lombardi', PhD Diss. (Frankfurt a. M, Bern and Cirencester, 1980), pp. 63ff.

[43] Pastor, *Die Geschichte*, v. 220ff.

[44] Vasari–Milanesi, v. 89; vi. 162ff.; compare Bandinelli's own account in A. Colasanti, 'Il memoriale di Baccio Bandinelli', *Repertorium für Kunstwissenschaft*, 28 (1905), 432ff.

doned his obligation, however, and it is tempting to imagine that
Baldassare Turini's consistent criticism of him was at least partly
motivated by a bias in favour of Sangallo and his followers, with
whose work Turini was naturally well acquainted. The contract with
Bandinelli, signed on 25 March 1536, had stipulated that the architectural elements of the tombs were to be executed by Lorenzetto
according to designs by Sangallo. Bandinelli, once again disenchanted
with the prospect of collaboration and intent on securing the commission for the monument of Duke Cosimo's father, Giovanni delle
Bande Nere (where he was to render in relief, we are told, the features
of Turini in close proximity to the hindquarters of a pig) finally
abandoned the papal project in 1541. Predictably, he was replaced by
Raffaello da Montelupo and Nanni di Baccio Bigi, who completed the
statue of Clement VII and carried out that of Leo X.

On 16 February 1538 a prominent acquaintance of Montelupo, the
scholar and artistic adviser Annibale Caro, had written him a letter
thanking him for drawings and reporting that 'Monsignor di Pescia
[Turini] took the drawing of the tomb to the Cardinal Ridolfi who
was pleased with it'.[45] The connection of Montelupo, Turini, Ridolfi,
and the drawing of a tomb at this date suggests that the drawing was
related to the project for the papal tombs in Santa Maria sopra
Minerva.

A drawing in Berlin which is in the style of Raffaello da Montelupo
and bears his name, does, in fact, clearly refer to the project and to
Sangallo's work in Santa Maria sopra Minerva. Its recto shows several
designs for tombs based on the sarcophagi in Michelangelo's New
Sacristy in San Lorenzo, Florence, as well as sketches of St Peter and
St Paul for the tomb of Clement VII. In addition to sketches for reliefs
(one representing Clement VII crowning the Emperor Charles V in
Bologna) the verso displays the seated figure of Clement VII as
executed by Bandinelli and Nanni di Baccio Bigi. Behind it, the artist
has indicated the *tribuna* that Sangallo had planned for the choir of
the church, a project that did not then come to fruition (Plate 25).[46]

The drawing, therefore, is a pastiche of the two projects, the papal
tombs and the projected choir. If this is, indeed, the drawing mentioned
in Caro's letter, then it would predate the final plans for the tombs

---

[45] A. Caro, *Lettere familiari*, ed. A. Greco (Florence, 1957), i. 66 (no. 37); Valone,
'Giov. Antonio Dosio', p. 11 n. 14.

[46] See D. Heikamp, 'Die Entwurfszeichnungen für die Grabmäler der Mediceer-Päpste
Leo X und Clemens VII', *Albertinerstudien* (1966), fasc. 3, pp. 141, 145.

and the *tribuna* and the participation of Montelupo in the project. Montelupo's inclusion of Sangallo's plans would, in that case, have implied to his potential patrons that he was abreast of recent developments and therefore qualified as an assistant. Although such a reconstruction of Montelupo's quest for involvement in the project is hypothetical, it may demonstrate how a struggling sculptor might approach the problem. We know from Caro's correspondence that Montelupo contributed to his collection of drawings and, on that level, they seem to have enjoyed a mutual friendship. They also discussed literary matters, and Caro expressed his appreciation of his friend by paying him a gracious, if rather ambiguous compliment, saying that Montelupo's mastery of the pen could not be considered inferior to his handling of the chisel.[47]

In times of meagre patronage the cultivation of such influential intermediaries as Caro would have been of some importance, as was the practice of dealing in antiques. Whereas Montelupo could approach Caro through their common interests, direct application to the members of the commission for a position that amounted to little more than that of a craftsman or stonemason, would have been less effective. One may also suppose that the intercession of Caro on behalf of his friend was matched by support from the shop-floor, and that Sangallo was in a position to exert some influence. Nanni and Raffaello could certainly be recommended on the grounds that their previous record had shown them capable of efficient collaboration and the latter, in particular, had by this time become something of a specialist in the completion of unfinished projects.

The Medici tombs of Santa Maria sopra Minerva are a good example of the manner in which commissions could be subcontracted within a system of patronage reflecting a variety of social motivation—from the need to express dynastic pretension to the financial reward of manual labour. Linking these two extremes are, on the one hand, the members of the commission, acting as patrons and performing a supervisory and administrative function, and, on the other, the artistic co-ordinator, Sangallo, who provides architectural plans, and who delegates and estimates the work carried out in the temporary workshop.

As was the case with work on St Peter's, the artistic relationships established by Sangallo's monopolization of patronage remained oper-

---

[47] Caro, *Lettere familiari*.

ative after his death, largely because the artists who had worked for
him had little to sustain them save the co-operative procedure to
which they had become accustomed. After the Sack of Rome, Sangallo
worked in Orvieto, where Clement VII had commissioned him to
build the Pozzo della Rocca, in order to ensure an adequate and
independent water supply for the city in which he had taken refuge.
At this time he also supplied alternative designs for the Altar of the
Magi with which Michele Sanmicheli da Verona had been inter-
mittently occupied since the early years of the century.[48] Sangallo's
position in Orvieto was strengthened by the election of Alessandro
Farnese, whose family had traditional links with the city. Sangallo
designed a palace there for Tiberio Crispo, an illegitimate relative of
Paul III who had been raised to the nobility of Orvieto.[49] In 1538
Simone Mosca, who had worked for Sangallo at Loreto and on other
occasions, was employed in Orvieto as 'Capo Maestro dell'Opera del
Duomo'. In the late 1530s and in the 1540s Mosca, his son Francesco,
and Montelupo executed the Altar of the Magi and continued to
collaborate on its counterpart on the other side of the Cappella Maggiore, the Altar of the Visitation.[50] Montelupo later succeeded his
compagno as *Capo Maestro* of the cathedral. When Sangallo died,
these sculptors found that their own, more indirect, relationship to
patrons in Rome was inadequate and that they were vulnerable to the
changing exigencies of courtly life. They therefore settled in a provincial centre where the ties of patronage established earlier by Sangallo
still continued to function.

It seems possible that the phenomenon of the *compagnia* was far
more common among artists of less than the first order than has
hitherto been thought. Partnerships among sculptors were, of course,
of common occurrence and a suitable example within the traditional
structure of guild organization is that of Donatello and Michelozzo
who submitted a joint tax return in 1427. But the formation of independent companies that might rival guild membership was generally
prohibited.[51] There were a number of exceptions—for example the

---

[48] Sangallo had already assisted Sanmicheli in 1513 by contributing designs for the
façade of the cathedral; L. Fumi, *Il duomo di Orvieto e i suoi restauri* (Rome, 1891),
p. 314; E. Langenskiöld, *Michele Sanmichele, the Architect of Verona* (Uppsala, 1938),
p. 4.

[49] Pastor, *Die Geschichte*, v. 13; P. Perali, *Orvieto* (Orvieto, 1919), pp. 175, 177.

[50] Vasari–Milanesi, vi. 545; Fumi, *Il duomo*, p. 336.

[51] H. McNeal Caplow, 'Sculptors' Partnerships in Michelozzo's Florence', *Studies in
the Renaissance*, 21 (1974), 145–73; V. Rutenberg, *Popolo e movimento popolare*

'Compagnia di San Luca' founded by the painters in 1350, and the 'Compagnia di Sant'Andrea de' Purgatori' of 1451 for the *sottoposti* of the Arte della Lana.[52] Ronald Weissman has expressed the view that the major sixteenth-century development of craft fraternities, particularly after the fall of the last Florentine republic in 1530, was due to the increasingly élitist and aristocratic nature of religious and neighbourhood confraternities, which accordingly tended to inhibit the membership of craftsmen. Compulsory membership and levied contributions enabled later craft associations to provide a form of social insurance,[53] which would have been of prime importance at a time when guilds began to play a smaller role in civic life. Their jurisdiction did not extend beyond their local base, and the itinerant artist travelling from commission to commission and meeting former associates in temporary workshops would naturally be inclined to join flexible companies. Such bonds increased the possibility of wider contacts and, in the case of larger sculptural projects, competition for patronage was more effectively met by the collaborative enterprise of the *compagnia*. Whether ostensibly religious or academic, it was a function of major confraternities such as the Congregazione dei Virtuosi al Pantheon[54] and the Compagnia di San Luca to act as a pool for patronage, in this role supplanting traditional guild and workshop structures.[55]

The *compagnie* discussed here evolved as a result of changes in the nature of patronage and were generally of an informal kind. On 2 February 1537, however, Simone Mosca, Raffaello da Montelupo, and a number of *scarpellini* came together at the Altare dell'Incoronata in the cathedral of Orvieto for a ceremony in which they gave oaths of allegiance to a formal brotherhood.[56] Little is known of what that entailed in practice: were codes of collaborative working methods formulated, and did a conscious reliance on communal artisanship

nell'Italia dell '300 e '400 (Bologna, 1971), pp. 60ff. The confraternity of San Marco was dissolved when it was about to become an unofficial guild of woolworkers: see R. Davidsohn, *Storia di Firenze* (Florence, 1973), vi. 213f.

[52] For the latter example, see R. F. E. Weissman, *Ritual Brotherhood in Renaissance Florence* (New York, 1982), pp. 65, 79, 86, 88.

[53] Ibid., pp. 163 n. 1, 201–3.

[54] J. A. F. Orbaan, 'Virtuosi al Pantheon', *Repertorium für Kunstwissenschaft*, 37 (1915).

[55] See J. Arnand, *L'Académie de Saint-Luc à Rome: Considérations historiques depuis son origine jusqu'à nos jours* (Rome, 1886), ch. 1; N. Pevsner, *Academies Past and Present* (Cambridge, 1940), pp. 44, 57ff.

[56] Perali, *Orvieto*, p. 179 (no source cited).

involve a rejection of patronage and of artistic ambition?[57] In Loreto the personalities of the artists receded behind the project itself. They suppressed individual expression, to the extent that authorship ceases to be of central importance. Nor is this a case of anonymous assistants working for a dominant master; these sculptors had already begun to work as independent masters, and the role of Sangallo is clearly to be understood as an organizational and supervisory one. The separation of the mental and manual processes of sculptural production never-theless relegated to the level of artisans a growing number of sculptors whose art had already implicitly or explicitly been allotted second place in the *paragone*. This social stigma led many artists, as was the case with Michelangelo, to oppose the manual and pecuniary connotations of the workshop, and to demonstrate a proficiency in the liberal arts. In his 'Memoriale', Bandinelli wrote that he would have preferred to attain immortality by wielding the pen rather than the chisel.[58] Montelupo's discourses with Annibale Caro and his send-ing him his drawings exemplify the artist's need to demonstrate intel-lectual creativity untainted by any association with trade. The aristo-cratic Tommaso de' Cavalieri, while taking drawing lessons with Michelangelo, would not have deigned to learn the skills of the sculp-tor. These examples are well known and many more could be added. Since they naturally apply more formidably to a sizeable and largely unexplored category of minor artists, it is plainly of value to examine the patterns of patronage and the workshop practice that governed their activities, in relation to the prevailing requirements of sixteenth-century art theory. *La buona maniera*, with its emphasis on grace and facility, the need to work from memory, and the application of sophisticated rhetorical devices, implied an analogy between artistic practice in the *arti di disegni* and the liberal arts that was hardly compatible with the sculptural procedure of the artists discussed here.[59]

---

[57] See, e.g., the letter of 26 Oct. 1550 to Benedetto Varchi (in Bottari–Ticozzi), *Raccolta*, i. 112–14 (No. L).

[58] Colasanti, 'Il memoriale', p. 430.

[59] See H. Miedema, 'On Mannerism and "maniera"', *Simiolus*, 10 (1978–9), 37ff.

Patronage and the Production of History: The Case of Quattrocento Milan

GARY IANZITI

FEW words are more fraught with difficulties, ambiguities, and misleading overtones than the English term 'patronage'. At its broadest, the word appears to signify a generic form of protection, a sense which is preserved in its French counterpart *patronage* ('protection accordée par un haut personnage'—*Grande Larousse*). But the English word also contains a whole series of specific meanings which either never existed in, or have largely disappeared from, the French. As Ronald Weissman has pointed out, these run all the way from the patronage of hotels and restaurants, to patronage of the arts, as well as to the special patron–client relationships which characterized ancient Roman society, and which sociologists like Boissevain believe can still be found, in one form or another, in many modern Mediterranean countries.

Indeed, the most striking feature of the English word patronage is its elasticity. The resilience of the term has recently received new confirmation in its extension into the field of Renaissance social history. Here the word patronage has come to be used to designate those personal ties of interest and obligation which were so effective in creating the cohesiveness of Renaissance socio-political networks. Nevertheless, Renaissance studies offer yet another example of the ambiguity referred to at the outset. For, while patronage has gained considerable ground as a sociological concept, it continues to be used by art historians and historians of culture in the more traditional sense of patronage of the arts. What has resulted is a kind of unacknowledged dichotomy.

Further light may be thrown on the question by briefly considering the equivalent terminology in other languages. Both French and Italian, for example, have words which convey the general sense of protection implied by the English term: French, *patronage*; Italian, *patrocinio*.

And in both languages the words preserve the technical sense desig-
nating patron–client relationships in ancient Rome. The similarity
with English, however, stops here: there has not occurred the same
overloading of meanings which characterizes our word patronage.
Neither the artistic nor the sociological extensions present in the
English have taken place. Thus, when an Italian wants to talk about
patronage of the arts, he adopts the word *mecenatismo* (cf. French,
mécènat; German, *Mäzenatentum*). And when he wants to talk about
patron–client relationships in a modern context, whether it be that of
Renaissance Florence or that of today's *Democrazia Cristiana* party,
he has at his disposal the word *clientelismo*.

The overlap of senses in the word patronage, as well as the inevitable
ambiguity, appear to be peculiar to English. No doubt the most obvious
way out of this difficulty lies in the refuge afforded by specialization.
Is it not to be expected that art historians, as well as historians of
literature, will be dealing with patronage as *mecenatismo*, while social
historians will focus on patronage as *clientelismo*? Perhaps, but are
there not areas, particularly on the borderlines between social, political, and cultural history, where something definite can be gained by
exploiting the ambiguities of the English term? In this chapter, I
presuppose an affirmative answer to this question, at least as far as it
concerns the problem of the writing of history in the Italian Renaissance.

At first glance the act of writing history, particularly that written
by the Italian humanists in the fifteenth century, may appear to fit
most appropriately, perhaps even exclusively, into the category of
patronage as *mecenatismo*. To the extent that it is considered at all,
such history is usually regarded as first and foremost a literary genre,
belonging to the forms of literature promoted by the munificence of
Renaissance patrons. Admittedly, exceptions are made for a few
notable figures whose works supposedly show a glimmer of modern
historical method. But the rest are seen chiefly as writers of elegant
Latin, usually contracted by a prince or other leading personage to
sing his praises to posterity.

This image matches with the interpretation of Italian humanism
itself as a movement of classical scholars whose main ambition was
to revive ancient literary forms. In its broadest terms, the humanist
movement might well be seen as characterized by its enthusiasm for
the classics, and many were those humanists who sought to curry the
favour of local rulers by turning out imitations of the *Lives* of

Suetonius, or the *Histories* of Sallust or Livy. In the sixteenth century, such exercises were to become a European fashion: the kings of France and England appointed official humanist historians to celebrate their royal houses, and to turn their account into a document of national, collective significance. These writers have been subsequently accused of being hacks who sold their talents to the highest bidder.[1]

Nevertheless, not all official humanist history was the product of mere *mecenatismo*. Particularly in dealing with the Quattrocento, when Renaissance patronage of the arts was still in its infancy, it is essential to pursue the enquiry beyond superficial appearances. Recent studies of Florentine, Venetian, and now Roman historiography in this period have stressed the importance of asking certain fundamental questions.[2] For example, what was the precise nature of the ties linking the humanist historian to the regime in power? Was there a formal commission, or appointment, and, if so, who were the contracting bodies, and what were the exact terms of the agreement? How closely was the writing of history controlled, and by what means? Finally, what was the purpose of history? Was it directed towards a restricted circle of courtly admirers, including perhaps the prince himself? Or was there a wider audience?

The answers have usually brought surprising results. To give only one example, it has sometimes been assumed that Lionardo Bruni's *Historia florentini populi*, written for the most part when Bruni was chancellor of Florence, was a work of official propaganda. Yet no evidence has ever been found of a commission, Bruni does not appear to have been paid for his work, and the Florentine *Signoria* made little or no effort to circulate, or later to publish it.[3] Similarly with Poggio Bracciolini's *Historia florentina*. Both works were first published (of all times and places) in Venice in 1476, and in Italian translation, not in the original Latin. This last point is important, for it is too often assumed that humanist history, because it was written in classicizing Latin, must have been intended for an élite audience of select learned

---

[1] See E. Cochrane, *Historians and Historiography in the Italian Renaissance* (Chicago, 1981), pp. x–xiii.

[2] See R. Fubini, 'Osservazioni sugli *Historiarum florentini populi libri XII* di Leonardo Bruni', in *Studi di storia medievale e moderna per Ernesto Sestan*, i (Florence, 1980), 403–48; A. Pertusi, 'Gli inizi della storiografia umanistica nel quattrocento', in A. Pertusi (ed.), *La storiografia veneziana fino al secolo XVI* (Florence, 1970), pp. 269–332; M. Miglio, *Storiografia pontificia del quattrocento* (Bologna, 1975); R. Fubini, 'Papato e storiografia nel quattrocento', *Studi medievali*, 18 (1977), 321–51.

[3] See Fubini, 'Osservazioni', pp. 429–33.

men. Not enough attention has been paid to the high frequency of translation into Italian, or rather into Tuscan—a practice that became common after the introduction of the printing press in the second half of the fifteenth century.

Another factor that often escapes notice is the large percentage of leading Quattrocento humanist historians who were at the same time employed in the administrative apparatus of government. These included not only the well-known examples of the Florentine chancellors (Bruni, Poggio, and later Bartolomeo Scala), but also key figures in other major centres such as Rome (Flavio Biondo, and later the secretaries of Pope Pius II, Jacopo Ammanati and Giovannantonio Campano), Naples (Panormita, Bartolomeo Facio), and Milan (Lodrisio Crivelli, Giovanni Simonetta). Such men by no means fall into the stereotype of the court historian. In general, they are not men of letters in search of a patron, they are full-time, professional bureaucrats whose livelihood depends chiefly on their skills as administrators. Sometimes they serve as secretaries and close collaborators of princes and popes. In this capacity, they share decision-making responsibility, and, to a varying degree, become the instruments of the prince's will. In some cases, they act as patrons of the arts, either in their own right, or through the power vested in them by the prince. In short, they are the mediators between the prince and his dependents and supporters. Clients of the prince themselves, they are also frequently the architects of the patron–client relationships upon which the prince's power rests.

That such men should also write history poses problems of a special nature. The ties of a humanist secretary to his prince can hardly be described in the traditional terms of *mecenatismo*. In fact, only in rare cases do we find evidence of a commission to write history, as in the instance of Facio, who worked under a king whose family had behind it a long tradition of royal historiography.[4] In general they were acting not on commission, but out of a commitment of both a personal and a professional origin. It is, in fact, impossible to distinguish between these two strains of motivation, so close is the identification in such figures between personal initiative and professional expediency. At its simplest, we might regard the secretary's writing of history as an extension of his official duties. These duties themselves, however, must not be regarded as a form of public service. At the higher echelons at

---

[4] See G. Resta's introduction to his edition of Panormita's *Liber rerum gestarum Ferdinandi Regis* (Palermo, 1968).

least, the status of the secretary depended to a large degree on his personal ties to the prince. These might be expressed by the establishment of family relationships, or by the secretary's accumulation of fiefs, ecclesiastical benefices, appointments, etc., for himself and for members of his immediate entourage. The important point is that the tie was of a personal as well as of a public nature, and thus the term bureaucrat itself is a somewhat misleading one. Ultimately, the secretary–historian was linked to the prince by ties of *clientelismo*.

Accordingly, the historiographical output of the Quattrocento secretaries will be viewed here not so much through the traditional optic of patronage of the arts as through that suggested by the relatively new area of patron–client relations. My thesis is that such history is best seen as both a product and an agent of such forces: a product in so far as it is the result of ties of clientship between prince and secretary, and an agent in so far as the history itself seems to be geared towards creating solidarity and consensus among the prince's clientele.

An enquiry of this kind must inevitably narrow its focus to a specific case. In the field of Renaissance studies, it has been customary to look to Florence as the testing ground for new ideas and interpretations. This is highly appropriate, for over the years Florence has provided many a detailed model for furthering our understanding of Renaissance culture and society. It is time, however, to ask whether the Renaissance really begins and ends with Florence, and whether, in some areas at least, our almost total preoccupation with this unique city has not resulted in some distortion. One of the main contentions of the present chapter is that the history of humanistic historiography cannot be written with reference to Florence alone. To do so would be to ignore forms of history which had a wide impact elsewhere in Italy, but whose presence in Florence was, for various reasons, minimal. The instance of the secretary–historian provides a typical case in point. For it was not in Florence, but in Milan, that such history reached its highest development. Accordingly, the rest of this chapter will concentrate on the problems surounding the rise of humanistic historiography in Sforza Milan in the years 1450–90, and even more specifically on the genesis of a single work: the *Commentaries* of the Sforza secretary, Giovanni Simonetta.

Though it might properly be described as the most important humanist history to emerge from Milan in the fifteenth century, Simonetta's work has not attracted much scholarly attention. It is often dismissed as a typical example of mere courtly history, and is indeed even sometimes associated with the *mecenatismo* of Ludovico il Moro, virtual ruler of Milan from 1480 to 1500. None the less, it can be shown that Simonetta's work belongs, at least in so far as its genesis and composition are concerned, to an earlier period: that corresponding to the reigns of Francesco Sforza (1450–66), and his son Galeazzo Maria (1466–76).

Any fair analysis, however, must begin with the position occupied by the Simonetta family under the Sforza rulers. Giovanni Simonetta was the younger brother of Cicco, who was from 1450 to 1479 the most powerful figure in the Sforza administration after the duke himself. Both Giovanni and Cicco were nephews of Angelo Simonetta, who had joined the entourage of the *condottiere* Muzio degli Attendoli, father of Francesco Sforza, at the beginning of the century. The origins of the Simonetta family in its native Calabria were relatively humble, but its fortunes rose with those of its Sforza employers. By the time Francesco Sforza had become Duke of Milan in 1450, the members of the Simonetta family found themselves at the head of the administration. Cicco, destined to become the most influential, was placed in charge of the Ducal Chancery, the hub of diplomacy and government. Giovanni was his closest assistant. Around themselves, they constructed what many have regarded as the first modern bureaucracy in Europe.[5]

Simonetta's history grew out of the chancery's efforts to deal with a number of problems that had plagued the regime from its inception. As an integral part of the ducal administration, the chancery was at the centre of the Sforza regime's struggle to establish and maintain control over the unruly Duchy. It must, in fact, be remembered that Francesco Sforza was essentially an upstart *condottiere* whose claims to Milan were of the most tenuous legal nature. Neither his marriage to Bianca Maria Visconti, nor the supposed 'donation' of her father Filippo Maria (d. 1447), were of sufficient legal weight to constitute an unquestionable right to the Duchy. Sforza's entry into the city at the beginning of 1450, as well as his stay thereafter, were only made possible through the recognition by an influential segment of the Milanese nobility, that his lordship was the sole alternative to utter chaos and eventual Venetian occupation of all or part of Lombardy. Beyond this recognition, and his own skills, Sforza had little in his

---

[5] See my article, 'A Humanist Historian and His Documents: Giovanni Simonetta, Secretary to the Sforzas', *Renaissance Quarterly*, 34 (1981), 492–501.

favour. It is true that his position in Milan was sanctioned and confirmed by the Milanese *popolo* in a solemn ceremony of 11 March 1450. But even after this date there continued to be many who questioned his right to rule. Their opposition drew strength from the Emperor's adamant refusal to invest Sforza with the ducal title, an act whose practical consequences may well have been slight, but whose moral implications were far-reaching. More threatening in real terms was the continued hostility to the regime of powerful states like Venice and Naples. And even when this hostility had finally been largely placated (by the late 1450s), there remained the constant threat of an internal collapse of the regime's support. There were crises at regular intervals: 1466, 1476, 1477–9. From these and other indications, it is evident that the proud and still powerful Milanese patriciate looked with a disdainful and suspicious eye upon their Sforza lords.[6]

In this precarious situation, it fell to the chancery to engineer some semblance of security for the struggling regime. A least two of its major areas of activity reflect this concern. The first is the well-studied area of Sforza diplomacy: the construction of a system of alliances with Italian and European powers. The second is the little-explored area of Sforza patronage: the distribution and manipulation of favours to create a clientele of firm supporters amongst the Milanese noble families. Both of these areas provide ground for speculation about the purposes of the Sforza historiographical project which was hatched in the chancery in the early 1450s and which continued to be of central concern to the regime down to the time of Ludovico il Moro. In the face of local factions or hostile foreign powers who could cite among other things the legal shortcomings of the Sforza position, it became essential to offer counter-arguments, especially in the form of an interpretation of Francesco Sforza's career that would legitimize his hold over Milan. That these counter-arguments should take the form of a humanist history was undoubtedly influenced by the fact that hostile powers like Naples were already promoting such history. As early as 1448, Bartolomeo Facio had begun his *De rebus gestis ab Alphonso Primo Neapolitanorum Rege commentariorum libri X*, which he completed in 1455. What was emerging was a battle for men's minds in which the Sforza entourage could not afford to be second best. Abroad the views of diplomats, statesmen, and foreign

---

[6] R. Fubini, 'Osservazioni e documenti sulla crisi del ducato di Milano nel 1477', in S. Bertelli and G. Ramakus (eds.), *Essays Presented to Myron P. Gilmore*, i (Florence, 1978), 47–103.

functionaries, at home the views of leading figures in the city and the Duchy had, if possible, to be influenced. Accordingly the chancery took upon itself the task of producing a history of the career of Francesco Sforza.[7]

The first stirrings in this direction date from the early 1450s, shortly after Sforza's occupation of Milan. The intention was to encourage the leading humanist Francesco Filelfo to compose a history *De vita et rebus gestis Francisci Sfortiae*. Filelfo was already engaged on his epic poem on a similar topic—the so-called *Sforziade*—and for both projects he seems to have sought financial support through the Simonetta brothers. Although there is no evidence of a commission for the history, it can hardly be doubted that Filelfo received aid in various forms. His ties with the Duke of Milan were those of *mecenatismo*, with the Simonetta brothers often acting as the brokers. This arrangement, however, did not bear the desired fruit. Filelfo abandoned his projected history and, by the late 1450s, efforts were under way to find another humanist author. Among the prospective candidates was, for example, Giovannantonio Campano, whose *Bracchi Perusini vita*, a history of the *condottiere* Braccio da Montone, completed in 1457, at first seemed to qualify him for the job. After due consideration, however, Campano's candidacy was rejected in favour of that of a protégé of Filelfo: Lodrisio Crivelli, who from 1460 to 1463 wrote the first books of his never-completed *De Vita et rebus gestis Francisci Sfortiae*.[8]

Crivelli was not only a humanist of some repute, he was also an employee of the chancery. The choice of such a man to write the history represented an internalization of the project, a shift, perhaps in the light of earlier failures, from the normal mechanism of *mecenatismo* to one more closely resembling that of *clientelismo*. At one stroke, it was decided to bypass the original plan calling for the services of a professional writer. The responsibility for penning the history was taken out of the hands of a humanist man of letters and put into those of a creature of the regime. It is important, in fact, to distinguish Crivelli from Filelfo. He was not an independent scholar contracted to write history, nor was his position in the chancery a reward for his

---

[7] See further my forthcoming article, 'The Rise of Sforza Historiography', in *Florence and Milan in the Renaissance* (to be published by the Harvard University Center for Italian Renaissance Studies, Villa I Tatti).

[8] See further my article, 'From Flavio Biondo to Lodrisio Crivelli: The Beginnings of Humanistic Historiography in Sforza Milan', *Rinascimento*, 20 (1980), 3–39.

willingness to undertake literary work on behalf of the regime. Crivelli
was a dependent of the duke whose ties ran through the new bureaucracy headed by the Simonetta clan. A member of an illustrious Milanese
family, Crivelli had been one of the first to voice his support for
Francesco Sforza during the tumultuous events of 1449–50. When
Sforza had gained the upper hand, he rewarded his supporters in
accordance with their station: Crivelli's participation in the regime
involved him in enlisting support for it amongst the nobility. His
association with the historiographical project gives a valuable indication of the project's role in connection with the Sforza clientele
network.

It was towards the end of the 1450s that Crivelli's normal administrative functions were apparently extended to include producing the
long-desired history. By taking this step the chancery was in part
rectifying its earlier effort to promote history through *mecenatismo*.
But there were other reasons why the concentration of the project
within the chancery was the most appropriate move. One of these was
certainly the need to establish more effective control over what was to
be said in the history. The presentation of Sforza's career and especially
the interpretation of the turbulent events attending on his seizure of
Milan in 1450, formed one of the most delicate issues in the complex
equilibrium of forces that held the regime in power. The chancery
could not afford to play with the chance that an independent humanist
might slip up, intentionally or unintentionally, in his account of what
had happened. What is more, men like Filelfo were not averse to
making threats in order to extract more money from the unfortunate
patron who had recourse to his services.

Financial considerations, indeed, may well have entered into the
decision to relocate the historiographical project exclusively within the
confines of the chancery. But even more telling is its own role as a
monopolizer and disseminator of information. For the chancery had,
among its many other duties, also that of propagating information in
support of current policy. It orchestrated the composition and delivery
in solemn circumstances of orations in praise of the duke, and saw to
the circulation of selected pieces of information, in fact news items,
which put current events in the best light possible from the regime's
point of view. All of this was part of the general drive to shape and
manipulate opinion amongst the more influential circles, both at home
and abroad. Such literature aimed at creating consensus and solidarity
among the duke's allies and clients. It provided a convenient rallying-

point for supporters, as well as a weapon to be used against similar propaganda emanating from rival states.

Such spur-of-the-moment propaganda forms the groundwork for the producing of history within the Sforza chancery. And just as the purposes of the history can be seen to run parallel to those of the propaganda, so there are less obvious links in the actual production process. Together with its almost daily output of propaganda, the chancery took upon itself the responsibility for assembling a set of raw materials from which the full-scale history was to be written. Under the direction of Cicco and Giovanni Simonetta, a kind of blueprint was drawn up, in the form of a rough narrative incorporating those documents and news items which had formed the material basis of the positions assumed *ad hoc* by the chancery in the day-to-day conduct of policy. From this blueprint, the humanist author was expected to weave a history conforming to classical literary standards. The final result was intended to lend a more dignified, coherent, and lasting form to what had previously been only dispersed and unsystematic propaganda.

The blueprint worked up in this fashion in the Sforza chancery was originally destined for Filelfo, who, like other humanists, referred to such material as 'commentaries'. When Filelfo bowed out of the enterprise, the commentaries were handed over to his successor. Crivelli in fact wrote his *De vita et rebus gestis Francisci Sfortiae* from a specific set of chancery materials that I have been able to identify. With their help, it is possible to reconstruct Crivelli's working methods, indeed to follow them step by step.

It may be stressed here that these techniques for the production of history were by no means limited to Sforza Milan. Many other centres used them, most notably Urbino, where Federigo da Montefeltro's secretary Pierantonio Paltroni compiled commentaries for the use of a whole array of humanist historians.[9] In short, in mid-to-late Quattrocento Italy there emerged a structure to cope with the production of a specific type of political, official historiography with a focus on contemporary events. The basic structure is articulated at three levels: first, the production of propaganda in the chancery; secondly, the compilation from this material of commentaries; thirdly, the contracting of a humanist to transmute the commentaries into acceptable, literary history.

[9] See W. Tommasoli's introduction to his edition of Paltroni's *Commentarii della vita et gesti dell'illustrissimo Federico Duca d'Urbino* (Urbino, 1966).

As we have seen in Sforza Milan, however, this structure is subject to adaptation. Crivelli's writing of the final product represents a breakdown of the third stage, and a consequent concentration of the entire project in the hands of the chancery. Under the pressure of the situation at Milan, *mecenatismo* gave way to the construction of the history by an employee of the chancery who was also a client of the duke.

It should be emphasized here that Crivelli's work never reached completion, nor was it published until Ludovico Antonio Muratori rediscovered it in the eighteenth century. Crivelli himself fell out of favour before he could finish the history: in 1463 he left Milan for good in what remain mysterious circumstances. He had at this time completed only two books. But despite its fragmentary state, the *De vita et rebus gestis* helps to clarify the processes which underlie the production of a specific type of humanistic historiography. More importantly still, it paves the way for a further understanding of Giovanni Simonetta's *De rebus gestis Francisci Sfortiae commentarii*.

The connection between Simonetta's work and that of Crivelli has never been clearly drawn, perhaps because of the tortured history of the composition and publication of the *Commentaries*. Simonetta appears to have written the work in the early 1470s, at the height of his family's fortunes. After the assassination of Galeazzo Maria in 1476, the Simonetta brothers gained virtual control under the nominal regency of Bona of Savoy, wife of the fallen duke. Not surprisingly, the coup of Ludovico il Moro was engineered largely against Cicco Simonetta, who was finally isolated, imprisoned, and executed in 1480. His brother Giovanni was stripped of his authority, and exiled and, though later recalled to Milan, was never reinstated in his former office. Yet with all this, Ludovico was impressed with Simonetta's recently completed *Commentaries*, and, after subjecting them to a thorough revision to bring them into line with his own policies, he had them published (in the original Latin) in 1483. Shortly thereafter, he commissioned a translation into Tuscan from no less than Cristoforo Landino. This appeared in 1490 after a second Latin edition of 1486.[10]

This publication history in particular has often led investigations on Simonetta's work down the wrong path. It has not been noticed

---

[10] See further my article, 'The First Edition of Giovanni Simonetta's *De rebus gestis Francisci Sfortiae commentarii*: Questions of Chronology and Interpretation', *Bibliothèque d'humanisme et Renaissance*, 44 (1982), 137–47.

that the *Commentaries* had their origins in an earlier project. As one of the leading figures in the chancery, Simonetta was in charge of assembling the blueprint that was to have served as the basis for Crivelli's history. When Crivelli left Milan, Simonetta probably maintained the direction of the enterprise, and eventually made the decision to write the work himself. The very title he adopted—commentaries—reveals the provenance of the work: it is an open admission of the chancery substratum, formerly only an intermediate stage, coming into the foreground. The cycle was thus completed: all the phases of historiographical activity were concentrated in the hands of a single figure. Giovanni Simonetta became not only client, secretary, and propagandist, but historian of the duke as well. Meanwhile, the figure of the humanist man of letters linked to the duke by ties of *mecenatismo* suffered a temporary eclipse.

Once again, this phenomenon is by no means limited to Milan. An important precedent existed in the *Commentaries* of Pope Pius II, a work written in the early 1460s and well known to Simonetta and to Sforza's entourage. Pius II's *Commentaries* were orchestrated along lines similar to those operative in Milan: they were built out of chancery sources assembled under the direction of the pope's closest associates, men like Jacopo Ammanati.[11] Pius II's work-plan also appears to have precluded *a priori* any need for the services of an outside humanist. The pope himself was to give high stylistic form to the rough notes prepared in the chancery by his secretaries.

These almost parallel developments in Rome and Milan suggest that the relocation of historiographical projects within the confines of the chancery was a structural rather than a casual evolution. The specific aims of a type of history generated specific forms of organization to produce it, eventually eliminating outmoded structures. Such history, as we have seen, was not primarily intended for the consumption of a court: its purpose was not to flatter, or glorify the prince to his face. Its mission lay squarely within the chancery programme of producing propaganda. Historiography was one way of using official material and policies to create an interpretation of the recent past that would be favourable to the interests of the regime in power. What was required was not so much literary elegance as the sharp and precise reflection of public policy. It was therefore only natural that the

---

[11] See R. Ceserani, 'Rassegna di studi piccolominiani', *Giornale storico della letteratura italiana*, 141 (1964), 279–81.

secretaries—those who had been in charge of formulating policy and who already held the pivotal role of assembling the materials of history and thus determining its content—should also undertake the actual writing. Or, if not they, then their chief himself, as in the case of Pius II.

Other developments encouraged this tendency. The rediscovery and re-evaluation of the *Commentaries* of Julius Caesar (which occurred at about this time) greatly aided the emergence of what was in fact a new genre. Caesar's *Commentaries* provided a useful classical precedent for the acceptability of apologetic, propagandistic history. Despite some obvious differences, both Simonetta and Pius II reflect Caesar's influence. His *Commentaries* became a model for this type of chancery history, acting both as a guide to the construction of political apology and as a source of specific techniques designed to create a persuasive, biased version of events.[12]

A second, and no less important development was the introduction of the printing press. Its capability of reaching a wider audience than ever before imagined not only contributed to the increasing importance of this type of writing, it also promoted a more stringent surveillance and thus tended to push the composition of the final product into more competent hands, that is, into the chancery.

Simonetta's *Commentaries* may be regarded as a paradigmatic work whose genesis, composition, publication, and circulation reflect a pattern that might be used to illuminate other examples of Quattrocento historiography. The foregoing remarks have tried to suggest that the way towards a fuller understanding of certain forms of humanistic historiography lies not in the traditional area of patronage of the arts, but rather in the relatively new field opened up by the social concept of patronage. Patronage as *clientelismo* helps us to formulate in a much clearer way how history such as that written by Simonetta was produced, and how it was meant to operate in a specific social and political context.

---

[12] See further V. Brown, 'Caesar', in F. E. Cranz and P. O. Kristeller (eds.), *Catalogus translationum et commentariorum*, iii (Washington, 1976), 87–139. On Caesar's techniques of persuasion, see M. Rambaud, *L'Art de la déformation historique dans les 'Commentaires' de César* (Paris, 1953).

Marx and the Study of Patronage in the Renaissance

MARGARET ROSE

IN view of the many references to Marx and Marxist theory made in debates on the nature of Renaissance patronage today, a short review of Marx's own statements on Renaissance art and society, and on patronage, was requested by the editors of this volume; it appears below, together with a bibliographical list of works relating to the Renaissance known to Marx.

To begin, one must make clear the fact that, despite the many uses of his name by Marxist historians of Renaissance art such as Frederick Antal, or by historians of the Renaissance who describe it as a 'transition from feudalism to capitalism', Marx himself neither spoke of the Italian Renaissance as such at any length, nor analysed in any depth the conditions in which it flourished. Those who have taken up this latter task have had, on the whole, to base their analyses on Marx's more general statements on the development of capitalism and the transition from feudalism, or on a few specific textual instances where he either relates those statements to fifteenth-century Italian society or speaks directly of it. Though infrequent and relatively undeveloped, Marx's specific comments on the development of capitalism in that society in *Capital I* (Chapter 26) and *Capital III* (Chapters 20 and 47) have, however, provided many students with the basis for analysing it as a transitional stage between feudalism and capitalism.[1] In addition to his remarks in *Capital I* and *III*, Marx's more recently discovered *Grundrisse* have also provided Renaissance studies with a new perspective on the growth of the Renaissance city. There, in shorthand fashion, he defines a major characteristic of the

---

[1] See for example, A. Heller, *Renaissance Man* (Budapest, 1967; tr. R.E. Allen, New York, 1981); *The Transition from Feudalism to Capitalism*, intr. Rodney Hilton (London, 1982); and E. Kamenka and R.S. Neale (eds.), *Feudalism, Capitalism and Beyond* (Canberra, 1975).

modern (capitalist) age as being the 'urbanization of the countryside',
in contrast to the 'ruralization of the city' typical of antiquity.[2] Application of this dictum to the Renaissance in general, without concern
for its clearly aphoristic character, may however lead not only to a
distortion of the differences that existed historically between Renaissance cities and their regions and modes of production, to which
Marx himself carefully alluded in *Capital III*,[3] but also to apparent
contradiction with his note on Italy in Chapter 26 of *Capital I*. There
he describes the way in which capitalism in Italy saw both the development of an urban proletariat and the return of that proletariat to
the country, following changes in the international market:

In Italy, where capitalist production developed earliest, the dissolution of
serfdom also took place earlier than elsewhere. The serf was emancipated in
that country before he had acquired any prescriptive right to the soil. His
emancipation at once transformed him into a free proletarian, who, moreover,
found his master ready waiting for him in the towns, for the most part handed
down as legacies from the Roman time. When the revolution of the world-
market, about the end of the fifteenth century, annihilated Northern Italy's
commercial supremacy, a movement in the reverse direction set in. The
labourers of the towns were driven *en masse* into the country and gave an
impulse, never before seen, to the *petite culture*, carried on in the form of
horticulture.

In addition to indicating in this note the unstable, transitional and
region-based character of the early capitalist period that accompanied
what is now understood as the Italian Renaissance, Marx had also
gone on, in the text itself, to date the beginning of that period from
the sixteenth century, and to conclude with the statement that it was
in fact in England that the 'classic form' of the expropriation of the
rural producer or peasant, and the beginnings of the urban proletariat
of which he had been speaking, was to be found.[4]

While such comparatively well-known passages show Marx to have
been interested in what we now call the Italian Renaissance—seeing
it as a period which could illustrate certain, but not all, aspects of the

---

[2] See the section of the *Grundrisse* entitled 'Formen die der kapitalistischen Pro-
duktion vorhergehen.'

[3] See both chs. 20 and 47. In ch. 20 of *Capital III*, for instance, Marx is especially
careful to point to the differences between specific towns and periods in the development
of trade and industry in the town.

[4] Ch. 47 of *Capital III* also refers, but only in passing, to the transitional and
exceptional character of urban development in Italy as contrasted with the conditions
in other, feudal, states.

modern capitalism which he was to analyse while living in London from 1849 on, earlier works from the 1840s also manifest a complex sense of that period as one which could illustrate characteristics of the transition between feudalism and capitalism that he found in his own early nineteenth-century Prussian society. These works range from extracts made for a thesis on Hegel and religion in 1841–2 to the *German Ideology* of 1845–6.

In these works of the early 1840s we find reference not only to his reading of Winckelmann, Lessing, and Hegel,[5] but also to extracts from von Rumohr, Grund, and Böttiger on early Christian and Renaissance art.[6] Made for a treatise on 'Hegel's hatred of Christian art' requested by Bruno Bauer in 1841–2, as part of Bauer's ongoing reinterpretation of Hegel as antipathetic to German pietism,[7] these extracts show Marx to have been concerned at that time with revealing a pagan base to Renaissance and pre-Renaissance Christian art which would also undermine the pietistic patronage of such art in his own time.[8] Written just after the promulgation by Friedrich Wilhelm IV of

[5] Read by Marx as early as 1837.

[6] These have been published in vol. iv, 1 of the new *Marx Engels Gesamtausgabe* (Berlin, 1976), and include extracts from Carl Friedrich von Rumohr's *Italienische Forschungen* of 1827–31, C. A. Böttiger's *Ideen zur Kunst-Mythologie* of 1826–36, and J. J. Grund's *Die Malerey der Griechen* of 1810–11.

[7] Bruno Bauer had parodied pietism and presented Hegel as a more radical 'Hellene' in his 'Letzte Posaune' ('Last Trump') of 1841. The treatise on Hegel and art to which Marx was to have contributed appeared as a sequel to the 'Last Trump' in 1842 and consisted of two parts (both thought to have been written by Bauer). The title of the first, by which the treatise is known, was 'Hegels Lehre von der Religion und Kunst von dem Standpunkt des Glaubens ausbeurteilt', and that of the second (which was to have been Marx's 'Hegel's Hatred of Christian Art and Religion'), 'Hegels Hass gegen die heilige Geschichte und die göttliche Kunst der heiligen Geschichtsschreibung'.

[8] Both Friedrich Wilhelm III and his son Friedrich Wilhelm IV admired and collected Christian art from the Middle Ages, the Renaissance, and the nineteenth century. In addition to their collecting, as Christian art, works of artists such as the young Raphael, the imitation by the German Nazarene artists (whom they also supported) of his Madonnas, and the description by Hegel of those works as the greatest yet produced by Christian art, led to the categorization of such Renaissance creations as Christian rather than pagan. That both Bauer and Marx considered their reinterpretation of the Christian art of their time as paganistic Hellenism to be radical, is evident both from Bauer's finished 1842 treatise and Marx's extracts for his unpublished contribution to it. It is also interesting to note that Friedrich Gottlieb Welcker (from whom Marx heard lectures on classical literature in 1835–6 at the same university in Bonn that Burckhardt later attended) was a friend of the Romantic A. W. von Schlegel, and was also involved with the Nazarene frescos painted on the walls of the university Aula in the 1820s and 1830s. Further details of these frescos, and of Marx's work on his treatise on 'Hegel's Hatred of Christian and Romantic Art', are given in ch. 3 of my *Marx's Lost Aesthetic* (Cambridge, 1984). Of interest in connection with Burckhardt's later writings on the Renaissance is the fact that he not only studied briefly in Bonn in 1841, but that he also

a new censorship law protecting both the court and the Christian religion from attack,[9] these extracts were also made by Marx at the time when the German Nazarenes, accused by Heine of resurrecting the fifteenth century in their own,[10] were being given new patronage by the Prussian court at the expense of Marx and his like.[11]

Moving on from this critique of feudal patronage and pietistic art to critiques of the Prussian court,[12] and then of the economy of capitalism,[13] Marx returned again, in his and Engels's *German Ideology* of 1845–6, to the art of the Renaissance and to an examination of the concept of the 'unique' artistic genius put forward, in his explanation of Raphael's greatness, by von Rumohr in his *Italienische Forschungen*.[14] Connecting this critique of uniqueness with that of the concepts of individuality and private property advanced by Max Stirner in his *Der Einzige und sein Eigentum*,[15] Marx continues on in this work to make the point, later taken up by Antal in his studies of Renaissance art, that even the greatest artists of the Renaissance were not merely unique individuals but were determined by material forces such as the technical advances in art made before their time, the organization of society into different classes, and the divisions of labour to be found not only in their particular region, but in those other regions with which theirs had trade or other such relationships.[16]

Written against a view proposed by an historian of art who had

came to know and befriend there the theologian, poet, and art historian Gottfried Kinkel, who was working on a history of paganism, and who was also to begin a history of Christian art, which first appeared in 1845 (see R. Meyer-Kraemer (ed.), *Briefe Jakob Burckhardts an Gottfried (und Johanna) Kinkel* (Basel, 1921)). Though Kinkel became too much of a radical for Burckhardt's liking at the time of the 1848 revolutions, and was imprisoned for his beliefs, he was one of those mocked by Marx in *The Great Men of Exile* of 1852 as a romantic revolutionary. What Marx might have thought of Burckhardt is difficult to say. Although the latter had sympathy neither for Kinkel's republicanism nor for the Communists of the time, he had (at least in his letters to Kinkel of the early 1840s) expressed his dislike of the pietism then prevalent in Prussia, and had even attempted to dissuade Kinkel from his study of theology.

[9] This censorship instruction was published at Christmas 1841.

[10] See Heine's *Reise von München nach Genua* of 1828.

[11] Marx attacked both the censorship laws and the Romanticism of the Prussian court in articles on censorship published in February and May of 1842 in the *Rheinische Zeitung*.

[12] See previous note.

[13] In his *Economic and Philosophic Manuscripts* of 1844.

[14] See especially von Rumohr's chapter: 'Was Raphael von allen neueren Künstlern auszeichnet.'

[15] See K. Marx and F. Engels, *The German Ideology* (Moscow, 1968), section on 'Saint Max'.

[16] Ibid., pp. 441–2.

acted as guide to Friedrich Wilhelm IV in Italy when the latter was Crown Prince, and who was also an adviser to Friedrich Wilhelm III on the purchase of Raphaels for the new National Gallery in Berlin,[17] Marx's comments in his *German Ideology* on the dependence of artists upon their society and its divisions of labour may also be read equally as comments on the aesthetic views and art policies of his own time— and on its own traditional feudal–capitalist character—as on the art and conditions of the Renaissance itself.[18] Hence, while later works such as *Capital I* and *III* show Renaissance Italy providing material for Marx's history of the development of the modern capitalism which he found in England in the 1850s and 1860s, his earlier *oeuvre* illustrates that the revival of some of its cultural forms, and the patronage of its Nazarene imitators in his native Prussia in the 1830s and 1840s, had led him not only to a new economic and political analysis of Renaissance art but also to a condemnation of its revival under the pietistic Prussian monarch Friedrich Wilhelm IV.[19]

To conclude this brief survey, it may be said that, although Marx's later comments on fifteenth-century Italy in *Capital* and elsewhere,[20] and his reading related to it,[21] show him to have maintained an interest in what is termed its Renaissance period, both his early and later works suggest that he was also concerned with the light it threw on the capitalistic and/or feudal conditions of his own time, be they the feudalism of early nineteenth-century Prussia, or the capitalist formations of his adopted Britain. Any thoroughgoing historical analysis of Renaissance societies based on Marx will have to take into account

---

[17] Von Rumohr is said to have arranged the purchase of two Raphaels for the Nationalgalerie, Berlin, in 1827.

[18] Like the early nineteenth-century Utopian socialist Claude Henri de Saint-Simon, Marx criticized the preservation of feudal relations of production by the capitalist industry of the nineteenth century, and regarded the French Revolution of 1789 as only having reformed in a limited manner the 'feudalism' represented by the *ancien régime*. For such reasons the 'modernism' of nineteenth-century industry was also regarded with some suspicion by Marx, as being of a limited nature. To the extent that the Prussian monarchy not only refused attempts to introduce constitutional government in Marx's time there, but had also sided with 'capitalist' industrialists over issues such as the revolt of the Silesian weavers in 1844 (when it sent in troops to put down the uprisings), it had also represented for Marx a 'feudalist–capitalist' society.

[19] See my book, *Marx's Lost Aesthetic*, ch. 3, for further discussion of this point.

[20] See the letter written by Marx to Engels from London on 25 Sept. 1857 (in Karl Marx and Frederick Engels, *Collected Works* (London, 1983), 40, pp. 186–7). Here Marx is recommending Machiavelli's *History of Florence* as a 'masterpiece' useful to Engels' history of the army, which again relates an aspect of the Italian Renaissance to a study of contemporary politico-economic problems.

[21] See Bibliographical list to this chapter.

the fact that Marx had studied them not merely for their own sake, but for the light they shed on the societies of his own time[22]. To what extent Marx's critical attitude to the latter influenced his reading of the Renaissance is yet another question for scholars to ask when reading Marx on the Renaissance.

BIBLIOGRAPHICAL LIST

This list of works owned by Marx relating to the Renaissance and Italy, and to early capitalist production, is selected from that given by Dr Bruno Kaiser in his *Ex Libris Karl Marx und Friedrich Engels. Schicksal und Verzeichnis einer Bibliothek* (Berlin, 1967).

Botta, Charles, *Histoire des peuples d'Italie* (Vols. 1–3; Paris, 1825).

Dickson, Adam, *De l'agriculture des anciens*, translated from the English (Vols. 1 and 2; Paris, 1804).

Dureau de la Malle (Adolphe Jules César Auguste), *Économie politique des Romains* (Vols. 1 and 2; Paris, 1840).

Guizot, *Histoire générale de la civilisation en Europe*, 5th edn (Paris, 1842).

Gulich, Gustav von, *Geschichtliche Darstellung des Handels, der Gewerbe und des Ackerbaus der bedeutendsten handeltreibenden Staaten unsrer Zeit* (Vols. 1 and 2; Jena, 1830).

Hallam, Henry, *View of the State of Europe during the Middle Ages*, 4th edn rev. and corr. in 3 vols. (Vol. 1, London, 1826). (Kaiser particularly notes, in mentioning the marginal notes to be found in Marx's copy, his critical comments on Hallam's presentation of Italian history. See *Ex Libris*, p. 85.)

Lange, Ludwig, *Römische Alterthumer* (Vol. 1; Berlin, 1856).

Laveleye, Émile, *La Lombardie et la Suisse* (1869). (Pencil marks by Marx largely in the section 'Économie rurale de la Lombardie'.)

Lièvre, Charles-Auguste le, *Le Travail et l'usure dans l'antiquité* (Paris, 1866), where the quotations from Dureau de la Malle (see above) are marked by Marx.

Loria, Achille, *La teoria del valore negli economisti italiani* (Bologna, 1882). (One of several works by Loria from the early 1880s.)

Machiavelli, Niccolò, *Tutte le opere. Cittadino e segretario Florentino*, divise in 2 tomi, e di nuovo con summa diligenza corrette e ristampate (Vols. 1 and 2; London, 1747). There are numerous annotations in Marx's hand to the 'History of Florence' in the first volume.

Mommsen, Theodor, *Römische Forschungen* (Vol. 1; Berlin, 1864).

Neigebaur, Johann Ferdinand, *Sicilien, dessen politische Entwickelung und jetztigen Zustände* (Leipzig, 1848).

---

[22] Many of the works written by Marx in Germany in the early 1840s refer obliquely rather than directly to their contemporary targets—one reason for this being the strengthening of censorship by Friedrich Wilhelm IV at the end of 1841.

Osiander, Heinrich Fredrich, *Ueber den Handelsverkehr der Völker*, 2nd edn (Vols. 1 and 2; Stuttgart, 1842).

Pecchio, Giuseppe (comte), *Histoire de l'économie politique en Italie, ou abrégé critique des économistes italiens. Précédée d'une introduction*, tr. Leonard Gallois (Paris, 1830).

Rossi, le comte Pellegrino Louis Edouard, *Cours d'économie politique* (Brussels, *c.* 1843) in J. A. Blanqui, *Histoire d'économie politique en Europe*.

Ungewitter, Fr. H., *Geschichte des Handels, der Industrie und Schiffahrt von der ältesten Zeiten an bis auf die Gegenwart* (1851).

In addition to the books owned by Marx listed above, Kaiser also gives those he left with Dr Roland Daniels in Cologne, noted by Daniels in 1850. Among the works listed by Daniels, and not discussed by Kaiser, can be found Machiavelli's *The Prince* in a German translation by Regis, published in Stuttgart and Tübingen in 1842, and in addition: Campanella's *La Cité du soleil*, tr. Villegardelle (Paris, 1840); Kannegiesser's *Italienische Grammatik* (Leipzig, 1845); Torquato Tasso's *La Gierusalemme Liberata*; Vols. 1, 2 and 4 of the 'opere' of Metastasio; Ariosto's *Orlando Furioso* and Goldini's *Scelta d'alcune commedie*.

Relevant works used by Marx for *Capital* and not already listed:

Anderson, Adam, *An historical and chronological deduction of the origin of commerce, from the earliest accounts to the present time* (London, 1764).

Augier, Marie, *Du crédit public et de son histoire depuis les temps anciens jusqu'à nos jours* (Paris, 1842).

Beccaria, Cesare, *Elementi di economia pubblica* (Milan, 1804).

Genovesi, Antonio, *Lezioni di economia civile* (Milan, 1803).

Hullmann, K. D., *Staedtewesen des Mittelalters* (Bonn, 1826–7). (It is Hullmann to whom Marx refers in Chapter 19 of *Capital III* in his footnote on the cash unions of Venice as an early form of Giro bank.)

Lancellotti, Secondo, *Farfalloni de gli Antichi Historici* (Venetia, 1636).

——, *Le Hoggidi, overo gli'ingegni non inferiori a passati* (Venetia, 1658).

Niebuhr, Berthold George, *Römische Geschichte* (Berlin, 1863).

Ortes, Gianmaria, *Della economia nazionale* (Vol. VII, 1777; Milan, 1804).

Pagnini, Gio. Francesco, *Saggio sopra il giusto pregio delle cose, la giusta valuta della moneta et sopra il commercio dei romani* (1751; Milan, 1803).

Verri, Pietro, *Meditazioni sulla economia politica* (1773; Milan, 1804).

(Those works published in Milan in 1803 or 1804 come from the series entitled 'Scrittori Classici Italiani di Economia Politica'.)

Index